Emerging Threats to Human Rights

Edited by HEATHER SMITH-CANNOY

EMERGING THREATS TO HUMAN RIGHTS

Resources, Violence, and Deprivation of Citizenship

TEMPLE UNIVERSITY PRESS
Philadelphia • *Rome* • *Tokyo*

TEMPLE UNIVERSITY PRESS
Philadelphia, Pennsylvania 19122
tupress.temple.edu

Library of Congress Cataloging-in-Publication Data

Names: Smith-Cannoy, Heather M., editor.
Title: Emerging threats to human rights : resources, violence, and deprivation of
    citizenship / edited by Heather Smith-Cannoy.
Description: Philadelphia, Pennsylvania : Temple University Press, [2019] |
    Includes bibliographical references and index. |
Identifiers: LCCN 2018046416 (print) | LCCN 2018058601 (ebook) |
    ISBN 9781439917206 (E-book) | ISBN 9781439917183 (cloth) |
    ISBN 9781439917190 (pbk.)
Subjects: LCSH: Human rights. | Human security. | Citizenship. | Refugees—Civil rights.
Classification: LCC JC571 (ebook) | LCC JC571 .E64 2019 (print) | DDC 323.4/9—dc23 LC
record available at https://lccn.loc.gov/2018046416

For my mom, Adele C. Smith, for always supporting me in every creative way she could come up with. I am grateful beyond words.

Contents

Figures and Tables

Figures

Tables

Acknowledgments

A t no point since we have been keeping records have more people crossed international borders in search of freedom and a better life. According to the United Nations High Commissioner for Refugees (2017), more than 65.6 million people were forcibly displaced in 2016, surpassing a record-breaking 65.3 million displaced people in the previous year. This work addresses some of the causes of this crisis and examines the human rights violations throughout the process of migration. So often the human rights violations that induce people to flee from their homes are examined in isolation from one another. In putting this project together, I wanted to think about the causes of flight—the intersections of these topics that pose catastrophic threats to the enjoyment of human rights today. Some of the threats to human rights in our age are similar to those confronted by past generations; indeed, this work shows that when conflict erupts into violence, people flee in search of safety and a better life. But some of the other threats to human rights that we examine here are distinct from those experienced by past generations. While environmental degradation threatened human well-being during the Industrial Revolution, for example, the specter of climate change and polluted drinking water are qualitatively different, threatening millions of lives today. This work also links citizenship to human rights and the possibility of flight. Having access to legal nationality is something that people often take for granted, but for those whose right to a formal, legal nationality is denied, a host of human rights violations may follow.

As of April 2018, there are many reasons to be skeptical and disheartened about the status of human rights in our world. But it is my hope that in reflecting on the causes of flight and the specter of rights violations throughout the process of migration, we can improve the conditions for the world's growing migrant population.

My sincere gratitude goes to all the scholars who contributed their work to this book and for their patience in the process of seeing my vision to press. In many ways this is a unique project, and for their efforts to wrestle with many moving parts and look across their own areas of expertise, I am especially grateful. Special thanks go to Tony Smith at University of California, Irvine, for his friendship and unwavering support. Aaron Javsicas, editor in chief at Temple University Press, deserves special recognition for his guidance and input. For my own substantive chapter in this work, I gratefully acknowledge the support of the American Philosophical Society.

I am especially indebted to my community of scholars in the Department of International Affairs department at Lewis and Clark College. I thank my dear friend and expert in Middle East politics Cyrus Partovi for forcing me to think about the intersection of migration and human rights and sparking my fascination with the topic of this book. A very special thanks goes to Bob Mandel for reading countless drafts and providing invaluable insights in the framing of this work. Special thanks also go to Elizabeth Bennett for being such a wonderful source of support and friendship. My research assistants, Laurel Olden and Maya Anthony-Crosby, deserve special recognition for helping me compile materials for Chapter 7. Over the years I have been inspired by the wonderful students who have taken my classes, worked as my research assistants, and generally forced me to think differently about the status of rights in the world. To them I am grateful.

Finally, when writing and thinking about human rights violations, it helps to have a supportive community of family and friends. That I am able to do this work that I love and continue to have a smile on my face is due in large part to them. I am forever grateful to my mom, Adele, for everything—far too much to say here. I thank my dad and stepmom, Larry and Veronika; I am not sure what I would do without their love, support, and guidance. A special thanks goes to the Maldonado family: Stacy, Michael, my beautiful little Emma, and her soon-to-be-born little sister, Riley. I also thank Jamie Flores and Candi Seibert-Flores; may everyone be lucky enough to have a friend family like we have found with them. In addition, I thank Lindsey Leighton, whose friendship has been invaluable in so many ways. We have been blessed to count the Robertsons—Nicola DeBolt, Steven, Duncan, and Sydney—as our dear friends during our time in Portland; I thank them. And most especially, I thank the two who have my heart, D.C. and Cole.

REFERENCE

United Nations High Commissioner for Refugees. 2017. "Global Trends: Forced Displacement in 2016." Available at http://www.unhcr.org/5943e8a34.pdf.

Emerging Threats to Human Rights

Introduction

Emerging Threats to Human Rights

I n recent years the international community has faced challenges that threaten the enjoyment of human rights in new and dramatic ways. With global temperatures rising, access to clean water dwindling, and communities being forced to make trade-offs between individual human rights and the protection of natural environments (Anton 2011; Steady 2009), the natural world is imperiled like never before. Such widespread environmental degradation threatens the basic human rights of a large proportion of the world's population. Populations in the Global South are particularly vulnerable to the effects of rising sea levels associated with climate change and to water pollution. When sea levels rise as a result of climate change, what will become of populations who call small island-nations their home? When water becomes too polluted to drink, where will communities go to secure new sources of fresh, drinkable water?

Beyond these challenges to our environment, which pose potentially catastrophic threats to the enjoyment of human rights on a large scale, the international community is facing a second threat, violence targeted at civilians. In September 2015 the lifeless body of a three-year-old Syrian refugee washed onto the shore of southern Turkey. Aylan Kurdi, his five-year-old brother, and his mother all died when the small boat they were on capsized en route to the Greek island of Kos. His father, Abdullah Kurdi, tried to save his family and explained that their dinghy hit large waves on the thirteen-mile journey down the Aegean, leading the trafficker whom he had paid sixty-one hundred dollars for safe passage to jump off in the hopes of swimming to safety ("That Little Syrian Boy" 2015). The image of Aylan's tiny body, face down in the waves, sparked outrage in the international community and a collective sense that something must be done to ease the suffering of the victims of state violence in Syria. Indeed, as rates of civil war and internal conflict have risen in the post–World War II period (Barbieri and Reuveny 2005), civilians find themselves choosing between remaining in their homes or fleeing in search of peace and a better life. Still other groups of people are persecuted by their own government for their race, religion, or other immutable characteristic. As migratory pressures have sparked xenophobic national responses, one particularly malicious human rights consequence has been government decisions to rescind or severely curtail citizenship for unpopular groups. In some cases, even when populations have resided in the country for centuries, government officials have decided to withdraw citizenship, leaving large groups of people without any form of official nationality documentation and rendering them stateless.

These threats to the environment and human security have been followed by record-breaking numbers of refugees, migrants, and stateless people. In 2016, the Office of the UN High Commissioner for Refugees (UNHCR) recorded the highest-ever number of forcibly displaced people—65.6 million (UNHCR 2017). In 2018 the UNHCR again recorded the highest-ever number of forcibly displaced people—68.3 million. This number includes both officially registered refugees (25.4 million) and the approximately 10 million stateless people who live in a legal limbo, denied access to citizenship and often to the most basic rights that citizenship confers (UNHCR 2018).

In bringing together scholars of resource dilemmas, violence, and citizenship, as well as lawyers and human rights practitioners, this book begins by identifying the core causes of human rights violations confronting our world today. The contributions collectively point to three significant and emerging causes of human rights violations: resource deprivation, violence, and the denial of nationality/citizenship. Though in some instances, which I discuss in subsequent sections, pairs of these topics are occasionally treated together, more often than not these topics are examined in isolation. One of the primary arguments this book advances is that there are novel insights to be gleaned through a careful examination of the intersections of these emerging threats to human rights. By dismissing the more traditional approaches to these topics and instead applying a human rights frame, this book sheds light on the important intersections between these issues. A second argument this book assesses is whether and to what extent these emerging threats to human rights serve as drivers of displacement.

Recent Patterns in Global Migration

People choose to leave or are forced to leave their homes for a variety of reasons.[1] Some people leave their country of origin in the hope of finding better economic opportunities abroad, choosing to take their chances that they can provide better situations for themselves and their families. For others the desire to cross an international border is motivated by the need to find sources of clean water and arable farmland, resources that may no longer be available in their country of origin. Still others flee for their lives, with little more than the clothes on their backs, as violence engulfs their communities. Violence can shape flight when it emanates from the state—that is, the government is targeting citizens, using weapons of war against its own civilians. Or violence leading to emigration can result from rebels, terrorist groups, or drug cartels, nonstate actors who make the prospect of safety at home all but impossible to imagine. Still others choose to flee after long, slow government policies to rescind their rights because of religious or racial difference culminate in unlivable conditions. For some, a collapsing or failed state can motivate the desire to leave, as the government loses the ability to ensure basic protections for the population.

While none of these factors should be understood as new drivers of migration, and the phenomenon of human movement across state borders is similarly as old as the concept of borders themselves, what is new are the scope and scale of migration. At the end of 2016, 65.6 million people were displaced from their homes, an increase of 300,000 people from the year before (UNHCR 2017, 2). This number includes people displaced within their own country, internally displaced people (IDP), who make up 40.3 million of the figure reported for 2016. In 2016 the top three migrant-producing countries were Syria (5.5 million displaced people), Afghanistan (2.5 million), and South Sudan (1.4 million) (3).

Though the UNHCR's work is focused on providing relief to refugees rather than other categories of migrants, its reports include data on stateless populations, groups that are of concern but fall short of the definition of refugees and asylum seekers (those who have yet to be designated as refugees but are seeking that status). A major challenge concerning stateless populations is that governments often do not know how large the populations of stateless migrants living within their borders really are. Without any formal method for counting these groups, even data obtained by the UNHCR are at best an approximation of the true population. The UNHCR estimates that there are 10 million stateless people, yet its data capture only 3.2 million, while the Institute on Statelessness and Inclusion (2014) suggests that the actual number of stateless people in the world is closer to 15 million. Groups in the "of concern" category do not meet the definition of refugee but may be former refugees, people in host countries displaced by refugees, or rejected asylum seekers (UNHCR 2017, 51). In 2016, there were more than 800,000 people in this category. The UNHCR reports that by the end of 2016, there were 2.8 million people awaiting asylum decisions (39).

International law treats classes of migrants very differently. For those who have a well-founded fear of being persecuted by their government, the 1951 Convention relating to the Status of Refugees (Refugee Convention) confers the possibility of asylum and refugee status in a host country. Political persecution is a very specific type of violation, and mere fear is generally not sufficient to meet this standard. In practice, for instance, this means that starvation resulting from state collapse would not trigger the protection of the refugee regime under international law. Migrants who flee in search of better economic opportunities or who migrate to eke out a living to avoid death are similarly not protected by international law. It would be erroneous, however, to crudely split the causes of migration, as Anna Lindley cautions against into two neat categories, "economic/voluntary" and "forced/political" (2014, 12). How, for example, can one characterize those who flee temporarily in response to a humanitarian disaster? Similarly, how should we label those who have been persecuted by their governments and who have lost their citizenship but for whom the UNHCR determines that their fear is short of well founded?

We take no normative position on whether flight is necessarily positive or negative as an end in and of itself, aiming not to fall victim to what Stephen Castles (2010) refers to as the sedentary bias in migration research—making the flawed assumption that all instances of human migration must be generated from crisis in one's country of origin. This, he argues, leads to one of two approaches to migration, both of which imply that migration is dysfunctional and problematic. The first approach suggests that there are root causes of migration such as poverty that must be "solved" to stop emigration from countries of origin. The second approach prioritizes tighter border controls in host countries, implying that if the borders are secure, then problematic migration will cease (Castles 2010, 1567). Instead, this book examines whether and to what extent patterns of rights violations in the country of origin can be systematically linked to migration while recognizing that for a variety of situations migration occurs in the absence of human rights deprivations at home.

Examining the relationship between human rights violations in the country of origin and the likelihood of migration is emerging as an important area of inquiry within both international relations and migration studies. Because the 1951 Refugee Convention carves out such narrow rules surrounding the extension of refugee status, we apply Alexander Betts's survival migration framework. Survival migrants are "people who are outside their country of origin because of an existential threat for which they have no access to a domestic remedy or resolution. . . . It is based on the recognition that what matters is not privileging particular causes of movement but rather clearly identifying a threshold of fundamental rights which, when available in a country of origin, requires that the international community allow people to cross an international border and receive access to temporary or permanent sanctuary" (Betts 2013, 5).

Betts asks that, if a government is no longer willing or able to protect the civil, political, or economic social and cultural rights of its people, might the international community expand the set of legally recognized reasons for individuals to cross international borders? With our examination of deprivation of resources, violence, and citizenship, we aim to dig into sources of rights violations that may pose the sort of existential threat to which Betts ascribes the label "survival migrant." He points to "new drivers of cross-border displacement," including "generalized violence, environmental change, and food insecurity—and their interaction—which underpin a significant and growing proportion of cross-border displacement in many parts of the world" (Betts 2013, 2). In this book, we take up his call to examine some of these other drivers of displacement.

Yet these are not the same types of violations he examines; ours is a test of the generalizability of the existential threat concept outside Africa, from which he generates all of his case studies, and beyond the failed-state designation. We extend his analysis beyond a consideration of failed states because we can envision many situations in which existential threats to human rights occur in functioning regimes. The effects of climate change, which could generate these sorts of threats to basic human rights to life, livelihood, and security of person, are certainly occurring in stable, functioning regimes. This book examines three categories that we suggest are emerging as central threats to human rights—deprivation of resources, violence, and the denial of nationality/citizenship.

Resources

Climate change and environmental degradation pose enormous challenges to the enjoyment of many basic human rights. In spite of the UN General Assembly recognition in 2010 that the right to water and sanitation is a human right, more than 783 million people lack access to clean water. Roughly 90 percent of wastewater is untreated globally, and up to 80 percent of wastewater in the Global South flows into lakes, rivers, and coastal zones; thus, water pollution is a growing threat to the environment (Corcoran et al. 2010).

While the possibilities of entire islands sinking into the ocean or mass environmental migration are often raised in public discourse to dramatize the human consequences of climate change and environmental degradation, in reality the human rights consequences of environmental degradation are more complex. For example, though micro-islands in the Pacific, such as Tuvalu, may indeed one day disappear as sea levels rise as a result of climate change, in the interim, populations living in Tuvalu experience coastal erosion, which creates internal population displacement as arable land shrinks, water resources dry up, and less land becomes habitable (McAdam 2012). In this way, human rights intersect with climate change in much subtler ways, causing people to be cut off from food and water supplies, disrupting agricultural practices, and potentially accelerating migration. In theory, human rights are imbued in all people as a consequence of their humanity and should not be conditioned by their nationality. In practice, this means that all people, regardless of gender, race, or ethnicity, have claims as rights holders to breathe clean air, to drink clean water, and to be consulted when states or corporations, as duty bearers, initiate projects that will affect people's enjoyment of these rights. As each of the contributing chapters on resources lays bare, however, these forces have dramatically different effects on rights holders in the Global South.

For states in the Global South, the competing demands of development, environmental protection, and human rights are in constant tension (Cameron 2010; McShane et al. 2011). When a large proportion of a state's population lives below the poverty line, government policies that favor economic growth and job creation may directly threaten preservation of natural resources. In this way the effects of climate change and environmental degradation may "compound pre-existing vulnerabilities" such as poor socioeconomic conditions, limited natural resources, and population growth (McAdam 2012, 10). When the Ecuadorian government permitted oil companies to drill and mine territory in the Amazon, the indigenous Sarakyus' ability to maintain their traditional way of life was put in jeopardy. But at the same time, excessive environmental protection may hinder the prospects for economic development because the costs of clean technologies may be prohibitive, particularly in developing societies (Costi 2003).

The authors in Part I differ in their assessment of whether and under what conditions the tensions between development, environmental protection, and human rights are resolvable. In Chapter 1, Michelle Scobie describes the environmental-justice perspective, which began in the 1970s in underrepresented minority communities in the United States in response to industrial zoning rules that exposed these groups to disproportionate levels of environmental pollutants. Globally, the environmental-justice perspective is now embodied in the response of the states of the Global South to the devastating effects of climate change. This perspective emphasizes that people of present and future generations are the rights holders and that the industrialized states and corporations, as duty bearers, are responsible for mitigating the effects of climate change. Her assessment is cautiously optimistic about the ability of developing states to navigate these tensions successfully and promote all of these values simultaneously.

In Chapter 2, Beatrice Lindstrom highlights the competing demands of environmental justice, human rights, and development in Haiti. As citizens of the poorest country in the Western Hemisphere, Haitians have become accustomed to nongovernmental actors serving as primary service providers. Yet when these nongovernmental actors are necessary partners in the process of development, how can states hold these organizations accountable when their practices sacrifice human rights? Lindstrom shows that coordination between grassroots nongovernmental organizations (NGOs) and a global litigation strategy has the potential to simultaneously maximize human rights.

In Chapter 3, Robert Mandel offers a very sobering take against the we-can-have-our-cake-and-eat-it-too approaches to balancing human rights, environmental protection, and development. He argues that when choices must be made between human rights and environmental protection in developed states, human rights often win for two reasons. The global spread of democracy prioritizes liberal, cosmopolitan values that privilege people and their right to consumption over the protection of the physical environment. Additionally, it takes time to recognize the effects of environmental degradation, far longer than it takes to witness human rights violations, allowing rights to take priority in national debates. Among developing countries in the Global South, he argues, the demands of survival and the quest for rapid economic growth swamp pressures to improve human rights or protect the environment. He cautions against the conclusion that we can harmoniously maximize human rights, environmental protection, and development simultaneously.

Violence

A second theme this book addresses is the human rights consequences of brute force and violence. By brute force, we mean physical coercion applied by either the state or organized nonstate actors on a civilian population. On a continuum of possible tools available for compelling an actor to change its course of action, brute force falls along the most severe end, involving the use of boots on the ground, the deployment of naval and air forces, and use of all means of hard power (Mandel 2015). In recent history (between 1989 and 2014) this form of organized violence against civilians has not accounted for the greatest number of fatalities; rather, state-on-state violence is responsible for the greatest share of fatalities during this period. But this form of one-sided violence, in which the state or an organized nonstate actor uses deadly force against a civilian population, accounted for 39 percent, or 706,106 deaths, between 1989 and 2014.[2] A steep spike in fatalities associated with one-sided violence occurred in 2014 and is largely attributable to the Syrian Civil War. Between 1989 and 2014 Africa was the deadliest region of the world for one-sided violence, followed by South and Central Asia and the Middle East (Melander 2015).

When armed actors use the tools of war against civilian populations, the most basic human rights of those civilian populations are imperiled. In seeking to root out threats to regime stability, a government may send troops to question, detain, and imprison civilians without due process. In Burma, government soldiers routinely engage in large sweeps of the minority Muslim Rohingya community, arresting, extorting, and detaining them en masse (Human Rights Watch 2012). Beyond the obvious deprivation of liberty that such detention entails, when large contingents of troops or armed groups intermix with civilian populations, the human rights of especially vulnerable populations may be at even greater risk. In weak states and among rebel groups, rape of women and girls is often used as a means to foster unit cohesion (Cohen 2013). Both governments and nonstate armed actors may also forcibly recruit child soldiers, depriving these children of their most basic rights (Pilisuk and Rountree 2015). Using their asymmetric power, armed actors may confiscate property and valuables or deprive civilians of means for supporting themselves and their families.

Beyond sending in troops, a government or a nonstate armed actor may direct the tools of war against civilian populations, resulting in devastating loss of life. Muammar Gaddafi, former head of the Libyan government, employed cluster munitions, rocket launchers, and mortars against civilian populations in Misrata during the Libyan Civil War (UN News 2011). Prior to the siege on Misrata, Gaddafi's forces had engaged in long-term detention and executions of perceived threats to his regime throughout the country (UN Human Rights Council 2012). Bashar Al Assad, president of Syria, employed chemical weapons against men, women, and children in at least 161 documented attacks through December 2015. These attacks have killed nearly 1,500 people and injured another 14,581 through exposure (Syrian American Medical Society 2016).

The contributors to Part II suggest that when the state or nonstate armed groups turn the weapons of war on civilian populations, forcing people to flee their homes and countries, these populations may experience new and distinct types of human rights violations. In Chapter 4, Kerstin Fisk examines the human security of refugees and asylum seekers in sub-Saharan Africa, illustrating that the traditional conception of refugees as threats to state security overlooks the refugees' own right to human security. Her case studies of Burundian refugees in Tanzania and Rwanda and refugees from Ethiopia and Democratic Republic of the Congo (DRC) in South Africa illustrate that even when refugees escape, they do not find safety in asylum countries. Burundian refugees in Tanzania and Rwanda were subject to attacks by forces loyal to the Burundian government even after they crossed into these neighboring countries. The South African government allowed the systematic targeting of refugees in violent attacks by xenophobic forces. Whether the perpetrators of violence are refugee senders or refugee hosts, Fisk shows that the human security of refugee populations is in jeopardy even when they are able to flee from violence at home.

In Chapter 5, Neil A. Englehart illustrates the ways in which cease-fires can exacerbate certain types of human rights abuses. Militants who are fighting government forces need civilian support and access to financing. These needs dictate the types of abuses these groups engage in—kidnapping and killing government officials both serve these ends. But once a cease-fire has been negotiated, the needs of these former militants change, and as Englehart shows, their patterns of human rights abuses do as well. When militants disarm as part of the terms of a cease-fire, they may stop engaging in the abuses that allowed them to fight the government, but they do not stop violating human rights. Englehart's analysis shows that cease-fire groups across Asia simply begin behaving like government-supported groups in their patterns of human rights abuses. His analysis demonstrates that cease-fires do not necessarily mean peace and safety for civilians. Instead, cease-fire groups adapt, behaving like government-supported groups, and subject civilians to the same sorts of human rights violations as government-supported groups.

Once intrastate violence has ceased, governments have many ways of moving forward: truth and reconciliation commissions can be used to uncover truth without prosecution, traditional prosecutions can be employed, or governments may simply opt to grant blanket amnesty and move forward. In Chapter 6, Brian Frederking and Max Aviles show that in countries undergoing democratic transitions, the use of truth-and-justice mechanisms (tribunals) has a marginal yet positive impact on human rights. Moreover, when these tribunals mete out punishment for state-sponsored violence rather than simply allow truth revelation in exchange for amnesty, human rights improve.

Collectively, the chapters in Part II suggest that there are reasons to fear new and distinct types of human rights violations once civilian populations successfully flee violence. Xenophobia, abuse at the hands of asylum governments, torture, restrictions on freedom of movement, and abuses of civil rights are all possible following the end of violence. Once state violence has ceased, cease-fires and transitional justice mechanisms may exacerbate and intensify new forms of violence against civilians.

Citizenship

Once those civilians manage to successfully escape dangerous or unhealthy conditions at home, what sorts of rights and opportunities can they expect to receive in countries of refuge? A critical element in understanding what rights and opportunities await migrants in countries of refuge is citizenship. If migrants have no realistic hope of naturalizing, they may remain detained in a refugee camp with minimal resources until they are able to return home. It is not uncommon for people to reside in this state of limbo for many years, unwelcome in their country of residence but unable to return home. For the Sahrawis, a group of 150,000 refugees living in camps in western Algeria since the late 1970s, the camps have become a way of life (Epatko 2013). In this regard, citizenship in international relations is paradoxical. While the international human rights regime is universal, ostensibly applying to all people as a consequence of their humanity, in reality, for migrants who flee their home to find refuge in another country, the rights and opportunities they can expect to receive vary considerably and are dependent, inter alia, on citizenship laws (see Chapter 9 for a discussion).

According to the UNHCR, 34,000 people were displaced from their homes each day in 2015 because of conflict or persecution. There are now 65.3 million forcibly displaced people in the world; of those 21.3 million are children (UNHCR 2015). Only 16.1 million people have obtained official refugee status through the UNHCR, and there are an additional 5.2 million Palestinian refugees, who are registered with the UN Relief and Works Agency (n.d.). These numbers matter for two reasons. First, the conflicts in Afghanistan and Syria and instability in Somalia have generated the highest number of forcibly displaced people on record. In short, these numbers are unprecedented. Second, the numbers represent individual lives, hopes, and dreams for the future. One cannot think about emerging threats to human rights without examining the greatest single threat to the enjoyment of human rights. Today, the realization of human rights is inextricably bound with questions of citizenship and nationality.

But Part III demonstrates that citizenship laws serve a dual purpose. Not only do rules governing the extension of citizenship carry with them important human rights consequences for migrants who successfully flee violence or environmental degradation, but the discriminatory deprivation of nationality may also serve as the initial impetus behind migration (van Waas 2008). Discriminatory deprivation of nationality is an especially cruel way for a government to use citizenship laws to discriminate against unpopular groups. When citizenship status or even permanent residency status is revoked on the basis of race, ethnicity, or any other immutable characteristic, the core rights that flow from citizenship or residency status are also revoked. People lose the ability to work, travel freely, go to school, and secure housing. Stateless people are often detained and held without cause as authorities attempt to sort out their status. Unlike refugees, who flee their country of nationality in search of safety but still retain their citizenship, those who have had their citizenship revoked (or those born without citizenship) have grim prospects in regard to their human rights.

And while the UNHCR reports that there are approximately 10 million stateless people in the world today, the real number is likely closer to 15 million (see Institute on Statelessness and Inclusion 2014). The overwhelming majority, some 97.6 percent, of the stateless people identified by the UNHCR reside in just twenty countries (van Waas, de Chickera, and Albarazi 2014). This concentration better reflects gaps in reporting than actual geographic distributions of stateless populations. For example, the UNHCR's official numbers include reports from just four of forty-seven of countries in sub-Saharan Africa and neglect 2.1 million Palestinians who have never been displaced from the West Bank or Gaza Strip but whose status is undoubtedly in question (van Waas, de Chickera, and Albarazi 2014).

In Chapter 7, I grapple with the human rights consequences of statelessness, examining the experience of Rohingya Muslims in the Greater Mekong Subregion. In 1982 the Burmese government started the process of eliminating citizenship status for the Rohingya, who had lived in Burma for more than two centuries. In the decades that followed, Rohingya human rights deteriorated precipitously, including the right to travel outside their village, freely marry, or work. As their rights evaporated and they became stateless, many Rohingya were left with little choice but to flee Burma, culminating in the 2015 Rohingya refugee crisis. I argue that a tragic and previously unappreciated human rights consequence of statelessness is an acute susceptibility to traffickers. I examine the links between Rohingya rights violations and the likelihood of trafficking, arguing that statelessness renders groups susceptible to traffickers.

Whereas stateless populations fare poorly in the Greater Mekong Subregion, as evidenced by the tragic experiences of the Rohingya, these populations do not necessarily fare better after arrival in the European Union (EU). In Chapter 8, Patricia Rodda and Charles Anthony Smith show that across Europe, states' immigration agendas conflict with a surprisingly underdeveloped European stateless regime. Rodda and Smith argue that unlike the EU's well-developed asylum and antitrafficking regimes, there has been no effort at the supranational level to harmonize statelessness determination procedures. The result is a patchwork approach to statelessness across Europe that has grave consequences for the human rights of stateless populations. As refugees and stateless people flood into Europe, these uneven procedures leave many in legal limbo, unable to work and susceptible to traffickers.

In Chapter 9, Jeannette Money and Shaina Western consider the characteristics of migrant-receiving countries that enhance or diminish the quality of refuge migrants arriving in new countries can expect to receive. They show that in spite of an international legal framework that emphasizes universal human rights, in reality refugees face a hierarchy of rights depending on the characteristics of the refuge country. Some governments provide high levels of resettlement support that allow migrants to integrate, develop job skills, and thrive; others allow migrants to eke out a living in a refugee camp; and still other governments simply detain and deport. Money and Western argue that when countries of refuge have a high level of human development, have a strong quality of governance, and provide access to citizenship, survival migrants are better equipped to thrive in their new countries. The authors' analysis suggests that migrants tend to settle in countries within the same region, meaning that today most flee and then resettle in the Middle East or sub-Saharan Africa. Countries with the fewest resources tend to be those that provide refuge most frequently, calling into question human rights that migrants can expect to receive, even after they have fled.

Human Rights: Looking across and between the Issues

Traditionally in international relations, resource deprivation, violence, and citizenship are not treated or examined together. Scholars interested in the politics of conservation and pollution may examine challenges that impede the negotiation of successful agreements or point to factors that hasten the collapse of such agreements (Battaglini and Harstad 2016; Susskind and Ali 2014; Gupta 2012). Similarly, scholars of state violence, in seeking to explain why a government might choose to take up arms against its civilian population or why civilians might choose to rebel against the government, identify the conditions under which such violence is most likely to occur (Collier 2006). In the statelessness and citizenship literature, those studying this phenomenon often adopt a legal framework, trying to understand how and why municipal or international law could permit such an outcome (van Waas 2008; Milbrandt 2011). Respectively, resource deprivation, violence, and citizenship are often examined within a conservation, security, and legal framework. Yet these traditional frameworks neglect the important human rights consequences associated with environmental scarcity/degradation, state violence, and deprivation of citizenship. By grouping these topics, not only can we more easily see the intersections between them, but we also can emphasize the human rights framework as a way to highlight these intersections.

   The 2005 Andijan massacre in Uzbekistan provides a good example of the value of grouping these topics together and the traction that can be gained by employing the human rights framework. Since independence in 1991, the government in Uzbekistan has remained a repressive, autocratic regime led in 2005 by Islam Karimov. Uzbek authorities became enraged in the early 2000s when a group of Muslim businessmen began distributing food and necessities to the struggling population of Uzbekistan. The government feared that because of this distribution of basic necessities, the people would shift their loyalty away from the government in favor of this group. In 2005 Karimov's government arrested the businessmen, leading to widespread protest in Andijan for their release in May 2005. The government responded by firing into the crowd of protesters, killing between 187 (government estimate) and 1,500 (Human Rights Watch estimate) (Human Rights Watch 2005). To defend its attack on the protesters to the rest of the world, Uzbek authorities claimed that the protesters were Islamic Fundamentalist terrorists, members of the Hizb ut-Tahrir.

   A more basic narrative for this story would suggest that a bad, autocratic government deprived its population of food and then used violence against the people for rising up in response to the policy. When we delve deeper into this example, we can see the value of grouping these topics together. The businessmen were motivated to distribute basic necessities to the poor as a consequence of their religious beliefs. As the government stopped providing basic necessities, the wealthy businessmen were compelled to step in and help the population. The failure to provide basic necessities, in this case the provision of food, if left unaddressed, would lead to malnutrition, disease, and possibly death. Such maladies inhibit the enjoyment of even the most basic aspiration for a full life. And one of the outcomes of this resource scarcity was state violence; the government responded to the uprising in support of the businessmen by firing into the crowd, depriving hundreds of people, perhaps even more than a thousand, of their lives. And why were people willing to challenge the government? Without food, their prospects for life were most certainly diminished. From a human rights perspective, the protesters were met with two unenviable options: risk being deprived of food or risk stepping into the government's crosshairs by challenging it to release the businessmen. Finally, the government attempted to use the narrative of us versus them, citizen versus terrorist, to justify its actions to a critical global community. Here the role of citizenship is critical: it was used by the government to justify killing Uzbeks.

   The value added in grouping these topics together is that we can make the human rights consequences of these emerging threats the central focus of our analysis. Additionally, when we emphasize rights rather than security, law, or conservation, we can examine the important ways in which these emerging threats to rights are connected. The primary argument this book advances is that in dismissing the traditional frameworks often applied to the environment, violence, and citizenship in favor of considering the human rights impact yields important insights into the ways in which these issues are interconnected in the real world.

Environment-Violence Connections

One branch of literature on environment-violence connection suggests that resource scarcity and environmental degradation can be a direct cause of state violence (Homer-Dixon 1994). When populations are deprived of basic necessities such as clean drinking water or food, they may take to the streets to protest and demand better provisions from their governments, as the Andijan Massacre aptly illustrates. Violence among groups may similarly erupt when water or arable farmland becomes scarce and groups must compete to obtain these resources. A different approach highlights the ways in which resource scarcity can be an intervening or indirect cause of violence, suggesting, for instance, that environmental scarcity can activate latent ethnic tensions, causing intraethnic violence to flare up (Baechler 1999). Still others suggest that resource scarcity and degradation are not necessarily a cause of violence, but populations may, through technological innovations, social institutions, or market mechanisms, avoid outright conflict in the face of environmental challenges. Though anecdotal evidence of the environment-violence connection abounds, a robust statistical relationship between these factors has yet to be identified in the literature (Bernauer, Bohmelt, and Koubi 2012).

The discussion in Part I reinforces many of the central findings in this literature but highlights the ways in which competition over resources is rarely confined to conflicts between local groups. The violence, conflict, and contestation over resources can ensnare states located thousands of miles apart and require the assistance and support of intergovernmental organization and NGOs, while pitting more-developed and less-developed countries against each other. The authors in Part I suggest that we expand our understanding of actors and forms of violence that emerge from conflicts over resources.

In Chapter 2, on the cholera epidemic in Haiti, Lindstrom shows that conflict over the source of water contamination can emerge between an intergovernmental actor (the UN) and the local population sickened by contaminated water. Here, the conflict over resources is not simply between domestic groups fighting for access to a dwindling resource. Instead, the conflict emerged because the UN needed to maintain a presence in Haiti to maintain order in the wake of violence. In Chapter 1, Scobie draws on the environmental-justice perspective to identify nontraditional actors involved in resource conflicts. She points to those who are socially more vulnerable and therefore least able to adapt to the consequences of climate change, as well as future generations, to understand locations of emerging sites of conflict over resources. These chapters suggest that the traditional way we have thought about a unidirectional environmental-violence link, invoking conflicting domestic actors over scarce resources, can miss the point. These conflicts can emerge between actors in far-flung places yet still call into question the enjoyment of basic human rights.

Violence-Citizenship Connections

Research on the connections between violence and flight are well developed in the scholarly literature, clearly establishing a relationship between violence, human rights abuses, and forced migration (Moore and Shellman 2004; Apodaca 1998; Schmeidl 1997). Yet across this literature there is a simple underlying assumption: once migrants flee from human rights abuses and violence in their country of origin, their prospects for a life with dignity ought to improve.

But again, the traditional framework misses important opportunities to tease out connections between violence, flight, migration, and prospects for human rights. In Chapter 4, Fisk forces the reader to think not about the security of the migrant-receiving states but rather about the human security of refugees and migrants who experience violent attacks even after they have fled. As refugees and migrants flood into host countries, their status as noncitizens creates a second set of threats: xenophobic violence. In Chapter 5, Englehart addresses the prospects for peace and human rights following the cessation of violence, challenging received wisdom that rights improve after cessation of hostilities. The implication is that, perhaps counterintuitively, fleeing one's country of origin even after the cessation of hostilities may improve one's rights prospects. Moreover, the causal relationship between citizenship and violence can go in the opposite direction. In Chapter 7, I show that when the government rescinded the citizenship of the Rohingya community in Burma, violence erupted between the Buddhist majority and the Rohingya. The intraethnic violence has today risen to what many observers consider a genocide against the Rohingya.

My argument is that dismissing the traditional frameworks (see Figure I.1) gives us traction in thinking about how human rights are imperiled across the issue areas; environmental degradation can be both a cause and consequence of violence. Deprivation of natural resources can spark violence both between groups and between people and their government. And simply fleeing violence at home does not necessarily improve prospects for rights

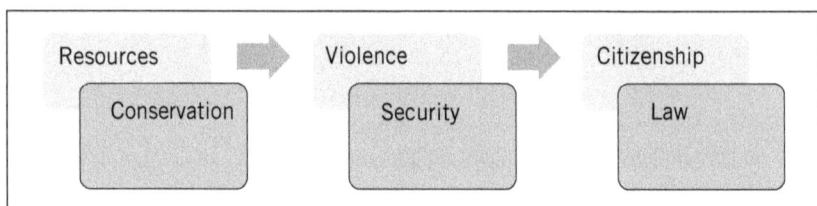

Figure I.1   Applying the human rights frame

abroad. As Money and Western suggest in Chapter 9, "Where those who seek refuge end up matters." This book addresses the issue of human rights at the intersections between the environment and violence, as well as between violence and citizenship.

This book addresses emerging threats to human rights that are vast and seemingly intractable. As the peril of our planet increases, populations are confronting difficult trade-offs: remaining in dirty, polluted environments and risking disease and death or fleeing in search of a better life. As civilians face unspeakable violence at the hands of both states and nonstate armed actors, they confront painful decisions about remaining at home or migrating. This book shows that once a difficult decision to migrate is made, naturalization and citizenship laws can obstruct the fulfillment of human rights in host countries. Emerging threats to human rights are displacing people at rates previously unexperienced, but by looking at some of the intersections between these areas, we can begin to think more systematically about the links between human rights and migration.

NOTES

1. The following is not a comprehensive list of the drivers of human migration.
2. As Erik Melander (2015) explains, this number is inflated because of the inclusion of the Rwandan genocide, which claimed approximately five hundred thousand lives.

REFERENCES

Anton, Donald. 2011. *Environmental Protection and Human Rights*. Cambridge: Cambridge University Press.
Apodaca, Claire. 1998. "Human Rights Abuse: Precursor to Refugee Flight?" *Journal of Refugee Studies* 11 (1): 80–93.
Baechler, Gunther. 1999. "Environmental Degradation and Violent Conflict: Hypotheses, Research Agendas and Theory-Building." In *Ecology, Politics and Violent Conflict*, edited by Mohamed Suliman, 76–112. London: Zed.
Barbieri, Katherine, and Rafael Reuveny. 2005. "Economic Globalization and Civil War." *Journal of Politics* 67 (4): 1228–1247.

Battaglini, Marco, and Bard Harstad. 2016. "Participation and Duration of Environmental Agreements." *Journal of Political Economy* 124 (1): 160–204.

Bernauer, Thomas, Tobias Bohmelt, and Vally Koubi. 2012. "Environmental Change and Violent Conflict." *Environmental Research Letters* 7 (1): 1–8.

Betts, Alexander. 2013. *Survival Migration: Failed Governance and the Crisis of Displacement.* Ithaca, NY: Cornell University Press.

Cameron, Edward. 2010. "Human Rights and Climate Change: Moving from an Intrinsic to an Instrumental Approach." *Georgia Journal of International and Comparative Law* 38 (3): 673–716.

Castles, Stephen. 2010. "Understanding Global Migration: A Social Transformation Perspective." *Journal of Ethnic and Migration Studies* 36 (10): 1565–1586.

Cohen, Dara Kay. 2013. "Explaining Rape during Civil War: Cross-National Evidence, 1980–2009." *American Political Science Review* 107 (3): 461–477.

Collier, Paul. 2006. "Economic Causes of Civil Conflict and Their Implications for Policy." In *Managing Global Chaos*, edited by Chester A. Crocker, Fen Osler Hampson, and Pamela Aall. Washington, DC: U.S. Institute of Peace.

Corcoran, Emily, Christian Nellemann, Elaine Baker, Robert Bos, David Osborn, and Heidi Savelli, eds. 2010. *Sick Water? The Central Role of Wastewater Management in Sustainable Development.* Nairobi, Kenya: United Nations Environment Programme.

Costi, Alberto. 2003. "Environmental Protection, Economic Growth, and Environmental Justice: Are They Compatible in Central and Eastern Europe?" In *Just Sustainabilities: Development in an Unequal World*, edited by Julian Agyeman, Robert D. Bullard, and Bob Evans, 289–310. Cambridge, MA: MIT Press.

Epatko, Larisa. 2013. "The 37-Year-Old Refugee Situation You Know Nothing About." *PBS News Hour*, October 25. Available at http://www.pbs.org/newshour/rundown/the-37-year-old-refugee-situation-you-know-nothing-about.

Gupta, Joyeeta. 2012. "Negotiating Challenges and Climate Change." *Climate Policy* 12 (5): 630–644.

Homer-Dixon, Thomas. 1994. "Environmental Scarcities and Violent Conflict: Evidence from Cases." *International Security* 1 (19): 5–40.

Human Rights Watch. 2005. "'Bullets Were Falling like Rain': The Andijan Massacre, May 13, 2005." June 6. Available at https://www.hrw.org/report/2005/06/06/bullets-were-falling-rain/andijan-massacre-may-13-2005.

———. 2012. "'The Government Could Have Stopped This': Sectarian Violence and Ensuing Abuses in Burma's Arakan State." August. Available at https://www.hrw.org/sites/default/files/reports/burma0812webwcover_0.pdf.

Institute on Statelessness and Inclusion. 2014. *The World's Stateless.* Oisterwijk, Netherlands: Wolf Legal.

Lindley, Anna. 2014. "Exploring Crisis and Migration: Concepts and Issues." In *Crisis and Migration: Critical Perspectives*, edited by Anna Lindley, 1–23. London: Routledge.

Mandel, Robert. 2015. *Coercing Compliance: State-Initiated Brute Force in Today's World.* Stanford, CA: Stanford University Press.

McAdam, Jane. 2012. *Climate Change, Forced Migration, and International Law.* Oxford: Oxford University Press.

McShane, Thomas, Paul D. Hirsch, Tran Chi Trung, Alexander N. Songorwa, Ann Kinzig, Bruno Monteferri, David Mutekanga, et al. 2011. "Hard Choices: Making Trade-Offs between Biodiversity Conservation and Human Well-Being." *Biological Conservation* 144 (3): 966–972.

Melander, Erik. 2015. "Organized Violence in the World, 2015: An Assessment by the Uppsala Conflict Data Program." Available at https://www.pcr.uu.se/digitalAssets/654/c_654446-l_1-k_ucdp-paper-9.pdf.

Milbrandt, Jay. 2011. "Statelessness." *Cardozo Journal of International and Comparative Law* 20 (75): 75–103.

Moore, Will, and Stephen Shellman. 2004. "Fear of Persecution: Forced Migration, 1951–1995." *Journal of Conflict Resolution* 48 (5): 723–745.

Pilisuk, Marc, and Jennifer Achord Rountree. 2015. *The Hidden Structure of Violence: Who Benefits from Global Violence and War.* New York: Monthly Review Press.

Schmeidl, Suzanne. 1997. "Exploring the Causes of Forced Migration: A Pooled Time-Series Analysis, 1971–1990." *Social Science Quarterly* 78 (2): 284–308.

Steady, Filomina Chioma, ed. 2009. *Environmental Justice in the New Millennium: Global Perspectives on Race, Ethnicity and Human Rights.* New York: Palgrave Macmillan.

Susskind, Lawrence, and Saleem Ali. 2014. *Environmental Diplomacy: Negotiating More Effective Global Agreements.* Oxford: Oxford University Press.

Syrian American Medical Society. 2016. "A New Normal: Ongoing Chemical Weapons Attacks in Syria." February. Available at https://www.sams-usa.net/wp-content/up loads/2016/09/A-New-Normal_Ongoing-Chemical-Weapons-Attacks-in-Syria.com pressed.pdf.

"That Little Syrian Boy: Here's Who He Was." 2015. *NPR*, September 3. Available at http://www.npr.org/sections/parallels/2015/09/03/437132793/photo-of-dead-3-year -old-syrian-refugee-breaks-hearts-around-the-world.

UNHCR (United Nations High Commissioner for Refugees). 2017. "Global Trends: Forced Displacement in 2016." Available at http://www.unhcr.org/5943e8a34.pdf.

———. 2018. "Figures at a Glance." Available at http://www.unhcr.org/en-us/figures-at -a-glance.html.

UN Human Rights Council. 2012. "Report of the International Commission of Inquiry on Libya." March 8. Available at https://www.ohchr.org/Documents/HRBodies/HR Council/RegularSession/Session19/A.HRC.19.68.pdf.

UN News. 2011. "Libya's Attacks on Civilians May Be International Crimes—UN Rights Chief." April 20. Available at http://www.un.org/apps/news/story.asp?NewsID= 38154#.WIOcUWb4VaU.

UN Relief and Works Agency. n.d. "What We Do." Available at https://www.unrwa.org/ what-we-do (accessed February 22, 2019).

van Waas, Laura. 2008. *Nationality Matters: Statelessness under International Law.* Antwerp, Belgium: Intersentia.

van Waas, Laura, Amal de Chickera, and Zahara Albarazi. 2014. "The World's Stateless: A New Report on Why Size Does and Does Not Matter." European Network on Statelessness, December 15. Available at http://www.statelessness.eu/blog/world %E2%80%99s-stateless-new-report-why-size-does-and-doesn%E2%80%99t-matter.

PART I | RESOURCES

Climate Change, Human Rights, and Migration

MICHELLE SCOBIE

There is a moral duty among human beings to provide solace to the suffering. Climate change threatens the human rights of present and future generations, including the right to life, privacy and a home, property, health, freedom of movement and of religion, adequate sanitation and food (Ford et al. 2016), medicine, clothing, water, housing, education, nationhood, development, and a series of cultural rights (Zellentin 2015). Climate change also endangers the rights of minorities and vulnerable groups to safe and healthy conditions of work, freedom of expression, self-determination, nondiscrimination, and procedural justice on climate-related issues (OHCHR 2015). The challenges around climate change and human rights resonate with the issues addressed in the other chapters in this book: water scarcity and human rights, balancing the rights of the environment and human development, violence motivated by resource scarcity, civil wars, statelessness, and migration. Climate change contributes to migration, but most environmental migrants come from, and sadly move to, places where they suffer from many of these issues. Climate change is a contextual reality within which the global sustainable development agenda is to be implemented. The Sustainable Development Goals (SDGs), seventeen global targets set by the United Nations General Assembly in 2015 related to social, economic, and environmental sustainability and development, directly address and provide a response to many of the problems and injustices caused by climate change. This chapter examines climate change, human rights and migration, the environmental justice and human rights responses to the injustices of climate change, and the multiple ways to understand the climate change–migration–human rights nexus.

Migration

Extreme or gradual-onset climatic events trigger the outward or internal displacement and migration of peoples. The International Organization for Migration (IOM), established in 1951, is the United Nations (UN) agency that manages global migration issues. It defines "migration" as the "movement of a person or a group of persons, either across an international border, or within a State. It is a population movement, encompassing any kind of movement of people, whatever its length, composition and causes; it includes migration of refugees, displaced persons, economic migrants, and persons moving for other purposes, including family reunification" (IOM, n.d.). "Internal migration" is a "movement of people from one area of a country to another for the purpose or with the effect of establishing a new residence. This migration may be temporary or permanent. Internal migrants move but remain within their country of origin (e.g. rural to urban migration)" (IOM 2008, 494). Internally displaced persons are "persons or groups of persons who have been forced or obliged to flee or to leave their homes or places of habitual residence, in particular as a result of or in order to avoid the effects of armed conflict, situations of generalized violence, violations of human rights or natural or human-made disasters, and who have not crossed an internationally recognized border" (OHCHR, n.d.b). The migrant has traditionally been recognized as a refugee under international law. According to the 1951 Convention relating to the Status of Refugees (Refugee Convention), Article 1A(2), as modified by the 1967 Protocol, a "refugee" is a person who, "owing to well-founded fear of being persecuted for reasons of race, religion, nationality, membership of a particular social group or political opinion, is outside the country of his nationality and is unable or, owing to such fear, is unwilling to avail himself of the protection of that country; or who, not having a nationality and being outside the country of his former habitual residence as a result of such events, is unable or, owing to such fear, is unwilling to return to it" (United Nations 1951, 14).

There are many factors that push persons to leave their country or place of abode and many other factors that encourage persons to move toward other places. Traditionally, triggers for migration have been related to economic, social, and political threats or opportunities. More recently, persons are displaced more often because of environmental change, but data are lacking on the number of persons within this category (IOM 2017, 40). Environmentally related displacement may not put persons within the category of refugees because of the missing element of "persecution." However, the duty of the international community to refugees and the rights of refugees are more clearly defined and systematically guaranteed than those of other migrants.

Migration involves three main groups of actors: vulnerable members of the migrant family and community who are not able migrate, the migrants, and those who receive the migrants in their new locations. Persons unable to migrate may be among the poorest, those with the least knowledge and finances and fewest connections and skills, and should not be forgotten when addressing climate migration (Geddes et al. 2012). Migrants are also vulnerable in their destination locations. They tend to move to the most affordable locations, which may also be the most vulnerable to climate change. Some migrants in megacities, for example, settle in coastal areas vulnerable to storm surges; others settle in flood-prone shanty dwellings (Black, Kniveton, and Schmidt-Verkerk 2011). Some migrants are at a disadvantage in the labor market because they may not speak the language, lack skills, or may not have regularized immigration and legal status in the destination country. Migrants may not have access to social services (Tanner et al. 2009) and may be pushed into the informal economy, which is less regulated; thus, these migrants may be open to exploitation.

Climate Change and Migration

How does climate change relate to migration? Climate variability and climate change have been among the factors pushing the displacement of peoples (McLeman and Smit 2006) because of the impacts on land, water, and the biosphere on which human existence depends (Smith et al. 2016). According to the Intergovernmental Panel on Climate Change (IPCC), the UN agency on climate change, the main cause of climate change is human-made greenhouse gas emissions from industrialized countries (Field et al. 2014). Climate change is responsible for more frequent extreme climatic events (hurricanes, cyclones, etc.), as well as slow-onset events such as rising sea levels, floods, water shortages, droughts, heat waves, desertification, the spread of vector-borne and tropical viruses (most recently zika and dengue), ocean acidification, glacial retreat, and loss of biodiversity (Adger et al. 2014). Rising sea levels and storm surges diminish arable land areas and cause desalination of freshwater reservoirs (Gemenne 2011a). Climate change affects health, human safety, and food security (Otto et al. 2017); triggers changes in disease and mortality patterns; causes food, water, and nutrition shortages; and increases the difficulty to provide adequate sanitation for human settlements (Costello et al. 2009). Collective violence may increase as rural communities compete for scarce farmland (Levy, Sidel, and Patz 2017), already in evidence in parts of the Middle East and North Africa (Sternberg 2012). This in turn triggers migration by what some have called "climate exiles" (Byravan and Rajan 2015).

The 2010 Cancun Outcome Declaration of the Conference of the Parties (COP) to the 1992 UN Framework Convention on Climate Change (UNFCCC) already recognized the need to address climate-related displacement, migration, and planned relocation (IOM 2017, 143–144). The UNFCCC 2015 Paris Agreement established a task force to develop recommendations for an integrated approach toward climate change–related displacement and migration. Its task is to recognize challenges and to propose solutions related to the legal, policy, and institutional dimensions of climate-induced migration (IOM 2017, 143–144). Although there has not yet been a drastic increase in climate migrants (Field et al. 2014), there is evidence of climate-related displacement.

There have been calls to provide a new legal framework for climate migrants (Skillington 2015), either under the UNFCCC (Warren 2016) or through a widening of scope of the 1951 Refugee Convention, therefore affording them the same immigration and asylum rights as other migrants (Biermann and Boas 2008; Williams 2008) or through a separate treaty (Kelman 2010; Smith and McNamara 2015). In principle, under the 1954 Convention relating to the Status of Stateless Persons (Statelessness Convention) and Articles 3.1 and 4.8 of the UNFCCC, there is space for developing protocols under international law for climate exiles suffering social effects of, for example, sea-level rise (Byravan and Rajan 2015). Perhaps because the term "refugees" relates more to persecuted persons, there is a trend away from this term in favor of "climate migrants" (Nicholson 2014; Bettini 2013). The status of these persons has not been resolved in international law and continues to be an unresolved problem for climate justice. The case of a Kirbati national in New Zealand illustrates this problem. In 2015 Ioane Teitiota was deported from New Zealand after a four-year battle to seek asylum as a climate refugee. He argued that sea levels are rising and making living on the island unsafe. The court hearing the matter found that his case was not covered by the Statelessness Convention, since he was not "being persecuted for reasons of race, religion, nationality, membership of a particular social group or political opinion" (Teitiota v. Chief Executive of the Ministry of Business Innovation and Employment 2013).

Some forecasting studies from the early 2000s created a sense of urgency and panic with estimates that as many as fifty million persons would be environmental refugees by 2010 (Myers 2005). This prompted calls for a widening of their protection under international refugee law (Biermann and Boas 2008). Larger developed states, however, have been reluctant to officially recognize "environmental refugees" as a specific class with special rights for fear of the legal obligations that come with the treatment of a wider definition of refugees (Skillington 2015). This raises new questions relating to the rights of climate migrants. Even without this international recognition, migrants are entitled to protection under several areas of human rights law.

Environmentally induced migration may be the result of a sudden disaster (Riede 2014), such as a flood, storm surge, earthquake, tsunami, or landslide that prompts sudden flows of persons (Gemenne 2010; Adger et al. 2014). Climate-induced migration may also be caused by less dramatic and more gradual situations such as droughts, water shortages, and coastal erosion caused by sea-level rise. There is ample evidence of negative impacts of climate change on different geographic groups, from those in remote island-states who face extreme weather events and gradual sea-level rise (Betzold 2015); to the urban poor who face thermal inequity with higher incidences of heat-associated health complications (Mitchell and Chakraborty 2015); to industrial waterfront communities vulnerable to storm surges and public health risks from open storage of hazardous materials during extreme events (Bautista, Osorio, and Dwyer 2015). In the Marshall Islands more frequent, longer, and unpredictable periods of drought and saltwater intrusion have caused crops to fail and food insecurity that threatens the inhabitants' right to nutrition (Ahlgren, Yamada, and Wong 2014). Communities in the Arctic (Bronen and Chapin 2013) and small island developing states (SIDS; Kelman 2015) are already being displaced by climate change.

Displaced persons are driven by direct and indirect pressures or triggers: climate, economic, social, and family (Marino and Lazrus 2015). Climate is not the sole cause of displacement of all climate migrants. In many cases it is difficult to isolate the environmental ground as the sole or main trigger (Ransan-Cooper et al. 2015). This has been another reason for the unwillingness by some to accept the climate-refugee approach to migration (Jakobeit and Methmann 2012) or to accept simplistic or alarmist approaches that climate change will necessarily lead to mass migration and security risks (Bettini, Nash, and Gioli 2017). One recent study on the Syrian crisis explained the complex motivations behind migration, discounting climate change as the main stressor for conflict and the need to abandon Syria (Selby et al. 2017).

Climate migrants may be seasonal migrants who have had to move to other agricultural areas because climate change negatively affected their traditional places of work (Turhan, Zografos, and Kallis 2015), or they may be permanent migrants. They may respond immediately or after a considerable period to the stimulus to migrate depending on their resilience to change or resources to finance the displacement (Stojanov et al. 2014). This makes their classification, measurement (Gemenne 2011b), and treatment more challenging. Migrants are described alternatively as victims, as threats to national security, as proactive adaptive agents, or even as subjects of political maneuver (Ransan-Cooper et al. 2015).

There are three categories of states with climate migrants or displaced persons: those that may totally disappear because of rising sea levels (some island-states), those where a significant part of the territory will disappear leaving an area incapable of supporting existing populations, and those where part of the territory is no longer arable or able to sustain livelihoods. The island-states most likely to be affected by rising sea levels are Tuvalu, with a population of approximately 11,000; Nauru 10,000; Kiribati, approximately 104,000; the Maldives, 341,000; and the Bahamas, approximately 321,000. For these states, climate change is an existential threat to the rights of its nationals to statehood. This dilemma creates moral climate duties (duties of states responsible for climate impacts to those affected by those impacts) for other states to mitigate and provide adaptation support.

There are two ways of looking at climate migrants: as victims or as active agents of adaptive change. First, migrants may be seen as groups of peoples that share a common identity particularly linked to geographic spaces. Climate events make those spaces inhospitable, forcing displacement that in some way leads to a destruction of part of their identity, culture, and livelihoods. Migration may lead to social tensions and even violence as migrants compete with settled communities for jobs and resources (McLeman and Smit 2006). Migrants can easily be branded scapegoats for negative and emerging economic, social, and cultural problems in the receiving state or community (Benjaminsen et al. 2012). Second, migrants can be seen as "proactive, self-determining and active agents of change," as a study on Pacific Islanders highlighted (Dreher and Voyer 2015). Climate migrants are the resilient persons who are able to adapt by migration. Migration may be a form of adaptation to economic changes (Hugo 2011) or evidence of educational and social aspirations. This latter view was common among inhabitants of Kiribati who migrated to Australia partly because of climate change.

Migration and Human Rights

Human rights law protects the fundamental freedoms of persons, groups, and peoples and is both national and international in scope. Human rights are universal or applicable to all human beings based on their inherent dignity; they are inviolable and inalienable; and they are interdependent or interlinked and can be achieved only collectively. The international human rights legal framework comprises nine key conventions or international agreements: the International Convention on the Elimination of All Forms of Racial Discrimination; the International Covenant on Civil and Political

Rights; the International Covenant on Economic, Social and Cultural Rights; the Convention on the Elimination of All Forms of Discrimination against Women; the Convention against Torture and Other Cruel, Inhuman or Degrading Treatment or Punishment; the Convention on the Rights of the Child; the International Convention on the Protection of the Rights of All Migrant Workers and Members of Their Families; the International Convention for the Protection of All Persons from Enforced Disappearance; and the Convention on the Rights of Persons with Disabilities.

The human rights law creates a framework of *rights holders*, who under international law are entitled to the protection of their rights, and *duty bearers*, who have an obligation to uphold these rights in areas within their jurisdiction and to cooperate with other national and international actors to ensure that they are also upheld in areas outside their jurisdiction. Each human being is a rights holder. Duty bearers include states as well as private actors, including transnational and national companies, especially in the field of climate change.

Migration raises many human rights issues. Migrants' rights include the right to live with their families and freedom of movement. Migrants should also receive respect, protection, assistance, and support (Article 16, Universal Declaration of Human Rights, 1948; Article 8, European Convention for the Protection of Human Rights and Fundamental Freedoms, 1950; Article 16, European Social Charter, 1961; Articles 17 and 23, International Covenant on Civil and Political Rights, 1966; Article 1, International Covenant on Economic, Social and Cultural Rights, 1966; and Article 17, American Convention on Human Rights, 1969) (IOM, n.d.). The right to freedom of movement includes three elements: "freedom to move within one's country (Art. 13(1), Universal Declaration of Human Rights, 1948: 'Everyone has the right to freedom of movement and residence within the borders of each state.'), the right to leave any country and the right to return to his or her own country (Art. 13(2), Universal Declaration of Human Rights, 1948: 'Everyone has the right to leave any country, including his own, and to return to his country.')" (IOM, n.d.). It is not clear that there is a duty among states to promote resettlement and migration, although at the local level it can be assumed that states have that responsibility to their citizens (Johnson 2012). In fact, the recent migrant crisis in Europe was evidence of the closing of the window of humanitarian support to block migrants coming from the Middle East and Africa (Webber 2017).

Climate Change, Migration, and Justice

Climate change is the cause of inequities and infringements on human rights that raise complex moral dilemmas. Climate justice is included in the preamble to the Paris Agreement as one of the pillars on which the work of the IPCC is built. The preamble states that the agreement is "noting the importance for some of the concept of 'climate justice,' when taking action to address climate change" (UNFCCC 2016). This section of the preamble addresses climate justice from an ethical perspective. States, however, have not established a legal regime of rights for climate-change victims.

Climate-change impacts are disproportionately borne by weaker members of the global community, those already disadvantaged by geography, age, gender, poverty, disability, and cultural and ethnic background and those from vulnerable locations in wealthier countries. Children and the aged are particularly vulnerable to heat mortality as temperatures rise (Gouveia, Hajat, and Armstrong 2003). Children in drought regions who have suffered malnutrition are less able to sustain adequate livelihoods when they become adults (Otto et al. 2017). Indigenous peoples, whose livelihoods and cultural and spiritual identity depend on the natural environment, are on the whole vulnerable to many of the impacts of climate change on their traditional lands and on their ability to have sustainable supplies of water and food. For example, in Nepal, the land poor were more likely to migrate or to be displaced (Massey, Axinn, and Ghimire 2010). Children, women, and the aged are among those less able to migrate when rural livelihoods are threatened or destroyed by climate change. Men are more likely to move to urban centers where they can earn money to send back to their families.

From an environmental-justice perspective, climate-change-triggered migration is an ethical and moral challenge (Tucker 2015; Jamieson 2014). Rights holders, which include vulnerable groups and future generations, have contributed least to climate change, but they often suffer disproportionate negative impacts, are more socially vulnerable, and are the least able to participate in adaptation policy (government decision making and implementation related to managing climate-change impacts), to adapt, and to be given redress (Davies et al. 2017, 245). Duty holders are those who have contributed most to the problem or those most able to assist the more vulnerable to reduce the negative consequences of climate change. Duty holders include states and private companies (such as fossil-fuel-producing companies; Frumhoff, Heede, and Oreskes 2015) but may also include individuals who are responsible for high levels of CO_2 emissions (Chakravarty et al. 2009). Identifying duty holders in climate redistributive justice is not simple (Gardiner 2013). Climate justice requires historic polluters to pay compensation or use a CO_2 budget or quota. This duty belongs to this generation and to particular states within this generation based on their historic responsibility for emissions (Knutti and Rogelj 2015). But the past offenders are no longer alive. Is it fair under the polluter-pays principle, under principles of compensatory rights or corrective justice (Nyinevi 2015), or perhaps even from a

criminal-responsibility perspective (McKinnon 2015) for present generations to pay for the climate liabilities (pecuniary responsibility for the negative climate impacts) of their predecessors? Under the beneficiary-pays principle, it is perhaps plausible that those who now enjoy the progress brought
by the industrialization that caused emissions should contribute to addressing the impacts of those emissions (Huseby 2015), but this argument may not
be fair.

However, these redistributive-justice arguments may not be relevant,
since the climate-change problem does not allow for duty or rights holders
to further pollute the earth (Forsyth 2014). From the perspective of rights
holders, it is not clear how the right to energy can be applied and propor-
tioned among existing populations and future generations (Schuppert and
Seidel 2015; McKinnon 2015) in the context of limited carbon budgets
(Knutti and Rogelj 2015). Justice also requires those least vulnerable to help
poorer global citizens use low-carbon pathways to development. The right to
development through traditional energy sources may be moot since that approach presupposes assets (carbon budgets or emission quotas) that can be
distributed, but there is no carbon budget for distribution if the world hopes
to stem the tide of climate change. To keep global warming below two degrees Celsius above preindustrial temperature levels, the global response
should include not only emission reductions but also the large-scale deployment of negative-emission technologies (Hetland et al. 2016).

Are these justice elements guaranteed under an international legal re-
gime for climate victims? International law is silent on rights and duties of
states toward climate-change victims (Kolmannskog and Myrstad 2009).
Generally, Article 2 of the UNFCCC binds states to address climate impacts.
The principles of customary environmental law related to state responsibility
and the no-harm rule also prescribe similar obligations. Signatory states to
UNFCCC Article 4 accept the duty to take adaptation action. The Warsaw
International Mechanism for Loss and Damage is an international response
to the climate-justice (Thompson and Otto 2015) or compensatory-justice
problem (Wallimann-Helmer 2015; Stabinsky and Hoffmaister 2015). This
mechanism was created to provide financing to developing states for adaptation to extreme events and slow-onset impacts (for example, desertification,
ocean acidification, sea-level rise, and glacial retreat). At the nineteenth
UNFCCC COP, states agreed to use the mechanism to improve the knowledge and understanding of risk-management approaches; strengthen syner-
gies and coordination among stakeholders; and provide finance, technology,
and capacity building for adaptation (UNFCCC 2014). Its mandate is to highlight the damage (recoverable and nonrecoverable), recognize those responsible, and determine fair remedies that should extend beyond physical loss to
include cultural loss (Zellentin 2015) and social fallouts from climate change.

Human Rights in Climate-Induced Migration

How do issues of climate change and climate migrants relate to human rights? Although this chapter focuses on moral responsibilities and human rights, the rights of nonhumans, future generations, and nature are also part of the climate change–human rights nexus, and similar stewardship responsibilities indirectly apply to these groups.

Several international resolutions and statements drawing attention to the nexus between human rights and climate change have been discussed in the literature (Davies et al. 2017). They all link climate-change impacts to the special plight of vulnerable populations. The 2007 Male' Declaration on the Human Dimension of Global Climate Change, adopted by SIDS, was the first intergovernmental statement to explicitly state that climate change had "clear and immediate implications for the full enjoyment of human rights" (Republic of Maldives 2007), especially the rights to life, health, well-being, and an adequate standard of living (OHCHR 2016). However, other documents also make reference to the link between human rights and the environment, such as the 1986 UN Declaration on the Right to Development; the 2003 UN Statement of Common Understanding on Human Rights Based Approaches to Development Cooperation and Programming (the Common Understanding); the 2010 UNFCCC COP 16 in Cancun ("Parties should, in all climate change related actions, fully respect human rights"); the 2012 Open Letter of the High Commissioner for Human Rights to all Permanent Missions in New York and in Geneva (to integrate human rights into the Rio+20 outcome document [Pillay 2012]); the 2030 Agenda for Sustainable Development (the seventeen SDGs to end poverty, fight inequality and injustice, and tackle climate change by 2030); the 2015 Paris Agreement of the UNFCCC COP 21 (UNFCCC 2016).

The 2015 Paris Agreement was an important milestone for international climate-change efforts with its target to keep global surface temperatures below 2 degrees Celsius and closer to 1.5 degrees Celsius. It requires states to take urgent action to help vulnerable communities. Although the Paris Agreement did not frame climate change within a rights-based approach, it highlighted the need to promote human rights, especially the rights of indigenous populations, women, and future generations. Notable in drawing attention to the climate change–human rights nexus was the advocacy of UNEP (2015) and UNICEF (2015) at the Paris UNFCCC 2015 COP. They focused on climate change, human rights, and the rights of the child, respectively. They all emphasized the global nature of the problem and the responsibility of the international community to take urgent action to reduce the impacts of climate change on vulnerable populations.

The Global Network for the Study of Human Rights and the Environment (GNHRE) network of scholars published its Declaration on Human

Rights and Climate Change (GNHRE 2015). It is one of the most thorough compilations of climate-related human rights and obligations. GNHRE noted that climate-related human rights are part of several international instruments. Many of the rights mentioned, however, are not universally recognized under international law, which, for example, does not yet recognize a right to an ecologically sound environment (Davies et al. 2017). This declaration is not a declaration in the legal sense under international law or an international statement of states but a private statement on the part of a group of scholars and activists. The international instruments referenced do not create legal obligations on states to recognize and protect the rights mentioned therein. The following are many of the international instruments on which the compilation of rights is based.

- The 2030 Sustainable Development Goals
- The Convention on the Elimination of All Forms of Discrimination against Women
- The Convention on the Rights of the Child
- The Draft United Nations Declaration on the Rights of Peasants
- The Earth Charter
- The International Covenant on Civil and Political Rights
- The International Covenant on Economic Social and Cultural Rights
- The International Labour Organization Convention No. 169
- The Nagoya Protocol
- The Rio Declaration on Environment and Development
- The Stockholm Declaration of the United Nations Conference on the Human Environment
- The United Nations Charter
- The United Nations Convention on the Law of the Sea
- The United Nations Declaration on the Rights of Indigenous Peoples
- The United Nations Framework Convention on Climate Change, the Kyoto Protocol, and the Paris Agreement
- The Universal Declaration of Human Rights
- The Universal Declaration of the Rights of Mother Earth
- The Vienna Declaration and Program of Action of the World Conference of Human Rights
- The World Charter for Nature

The declaration is helpful because it includes the rights of the environmental migrants, those unable to migrate, and in some cases the rights of the receiving populations. It references many of the climate-related rights discussed in this book. It lists the human rights specifically related to climate change.

- The right of future generations to a planetary climate suitable to equitably meet their ecologically responsible needs
- The rights of climate migrants to a safe, secure receiving environment
- The rights of locals to adequate systems to manage the use of limited resources between the local populations and migrants
- The rights of locals to systems to ensure that migration is not a source of conflict over resources, culture, or security
- The rights of locals to administrative and legal systems to reduce potential conflicts caused by the introduction of climate migrants into a local community
- The right of present generations to a planetary climate suitable to equitably meet their ecologically responsible needs
- The right to a just transition toward a sustainable society based on inclusion and distributive justice
- The right to a secure, healthy, and ecologically sound earth system
- The right to active, free, and meaningful participation in planning and decision-making activities and processes that may have an impact on the climate
- The right to associate freely and peacefully with others and to gather peacefully in public spaces for purposes of protecting the climate or the rights of those affected by climate harm
- The right to be free from dangerous anthropogenic interference with the climate system
- The right to climate and human rights education
- The right to effective remedies and redress in administrative or judicial proceedings for climate harm or the threat or risk of such harm, including modes of compensation
- The right to fairness, equity, and justice in all climate resilience, adaptation, and mitigation efforts
- The right to fairness, equity, and justice in respect responses to the threat of climate change
- The right to hold and express opinions and to disseminate ideas and information regarding the climate
- The right to information about, and to participation in, decision-making processes related to alterations made to the physical environments people rely on for their health and survival
- The right to international solidarity and timely assistance in the event of climate-change-driven catastrophes

- The right to investments in adaptation and mitigation to prevent the deleterious consequences of anthropogenic climate change
- The right to protection from deleterious impacts caused by adaptation and mitigation efforts to develop climate resilience and climate-geoengineering technologies
- The right to the highest attainable standard of health, free from environmental pollution, degradation, and harmful emissions
- The right to timely, clear, understandable, and easily available information concerning the climate
- The rights of indigenous peoples to participate in the protection of their rights to their lands, territories, natural resources, tenure rights, and cultural heritage
- The rights of indigenous peoples, women, and other underrepresented groups to equality of meaningful participation in climate-change policy and activities and to procedural justice related to climate change
- The rights of migrants to their ethnic and religious traditions
- The rights of migrants to protection from labor and economic exploitation within the informal economy of their receiving communities

The declaration implicitly identifies duty holders and defines their responsibilities under human rights laws and norms. The following are the responsibilities of climate-justice duty holders.

- Persons have a moral responsibility to avoid and/or to minimize practices known to contribute to climate damage.
- Persons have a moral responsibility to ensure that climate-related actions promote gender equality and the full and equal participation of women.
- Persons have a moral responsibility to ensure that climate-related actions promote intergenerational equity.
- Persons, in all climate-change-related actions, have a duty to respect, protect, promote, and fulfill the rights of indigenous peoples related to climate change, including indigenous traditional knowledge and indigenous customary laws.
- States and business enterprises have a duty to protect the climate and to respect the rights of individuals related to climate change.
- States have a duty to ensure international cooperation with other states and international organizations and agencies for the purpose of respecting the climate-related human rights, even outside their jurisdiction.

- States have a duty to provide assistance and solidarity to climate refugees.
- States have a duty to respect and ensure the right to a secure, healthy, and ecologically sound environment and to adopt the requisite administrative, legislative, and procedural measures.
- States have a moral responsibility to ensure that climate-related actions promote intergenerational equity, a just transition of the workforce that creates decent work.
- States have a moral responsibility to ensure that climate-related actions promote food sovereignty.
- States have a moral responsibility to respect the rights to assistance and solidarity and to create the necessary legal frameworks to assist and support climate refugees.

The Human Rights–Based Approach to Climate Change

The previous sections illustrate the link between climate change, migration, and human rights. The international response to climate change has been led by the IPCC, which laid a good scientific foundation for adaptation and mitigation. However, another possible perspective on climate change is to approach all climate-change policy from the human rights perspective. The Office of the High Commissioner for Human Rights (OHCHR) is the UN agency tasked with the promotion and protection of human rights. In 2012, the OHCHR commissioned a special rapporteur on human rights and the environment to sensitize the global-policy community on the rights and obligations related to the enjoyment of a safe, clean, healthy, and sustainable environment and to promote best practices in environmental policy making and human rights. The OHCHR promotes a human rights–based approach (HRBA) to climate policy at both global and local levels (OHCHR, n.d.a). Ambitiously, in an open letter to state parties to the UNFCCC in October 2014, the OHCHR special rapporteur suggested that the main objective of policies to address climate change should be to secure human rights and that the international human rights legal framework should guide all climate-change policies and programs (OHCHR 2015).

The HRBA advocates for mechanisms to allow individuals to make claims and duty holders to meet obligations. In practice, the HRBA allows already-employed human rights operational paradigms, which help the socially and economically poor and vulnerable, to be applied to those made vulnerable by climate change. The approach is buttressed by many of the international and national laws, norms, and principles discussed previously and create positive and negative obligations for duty bearers (to enforce the rights and to abstain from violating them) and substantive and procedural rights on rights bearers and insists on the national implementation of a rights-based approach to climate change. This ensures that climate-related human rights are among the most guaranteed under the majority of domestic constitutional systems. Their inviolability will then give them higher value and precedence over contractual, environmental, and other civil rights. The HRBA highlights four perspectives:

- Climate-change impacts disproportionately affect the human rights of vulnerable groups that heavily depend on the environment.
- Climate justice has global implications with duties of states to redress collective vulnerabilities of communities and states through mitigation targets, international cooperation, technology transfer, capacity building, and sustainable development.
- Climate rights include procedural justice in climate-change governance for the vulnerable groups (participation in policy making, consultation, and access to information and legal services).
- There is a potential conflict between policy to secure basic human rights and the climate-change measures that may infringe on those rights (impacts of new protected areas on community livelihoods).

The HRBA is not without its critics. From a legal and constitutional perspective, the HRBA raises but does not resolve the difficulty of competition in the application of rights: for example, the right to property versus the right to conserve a protected area in climate policy related to the establishment of protected areas in traditional fishing grounds in coastal estuaries. Furthermore, the legal solution for each case will involve law and fact through dispute-settlement mechanisms not easily accessible by those most affected. At the international level, the human rights framework is not a seamless coherent network of rights. Rights are recognized by various state signatories from different conventions and implemented and enforced to varying degrees by different nations. There is no single HRBA to apply to the global problem of climate change. Many argue that using the rights-based approach may not be the most effective way to protect the vulnerable. Although rights are identifiable, the systems to enforce them at a national level depend on states developing and enforcing national laws that cannot be guaranteed. Thus, the HRBA has been criticized for being too limited and legalistic: it does not provide resources, concrete solutions, or guidance concerning the dilemma faced by the vulnerable (Cameron 2010). It can also be argued that HRBA gives a useful analytical framework of principles, standards, and values for development planning and environmental governance when development resources are to be applied to climate change.

There is a debate concerning whether to link climate change and human rights to migration and climate refugees. The refugee approach, some argue,

can be analytically flawed since most climate displacements are within national boundaries (Tacoli 2009). Also, putting climate change under a migration lens depoliticizes global warming, leaving the duties of rights bearers and
issues of retributive and restorative justice entirely out of the political discourse (Methmann 2014; Bettini, Nash, and Gioli 2017). The declaration of
the GNHRE, for example, hardly stresses mitigation as among the main ways
to address climate-related human rights. When climate migrants are treated
as passive and helpless victims to fear or protect (Bettini 2013), the discussion
takes the international spotlight away from the duty holders and issues of
inequality and structural injustices in the global economic system toward a
sometimes immobilizing global focus on helping the victims be resilient (Bettini, Nash, and Gioli 2017). Using the term "refugees" ignores the duty of
emitters to accept the displaced in accordance with the historic emissions of
the emitters and to provide development support in relation to their contribution to climate change (Loewe 2014) and their obligations under the
UNFCCC. Rather, the refugee regime does not attribute culpability to emitters or provide a duty of restorative justice to the migrants. Furthermore, the
"migrant" or "refugee" label may introduce a stigma and a "fear of refugees"
into migrant management. One alternative is framing climate migration
within rational choice, adaptation, and resilience debates (Felli 2013) rather
than within rights and justice. This is likely to move the fear-of-refugees discussions toward rational-adaptation strategy and resilience perspectives. This
approach may make relocation more globally and socially acceptable (Methmann and Oels 2015) and include options such as dual and even deterritori-
alized citizenship (Marshall 2015) or other special mobility rights for climate
migrants. Finally, one of the underlying assumptions in climate migration is
contestable: Do those disadvantaged by climate change necessarily have a
right to occupy space in another state? Put differently, is there a right to the
world, to mobility, and to a share in the earth's resources for migrants (Nevins
2017)? There is as yet no international recognition of this as a human right
(Nevins 2017), and thus building human rights on the grounds of climate
migration may also be contestable. Migrants have rights because they are human persons, above and beyond the trigger that caused their rights to be in-
fringed on.

The Agenda for Sustainable Development, though not couched along the
lines of an HBRA to climate change, has the potential to address many of the
critical issues for climate migrants.

Sustainable Development Goals

Like climate change, climate justice, and human rights, the SDGs are truly
global, apply to all states, and are part of the UN 2030 Development Agenda

that will guide the development community's policy and funding until 2030. The seventeen SDGs replace the eight Millennium Development Goals (MDGs) that steered global policy from September 2000 to 2015. Although the UNFCCC is the main instrument for managing the global response to climate change, the wider global development agenda is explicitly committed to protecting humanity and the environment against the many negative impacts of climate change. Internal and external climate migrants become displaced to avoid poverty, inequality, and insecurity. Solving these through the global SDGs agenda directly addresses many of the root causes of climate-induced migration. Enshrined in the SDGs is a global response to the climate-change/human-suffering dilemma. Climate-change impacts retard sustainable development trajectories, both because of the direct harm caused by climate change and because of forgone development opportunities (Stabinsky and Hoffmaister 2015). Mitigation and adaptation measures also affect sustainable development efforts both positively, with what some refer to as "co-benefits," and negatively, what the IPCC Fifth Assessment Report (AR5) refers to as maladaptation (Field et al. 2014). Specifically, goal 1 of the SDGs is to "end poverty in all its forms everywhere"; goal 10 is to "reduce inequality within and among countries"; and goal 16 is to "promote just, peaceful and inclusive societies."

Goal 13, the SDG climate-change goal ("take urgent action to combat climate change and its impacts"), includes several targets related to procedural and distributive climate justice:

- Strengthen resilience and adaptive capacity
- Mainstream climate-change measures into national policy
- Improve education on climate-change adaptation, mitigation, and early warning
- Fully operationalize the Green Climate Fund (by implementing pledges to mobilize $100 billion annually by 2020)

The purpose of the Green Climate Fund, for example, is directly linked to climate justice: to support climate-change mitigation and adaptation in developing countries, least-developed countries (LDCs), and SIDS especially for the benefit of women, youth, and marginalized groups and communities.

Several other goals and targets of the SDG agenda address many of the equity and justice challenges caused by climate change. Goal 2, on food security, addresses the right to safe, nutritious, and sufficient food for all. This is influenced by climate change and weather patterns that can affect agriculture and yields (Porter et al. 2014). Goal 6, on clean water and sanitation, addresses equity in access to drinking water and capacity building for improving water and sanitation management, areas that the IPCC recognizes as threatened by climate change (Jiménez Cisneros et al. 2014). Goal 7, on affordable and clean energy, highlights the importance of supporting developing countries in establishing sustainable energy services to reduce resource inequity and energy poverty, which is tied to the global efforts that IPCC considers key to reducing emissions (Bruckner et al. 2014). Goal 8, on decent work and economic growth, recognizes the importance of ensuring that development does not fuel unsustainable consumption and production. Target 8.4 specifically seeks to decouple economic growth from environmental degradation (Seto et al. 2014; Clarke et al. 2014). Target 9.1 of goal 9, on industry, innovation, and infrastructure, focuses on the need for sustainable infrastructure to support human well-being in an equitable manner for the benefit of all, especially by providing financial, technological, and technical support to LDCs, landlocked developing countries (LLDCs), SIDS, and African countries (target 9.a). These targets also relate to the right to decent living conditions (Denton et al. 2014), the absence of which is often a migration trigger. Goal 11, on sustainable cities and communities, which addresses the right to adequate, safe, and affordable housing (target 11.1), green and public spaces (target 11.7), and basic services for all, including public transport and municipal and other waste management (Smith et al. 2014; Adger et al. 2014; Arent et al. 2014; Olsson et al. 2014; Dasgupta et al. 2014; Revi et al. 2014), also relates to climate change; these issues are addressed by the AR5. The recommendations of the IPCC's AR5 are also part of goal 12, on responsible consumption and production, which recognizes the responsibility to significantly reduce air, water, and soil pollution to remove adverse impacts on human health in consonance with the environmental-justice principle of the right of all to ecosystem services (Fleurbaey et al. 2014).

Goal 14, on marine life, addresses the rights of access of artisanal fishers to marine resources and markets (target 14.b) and of future generations to marine resources by promoting the restoration of marine and coastal ecosystems (target 14.2) that are already showing high rates of degradation from global warming and ocean acidification (Pörtner et al. 2014). Goal 15, on terrestrial ecosystems, focuses on the equitable sharing of benefits from and access to genetic resources (target 15.6) and on supporting local communities' efforts toward sustainable livelihood as alternatives to trafficking in protected species (target 15.c). The AR5 stressed the importance of reducing nonclimate stresses to ecosystems and finding ways to promote the restoration of systems degraded by climate-change impacts. Goal 17, on implementation, addresses the need to encourage financing, technology transfer and cooperation, capacity building, and partnerships to assist highly indebted poor countries (HIPC), LDCs, and developing states more generally. This is in accord with the IPCC, which recognizes the importance of international climate cooperation to preserve the global commons (Stavins et al. 2014).

Goal 17 recognizes the responsibility of rights holders to cooperate to achieve the sustainable development goals that are threatened inter alia by climate change.

The human rights affected by climate change can be protected by global efforts toward sustainable development. The cases of the Inuit population in Alaska and the migrants from Mauritius are a good reminder of the complexity of the human rights and climate-induced migration nexus but also the complexity of links between them and sustainable development. Arguably, migrants and those unable to leave are faced with many of the sustainable development challenges addressed in this section.

Human Rights in Climate-Induced Migration

Ocean warming and melting polar ice cause sea-level rise that threatens the territorial integrity of low-lying SIDS. In 2007, SIDS signed the Male' Declaration on the Human Dimension of Global Climate Change, which explicitly references the human right to an environment that can support communities. In that declaration, SIDS representatives stated that "climate change has clear and immediate implications for the full enjoyment of human rights including inter alia the right to life, the right to take part in cultural life, the right to use and enjoy property, the right to an adequate standard of living, the right to food, and the right to the highest attainable standard of physical and mental health."

Republic of Mauritius is a SIDS in the Southwest Indian Ocean with high levels of internal and external migrants who migrate to obtain a better standard of living in other parts of Mauritius and other countries. It is a parliamentary republic with a population of approximately 1.2 million people and a per capita gross domestic produce of about US$11,700. It is an archipelago comprising several islands, sandbanks, and islets with a land area of 2,040 square kilometers and an ocean area of 2.3 million square kilometers. Mauritius's economy is classed as upper middle income by the World Bank. Today it has diversified from its traditional agriculture base toward tourism, textiles, sugar, information and communication technology, and financial services. Its small and geographically dispersed population is vulnerable to many of the effects of climate change discussed earlier. In Mauritius, climate-induced migration is often caused by extreme and gradual climatic events such as floods, cyclones, landslides, and droughts. As in many SIDS, climate and environmental stressors are unlikely to lead to large-scale external migration but may contribute to social and economic displacement of persons and competition for resources in destination communities.

The Mauritius case illustrates three issues. First, it is difficult to attribute all migration from the island, and from SIDS in general, solely or principally to climate change. Second, the human rights challenges faced by migrants from Mauritius are similar in many instances to those of migrants more generally. Some migrant (and nonmigrant) households may experience environmental risks at their destination because they have fewer assets and resources and live in poor conditions. One recent study noted that "almost 55 per cent of migrant respondents said that they had been affected by torrential rain, while this figure is 40 per cent of non-migrant households" (Sultan 2017, 28, 31). Migrants may suffer landslides, flooding, droughts, and lack of infrastructure. Migrants tend to have lower incomes than nonmigrants and less ability to invest in entrepreneurial and trade activities. They also report security threats, discrimination, and less ability to access housing. In the case of SIDS, internal migrants are subject to the same environmental stressors in their destination locations because the entire country is often subject to the same environmental events, such as torrential rain, flood, and droughts. When migrants are displaced, however, they may move to areas with better infrastructure that are less likely to be as seriously affected. Third, and somewhat surprisingly, in some cases, migration prompted by environmental stressors and climate change is seen as a positive adaptation strategy (Sultan 2017). For some migrants, climate impacts are the stimulus for an improved standard of life. Internal migrants generally have improved living conditions and access to health care, safe drinking water, and electricity and energy services.

Although very different from Mauritius, another interesting case study on climate and human rights is that of the Inuit population in Canada and the United States. The Inuit are indigenous peoples of the Arctic who live in Greenland, Canada, and Alaska and number at least 155,000. The Arctic temperatures have increased by 2.0–3.5 degrees Celsius since 1970 (Larsen et al. 2014). Ice has been thinning or detaching from larger masses and leaving local hunters stranded. Traditional species, including seals, walruses, and polar bears, are decreasing in numbers, as are fish stocks, which affect food security and tourism in the area. Melting ice also has made Inuit homes more vulnerable to storm surges and erosion. The thawing of permafrost has caused infrastructure damage to buildings, roads, and pipelines in polar regions (Larsen et al. 2014). Warmer weather is affecting Inuit traditional hunting practices, livelihoods, and physical property. Residents of the town of Shishmaref, Alaska, which has a population of 563, held a council village vote in 2016 on whether to relocate. Most of the council members were in favor. The island on which the town is built is subject to erosion and flooding caused by sea ice thawing earlier and freezing later than ever before as a result of warmer temperatures. Some villagers have lost homes to erosion and beach slumping. One village hunter lost his life when he fell through ice that was supposed to be solidly frozen for the time of year that he went hunting

(Sutter 2017). Villagers argue that climate change is forcing them to give up their livelihoods and identity and is affecting their social, mental, and cultural health and well-being (Durkalec et al. 2015). Traditional knowledge related to the environment can no longer guide hunting practices because of unpredictable temperatures and precipitation. The community, however, does not have the funding to relocate the entire village, and many do not want to leave their traditional homeland (Sutter 2017). The Inuit see climate change as a human rights issue, and in 2005, they presented a petition to the Inter-American Commission on Human Rights, the international organization responsible for the stewardship of human rights in the American region. The petition argued that climate change affected their rights and brought visibility to the challenge of climate change for indigenous populations.

These two cases of climate impacts in vulnerable communities illustrate the complexity of perspectives, human rights challenges, and solutions to climate change. In Mauritius, climate change is another trigger for migration, although migration does not always solve some of the human rights infringements faced by migrants. In Shismaref, for example, many villages do not consider migration as an adaptation solution since they do not want to abandon their traditional ways of life and sources of livelihood.

Conclusion

The impacts of climate change on human settlements (Arent et al. 2014; Dasgupta et al. 2014; Revi et al. 2014); on human health, well-being, livelihoods, and security (Smith et al. 2014; Adger et al. 2014; Olsson et al. 2014); and on human migration and displacement (Oppenheimer et al. 2014) are confirmed by science. So is the special vulnerability of some regions, including polar regions (Larsen et al. 2014) and small islands (Nurse et al. 2014). One solution to avoid some of the negative consequences of climatic impacts has been displacement and migration. Conceptually, considering migration and migrants as refugees within climate discourses may have some unwanted consequences. It may mask some of the environmental-justice duties of polluters, but it may also be too simplistic in its approach toward displaced persons, viewing them necessarily as victims or potential troublemakers rather than as persons seeking opportunities elsewhere, just as many other migrants do for nonclimate reasons.

Recognizing the human rights associated with climate impacts is an important part of the climate-change puzzle. Addressing the sustainable development problems behind many of these impacts, which the SDGs are meant to do, is a structured and coherent way to address many injustices faced by the three groups of persons identified in the human rights–migration nexus: the migrants, those not able to migrate, and those in the destination communities. The following fifteen years of the UN's Sustainable Development Agenda may be able to go further than the climate community has done in protecting those most affected and most vulnerable to climate change. This global development project will add resources and provide renewed impetus to climate solutions (Fridahl and Linner 2016; Markandya et al. 2015). This global shift is, however, only the start; each country must develop its own policy, legislative, and institutional framework to effect the declarations, resolutions, goals, and targets to protect the rights of those most vulnerable to climate change.

REFERENCES

Adger, W. Neil, Juan M. Pulhin, Jon Barnett, Geoffrey D. Dabelko, Grete K. Hovelsrud, Marc Levy, Ursula Oswald Spring, and Coleen H. Vogel. 2014. "Human Security." In *Climate Change, 2014: Impacts, Adaptation, and Vulnerability; Part A: Global and Sectoral Aspects*, edited by Christopher B. Field, Vicente R. Barros, David J. Dokken, Katharine J. Mach, Michael D. Mastrandrea, T. Erin Bilir, Monalisa Chatterjee, et al., 755–791. Cambridge: Cambridge University Press.

Ahlgren, Ingrid, Seiji Yamada, and Allen Wong. "Rising Oceans, Climate Change, Food Aid, and Human Rights in the Marshall Islands." *Health and Human Rights* 16, no. 2 (2014): 69–81.

Arent, Douglas J., Richard S. J. Tol, Eberhard Faust, Joseph P. Hella, Surender Kumar, Kenneth M. Strzepek, Ferenc L. Tóth, and D. Yan. 2014. "Key Economic Sectors and Services." In *Climate Change, 2014: Impacts, Adaptation, and Vulnerability; Part A: Global and Sectoral Aspects*, edited by Christopher B. Field, Vicente R. Barros, David J. Dokken, Katharine J. Mach, Michael D. Mastrandrea, T. Erin Bilir, Monalisa Chatterjee, et al., 659–708. Cambridge: Cambridge University Press.

Bautista, Eddie, Juan Camilo Osorio, and Natasha Dwyer. 2015. "Building Climate Justice and Reducing Industrial Waterfront Vulnerability." *Social Research* 82 (3): 821–838.

Benjaminsen, Tor A., Koffi Alinon, Halvard Buhaug, and Jill Tove Buseth. 2012. "Does Climate Change Drive Land-Use Conflicts in the Sahel?" *Journal of Peace Research* 49 (1): 97–111.

Bettini, Giovanni. 2013. "Climate Barbarians at the Gate? A Critique of Apocalyptic Narratives on 'Climate Refugees.'" *Geoforum* 45:65–74.

Bettini, Giovanni, Sarah Louise Nash, and Giovanna Gioli. 2017. "One Step Forward, Two Steps Back? The Fading Contours of (In)Justice in Competing Discourses on Climate Migration." *Geographical Journal* 183 (4): 348–358.

Betzold, Carola. 2015. "Adapting to Climate Change in Small Island Developing States." *Climatic Change* 133 (3): 481–489.

Biermann, Frank, and Ingrid Boas. 2008. "Protecting Climate Refugees: The Case for a Global Protocol." *Environment: Science and Policy for Sustainable Development* 50 (6): 8–17.

Black, Richard, Dominic Kniveton, and Kerstin Schmidt-Verkerk. 2011. "Migration and Climate Change: Towards an Integrated Assessment of Sensitivity." *Environment and Planning A* 43 (2): 431–450.

Bronen, Robin, and F. Stuart Chapin III. 2013. "Adaptive Governance and Institutional Strategies for Climate-Induced Community Relocations in Alaska." *Proceedings of the National Academy of Sciences of the United States of America* 110 (23): 9320–9325.

Bruckner, Thomas, Igor Alexeyevich Bashmakov, Yacob Mulugetta, Helena Chum, Angel de la Vega Navarro, James Edmonds, Andre Faaij, et al. 2014. "Energy Systems." In *Climate Change 2014: Mitigation of Climate Change*, edited by Ottmar Edenhofer, Ramó Pichs-Madruga, Youba Sokona, Jan C. Minx, Elli Farahani, Susanne Kadner, Kristin Seyboth, et al., 511–598. Cambridge: Cambridge University Press.

Byravan, Sujatha, and Sudhir Chella Rajan. 2015. "Sea Level Rise and Climate Change Exiles: A Possible Solution." *Bulletin of the Atomic Scientists* 71 (2): 21–28.

Cameron, Edward. 2010. "Human Rights and Climate Change: Moving from an Intrinsic to an Instrumental Approach." *Georgia Journal of International and Comparative Law* 38 (3): 673–716.

Chakravarty, Shoibal, Ananth Chikkatur, Heleen de Coninck, Stephen Pacala, Robert Socolow, and Massimo Tavoni. 2009. "Sharing Global CO_2 Emission Reductions among One Billion High Emitters." *Proceedings of the National Academy of Sciences* 106 (29): 11884–11888.

Clarke, Leon, Kejun Jiang, Keigo Akimoto, Mustafa Babiker, Geoffrey Blanford, Karen Fisher-Vanden, Jean-Charles Hourcade, et al. 2014. "Assessing Transformation Pathways." In *Climate Change 2014: Mitigation of Climate Change*, edited by Ottmar Edenhofer, Ramó Pichs-Madruga, Youba Sokona, Jan C. Minx, Elli Farahani, Susanne Kadner, Kristin Seyboth, et al., 413–510. Cambridge: Cambridge University Press.

Costello, Anthony, Mustafa Abbas, Adriana Allen, Sarah Ball, Sarah Bell, Richard Bellamy, Sharon Friel, et al. 2009. "Managing the Health Effects of Climate Change." *The Lancet* 373 (9676): 1693–1733.

Dasgupta, Purnamita, John F. Morton, David Dodman, Baris Karapinar, Francisco Meza, Marta G. Rivera-Ferre, A. Toure Sarr, and Katharine E. Vincent. 2014. "Rural Areas." In *Climate Change 2014: Impacts, Adaptation, and Vulnerability; Part A: Global and Sectoral Aspects*, edited by Christopher B. Field, Vicente R. Barros, David J. Dokken, Katharine J. Mach, Michael D. Mastrandrea, T. Erin Bilir, Monalisa Chatterjee, et al., 613–657. Cambridge: Cambridge University Press.

Davies, Kirsten, Sam Adelman, Anna Grear, Catherine Iorns Magallanes, Tom Kerns, and S. Ravi Rajan. 2017. "The Declaration on Human Rights and Climate Change: A New Legal Tool for Global Policy Change." *Journal of Human Rights and the Environment* 8 (2): 217–253.

Denton, Fatima, Thomas J. Wilbanks, Achala C. Abeysinghe, Ian Burton, Qingzhu Gao, Maria Carmen Lemos, Toshihiko Masui, Karen L. O'Brien, and Koko Warner. 2014. "Climate-Resilient Pathways: Adaptation, Mitigation, and Sustainable Development." In *Climate Change 2014: Impacts, Adaptation, and Vulnerability; Part A: Global and Sectoral Aspects*, edited by Christopher B. Field, Vicente R. Barros, David J. Dokken, Katharine J. Mach, Michael D. Mastrandrea, T. Erin Bilir, Monalisa Chatterjee, et al., 1101–1131. Cambridge: Cambridge University Press.

Dreher, Tanja, and Michelle Voyer. 2015. "Climate Refugees or Migrants? Contesting Media Frames on Climate Justice in the Pacific." *Environmental Communication: A Journal of Nature and Culture* 9 (1): 58–76.

Durkalec, Agata, Chris Furgal, Mark W. Skinner, and Tom Sheldon. 2015. "Climate Change Influences on Environment as a Determinant of Indigenous Health: Relationships to Place, Sea Ice, and Health in an Inuit Community." *Social Science and Medicine* 136–137 (supplement C): 17–26.

Felli, Romain. 2013. "Managing Climate Insecurity by Ensuring Continuous Capital Accumulation: 'Climate Refugees' and 'Climate Migrants.'" *New Political Economy* 18 (3): 337–363.

Field, Christopher B., Vincente R. Barros, Michael D. Mastrandrea, Katharine J. Mach, Mohamed A.-K. Abdrabo, W. Neil Adger, Yury A. Anokhin, et al. 2014. "Summary for Policymakers." In *Climate Change, 2014: Impacts, Adaptation, and Vulnerability; Part A: Global and Sectoral Aspects*, edited by Christopher B. Field, Vicente R. Barros, David J. Dokken, Katharine J. Mach, Michael D. Mastrandrea, T. Erin Bilir, Monalisa Chatterjee, et al., 1–32. Cambridge: Cambridge University Press.

Fleurbaey, Marc, Sivan Kartha, Simon Bolwig, Yoke Ling Chee, Ying Chen, Esteve Corbera, Franck Lecocq, et al. 2014. "Sustainable Development and Equity." In *Climate Change 2014: Mitigation of Climate Change*, edited by Ottmar Edenhofer, Ramó Pichs-Madruga, Youba Sokona, Jan C. Minx, Elli Farahani, Susanne Kadner, Kristin Seyboth, et al., 238–350. Cambridge: Cambridge University Press.

Ford, James D., Joanna Petrasek Macdonald, Catherine Huet, Sara Statham, and Allison MacRury. 2016. "Food Policy in the Canadian North: Is There a Role for Country Food Markets?" *Social Science and Medicine* 152:35–40.

Forsyth, Tim. 2014. "Climate Justice Is Not Just Ice." *Geoforum* 54:230–235.

Fridahl, Mathias, and Björn-Ola Linnér. 2016. "Perspectives on the Green Climate Fund: Possible Compromises on Capitalization and Balanced Allocation." *Climate and Development* 8 (2): 105–109.

Frumhoff, Peter C., Richard Heede, and Naomi Oreskes. 2015. "The Climate Responsibilities of Industrial Carbon Producers." *Climatic Change* 132 (2): 157–171.

Gardiner, Stephen M. 2013. *A Perfect Moral Storm: The Ethical Tragedy of Climate Change, Environmental Ethics and Science Policy Series*. New York: Oxford University Press.

Geddes, Andrew, W. Neil Adger, Nigel W. Arnell, Richard Black, and David S. G. Thomas. 2012. "Migration, Environmental Change, and the 'Challenges of Governance.'" *Environment and Planning C: Government and Policy* 30 (6): 951–967.

Gemenne, François. 2010. "What's in a Name: Social Vulnerabilities and the Refugee Controversy in the Wake of Hurricane Katrina." In *Environment, Forced Migration and Social Vulnerability*, edited by Tamer Afifi and Jill Jäger, 29–40. Berlin: Springer Berlin Heidelberg.

———. 2011a. "Climate-Induced Population Displacements in a 4°C+ World." *Philosophical Transactions of the Royal Society A: Mathematical, Physical and Engineering Sciences* 369 (1934): 182–195.

———. 2011b. "Why the Numbers Don't Add Up: A Review of Estimates and Predictions of People Displaced by Environmental Changes." *Global Environmental Change* 21 (supplement 1): S41–S49.

GNHRE (Global Network for the Study of Human Rights and the Environment). 2015. "Declaration on Human Rights and Climate Change." Available at http://gnhre.org/declaration-human-rights-climate-change.

Gouveia, Nelson, Shakoor Hajat, and Ben Armstrong. 2003. "Socioeconomic Differentials in the Temperature-Mortality Relationship in São Paulo, Brazil." *International Journal of Epidemiology* 32 (3): 390–397.

Hetland, Jens, Ping Yowargana, Sylvain Leduc, and Florian Kraxner. 2016. "Carbon-Negative Emissions: Systemic Impacts of Biomass Conversion: A Case Study on CO_2 Capture and Storage Options." *International Journal of Greenhouse Gas Control* 49:330–342.

Hugo, Graeme. 2011. "Future Demographic Change and Its Interactions with Migration and Climate Change." *Global Environmental Change* 21 (supplement 1): S21–S33.

Huseby, Robert. 2015. "Should the Beneficiaries Pay?" *Politics, Philosophy and Economics* 14 (2): 209–225.

IOM (International Organization for Migration). 2008. *World Migration, 2008: Managing Labour Mobility in the Evolving Global Economy.* Vol. 4. London: Hammersmith Press.

———. 2017. *World Migration Report, 2018.* Geneva, Switzerland: International Organization for Migration.

———. n.d. "Key Migration Terms." Available at https://www.iom.int/key-migration -terms (accessed December 21, 2018).

Jakobeit, Cord, and Chris Methmann. 2012. "'Climate Refugees' as Dawning Catastrophe? A Critique of the Dominant Quest for Numbers." In *Climate Change, Human Security and Violent Conflict: Challenges for Societal Stability,* edited by Jürgen Scheffran, Michael Brzoska, Hans Günter Brauch, Peter Michael Link, and Janpeter Schilling, 301–314. Berlin: Springer Berlin Heidelberg.

Jamieson, Dale 2014. *Reason in a Dark Time: Why the Struggle against Climate Change Failed—and What It Means for Our Future.* New York: Oxford University Press.

Jiménez Cisneros, Blanca E., Taikan Oki, Nigel W. Arnell, Gerardo Benito, J. Graham Cogley, Petra Döll, Tong Jiang, and Shadrack S. Mwakalila. 2014. "Freshwater Resources." In *Climate Change 2014: Impacts, Adaptation, and Vulnerability; Part A: Global and Sectoral Aspects,* edited by Christopher B. Field, Vicente R. Barros, David J. Dokken, Katharine J. Mach, Michael D. Mastrandrea, T. Erin Bilir, Monalisa Chatterjee, et al., 229–269. Cambridge: Cambridge University Press.

Johnson, Craig A. 2012. "Governing Climate Displacement: The Ethics and Politics of Human Resettlement." *Environmental Politics* 21 (2): 308–328.

Kelman, Ilan. 2010. "Hearing Local Voices from Small Island Developing States for Climate Change." *Local Environment* 15 (7): 605–619.

———. 2015. "Difficult Decisions: Migration from Small Island Developing States under Climate Change." *Earth's Future* 3 (4): 133–142.

Knutti, Reto, and Joeri Rogelj. 2015. "The Legacy of Our CO_2 Emissions: A Clash of Scientific Facts, Politics and Ethics." *Climatic Change* 133 (3): 361–373.

Kolmannskog, Vikram, and Finn Myrstad. 2009. "Environmental Displacement in European Asylum Law." *European Journal of Migration and Law* 11 (4): 313–326.

Larsen, Joan Nymand, Oleg A. Anisimov, Andrew Constable, Anne B. Hollowed, Nancy Maynard, På Prestrud, Terry D. Prowse, and John M. R. Stone. 2014. "Polar Regions." In *Climate Change 2014: Impacts, Adaptation, and Vulnerability; Part B: Regional Aspects,* edited by Vicente R. Barros, Christopher B. Field, David J. Dokken, Michael D. Mastrandrea, Katharine J. Mach, T. Erin Bilir, Monalisa Chatterjee, et al., 1567–1612. Cambridge: Cambridge University Press.

Levy, Barry S., Victor W. Sidel, and Jonathan A. Patz. 2017. "Climate Change and Collective Violence." In *Annual Review of Public Health,* vol. 38, edited by J. E. Fielding, 241–257. Palo Alto, CA: Annual Reviews.

Loewe, Daniel. 2014. "Refugiados climáticos: ¿Quién debe cargar los costos?" [Climate refugees: Who should bear the costs?]. *REMHU: Revista Interdisciplinar da Mobilidade Humana* [Interdisciplinary journal of human mobility] 22 (43): 169–187.

Marino, Elizabeth, and Heather Lazrus. 2015. "Migration or Forced Displacement? The Complex Choices of Climate Change and Disaster Migrants in Shishmaref, Alaska and Nanumea, Tuvalu." *Human Organization* 74 (4): 341–350.

Markandya, Anil, Alessandro Antimiani, Valeria Costantini, C. Martini, Alessandro Palma, and M. C. Tommasino. 2015. "Analyzing Trade-Offs in International Climate Policy Options: The Case of the Green Climate Fund." *World Development* 74:93–107.

Marshall, Nicole. 2015. "Toward Special Mobility Rights for Climate Migrants." *Environmental Ethics* 37 (3): 259–276.

Massey, Douglas S., William G. Axinn, and Dirgha J. Ghimire. 2010. "Environmental Change and Out-Migration: Evidence from Nepal." *Population and Environment* 32 (2): 109–136.

McKinnon, Catriona. 2015. "Climate Justice in a Carbon Budget." *Climatic Change* 133 (3): 375–384.

McLeman, Robert, and Barry Smit. 2006. "Migration as an Adaptation to Climate Change." *Climatic Change* 76 (1): 31–53.

Methmann, Chris. 2014. "Visualizing Climate-Refugees: Race, Vulnerability, and Resilience in Global Liberal Politics." *International Political Sociology* 8 (4): 416–435.

Methmann, Chris, and Angela Oels. 2015. "From 'Fearing' to 'Empowering' Climate Refugees: Governing Climate-Induced Migration in the Name of Resilience." *Security Dialogue* 46 (1): 51–68.

Mitchell, Bruce C., and Jayajit Chakraborty. 2015. "Landscapes of Thermal Inequity: Disproportionate Exposure to Urban Heat in the Three Largest US Cities." *Environmental Research Letters* 10 (11): 1–11.

Myers, Norman. 2005. "Environmental Refugees: An Emergent Security Issue." Paper presented at 13th Meeting of the OSCE Economic Forum, Session III (Environment and Migration), Prague, May 23.

Nevins, Joseph. 2017. "The Right to the World." *Antipode* 49 (5): 1349–1367.

Nicholson, Calum T. M. 2014. "Climate Change and the Politics of Causal Reasoning: The Case of Climate Change and Migration." *Geographical Journal* 180 (2): 151–160.

Nurse, Leonard A., Roger F. McLean, John Agard, Lino Pascal Briguglio, Virginie Duvat-Magnan, Netatua Pelesikoti, Emma Tompkins, and Arthur Web. 2014. "Small Islands." In *Climate Change 2014: Impacts, Adaptation, and Vulnerability; Part B: Regional Aspects*, edited by Vicente R. Barros, Christopher B. Field, David J. Dokken, Michael D. Mastrandrea, Katharine J. Mach, T. Erin Bilir, Monalisa Chatterjee, et al., 1613–1654. Cambridge: Cambridge University Press.

Nyinevi, Christopher Y. 2015. "Universal Civil Jurisdiction: An Option for Global Justice in Climate Change Litigation." *Journal of Politics and Law* 8 (3): 135–148.

OHCHR (Office of the High Commissioner for Human Rights). 2015. "Understanding Human Rights and Climate Change." Available at https://www.ohchr.org/Documents/Issues/ClimateChange/COP21.pdf.

———. 2016. "Report of the Special Rapporteur on the Issue of Human Rights Obligations relating to the Enjoyment of a Safe, Clean, Healthy and Sustainable Environment." Available at https://digitallibrary.un.org/record/831230/files/A_HRC_31_52-EN.pdf.

———. n.d.a. "Human Rights and Climate Change." Available at http://www.ohchr.org/ EN/Issues/HRAndClimateChange/Pages/HRClimateChangeIndex.aspx (accessed December 21, 2018).

———. n.d.b. "Questions and Answers about IDPs." Available at http://www.ohchr.org/ EN/Issues/IDPersons/Pages/Issues.aspx (accessed December 21, 2018).

Olsson, Lennart, Maggie Opondo, Petra Tschakert, Arun Agrawal, Siri Eriksen, Shiming Ma, Sumaya Zakieldeen, Etienne Piguet, Rita Sharma, and Anna Kaijser. 2014. "Livelihoods and Poverty." In *Climate Change 2014: Impacts, Adaptation, and Vulnerability; Part A: Global and Sectoral Aspects*, edited by Christopher B. Field, Vicente R. Barros, David J. Dokken, Katharine J. Mach, Michael D. Mastrandrea, T. Erin Bilir, Monalisa Chatterjee, et al., 793–832. Cambridge: Cambridge University Press.

Oppenheimer, Michael, Maximiliano Campos, Rachel Warren, Joern Birkmann, George Luber, Brian O'Neill, and Kiyoshi Takahashi. 2014. "Emergent Risks and Key Vulnerabilities." In *Climate Change 2014: Impacts, Adaptation, and Vulnerability; Part A: Global and Sectoral Aspects*, edited by Christopher B. Field, Vicente R. Barros, David J. Dokken, Katharine J. Mach, Michael D. Mastrandrea, T. Erin Bilir, Monalisa Chatterjee, et al., 1039–1099. Cambridge: Cambridge University Press.

Otto, Ilona M., Diana Reckien, Christopher P. O. Reyer, Rachel Marcus, Virginie Le Masson, Lindsey Jones, Andrew Norton, and Olivia Serdeczny. 2017. "Social Vulnerability to Climate Change: A Review of Concepts and Evidence." *Regional Environmental Change* 17 (6): 1651–1662.

Pillay, Navanethem. 2012. Open letter to all permanent missions in New York and in Geneva. March 30. Available at https://www.ohchr.org/Documents/Issues/ Development/OpenLetterHC.pdf.

Porter, John R., Liyong Xie, Andrew J. Challinor, Kevern Cochrane, S. Mark Howden, Muhammad Mohsin Iqbal, David B. Lobell, and Maria I. Travasso. 2014. "Food Security and Food Production Systems." In *Climate Change 2014: Impacts, Adaptation, and Vulnerability; Part A: Global and Sectoral Aspects*, edited by Christopher B. Field, Vicente R. Barros, David J. Dokken, Katharine J. Mach, Michael D. Mastrandrea, T. Erin Bilir, Monalisa Chatterjee, et al., 485–533. Cambridge: Cambridge University Press.

Pörtner, Hans-Otto, David M. Karl, Philip W. Boyd, William Cheung, Salvador E. Lluch-Cota, Yukihiro Nojiri, Daniela N. Schmidt, et al. 2014. "Ocean Systems." In *Climate Change 2014: Impacts, Adaptation, and Vulnerability; Part A: Global and Sectoral Aspects*, edited by Christopher B. Field, Vicente R. Barros, David J. Dokken, Katharine J. Mach, Michael D. Mastrandrea, T. Erin Bilir, Monalisa Chatterjee, et al., 411–484. Cambridge: Cambridge University Press.

Ransan-Cooper, Hedda, Carol Farbotko, Karen E. McNamara, Fanny Thornton, and Emilie Chevalier. 2015. "Being(s) Framed: The Means and Ends of Framing Environmental Migrants." *Global Environmental Change: Human and Policy Dimensions* 35:106–115.

Republic of Maldives. 2007. "Male' Declaration on the Human Dimension of Global Climate Change." Available at http://www.ciel.org/Publications/Male_Declaration _Nov07.pdf.

Revi, Aromar, David E. Satterthwaite, Fernando Aragón-Durand, Jan Corfee-Morlot, Robert B. R. Kiunsi, Mark Pelling, Debra C. Roberts, and William Solecki. 2014. "Urban Areas." In *Climate Change 2014: Impacts, Adaptation, and Vulnerability; Part A: Global and Sectoral Aspects*, edited by Christopher B. Field, Vicente R.

Barros, David J. Dokken, Katharine J. Mach, Michael D. Mastrandrea, T. Erin Bilir, Monalisa Chatterjee, et al., 535–612. Cambridge: Cambridge University Press.

Riede, Felix. 2014. "Towards a Science of Past Disasters." *Natural Hazards* 71 (1): 335–362.

Schuppert, Fabian, and Christian Seidel. 2015. "Equality, Justice and Feasibility: An Ethical Analysis of the WBGU's Budget Approach." *Climatic Change* 133 (3): 397–406.

Selby, Jan, Omar S. Dahi, Christiane Fröhlich, and Mike Hulme. 2017. "Climate Change and the Syrian Civil War Revisited." *Political Geography* 60 (supplement C): 232–244.

Seto, Karen Ching-Yee, Shobhakar Dhakal, Anthony Bigio, Hilda Blanco, Gian Carlo Delgado, David Dewar, Luxin Huang, et al. 2014. "Human Settlements, Infrastructure and Spatial Planning." In *Climate Change, 2014: Mitigation of Climate Change*, edited by O. Edenhofer, R. Pichs-Madruga, Y. Sokona, E. Farahani, S. Kadner, K. Seyboth, A. Adler, et al., 923–1000. Cambridge: Cambridge University Press.

Skillington, Tracey. 2015. "Climate Justice without Freedom: Assessing Legal and Political Responses to Climate Change and Forced Migration." *European Journal of Social Theory* 18 (3): 288–307.

Smith, Kirk R., Alistair Woodward, Diarmid Campbell-Lendrum, Dave D. Chadee, Yasushi Honda, Qiyong Liu, Jane M., Boris Revich, and Rainer Sauerborn. 2014. "Human Health: Impacts, Adaptation, and Co-benefits." In *Climate Change, 2014: Impacts, Adaptation, and Vulnerability; Part A: Global and Sectoral Aspects*, edited by Christopher B. Field, Vicente R. Barros, David J. Dokken, Katharine J. Mach, Michael D. Mastrandrea, T. Erin Bilir, Monalisa Chatterjee, et al., 709–754. Cambridge: Cambridge University Press.

Smith, Pete, Steven J. Davis, Felix Creutzig, Sabine Fuss, Jan Minx, Benoit Gabrielle, Etsushi Kato, et al. 2016. "Biophysical and Economic Limits to Negative CO_2 Emissions." *Nature Climate Change* 6:42–50.

Smith, Roy, and Karen E. McNamara. 2015. "Future Migrations from Tuvalu and Kiribati: Exploring Government, Civil Society and Donor Perceptions." *Climate and Development* 7 (1): 47–59.

Stabinsky, Doreen, and Juan P. Hoffmaister. 2015. "Establishing Institutional Arrangements on Loss and Damage under the UNFCCC: The Warsaw International Mechanism for Loss and Damage." *International Journal of Global Warming* 8 (2): 295–318.

Stavins, Robert, Ji Zou, Thomas Brewer, Mariana Conte Grand, Michel den Elzen, Michael Finus, Joyeeta Gupta, et al. 2014. "International Cooperation: Agreements and Instruments." In *Climate Change, 2014: Mitigation of Climate Change*, edited by O. Edenhofer, R. Pichs-Madruga, Y. Sokona, E. Farahani, S. Kadner, K. Seyboth, A. Adler, et al., 1001–1082. Cambridge: Cambridge University Press.

Sternberg, Troy. 2012. "Chinese Drought, Bread and the Arab Spring." *Applied Geography* 34 (supplement C): 519–524.

Stojanov, Robert, Ilan Kelman, Shawn Shen, Barbora Duzi, Himani Upadhyay, Dmytro Vikhrov, G. J. Lingaraj, and Arabinda Mishra. 2014. "Contextualising Typologies of Environmentally Induced Population Movement." *Disaster Prevention and Management* 23 (5): 508–523.

Sultan, Riad. 2017. *Assessing the Climate Change–Migration Nexus through the Lens of Migrants: The Case of the Republic of Mauritius*. Geneva: International Organization for Migration.

Sutter, John D. 2017. "Tragedy of a Village Built on Ice." *CNN*, March 29. Available at http://edition.cnn.com/2017/03/29/us/sutter-shishmaref-esau-tragedy/index.html.

Tacoli, Cecilia. 2009. "Crisis or Adaptation? Migration and Climate Change in a Context of High Mobility." *Environment and Urbanization* 21 (2): 513–525.

Tanner, Thomas, Tom Mitchell, Emily Polack, and Bruce Guenther. 2009. "Urban Governance for Adaptation: Assessing Climate Change Resilience in Ten Asian Cities." *IDS Working Papers* 2009 (315): 1–47.

Teitiota v. Chief Executive of the Ministry of Business Innovation and Employment. 2013. NZHC 3125.

Thompson, Allen, and Friederike E. L. Otto. 2015. "Ethical and Normative Implications of Weather Event Attribution for Policy Discussions concerning Loss and Damage." *Climatic Change* 133 (3): 439–451.

Tucker, Mary Evelyn. 2015. "Can Science and Religion Respond to Climate Change?" *Zygon* 50 (4): 949–961.

Turhan, Ethemcan, Christos Zografos, and Giorgos Kallis. 2015. "Adaptation as Biopolitics: Why State Policies in Turkey Do Not Reduce the Vulnerability of Seasonal Agricultural Workers to Climate Change." *Global Environmental Change: Human and Policy Dimensions* 31:296–306.

UNEP (United Nations Environment Programme). 2015. "Climate Change and Human Rights." Available at https://web.law.columbia.edu/sites/default/files/microsites/climate-change/climate_change_and_human_rights.pdf.

UNFCCC (United Nations Framework Convention on Climate Change). 2014. "Report of the Conference of the Parties on Its Nineteenth Session, Held in Warsaw from 11 to 23 November 2013: Addendum, Part Two: Action Taken by the Conference of the Parties at Its Nineteenth Session." Available at https://unfccc.int/sites/default/files/resource/docs/2013/cop19/eng/10a01.pdf.

———. 2016. "Report of the Conference of the Parties on Its Twenty-First Session, Held in Paris from 30 November to 13 December 2015: Addendum, Part Two: Action Taken by the Conference of the Parties at Its Twenty-First Session." Available at https://unfccc.int/resource/docs/2015/cop21/eng/10a01.pdf.

UNICEF (United Nations International Children's Emergency Fund). 2015. "Unless We Act Now: The Impact of Climate Change on Children." Available at https://www.unicef.org/publications/files/Unless_we_act_now_The_impact_of_climate_change_on_children.pdf.

United Nations. 1951. "Convention relating to the Status of Refugees." Available at https://www.unhcr.org/protect/PROTECTION/3b66c2aa10.pdf.

Wallimann-Helmer, Ivo. 2015. "Justice for Climate Loss and Damage." *Climatic Change* 133 (3): 469–480.

Warren, Phillip Dane. 2016. "Forced Migration after Paris COP21: Evaluating the 'Climate Change Displacement Coordination Facility.'" *Columbia Law Review* 116 (8): 2103–2144.

Webber, Frances. 2017. "Europe's Unknown War." *Race and Class* 59 (1): 36–53.

Williams, Angela. 2008. "Turning the Tide: Recognizing Climate Change Refugees in International Law." *Law and Policy* 30 (4): 502–529.

Zellentin, Alexa. 2015. "Climate Justice, Small Island Developing States and Cultural Loss." *Climatic Change* 133 (3): 491–498.

2

Right to Water

Remedying Violations by Nonstate Actors

Beatrice Lindstrom

It is with great sadness that I write you this letter to remind
you that human rights are something that all people must
respect no matter how powerful you are.
—Cholera survivor Viengeméne Ulisse, letter to the UN
    Security Council, December 10, 2015

The small island-state of Haiti has contended with a history of natural disasters, entrenched poverty, and political turmoil that has spurred survival migration. While many of the rights violations causing Haitians to seek refuge abroad are a result of state-sponsored violence or a failure of the state to fulfill economic and social rights, recent calamities have also laid bare the prominent role of nonstate actors in shaping the conditions that lead to migration.

One of the worst disasters in Haiti's recent history was caused by recklessness in international development cooperation. More than ten thousand Haitians have died and more than eight hundred thousand have been sickened by cholera introduced to Haiti by United Nations (UN) peacekeepers, who contaminated Haiti's largest river with untreated human waste from one of its bases. The cholera crisis in Haiti is an acute example of how nonstate actors—even ones engaged in well-intentioned development cooperation—can cause violations of human rights such as the right to water. As cross-border cooperation increases, nonstate actors such as international organizations, international financial institutions, and multinational corporations command enormous power and resources that affect the realization of human rights worldwide. When such rights violations occur, they can paradoxically contribute to the conditions that spur cross-border migration. Unless such harms are remedied in the places where they occur, they may contribute to a continued rise in cross-border flight.

This chapter looks beyond the traditional paradigm of human rights law as a body of law that governs relations between states and individuals to explore the rights and obligations that inure when the duty bearers are non-state actors. After briefly discussing the recent emergence of the human right to water, the chapter delves into the relatively murkier area of defining human rights obligations in the context of development cooperation. Using the Haiti cholera epidemic as a case study, the chapter demonstrates that barriers to obtaining remedies for nonstate human rights violations are amplified by underlying structural deficiencies and power dynamics that limit access to judicial accountability mechanisms and complicate opportunities for political accountability.

Yet the Haiti cholera case is also an example of how innovative advocacy strategies that take advantage of the interconnectedness of this globalized world can pry open the doors to new opportunities for rights enforcement. The chapter chronicles the efforts of cholera victims to hold the UN accountable through a vast range of innovative and interconnected strategies—from employing visual media campaigns to suing the UN in court. In this new world order, transnational partnerships, the Internet, and social media are empowering rights holders such as Viengeméne Ulisse to hold one of the most powerful organizations in the world accountable under human rights law.

From Need to Right: Evolution of a Legal Right to Water

Today, one in nine people globally lacks access to safe water (World Health Organization and UNICEF 2017, 3). The impact is especially harsh on women and children, who collectively spend 125 million hours each day collecting water (UNICEF 2016). An average of four thousand children die per day as a result of lack of access to clean water (Winkler 2012, 5). While these astounding statistics conjure images of a drought-filled world, the global water crisis is not a result of physical scarcity. It is "rooted in power, poverty and inequality" that determine how water is allocated and prioritized (7).

Despite its centrality to human survival, access to safe water has only recently been recognized as a human right in formal human rights instruments. The right to water is notably absent from direct articulation in seminal human rights documents such as the Universal Declaration of Human Rights and the International Covenant on Economic, Social and Cultural Rights (ICESCR). Inga Winkler (2012, 10) posits that such an express recognition is absent because water was long taken for granted to be as freely available as the air we breathe and therefore was not thought to necessitate codification as a right. Water access was especially not an issue in the developed countries that led the codification of human rights. As industrialization, commodification, and climate change have contributed to the emergence of the global water crisis, however, an urgent need for human rights law to keep pace has spurred a series of developments toward the recognition of the right to water as legally binding (9).

Access to safe water first emerged as a human right in discussions at international conferences in the 1970s (Salman and McInerney-Lankford 2004). In 2002, thirty-five years after the ICESCR took effect, the Committee on Economic, Social and Cultural Rights (ESCR Committee) issued a General Comment that for the first time recognized the human right to water as a separate right within the ICESCR framework. Reasoning that the right to water is inextricably linked to a series of rights expressly articulated in the treaty, including the right to health, food, and attainment of an adequate standard of living, the ESCR Committee interpreted the ICESCR to implicitly "entitle everyone to sufficient, safe, acceptable, physically accessible and affordable water for personal and domestic uses" (Committee on Economic, Social and Cultural Rights 2003). While the ESCR Committee does not have the authority to create new obligations, General Comment No. 15 is an authoritative interpretation of the ICESCR and laid important normative groundwork for a full recognition of the right.

In 2010, the UN General Assembly formally "recognise[d] the right to safe and clean drinking water and sanitation as a human right that is essential for the full enjoyment of life and all human rights" (United Nations General Assembly 2010, 2). The resolution does not have binding legal force on its own, but the use of the word "recognise" signals that member states viewed the resolution as a codification of an existing right rather than creation of a new one (Winkler 2012, 78). Moreover, the resolution was adopted without any votes against it (though seventy states abstained or were absent), indicating widespread state support (10). Later the same year, the UN Human Rights Council affirmed the legally binding nature of the right in a resolution adopted by consensus. The right to water is also protected in relation to specific populations in the Convention on the Elimination of All Forms of Discrimination against Women and the Convention on the Rights of the Child, as well as in various regional documents, including the African Charter on the Rights and Welfare of the Child, the Arab Charter on Human Rights of the League of Arab States, and the San Salvador Protocol to the American Convention on Human Rights (56–57).

The recognition of a human right to water creates duties of states to (1) respect the right to water by refraining from interfering with enjoyment of water, (2) protect against violations by nonstate actors, and (3) progressively realize the right to water by applying maximum available resources and by prioritizing essential levels of access to the most marginalized (United Nations 2014). Ultimately, states are obligated to fully realize the right to water by ensuring access to sufficient, safe, acceptable, accessible, and affordable water and sanitation services for all. As Winkler notes, the recognition of the right to water has significant implications for distribution; it requires prioritizing the basic needs of the marginalized and disempowered over allocations based on wealth and power. Moreover, it means that violations of the right to water entitle rights holders to effective remedies (Winkler 2012, 1).

The Rise of Nonstate Actors

The Role of Nonstate Actors in Realizing the Right to Water

Human rights law's traditional focus on the duties of states in regard to individual rights holders does not fully address the challenges of rights realization in a globalized world. As discussed in the Introduction, nonstate actors have an increasingly harsh impact on access to environmental resources that are key to rights enjoyment, including clean water. Corporations have been responsible for releasing toxins into major waterways, monopolizing water rights, privatizing water distribution, and depleting water supplies. Globalization has also given rise to increased interconnectedness and fostered a culture of global responsibility, beyond the private sector, that in turn has spurred growth in development cooperation.[1] In this context, nonprofit nonstate actors such as international organizations, international financial institutions, and nongovernmental organizations (NGOs) have tremendous impacts on human rights. As Amir Attaran notes, "There are probably very few people living in poor countries who, by a certain age, have not been educated in a school, treated in a clinic, traveled on a road, or partaken of some food or drink, paid for in part by foreign aid" (2006, 1).

The role of nonstate actors in development cooperation is readily apparent in Haiti, one of the most water-insecure countries in the world. In 2015, half of the Haitian population lacked regularized access to an improved water source protected from outside contamination such as fecal matter (UNICEF and World Health Organization 2015, 63). The government's ability to address this chronic violation is limited by a history of debt service, corruption, lack of resources, and limited technical expertise. In 2015, its budget for *all* government services was approximately $2 billion, placing a national water and sanitation system priced at $2.2 billion out of reach without external support.[2]

However, nonstate actors participating in development cooperation command enormous resources (Satterthwaite 2011, 880–882). Following the 2010 earthquake, foreign donors pledged $6.04 billion in aid—three times the national budget. The vast majority of this aid bypassed the government completely and was channeled through nonstate actors: 99 percent of relief aid and 90 percent of reconstruction aid went to projects and programs run by multilateral agencies, foreign NGOs, and private contractors (Office of the Special Envoy for Haiti 2012). Haiti is believed to have the highest number of NGOs per capita in the world, earning it the nickname "Republic of NGOs."[3] The UN has a strong presence in Haiti, with eight different civilian and military missions in the country since 1993. The UN Stabilization Mission in Haiti (MINUSTAH) was in the country for thirteen years, despite the absence of any recognized armed conflict in Haiti for more than fifty years. The mission had an expansive mandate, including training and supplementing the national police force; building up the rule of law; assisting with organization and implementation of elections at all levels of government; and promoting human rights. In October 2017, MINUSTAH transitioned to a smaller successor mission focused on rule of law and promotion of justice, the UN Mission for Justice Support in Haiti (MINUJUSTH).

These nonstate actors are primary service providers and perform traditional government functions. Their budgets often exceed those of the government agencies whose tasks they are carrying out. Thus, they play a powerful role in setting priorities, designing projects, and overseeing implementation of policies that determine the fulfillment of human rights at various levels. When development cooperation is carried out in a way that builds the capacity of the state to meet needs in the long run, it can contribute decisively to the fulfillment of human rights. But when development cooperation does not employ a human rights–based approach that prioritizes capacity building and empowerment, it can undermine long-term fulfillment of human rights (Concannon and Lindstrom 2011). For example, in the water sector, nonstate actors tend to prioritize piecemeal and short-term projects, such as installing a water pump or providing water treatment tablets, over investing in public water treatment and delivery systems. When these actors leave Haiti, their projects often go with them, either ending from lack of continued funding or falling into disrepair from lack of technical expertise or resources for maintenance.

Moreover, the ability of developing-country governments to fulfill rights can also be hampered by nonstate actors whose support is determined by a range of diverse interests, including political interests of donor countries. For example, in 1998, the Inter-American Development Bank (IDB) approved a loan of fifty-four million dollars to fund a massive water project that would have transformed access to clean water in Haiti (Center for Human Rights and Global Justice et al. 2008). As internal documents obtained through the Freedom of Information Act requests have revealed, however, disbursal of the loans was blocked by the United States as a way to pressure the Haitian government to meet its political demands on other fronts (11–14). This action violated the IDB charter, but insufficient accountability

mechanisms meant that neither the Haitian government nor the rights holders who would have benefited from the project had a means to challenge it.

Faulty executions of development projects—no matter how well intended—can also directly cause human rights violations. As Attaran notes,
"It would be naïve to imagine that, in such a sweeping enterprise, led by ordinary, fallible men and women, *nowhere* has a foreign aid scheme made an
unfortunate error that foreseeably harmed its intended beneficiaries" (2006,
1–2). A few examples underscore this reality. In Bangladesh, UNICEF spon-
sored a massive tubewell project in the 1970s that exposed an estimated seventy million people to toxic levels of arsenic, causing the largest mass poisoning of a population in history (though the foreseeability of the presence of
arsenic in the ground is debated). In Kosovo, the UN Mission in Kosovo (UN-
MIK) housed hundreds of displaced Roma families on toxic wastelands that
leached lead for more than ten years, resulting in widespread paralysis, mis-
carriages, deformities, and death from lead poisoning. In Haiti, MINUSTAH
discharged untreated human waste into the primary water source, contami-
nating it with cholera and unleashing the worst cholera epidemic in the world.
These situations evince the need to clarify nonstate actors' obligations and
rights holders' options for enforcement under human rights law.

Human Rights Obligations of Nonstate Actors

While the impact of nonstate actors on the human rights of host-country
nationals is clear, their obligations under human rights law are less so. Corporations, international organizations, and international financial institutions are not parties to the human rights treaties that protect the right to
water; nor are they bound by the UN resolutions that expound the right.
Moreover, while nonstate actors are generally bound by customary international law, it is not clear that state practice with regard to the right to water
has reached the consistency required to constitute custom (Winkler 2012).
Thus, the main sources of state human rights obligations do not readily apply
to nonstate actors.

Nonetheless, there exist various reasons for concluding that nonstate actors have some duties under human rights law. At a minimum, they are obligated to *respect* human rights in their operations—in other words, they
must refrain from directly causing human rights violations. In the case of
multinational corporations, this principle is enshrined in the UN "Guiding
Principles on Business and Human Rights," which articulate a corporate
responsibility to respect human rights and to exercise due diligence to avoid
any action that would result in human rights abuses in the scope of their
operations, including their supply chain (United Nations 2011). International organizations are similarly obligated to respect human rights. Those

that are a part of the UN system have adopted a commitment to using a human rights–based approach in their work (Concannon and Lindstrom 2011). Since international organizations are made up of member states with their own human rights obligations, they are also arguably transitively bound by human rights law to the extent that their members are (Mégret and Hoffmann 2003, 317). The imperative for the UN to comply with human rights law also comes from its constituent document itself (Dannenbaum 2010; Paust 2010). Article 55 of the UN Charter identifies the promotion of human rights as one of the UN's core functions and "entails a duty on the part of the U.N. and its agents to respect the international human rights law that it promotes" (Transnational Development Clinic, Global Health Justice Partnership, and Association Haïtienne de Troit de l'Environnement 2013, 35). The case is less clear regarding NGOs that do not have international legal personality, though many large humanitarian NGOs have also committed to employing a human rights–based approach in their work (Concannon and Lindstrom 2011).

Moreover, international organizations and other nonstate actors engaged in development cooperation have a particularly high onus to comply with human rights law even where they are not legally bound to do so. Respect for human rights is consistent with the "do no harm" principle that undergirds humanitarian work. Further, these actors rely on moral credibility to attract the financial and political support to function, and being seen as a violator of human rights is hardly consistent with standing on the moral high ground. The UN in particular has a heightened need to avoid causing or contributing to human rights violations because its legitimacy and effectiveness as a promoter of human rights depend on it (Darrow and Arbour 2009, 461). This normative incentive for compliance also creates opportunities to engage the UN on accountability outside the strictly legal avenues.

The UN's Human Rights Violations in Haiti

Introduction of Cholera and Violation of the Right to Water

The UN's introduction of cholera to Haiti illustrates the challenges and opportunities of enforcing human rights against nonstate actors. Cholera first appeared in Haiti in 2010 in the sleepy village of Meille, where the major source of activity at the time was a MINUSTAH base (Ivers and Walton 2012). The base sat perched on the banks of a tributary that feeds into the Artibonite River, Haiti's largest waterway that tens of thousands rely on as their primary water source for drinking, washing, and irrigation. Shortly before the outbreak, a new rotation of peacekeepers arrived at the base from Nepal, where cholera is endemic (Cravioto et al. 2011). The soldiers were not tested or treated for cholera ("Haiti Cholera Outbreak" 2010). Improper sewage management on the base caused untreated human waste to flow from the base into the Meille tributary. Journalists who investigated the situation uncovered overflowing septic tanks and broken sewage pipes leaking foulsmelling liquids into the tributary ("UN Investigates" 2010; Katz 2013). Once the cholera bacteria entered the tributary, they contaminated the Artibonite River system and spread like wildfire throughout the country. In the first week of the outbreak, Haiti's Ministry of Public Health recorded more than one thousand cases and 135 deaths. By mid-November 2010, one month into the outbreak, more than one thousand people had died and cholera had spread to all ten of Haiti's geographic departments (Cravioto et al. 2011, 21).

The UN responded to the strong circumstantial evidence with outright denial. The UN spokesperson in Haiti issued press statements claiming that sanitation on the base was compliant with international standards. Efforts to identify the source were expressly discouraged as not a priority (Frerichs 2016, 89). For example, the Pan-American Health Organization's senior program manager, speaking at a MINUSTAH press conference, dismissed the evidence of UN responsibility as "simply rumors. . . . There is no agent, no entity, no person, no structure that is responsible for the introduction of cholera in Haiti. . . . There is nothing more to say on this and all attempts at stigmatization, pointing fingers, identifying [the source] are erroneous" (Thieren 2010; my translation). The UN spokesperson echoed this view, stating that "from our point of view, [the origin] really doesn't matter" (McNeil 2010). When protests erupted around Haiti, the spokesperson dismissed them as "not genuine," politically motivated efforts to disrupt upcoming elections (Archibold 2010). In November 2010, as the death toll was soaring, Edmond Mulet, the head of MINUSTAH, told a *Time* magazine reporter that "it's really unfair to accuse the U.N. for bringing cholera into Haiti" (Desvarieux 2010). This view was echoed in the international media. The *New York Times* science and health writer Donald McNeil (2010) epitomized this view in an op-ed titled "Cholera's Second Fever: An Urge to Blame," where he cautioned against blaming the UN on the grounds that fault "often lies just as much with the victims as with the vectors, since, as in syphilis's case, they are careless about whom they cavort with, and with cholera, they must lack good sanitation for it to spread."

In the face of this intransigence, the Haitian government requested support from the French government, and they jointly appointed an investigatory team led by global cholera expert Renaud Piarroux. Piarroux's team concluded that there was "no doubt" that cholera had been imported to Haiti by MINUSTAH and that the epidemic "started around the camp of MINUSTAH and was spread explosively due to massive contamination of the water in the Artibonite River and one of its tributaries with feces of patients with cholera." He also noted the possibility that MINUSTAH had intentionally covered up its actions: "It cannot be ruled out that steps were taken to remove feces and erase traces of an epidemic of cholera among the soldiers" (Piarroux 2011).

Finally, in December 2010, the UN secretary-general relented to public pressure and announced the establishment of an Independent Panel of Experts to investigate and determine the origins of cholera in Haiti, which released its report in May 2011. It found that the pipes on the MINUSTAH base were "haphazard, with significant potential for cross-contamination," and that the base routinely disposed of untreated fecal waste in unprotected, open-air pits dug directly into the ground that created a serious risk of overflow (Cravioto et al. 2011, 22–23). It concluded that the "evidence overwhelmingly supports" that "the outbreak was caused by bacteria introduced into Haiti as a result of human activity; more specifically by the contamination of the Meye Tributary System" with a South Asian strain of cholera (29). Subsequent genetic studies presented "irrefutable molecular evidence" that the strain of cholera in Haiti is identical to the one in Nepal (Hendriksen et al. 2011; Sontag 2012). In March 2013, the panelists released a second article clarifying their findings in light of the overwhelming scientific evidence, specifying that "the preponderance of the evidence and the weight of the circumstantial evidence does lead to the conclusion that personnel associated with the Mirebalais MINUSTAH facility were the most likely source of introduction of cholera into Haiti" (Lantagne et al. 2014, 163). Today, no serious debate remains about the origins of cholera in Haiti, and even the UN has stopped publicly denying responsibility.

Violations of the Right to an Effective Remedy

The introduction of cholera constitutes violations of, inter alia, the rights to water, health, life, and an adequate standard of living (Freedman 2016). Under human rights law, victims of rights violations must have access to procedures through which they can submit complaints and must be assured of the fair, transparent, and impartial adjudication of their claims, as well as substantive remedies. Yet hurdles to fulfilling the right to an effective remedy are particularly pronounced where nonstate actors are concerned. The Convention on the Privileges and Immunities of the United Nations (CPIUN), a multilateral treaty signed by most UN member states, effectively protects the UN from suit in national courts by granting sweeping immunity "from all forms of legal process." In exchange, the convention also mandates that the UN "shall make provisions for appropriate modes of settlement" of third-party claims filed against it. In the context of peacekeeping, this clause is operationalized through local claims units—opaque administrative offices in peacekeeping missions that unilaterally review and decide whether to settle claims. The Status of Forces Agreements (SOFA) between the UN and host countries require that third-party claims for personal injury, illness, or death that cannot be resolved through this system be decided by a standing claims commission (United Nations and Government of Haiti 2004). As the introduction to the CPIUN notes, these requirements refect an "acknowl-edgment of the right of access to court as contained in all major human rights instruments" (Reinisch, n.d.). In practice, however, the UN has never established such a commission in Haiti or in any country that has hosted a peacekeeping operation, despite signing thirty-two SOFAs promising to do so (Transnational Development Clinic, Global Health Justice Partnership, and Association Haïtienne de Troit de l'Environnement 2013, 42). This ef-fectively leaves victims of UN-caused injuries without an independent fo-rum in which to seek redress.

In the late summer of 2011, as the first anniversary of the outbreak ap-proached without the UN accepting responsibility, the Bureau des Avocats Internationaux (BAI), one of Haiti's principal human rights organizations, began working with victims of cholera in rural Haiti to develop a legal strat-egy for accountability. Through a grassroots outreach effort, the BAI con-nected with victims who had been sickened by cholera or lost family to the disease. They partnered with community organizers and international vol-unteers to prepare and file formal legal claims in accordance with the UN's obligations to provide appropriate modes of settlement under the CPIUN. In November 2011, the BAI and its U.S.-based partner, the Institute for Jus-tice and Democracy in Haiti (IJDH), submitted five thousand claims to MINUSTAH's claims unit in Haiti and UN headquarters in New York. The claims alleged both tort and human rights violations and sought as remedies (1) compensation, (2) investment in clean water and sanitation infrastruc-ture to control the epidemic, and (3) a public acceptance of responsibility for the cholera outbreak. Additionally, they requested that the UN establish a standing claims commission as required by the SOFA to adjudicate the claims. The filing of the claims generated significant media attention.

The UN's response took fifteen months and amounted to a two-line dis-missal: "Consideration of these claims would necessarily include a review of political and policy matters. Accordingly, these claims are not receivable pursuant to Section 29 of the Convention" (O'Brien 2013a). The claimants challenged the response, requesting that the UN provide legal justification for its position and again requesting that the claims be referred to indepen-dent adjudication before a claims commission or, alternatively, be submitted to arbitration or mediation. The UN denied those requests, repeating verba-tim the assertion from the previous letter that the claims were "not receiv-able" and declaring that "there is no legal basis for the United Nations to establish such a commission in respect of claims that are not receivable" (O'Brien 2013b).

Reclaiming Rights

Bringing the Legal Case to the Court of Public Opinion

In decades past, the UN's dismissal of the victims' claims may have been the end of the story. But in the age of interconnectedness and telecommunications, the victims' advocates were able to shine a spotlight on the UN's response and bring it to international scrutiny. As Kristina Dauguirdas notes, "Once the UN had publicly provided a reason (however thin) for denying the petition, transnational actors were in a position to evaluate the UN's position" (2014, 1003). The case that the UN had deemed closed in its third-party claims process was reopened at international law conferences, in law review articles, and in academic discussions where legal experts denounced the UN's response. In August 2013, Yale Law School and School of Public Health, in partnership with L'Association Haïtienne de Droit de l'Environnement, a nonprofit environmental law group in Haiti, released a critical report concluding that "the UN's ongoing unwillingness to hold itself accountable to victims violates its legal obligations under international law" (Transnational Development Clinic, Global Health Justice Partnership, and Association Haïtienne de Troit de l'Environnement 2013, 4). Frédéric Mégret (2013) rejected the notion that the cholera claims could be characterized as anything but private law claims. Jeremy Waldron (2015) castigated the UN's "shabby formalistic maneuvers to avoid the very principles of the Rule of Law that they urge on the rest of the world." José Alvarez highlighted the contradiction that "an organization that has committed itself at the highest levels to the promotion and fulfillment of the rule of law apparently sees no contradiction in promoting accountability—including legal accountability—in others while refusing to address how the national or international law applies to itself in this case" (2014, 23).

This rebuke reverberated in the international media. Media outlets around the world condemned the UN's reliance on an unexplained technicality to rebuff the claims, running headlines such as "U.N. Hypocrisy in Haiti" (Krishnaswami and Ahmad 2013), "Double Standards" (2013), and "In Haiti the UN's Behaviour Is a Far Cry from Being the Conscience of the World" (Birrell 2013).[4] The *Washington Post* opined that "by refusing to acknowledge responsibility, the United Nations jeopardizes its standing and moral authority in Haiti and in other countries where its personnel are deployed" (Washington Post Editorial Board 2013), and the *New York Times* urged the organization to "acknowledge responsibility, apologize to Haitians and give the victims the means to file claims against it for the harm they say has been done them" (New York Times Editorial Board 2013). This marked a major shift in the narrative around the UN's responsibility to the victims. As Alvarez observed, "The United Nations' handling of the allegations that its peacekeepers in Haiti are responsible for the largest number of cholera cases and deaths in the world [became] a public relations as well as public health disaster" (2014, 22).

Bringing the Legal Case to U.S. Court

The UN's refusal to provide victims with an avenue to seek remedies—and the broad agreement among international legal experts that this amounted to a breach of its treaty obligations—also set the stage for a challenge to the UN's immunity in court. In October 2013, BAI and IJDH filed an unprecedented class-action lawsuit against the UN, MINUSTAH, and their leadership in federal court in New York, where the UN is headquartered (Georges v. United Nations 2013). The case argues that the UN's immunity must be read in the context of its obligation to settle claims out of court and that the refusal to do so amounts to a breach of treaty and a failure to fulfill a condition precedent to its immunity. In January 2015, the District Court dismissed the suit, holding that the UN enjoyed immunity pursuant to the CPIUN. Victims appealed the dismissal, supported by eighty-three organizations and prominent individuals from around the world, including human rights organizations and former UN officers, who filed six amicus curiae briefs (Georges v. United Nations 2015). On August 19, 2016, the appellate panel affirmed the District Court's dismissal, holding that the obligation to settle claims did not constitute a condition precedent to immunity and that the plaintiff-appellants lacked standing to raise material breach (Georges v. United Nations 2016).

While the case lost in court, the act of taking the cholera victims' claims to court has significantly affected the political context of the issue. The litigation sustained public attention and created important leverage to place political pressure on the UN Secretariat and member states to provide remedies to victims out of court (Freedman 2016). The lawsuit also helped shift the lens through which cholera victims were viewed in the international public discourse, from passive recipients of aid gone wrong to active rights holders entitled to justice.

Building the Moral Case for Remedies

The litigation also provided an important pillar for organizing a broad movement for justice. Through an informal network of victims' groups, Haitian grassroots activists, lawyers, journalists, academics, filmmakers, medical and public health professionals, and political leaders, BAI and IJDH nurtured a vast advocacy campaign to raise public awareness, build solidarity, and influence decision makers to respond justly to the ongoing crisis. An essential component of the campaign has centered on using social media, video, art, and the Internet to bring the resistance of Haitian victims and activists—expressed primarily through organizing and protests in the streets of Haiti—to the halls of power in New York, Geneva, and Washington. For example, in October 2015, on the fifth anniversary of the introduction of cholera, victims' groups partnered with activists and artists to paste large portraits of cholera victims on the gates of MINUSTAH's headquarters in Port-au-Prince. International partners displayed identical exhibits at UN headquarters in New York and Geneva. They also published the campaign online on the website www.facejustice.org and circulated it on social media using the hashtag #FaceJustice. The calls to "face justice" were also printed on postcards handed directly to UN Security Council delegates as they exited a meeting on MINUSTAH's mandate renewal. Then, to mark Human Rights Day the same year, cholera victims wrote twenty-five hundred letters (including the one by Viengeméne Ulisse quoted earlier) to the UN Security Council, describing the impacts of cholera and their demands for justice. IJDH engaged volunteers from the Haitian American diaspora to translate a selection of the letters into English. BAI and IJDH delivered the letters electronically to the members of the Security Council in New York and to their embassies in Haiti.

International solidarity campaigns have been critical to raising the profile of the cholera issue outside Haiti. For example, in November 2012, forty-eight human rights groups signed a letter asking the UN secretary-general to respond to victims' claims. Thirty thousand people have signed an Avaaz .org petition that calls on the UN to eliminate cholera in Haiti. Four hundred thousand people viewed and shared *Baseball in the Time of Cholera*, a documentary about the human impacts of cholera on one family in Haiti, and another documentary by Al Jazeera ("Haiti in a Time of Cholera" 2013) won Peabody and Emmy Awards for its depiction of the crisis and efforts to hold the UN accountable. This public pressure in turn generated public outrage among lawmakers and decision makers. For example, in July 2016, 160 members of the U.S. Congress signed letters demanding U.S. government leadership in securing UN fulfillment of its "moral and legal obligations." The campaign has also increasingly persuaded individual UN officers to call for a more just UN response. In October 2013, the high commissioner for human rights publicly expressed her view that victims should receive compensation (Associated Press 2013).

Engaging the UN Human Rights System

BAI and IJDH also formally engaged the UN human rights system by making stakeholder submissions to treaty committees, the Universal Periodic Review, and UN Special Procedures. In the summer of 2014, they submitted a formal request for a letter of allegation to the special rapporteur on the human right to safe drinking water and sanitation that eventually led to a major turning point in the advocacy. The allegation letter process allows victims of rights violations to submit complaints to the UN's Special Procedures, which in turn files official letters of allegation with the respective government if there is evidence that human rights have been violated. In the Haiti case, the special rapporteur on water joined with the independent expert on human rights in Haiti, the special rapporteur on the right to health, and the special rapporteur on the right to housing to send a joint letter to the UN secretary-general (Farha et al. 2014). This marked the first time that Special Procedures had filed an allegation letter against the UN Secretariat, and it made headlines when released publicly. Importantly, the allegation letter forced the Secretariat to attempt to further justify its position on cholera. The response, however, still sidestepped the central question presented by the special rapporteurs concerning what the UN was doing to respect the victims' right to an effective remedy (Alston 2018, 15–48).

The group of special rapporteurs—now joined also by the special rapporteur on extreme poverty—did not relent. In a second letter, they stressed that "the effective denial of the fundamental right of the victims of cholera to justice and to an effective remedy is difficult to reconcile with the United Nations' commitment to 'promote and encourage respect for human rights.'" They also underlined the broader implications of the case for the UN's legitimacy: "The non-receivability approach undermines the reputation of the United Nations, calls into question the ethical framework within which its peace-keeping forces operate, and challenges the credibility of the Organization as an entity that respects human rights" (Farha et al. 2015). In his response to this letter, the deputy secretary-general acknowledged for the first time the UN's human rights obligations in the situation and invited further conversation on what more the UN should be doing, signaling a potential new opening to discussing remedies for victims (Alston 2018, 53–54).

These efforts coincided with a widespread demand for greater transparency and civil-society participation in the selection process for the UN's secretary-general. For the first time in the organization's history, the General Assembly required candidates for secretary-general to publicly post their qualifications and hosted a series of webcasted dialogues in which candidates answered member-state and civil-society questions about their positions.

Taking advantage of this opportunity, IJDH lobbied member states, media, and other civil-society partners to raise the cholera issue at such public discussions and publicized their responses over social media. By the time the Security Council began its official straw polling to narrow down the candidate list in July 2016, more than half the candidates had publicly expressed support for remedies for cholera victims. This support for a more just response from these secretary-general candidates in turn spurred calls on Secretary-General Ban Ki-moon to address the issue before he left office in December 2016, including in prominent outlets such as the *New York Times* (New York Times Editorial Board 2016) and the leading medical journal the *Lancet* (Lancet Editorial Board 2016).

A Breakthrough

In August 2016, the campaign culminated in a major breakthrough. The UN special rapporteur on extreme poverty and human rights followed the letter to the secretary-general with a scathing report to the General Assembly that deplored the UN's approach to the issue as "morally unconscionable, legally indefensible and politically self-defeating" (Alston 2016, 2). An advance copy of the report was leaked to Jonathan Katz, one of the journalists who had first uncovered the waste leaking from the UN base in 2010. When Katz contacted the UN for comment, the UN's response presented a radical shift in position: "Over the past year the UN has become convinced that it needs to do much more *regarding its own involvement* in the initial outbreak and the suffering of those affected by cholera" (Katz 2016; emphasis added). The headline "U.N. Admits Role in Cholera Epidemic in Haiti" ran on the front page of the *New York Times* (Katz 2016), and the news was echoed in outlets around the world for days to follow. Importantly, the UN also committed to rolling out a "significant new set of actions" within two months, which would "provide material assistance and support to those Haitians most directly affected by cholera." The UN also stated that "these efforts must include, as a central focus, the victims of the disease and their families" (Lederer 2016).

As Mario Joseph, the BAI managing attorney who had been leading the fight for justice from Haiti told the press, this was "a major victory for the thousands of Haitians who have been marching for justice, writing to the UN and bringing the UN to court. It is high time for the UN to make this right and prove to the world that 'human rights for all' means for Haitians too" (Carasik 2016). Finally, after nearly six years of advocating for an admission of truth, compensation, and cholera elimination, the campaign for justice was making concrete advances. In December 2016, the secretary-general followed the acknowledgment of the UN's role with a formal apology issued before the General Assembly in Haitian Creole, French, and English and launched a four hundred million–dollar program, "New Approach to Cholera in Haiti," with the twin goals of controlling and eliminating cholera and providing material assistance to those most affected by the epidemic. If fully implemented, this plan could revolutionize access to clean water, sanitation, and health; save thousands of lives per year that have recently been lost to waterborne diseases including cholera; and provide much-needed remedies to households that have been devastated by the disease.

The need for follow-through on the new approach is particularly urgent, as Haitians who have migrated abroad to escape the scourge of cholera and other rights violations are being forced to return home to continued life-threatening conditions. In particular, the United States, which is home to the largest Haitian diaspora, decided in November 2017 to rescind temporary protected status (TPS) for Haiti. The TPS program granted fifty thousand Haitians the legal status to live and work in the United States following the devastating earthquake of 2010. The U.S. government frequently cited the subsequent cholera epidemic as additional justification for extending TPS, and its decision to rescind the program in the context of the continued epidemic was widely criticized by activists, members of Congress, state officials, and others. Tens of thousands of people may now face deportation to Haiti when the program is set to end in July 2019. By funding and implementing the cholera response, the UN and its members can take concrete action to ensure that one of the key conditions that spurred the migration is resolved. In the long term, this would reduce the structural inequality that results in Haiti's outsized vulnerability to rights violations. Doing so would also have implications far beyond Haiti; it would mark a historical step in the evolution of the human right to water and the obligation of nonstate actors to provide effective remedies for rights violations around the world.

Lessons from Haiti: Securing Remedies for Human Rights Violations by Nonstate Actors

The Haiti cholera crisis demonstrates the particular challenges and opportunities that arise when human rights are violated through the actions of nonstate actors. Understanding these dynamics is essential to more effectively addressing these emerging threats to human rights.

Barriers to Justice

As Riccardo Pavoni observes, in the cholera case, "the UN's defense does not rely on arguments that exclude the existence of primary obligations on the

Organization in the area of international human rights law or that suggest difficulties in establishing that the acts leading up to the Haiti cholera tragedy should be attributed to the UN" (2015, 19–20). Instead, the central point of contention between the UN and the victims and their allies seems to be whether and how the UN can be held accountable for harms that the organization no longer seriously contests that it inflicted. The Haiti cholera dispute reflects a culture clash between the traditional system in which nonstate actors operate outside the reach of formal accountability structures and today's "alternative human rights universe," in which states and nonstate actors alike are expected to provide remedies to those whom they harm (Alvarez 2014, 25).

The immense obstacles to justice faced by cholera victims are symptomatic of the limitations of the traditional system in securing human rights accountability from nonstate actors. These barriers can be characterized as legal, political, and conceptual in nature. The legal barriers stem from a lack of robust grievance mechanisms through which claims can be reviewed, coupled with immunities and jurisdictional limitations that foreclose actions against international organizations in national courts. This obstacle to accountability is particularly problematic from a human rights point of view because it is inconsistent with the human right to an effective remedy that includes a right to a fair, independent, and transparent adjudication of claims.

The lack of direct accountability relationships between international organizations and the people who are affected by their operations also imposes unique political barriers to accountability. Nonstate actors are politically accountable to their member states, funders, creditors, shareholders, and to some extent the host-state government whose cooperation and consent are both pragmatically and politically important. But they lack the type of accountability relationship to individuals in host countries that exists between governments and their polity. Individuals affected by international organizations do not have agency to set the terms of their operations or direct outcomes. Moreover, nonstate actors' headquarters and decision makers are often located in far-flung places that are difficult to access both physically and politically. This dynamic is especially pronounced in the Haiti-cholera context, where the lack of accountability by MINUSTAH has spurred a widespread perception among Haitians that MINUSTAH, and now its successor mission MINUJUSTH, is an "occupation force."

Finally, on the conceptual level, accountability is decelerated by a general reluctance among those who value development cooperation to demand accountability when humanitarian actors such as the UN commit wrongs. This was evident in the early stages of the cholera advocacy, in the reluctance to investigate the source despite the strong circumstantial evidence, and the initial tendency in the media to frame cholera victims as blame throwing, discontented recipients of aid rather than as rights holders. Over time, persistent advocacy to reframe the issue in human rights terms has largely succeeded in transforming this narrative, which in turn has paved the way for new opportunities for political and legal accountability.

Opportunities for Justice

The strategies employed by advocates for cholera victims also reflect the opportunities that are presented by today's alternate human rights universe. In this universe, global interconnectedness and access to communications have enabled rights holders and their civil-society partners to form powerful transnational and interdisciplinary alliances with the ability to relentlessly focus attention on rights violations, generate cross-boundary political and legal discourse, and demand justice in multifarious ways. Through the employment of a vast network that spans from the grassroots in Haiti to the halls of academia and power, rights holders can seek to enforce the rule of law against violators by using a range of new tools, including private litigation, "media savvy mobilizations of shame," and other forms of public pressure (Alvarez 2014, 25). In this way, the playing field is beginning to even as individuals are empowered to demand accountability through public pressure.

These innovative tools to generate public pressure are particularly effective in regard to nonstate actors that depend on moral authority and credibility for legitimacy. International organizations like the UN depend on voluntary cooperation and contributions to function and can succeed in their mission only if they retain legitimacy. As Waldron (2015) warns, "UN officials should not be surprised if, as things progress along these lines, other countries become increasingly reluctant to accept lectures from its officials and agencies on the importance of the Rule of Law." Indeed, as Special Rapporteur Philip Alston summarized in his report to the General Assembly:

> What is at stake is the Organization's overall credibility in many different areas. Its existing position on cholera in Haiti is at odds with the positions that it espouses so strongly in other key policy areas. It has a huge amount to gain by rethinking its position and a great deal to lose by stubbornly maintaining its current approach. (2016, 20)

Certainly, the cholera case may be unique in that several factors have aligned to make the case particularly compelling in the court of public opinion: it involved a massively lethal harm, a legally and morally objectionable response, and a nonstate actor whose legitimacy is particularly tied up with its moral authority as a promoter of human rights. Because of the diverse nature of nonstate actors' operations in development cooperation, the options for accountability will depend on the circumstances. Still, the cholera case reveals new prospects and possibilities for alleviating human suffering through individual action and innovative solutions. The world in which the UN developed its "deny-and-ignore" policy has passed. Such a policy is no longer tenable in the age of interconnectedness, networked advocacy, social media, and increased skepticism of institutions. The cholera campaign has both revealed this shift and developed a template for victims of nonstate actor violations to navigate it successfully. It is difficult to envision that a few decades ago the cholera victims' claims would be able to overcome institutional intransigence, but successful claims will hopefully be routine a decade hence.

If the efforts to uphold Haitians' human right to water are to succeed, they will ultimately need to involve governments. The Haitian government must exercise leadership in favor if its citizens and supply political support, oversight, and technical expertise to ensure that any reparations are sustainable and build the government's capacity rather than undermine it. Other states will need to provide buy-in and political support and ultimately supply funding for compensation and water and sanitation infrastructure. Still, the cholera case is remarkable as a sign of how human rights in a globalized world can transcend the individual-state dynamic and empower individuals to hold nonstate violators responsible for human rights violations.

NOTES

1. Between 2000 and 2013, official development assistance increased by 66 percent. See OECD 2014.

2. This equates to approximately ten days of the budget for New York City. See City of New York 2018.

3. The exact numbers of NGOs operating in Haiti is unknown. Most do not register with the government, despite legal requirements to do so, because the process is arduous. In 2005, only 346 were registered with the government, but some estimate that the actual number is as high as 10,000. Schuller 2007, 96, 98–99.

4. The *Trinidad Express* noted, "The UN's reputation as a well-meaning, honest broker to the world now stands to be savaged by this decision to refuse compensation to the 5,000 Haitian claimants for the cholera epidemic which has been scientifically traced to infection from Nepalese UN peacekeepers who were brought in following the earthquake" ("Immunity with Impunity" 2013). Jake Johnston (2013) asserted, "The UN's responsibility for introducing cholera . . . [has] been a defining feature of [MINUSTAH's] time in Haiti. . . . Part of MINUSTAH's mandate in Haiti is ostensibly to strengthen the rule of law, support the Haitian justice system and help protect human rights. Talk about a setting a poor example—it's no wonder that polls find a majority of Haitians want MINUSTAH to leave Haiti and to compensate victims of cholera." According to the *Economist*, "Even as Haitians have been outraged by MINUSTAH's wrongdoing, they have become increasingly doubtful of the benefits it provides. . . .

Only the UN can restore MINUSTAH's legitimacy" ("First, Do No Harm" 2012). And Deborah Sontag (2012) reported, "The issue has strained the peacekeepers' relationship with the Haitians they are protecting in an eight-year mission to stabilize the politically volatile nation."

REFERENCES

Alston, Philip. 2016. "Report of the Special Rapporteur on Extreme Poverty and Human Rights." August 26. Available at http://daccess-ods.un.org/access.nsf/Get?Open& DS=A/71/367&Lang=E.

———. 2018. "Extracting Accountability: Special Rapporteurs and the United Nations' Responsibility for Cholera in Haiti." New York University School of Law Public Law and Legal Theory Research Paper Series, Working Paper no. 18-10. Available at https://papers.ssrn.com/sol3/Delivery.cfm/SSRN_ID3125084_code419245.pdf ?abstractid=3125084&mirid=1&type=2.

Alvarez, José. 2014. "The United Nations in the Time of Cholera." *AJIL Unbound* 108:22–29.

Archibold, Randal C. 2010. "Officials in Haiti Defend Focus on Cholera Outbreak, Not Its Origins." *New York Times*, November 17. Available at https://www.nytimes.com/2010/11/17/world/americas/17haiti.html.

Associated Press. 2013. "UN Official Pushes Compensation for Haiti Victims." *New Zealand Herald*, October 9. Available at https://www.nzherald.co.nz/world/news/article.cfm?c_id=2&objectid=11137337.

Attaran, Amir. 2006. "Will Negligence Law Poison the Well of Foreign Aid? A Case Comment on: Binod Sutradhar v. Natural Environment Research Council." *Global Jurist Advances* 6:1535–1661.

Birrell, Ian. 2013. "In Haiti the UN's Behaviour Is a Far Cry from Being the Conscience of the World." *The Guardian*, March 3. Available at https://www.theguardian.com/commentisfree/2013/mar/03/haiti-un-conscience-cholera-responsibility.

Carasik, Lauren. 2016. "The United Nations Comes Clean." *Foreign Affairs*, August 29. Available at https://www.foreignaffairs.com/articles/haiti/2016-08-29/united-nations-comes-clean.

Center for Human Rights and Global Justice, Partners in Health, Robert F. Kennedy Memorial Center for Human Rights, and Zanmi Lasante. 2008. "Wòch Nan Soley: Denial of the Right to Water in Haiti." Available at https://act.pih.org/page/-/reports/Haiti_Report_FINAL.pdf.

Chery, Dieu Nalio. 2012. "Clinton: U.N. Soldier Brought Cholera to Haiti." *USA Today*, March 7. Available at http://www.usatoday.com/news/world/story/2012-03-07/haiti-cholera/53402748/1.

City of New York. 2018. "Fact Sheet: Mayor de Blasio Releases Preliminary Budget for Fiscal Year 2019." February 1. Available at https://www1.nyc.gov/office-of-the-mayor/news/077-18/fact-sheet-mayor-de-blasio-releases-preliminary-budget-fiscal-year-2019#/0.

Committee on Economic, Social and Cultural Rights. 2003. "Substantive Issues Arising in the Implementation of the International Covenant on Economic, Social and Cultural Rights: General Comment No. 15." Available at https://www2.ohchr.org/english/issues/water/docs/CESCR_GC_15.pdf.

Concannon, Brian, Jr., and Beatrice Lindstrom. 2011. "Cheaper, Better, Longer-Lasting: A Rights-Based Approach to Disaster Response in Haiti." *Emory International Law Review* 25:1145–1191.

Cravioto, Alejandro, Claudio F. Lanata, Daniele S. Lantagne, and G. Balakrish Nair. 2011. "Final Report of the Independent Panel of Experts on the Cholera Outbreak in Haiti." Available at http://www.un.org/News/dh/infocus/haiti/UN-cholera-report -final.pdf.

Dannenbaum, Tom. 2010. "Translating the Standard of Effective Control into a System of Effective Accountability." *Harvard International Law Journal* 51:323–327.

Darrow, Mac, and Louise Arbour. 2009. "The Pillar of Glass: Human Rights in the Development Operations of the United Nations." *American Journal of International Law* 103 (3): 446–506.

Dauguirdas, Kristina. 2014. "Reputation and Responsibility of International Organizations." *European Journal of International Law* 25 (4): 991–1018.

Desvarieux, Jessica. 2010. "At the Heart of Haiti's Cholera Riots, Anger at the U.N." *Time*, November 22. Available at http://content.time.com/time/world/article/0,8599, 2032437,00.html.

"Double Standards." 2013. *The Economist*, March 2. Available at https://www.economist .com/the-americas/2013/03/02/double-standards.

Farha, Leilani, Philip Alston, Gustavo Gallón, Dainius Puras, and Léo Heller. 2015. Letter to UN Secretary-General. October 23. Available at https://spdb.ohchr.org/ hrdb/31st/public_-_OL_Other_(7.2015).pdf.

Farha, Leilani, Gustavo Gallón, Dainius Puras, and Catarina de Albuquerque. 2014. Letter to the UN Secretary-General. September 25. Available at https://www.scribd .com/document/261396799/SR-Allegation-Letter-2014.

"First, Do No Harm: The UN in Haiti." 2012. *The Economist*, April 28. Available at https://www.economist.com/the-americas/2012/04/28/first-do-no-harm.

Freedman, Rosa. 2016. "UN-Accountable? A Response to Devika Hovell." *AJIL Unbound* 110:8–12. Available at https://www.cambridge.org/core/journals/american-journal -of-international-law/article/unaccountable-a-response-to-devika-hovell/E4D49D 01C242AFE36DEFF267CD971A3C.

Frerichs, Ralph R. 2016. *Deadly River: Cholera and Cover-Up in Post-earthquake Haiti.* Ithaca, NY: Cornell University Press.

Georges v. United Nations. 2013. Complaint no. 13-cv-7146-JPO.

Georges v. United Nations. 2015. 84 F. Supp. 3d 246 (S.D.N.Y.).

Georges v. United Nations. 2016. 834 F.3d 88 (2d Cir.).

"Haiti Cholera Outbreak: Nepal Troops Not Tested." 2010. *BBC News*, December 8. Available at https://www.bbc.com/news/world-south-asia-11949181.

"Haiti in a Time of Cholera." 2013. *Al Jazeera*, August 29. Available at https://www .aljazeera.com/programmes/faultlines/2013/08/2013828102630903134.html.

Hendriksen, Rene S., Lance B. Price, James M. Schupp, John D. Gillece, Rolf S. Kaas, David M. Engelthaler, Valeria Bortolaia, et al. 2011. "Population Genetics of *Vibrio cholerae* from Nepal in 2010: Evidence on the Origin of the Haitian Outbreak." *mBio*, August 23. Available at https://mbio.asm.org/content/2/4/e00157-11.

"Immunity with Impunity." 2013. *Trinidad Express*, March 13. Available at http://www .ijdh.org/2013/03/topics/health/immunity-with-impunity.

Ivers, Louise C., and David A. Walton. 2012. "The 'First' Case of Cholera in Haiti: Lessons for Global Health." *American Journal of Tropical Medicine and Hygiene* 86 (1): 36–38.

Johnston, Jake. 2013. "When Will the United Nations Pay for Its Actions in Haiti?" *Caribbean Journal*, March 1. Available at http://www.caribjournal.com/2013/03/01/ op-ed-when-will-the-united-nations-pay-for-its-actions-in-haiti.

Katz, Jonathan. 2013. *The Big Truck That Went By: How the World Came to Save Haiti and Left Behind a Disaster*. New York: Palgrave Macmillan.

———. 2016. "U.N. Admits Role in Cholera Epidemic in Haiti." *New York Times*, August 17. Available at https://www.nytimes.com/2016/08/18/world/americas/united-nations-haiti-cholera.html.

Krishnaswami, Charanya, and Muneer I. Ahmad. 2013. "U.N. Hypocrisy in Haiti." *Washington Post*, March 21. Available at https://www.washingtonpost.com/opinions/un-hypocrisy-in-haiti/2013/03/21/1b3c9a10-8d87-11e2-9f54-f3fdd70acad2_story.html.

Lancet Editorial Board. 2016. "Dear Mr Ban Ki-moon." *The Lancet* 387 (10036): 2352. Available at http://www.thelancet.com/journals/lancet/article/PIIS0140-6736(16)30778-4/fulltext?rss=yes.

Lantagne, Daniele, G. Balakrish Nair, Claudio F. Lanata, and Alejandro Cravioto. 2014. "The Cholera Epidemic in Haiti: Where and How Did It Begin?" In *Current Topics in Microbiology and Immunology*, vol. 379, *Cholera Outbreaks*, edited by G. Balakrish Nair and Yoshifumi Takeda, 145–164. Berlin: Springer.

Lederer, Edith M. 2016. "UN to Provide 'Material Assistance' to Haiti Cholera Victims." *Associated Press*, August 19. Available at https://www.apnews.com/663582bd89274793ba610420a6a41708.

McNeil, Donald G., Jr. 2010. "Cholera's Second Fever: An Urge to Blame." *New York Times*, November 20. Available at http://www.nytimes.com/2010/11/21/weekinreview/21mcneil.html.

Mégret, Frédéric. 2013. "La responsabilité des Nations Unies aux temps du choléra" [The responsibility of the United Nations in the time of cholera]. *Revue belge de droit international* [Belgian review of international law] 46 (1): 161–189.

Mégret, Frédéric, and Florian Hoffmann. 2003. "The UN as a Human Rights Violator? Some Reflections on the United Nations' Changing Human Rights Responsibilities." *Human Rights Quarterly* 25:316–318.

New York Times Editorial Board. 2013. "Haiti's Imported Disaster." *New York Times*, October 12. Available at http://www.nytimes.com/2013/10/13/opinion/sunday/haitis-imported-disaster.html.

———. 2016. "The Cholera Epidemic the U.N. Left Behind in Haiti." *New York Times*, July 6. Available at http://www.nytimes.com/2016/07/06/opinion/the-cholera-epidemic-the-un-left-behind-in-haiti.html.

O'Brien, Patricia. 2013a. Letter to Brian Concannon. February 21. Available at http://www.ijdh.org/wp-content/uploads/2011/11/UN-Dismissal-2013-02-21.pdf.

———. 2013b. Letter to Brian Concannon. July 5. Available at http://www.ijdh.org/wp-content/uploads/2013/07/20130705164515.pdf.

OECD (Organisation for Economic Co-operation and Development). 2014. "Development Aid Stable in 2014 but Flows to Poorest Countries Still Falling." Available at http://www.oecd.org/dac/stats/development-aid-stable-in-2014-but-flows-to-poorest-countries-still-falling.htm.

Office of the Special Envoy for Haiti. 2012. "Can More Aid Stay in Haiti and Other Fragile Settings?" Available at http://www.lessonsfromhaiti.org/download/Report_Center/osereport2012.pdf.

Paust, Jordan J. 2010. "The U.N. Is Bound By Human Rights: Understanding the Full Reach of Human Rights, Remedies, and Nonimmunity." *Harvard International Law Journal* 51. Available at http://www.harvardilj.org/wp-content/uploads/2010/09/HILJ-Online_51_Paust.pdf.

Pavoni, Riccardo. 2015. "Choleric Notes on the Haiti Cholera Case." *International Law Quarterly* 1:19–20. Available at http://www.qil-qdi.org/choleric-notes-on-the-haiti-cholera-case.

Piarroux, Renaud. 2011. "Mission Report on the Cholera Epidemic in Haiti." Translated by R. R. Frerichs. Available at http://www.ph.ucla.edu/epi/snow/cholera_haiti_piarrouxreport.html.

Reinisch, August. n.d. "Convention on the Privileges and Immunities of the United Nations: Introductory Note." Audiovisual Library of International Law. Available at http://legal.un.org/avl/ha/cpiun-cpisa/cpiun-cpisa.html (accessed December 24, 2018).

Salman, Salman M. A., and Siobhan McInerney-Lankford. 2004. *The Human Right to Water: Legal and Policy Dimensions.* Washington, DC: World Bank.

Satterthwaite, Margaret L. 2011. "Indicators in Crisis: Rights-Based Humanitarian Indicators in Post-earthquake Haiti." *Journal of International Law and Policy* 43:880–882.

Schuller, Mark. 2007. "Invasion or Infusion? Understanding the Role of NGOs in Contemporary Haiti." *Journal of Haitian Studies* 13 (2): 96–119.

Sontag, Deborah. 2012. "In Haiti, Global Failures on a Cholera Epidemic." *New York Times,* March 31. Available at https://www.nytimes.com/2012/04/01/world/americas/haitis-cholera-outraced-the-experts-and-tainted-the-un.html.

Thieren, Michel. 2010. "Point de presse des Nations Unies en Haiti" [United Nations press briefing in Haiti]. *ReliefWeb,* October 28. Available at https://reliefweb.int/report/haiti/point-de-presse-des-nations-unies-en-haiti-jeudi-28-octobre-2010.

Translational Development Clinic, Global Health Justice Partnership, and Association Haïtienne de Troit de l'Environnement. 2013. "Peacekeeping without Accountability: The United Nations' Responsibility for the Haitian Cholera Epidemic." Available at https://law.yale.edu/system/files/documents/pdf/Clinics/Haiti_TDC_Final_Report.pdf.

UNICEF (United Nations Children's Fund). 2016. "Collecting Water Is Often a Colossal Waste of Time for Women and Girls." August 29. Available at https://www.unicef.org/press-releases/unicef-collecting-water-often-colossal-waste-time-women-and-girls.

UNICEF and World Health Organization. 2015. "Progress on Sanitation and Drinking Water." Available at https://washdata.org/report/jmp-2015-report.

"UN Investigates Cholera Spread in Haiti." 2010. *Al Jazeera,* October 27. Available at https://www.youtube.com/watch?v=gk-2HyQHUZ0.

United Nations. 2011. "Guiding Principles on Business and Human Rights." Available at http://www.ohchr.org/Documents/Publications/GuidingPrinciplesBusinessHR_EN.pdf.

———. 2014. "Report of the Special Rapporteur on the Human Right to Safe Drinking Water and Sanitation, Catarina de Albuquerque." June 30. Available at http://www.un.org/ga/search/view_doc.asp?symbol=A/HRC/27/55.

United Nations General Assembly. 2010. "The Human Right to Water and Sanitation." A/Res/64/292. August 30. Available at https://berkleycenter.georgetown.edu/publications/united-nations-resolution-64-292-the-human-right-to-water-and-sanitation.

United Nations and Government of Haiti. 2004. "Agreement between the United Nations and the Government of Haiti concerning the Status of the United Nations Operations in Haiti." Available at http://www.ijdh.org/wp-content/uploads/2014/03/MINUSTAH-SOFA-English.pdf.

Waldron, Jeremy. 2015. "The UN Charter and the Rule of Law." Address at "The Pre and Post UN Charter Order" conference, November 1, New York University School of Law.

Washington Post Editorial Board. 2013. "United Nations Must Admit Its Role in Haiti's Cholera Outbreak." *Washington Post*, August 16. Available at http://articles.washingtonpost.com/2013-08-16/opinions/41417425_1_cholera-outbreak-united-nations-haiti-and-haitians.

Winkler, Inga. 2012. *The Human Right to Water*. Oxford: Hart.

World Health Organization and UNICEF. 2017. "Progress on Drinking Water, Sanitation and Hygiene." Available at https://apps.who.int/iris/bitstream/handle/10665/258617/9789241512893-eng.pdf.

3

Protecting People or Land?

Global Trade-Offs between Safeguarding Human Rights and Physical Environments

ROBERT MANDEL

This chapter analyzes global trade-offs between physical environment and human rights protection, reasons they are ignored and skewed, significant consequences, and potential remedies. It seems crucial to question fundamentally the naïve belief that protecting people and their natural habitats can both be maximized simultaneously. Neither protecting the physical environment nor protecting human rights should be thought about in isolation, as critical interconnections exist in causes and consequences of disruptions and associated management strategies. Just as environmental degradation or human rights violation can link up with regional violence, undesired migration, and changes in the meaning of citizenship and the viability of the social contract, so attempts to repair such environmental degradation or human rights violation can inadvertently connect with destabilizing each of these areas. The tendency of many writers to focus on just one facet of this complex interactive web on which they have expertise and interest has tended to limit understanding of what is transpiring and to distort subsequent remedial strategies. Although the physical environment–human rights trade-offs discussed in this chapter create tensions that are only occasionally severe enough to trigger violence, citizenship changes, and ultimately out-migration of people from their countries as a result of perceived injustice, these trade-offs are nonetheless highly significant in their broader implications. Thus, the interrelationship specifically between environmental and human rights thrusts, in the wider context of pressing concerns about violence, migration, and citizenship, needs more holistic and integrative analysis.

Because of growing globalization, both policy makers and citizens are reluctant to recognize and manage existing trade-offs in the context of resource scarcity between protecting physical environments and protecting human rights. Human rights protection entails safeguarding basic freedoms to which all people are entitled. The human "right to choose" has always been a fundamental component of human rights and indeed is mentioned explicitly in the United Nations (UN) Universal Declaration of Human Rights (United Nations 1948). Physical environment protection entails conserving and maintaining sustainable access to natural resources and minimizing land, water, and air-quality degradation. Safeguarding endangered species, promoting biodiversity, moderating human population density, and minimizing toxic pollution have always been key elements of this thrust.

This analysis highlights the dangers of ignoring the serious trade-offs between human rights and environmental protection, as attempts to maximize them simultaneously would doom both ends. Indeed, "win–win scenarios, where both natural resources are conserved and human well-being is improved in specific places over time, have been difficult, if not almost impossible, to realize" (McShane et al. 2011, 270). Many environmentalists believe that technological advancements cannot overcome the earth's "carrying capacity" (Meadows et al. 1972, 91; Meadows, Randers, and Meadows 2004, x), so if too many people consume and produce too much, human rights may need to be sacrificed to keep the environment safe. Many human rights advocates argue that the freedom to choose should be unrestricted unless other people are directly hurt (see Lin and Allhoff 2008), downplaying protection of other species and the global ecosystem; but when unrestricted free choice prevails, individual citizens can cause a loss of biodiversity, driven by the emphasis on private gains over broader social costs and undercutting not only environmental protection ends but also human lives and livelihoods (Perrings 2014, 68, 149, 479). Indeed, "unrestrained exercise of our liberties does not bring us real freedom" because of negative ecological consequences related to our choices (Ophuls and Boyan 1992, 195). Thus, both national governments and international organizations managing human rights and physical environments find they have to make painful choices and troublesome ranking of priorities, ones likely to be unpopular with advocates of both causes.

Global Physical Environment–Human Rights Protection Trade-Offs

Significant trade-offs between physical environment protection and human rights protection apply to many different areas, including resource consumption and production (with the industrialized world and the Global South facing starkly different dilemmas), resource distribution, population, food, and energy issues. This is not to say that global environmental threats such as climate change (discussed in Chapter 1) or water-based infectious disease (discussed in Chapter 2) cannot associate with human rights shortcomings or that human rights violations cannot negatively affect environmental sustainability; rather, the claim here is that simultaneously maximizing environment and human rights protection is rarely possible, and consequently relative prioritization is usually necessarily. Despite being ubiquitous, explicit societal recognition of these crucial trade-offs remains decidedly inadequate.

Regarding resource consumption and production, most individuals and most societies in today's world seem bent on economic growth (Winship 2013). This is evidenced by the public and private choices being made by governments and citizens in the Global South, where short-term economic benefits are driving many to knowingly choosing rapid environmentally destructive industrial growth—spurred on by Western-controlled organizations such as the World Bank in their support for large infrastructure projects—over slower environmentally sensitive modernization, and in the Global North, where consumption rates continue to dramatically outpace those in the Global South. Supporting such policy choices, many growth economists have assumed that "technological progress overrides the effects of diminished and degraded natural capital" pertaining to physical environment assets (Perrings 2014, xix). Key trade-offs exist between economic growth and environmental protection, despite persistent difficult-to-overcome minority beliefs promoted by many conservation organizations that "much that is needed in the way of conservation of natural resources and protection of the environment will enhance the efficiency, productivity and competitiveness of our economy" (Church 1992) and that "institutional reform provides the promise of overcoming trade-offs between economic and environmental policy goals" (Feiock and Stream 2001, 318).

Many of the world's citizens feel empowered because the increased wealth they accrue increases their sense of freedom, self-sufficiency, and range of choice, and they would be reluctant to compromise or sacrifice such advantages to promote long-range environmental protection. The kinds of steps such individuals seem likely to take if aware of environmental degradation and pollution are decidedly cosmetic, such as buying "green" products or engaging in recycling efforts while refusing to cut their consumption in any truly meaningful way. Government policy makers in such societies generally trust that technological advances, not belt-tightening conservation, is the key to maintaining plentiful clean air and water, arable land to grow crops, minimal harmful pollution, and an overall healthy and resilient environment. For example, when wealthy societies have faced water scarcity, rather than infringe on human rights and try to reduce water consumption per capita, they have often turned to methods like energy-intensive desalinization of ocean water (Israel) or energy-intensive conversion of urine into drinking water (California).

Within advanced industrial societies, with customarily high value placed on individual human rights, high levels of resource consumption and production, and high dependence on externally derived natural resources, the trade-offs between protection of the physical environment and human rights are especially acute. Despite lip service to environmental concerns and willingness to undertake cosmetic environmental protection steps, citizens of these countries usually are steadfast in their unwillingness to make significant sacrifices in their freedoms and their quest for materialistic lifestyles to protect physical environments (see Dewan 2009). For example, concern about climate change has not caused citizens of these wealthy countries to be willing to give up their freedom to purchase and drive pollution-generating and resource-draining, gas-guzzling sport utility vehicles, whose sales have recently been booming globally. Protection of the natural environment would occur only in the unlikely event that high living standards could be maintained even under resource scarcity where quantities of needed raw materials are limited and prices skyrocket.

Within the Global South, where both individual human rights and environmental protection often take a back seat to promoting survival needs and the quest for rapid economic development, getting either one to be high priority on national governments' policy agenda may depend on their perceived noninterference with industrial growth. Resentment occurs in developing countries because both human rights and environmental protection are being heavily pushed by Western organizations that make little attempt to adapt their strongly held ideas to the context of the distinctive culture and values of affected societies. For example, highly capital-intensive Western agricultural technologies exported to the Global South to improve food production consistently fail to take into account the high unemployment rates in developing countries (calling for more labor-intensive solutions) and the cultural disruption to traditional modes of human interaction introduced by efficient farm machinery. Moreover, such environmental policies can stunt developing countries' economic development and the freedom of their citizens to make unfettered consumption choices (Roberts 2011). In many countries at or near the bottom of the global pecking order, religious beliefs prevent human rights advancement, and economic dependence on revenues from raw materials exports prevents environmental protection advancement. In other developing countries that have achieved greater industrialization, such as India, Brazil, and China, protecting human rights to choose has caused much environmental damage, such as destruction of tropical rain forests and generation of toxic pollution for short-term profits. Under resource scarcity, these protection trade-offs would intensify and the ability to safeguard either human or environmental protection could precipitously decline.

In regard to resource distribution, in line with globalization pressures, most human rights advocates suggest those who can afford it share resources with those in dire need (see, e.g., Soroos 1977; "Rio + 20" 2012), particularly if outsiders perceive people to be in dire straits as a result of natural disasters or circumstances beyond their control. Such resource sharing usually entails aid from public national governments or international organizations and humanitarian assistance combined with philanthropic efforts by private nonstate groups and individuals. For some observers, resource sharing is mostly the responsibility of wealthy countries in the Global North, in part because of their legacy of overseas colonial rule that such analysts feel was responsible for the plight of the Global South; although the advanced industrial societies do not have plentiful excess raw materials that they could easily share with the developing world, the thought here is that they could at least share technology and monetary aid that could help recipients better manage their own resources. However, in stark contrast, some key environmental protection advocates argue that such resource sharing reduces the accountability and "intrinsic responsibility" of aid recipients (Hardin 1986, 97), leading to magnified irresponsible future local environmental degradation (such as when aid to chronic drought victims exacerbates population-ecosystem imbalances) because of the assumption that the outside world will always bail out needy developing-country recipients if they mismanage their resources.

In regard to population, providing family-planning information along with contraceptives to needy expanding populations in the Global South might theoretically seem to improve environmental protection by reducing undesired high population growth rates and to improve human rights by giving people more choices and control over their reproduction. However, in practice, global population-control programs have imperialistically violated human reproductive rights in many countries (Connelly 2010) and have not worked well globally to reduce birth rates—and show little promise of working a lot better in the future. Because valuing children is prevalent in affected countries, men rather than women control the decision in many societies, and it is commonly perceived that having children is necessary to help provide income given rampant human poverty. Despite the widespread global availability of contraceptives and family planning, population growth rates in some of the poorest countries in the world continue "at the relatively rapid pace of 2 to 3 percent a year. . . . It remains difficult to imagine how much

longer these high growth rates can be sustained in countries where governments and other institutions tend to be weakest and most stressed by rapid
change, and where critical natural resource bases are dangerously degraded"
(Engleman et al. 2005, 26). Thus, societies deciding to emphasize the human
procreation right even in the face of dramatic overpopulation pressures can
lead in many overpopulated areas to dramatic deterioration of environmental conditions.

In regard to food, expanding "fair-trade" organic agricultural production might theoretically be better for environmental protection and also be
far better for the human rights treatment of agricultural workers. However,
in practice, this food-growing approach has been so co-opted by large oli-
gopolistic multinational corporations that its contribution to human rights
is questionable (Engler 2012). This approach has not worked well to satisfy
global consumption desires because such production is less efficient than
traditional modes in the volume of crops produced and the amount of arable
land available globally is shrinking so rapidly that high-efficiency production
is needed to feed a growing global population. Protecting the land through
sustainable agricultural production practices can ultimately hurt the basic
human needs of the poorest segments of the global population—particularly
the increasing numbers who find themselves living in urban areas—because
they end up having to pay more for the less abundant and less efficiently
grown food products. Moreover, whenever people in many countries are
given free choice and ready access to food, once again this right is likely to be
abused—as evidenced by the April 2016 finding that for the first time in
world history there were more adults in the world classified as obese than as
underweight ("More Obese People" 2016)—and trigger environmental overexploitation. Finally, globalization of food production to suit human needs
and desires frequently has displaced native with nonnative species and thus
may end up compromising ecosystem resiliency (Perrings 2014, 240).

In regard to energy, reducing reliance on traditional fossil fuels could
theoretically both help expand environmental protection and reduce human
rights violations of miners and agricultural workers who operate in dangerous and unsanitary conditions. However, in practice, moving to alternative
energy sources such as solar, wind, and water involves key limitations: for
example, such alternative-energy sources rely on scarce, nonrenewable rare-
earth minerals (located in politically volatile parts of the world and increasingly heavily controlled by China), and such reliance could end up "replacing
oil addiction with metals dependence" (Ngai 2010) and with supply inade-
quacy. Specifically, given today's globally skyrocketing energy demands, "the
world will need significantly increased energy supply in the future, especially
cleanly-generated electricity" (World Nuclear Association 2018), and inter-
mittent renewable energy sources such as solar and wind are rather costly per

output unit and so cannot by themselves satisfy global energy needs. More-over, states downplay energy conservation and belt tightening in favor of end-lessly hunting for new and better energy sources to promote human expan-sion and freedom to choose. More efficient energy-extraction technologies and lower energy prices frequently occur at the same time as increasingly devastating and misunderstood impacts on the global physical environment. Unlike in food production, rising energy demands are less a function of global population growth than of global industrialization growth.

Common Skewing of Physical Environment–Human Rights Protection Trade-Offs

Two forces highly skew the trade-offs between protecting physical environ-ments and protecting human rights. First, because democracy through its checks and balances focuses exclusively on competing human needs and desires, human rights inherently assume a higher position than environ-mental protection. Indeed, it is quite common to consider protection of per-sonal rights to be the primary function of democratic governance (see, e.g., Behrouzi 2006; El Amine 2016). Second, it takes much longer for humans to recognize environmental degradation and pollution than human rights abuses, so remedial action for human rights abuses is likely to occur much more quickly than for environmental degradation and pollution. Both forces favor human rights over environmental protection under resource scarcity when a choice has to be made.

The worldwide spread of democracy, accelerated through globalization of liberal internationalist norms, skews decision making regarding these trade-offs in three ways. First, only humans are represented and have a voice within democratic systems. Although some analysts in environmental law think objects in nature should have rights and be given a voice (even though they cannot vote), just as unborn babies are (Stone 2010), this argument is largely rejected even by the most open-minded yet species-centric citizens, who believe that only people of all races, genders, and income levels should have any right to influence political decisions. Second, within many democ-racies, citizens are encouraged to insist on the protection of their rights and privileges—especially reproductive and consumptive rights—no matter what the circumstances. The result is that environmental protection initia-tives receive wide popular support only in circumstances when they do not constrain or significantly interfere with human choices:

> The truth, of course, is that most of us care more about our standard
> of living than we do about the health of some species we seldom if

ever see. And the truth, even harder to admit, is that most of us care more about our own welfare than we do about that of persons living three or four or five generations hence. If protecting the planet, for future generations and for other species, depended on changing these operational values, then we would be in deep trouble. . . . Think whatever you wish about the moral standing of these operational values—this is the reality. (Church 1992)

Third, because elected leaders serve short terms in office, policy makers benefit more from focusing on short-term problems with quick fixes, not long-term issues that cannot possibly be resolved during their term in office. Even when environmental degradation, resource scarcity, or pollution is severe, citizens tend to prefer options that preserve—for better or for worse—their right to choose how to respond and specifically how to change their lifestyle (see Ophuls and Boyan 1992, chap. 4).

The imbalance in the psychological time lags (Mandel 1988, 32–35) involved in policy makers and the mass public recognizing dangers in these two protection areas also skews these trade-offs. When human rights are violated, in open societies usually political leaders and the public quickly notice the violations, partly because the anthropocentric media seem to enjoy publicizing them and amplifying this resentment. In contrast, when physical environments are abused, often the degradation or pollution increase is gradual and relatively invisible, and as a result it can remain undetected for quite some time. Even when countries have extensive environmental monitoring, negative ecosystem effects that occur in remote areas can be missed. Within most societies, leaders and citizens respond to what they can tangibly see directly around them, not what abstruse prognosticators tell them is occurring in distant places or has a high probability of happening in the future; so there is often widespread disbelief and disregard about environmentalists' doom-and-gloom claims about deteriorating ecosystems than about human rights advocates' reports of growing freedom violations around the world. Given that an increasing proportion of people are living in dense urban or suburban areas, they seem quite likely not to notice subtle changes in the natural environment (such as climate change).

Widespread Downplaying of Physical Environment–Human Rights Protection Trade-Offs

Optimists insist that physical environment–human rights trade-offs are not inescapable, evidencing a we-can-have-our-cake-and-eat-it-too mentality, claiming both types of protection can be maximized at once. Especially among international organizations, including multilateral and bilateral aid agencies and conservation organizations, "win–win language"—which has "the appearance of being ethical, efficient, and highly marketable"—is a common depiction of the joint pursuit of biodiversity conservation and human well-being (McShane et al. 2011, 967). For example, in 2016 the United Nations Human Rights Office of the High Commissioner for Human Rights and the United Nations Environment Programme jointly asserted that "biodiversity and human rights are closely intertwined" in that "the diversity of all forms of life on our planet and ecosystem services such as provision of food, pollination of crops and fulfilment of people's cultural life are necessary for enjoying a broad range of human rights such as right to food, right to health and cultural rights" (Stockholm Resilience Centre 2016).

Pollyanna-like underlying assumptions play a key role here. One analyst contends the two protection objectives are naturally reinforcing:

> Human rights laws may also present important opportunities for gaining better environmental protection. Intuitively, people support the fundamental human right to enjoy minimum amounts of air and water free of contamination; to grow crops in a stable climate system on land protected from harmful ultraviolet radiation; in short, to live and raise their children in an environment conducive to human life and health.
>
> Regardless of whether the human right to a healthy environment is recognized, however, the relationship between environmental protection and human rights is a natural one. (Hunter 1999)

Other observers assert that any alleged discrepancies between protecting physical environments and protecting human rights can be overcome with prudent choices involving environmental techniques facilitating human rights protection (Anton and Shelton 2011). Still others contend that people can be educated to voluntarily make choices in their consumption and production that do not harm the physical environment; equitable redistribution of resources even under scarcity can move everyone in the direction of attaining the basic human rights and free choices currently enjoyed by people in advanced industrial societies; and technology and human ingenuity can devise satisfactory solutions maximizing both kinds of protection without significant compromise.

Such rosy perspectives might certainly be feasible where resources are abundant; where levels of population, pollution, and environmental degradation are low and under control; and where resource substitution—replacing less available with more available raw materials—is easy (see Zetland 2011). Within such settings, trial-and-error experimentation would be inexpensive, and through that process one might find ways to prevent both physical environment and human rights abuses. However, that propitious set of circumstances decidedly does not characterize today's world.

Government policy makers lack incentives to highlight physical environment–human rights protection trade-offs, for explicitly identifying such trade-offs in domestic or foreign policy could increase the frustration and anger of both environment and human rights advocates, who might feel that doing so can simply be used as yet another excuse for inaction. It is much more appealing for national leaders to insist that they can pursue both agendas at the same time.

Similarly, private citizens do not seem to want such trade-offs to be highlighted, perhaps because unrecognized contradictions exist in their own choices. For example, while most people claim not only to value their own rights but also to respect the rights of others, often when they want to relax or go on vacation, they prefer locations where few other humans are present because they fear that these people will be irresponsible and ruin the natural environment around them. Similarly, people support the protection of particularly appealing species or locales until or unless their jobs are threatened, the price of goods and services they think they need goes up too high, and/ or dependence on unreliable foreign resources takes perceived vulnerability too far, at which point they become willing to exploit such locales or species for their own use.

Consequences of Ignoring Physical Environment–Human Rights Protection Trade-Offs

Ignoring physical environment–human rights trade-offs will not make them go away. The track record of outcomes from pursuing both kinds of protection simultaneously has been dismal: "After more than 20 years of international conservation experience, initiatives that produce win–win outcomes appear to be the exception as opposed to the rule; only rarely have initiatives realized outcomes that demonstrate how natural resources can be managed in ways that achieve benefits for local people while sustaining local and global biodiversity conservation values" (McShane et al. 2011, 967). Often contradicting the win-win rhetoric has been the painful reality of difficult choices faced by affected societies: "When losses are experienced where only gains were promised, the result can be disillusionment and alienation of the very people and groups whose support is essential for long-term success" (Hirsch and Brosius 2013, 101). As environment and human rights protection challenges become more inescapably global than local or regional, unresolved trade-offs seem likely to become more difficult to manage and resolve because of the larger number of intractable differing interests and the debilitating noncompliance among parties who could sink collective agreements.

If mismanaged, global resource scarcity can lead to a widespread feeling of vulnerability, as societies feel increasing pressure to be highly externally dependent on unreliable foreign sources for vital raw materials. This vulnerability can interfere with human rights in the political and economic spheres, as societies feel forced to deal with unsavory trading partners and accept externally imposed limitations on the quantity and price of what is available. This pattern seems especially evident in the high-tech industry, where rare-earth minerals necessary for mobile digital devices and computers have to be obtained from places such as the Democratic Republic of the Congo. Given rising globalized interdependence, multinational corporations are often blamed for not holding up the highest human rights standards, even though they operate in countries with very different human rights norms, and not providing secure low-cost access to resources deemed vital, even though often this is the result of government decisions beyond policy makers' control. The common view here is that "the flight of many MNCs [multinational corporations] to the interior of Third World countries to avoid visibility, regulations, liability, and environmental pollution accountability directly contributes to human rights and ecological rights violation" (Adeola 2000, 701). This feeling of national vulnerability can also lead to human rights curtailment, illustrated by the gas rationing in the United States following the resource scarcity imposed by the 1973–1974 Arab oil embargo, restricting human freedom to choose.

The trade-offs between protection of physical environments and protection of human rights appear to be most acute during environmental crises characterized by high threat, short decision time, and surprise. For example, during severe natural disasters, whose human and economic costs have increased recently as a result of human choices to reside in more eco-vulnerable areas and of lower ecosystem resiliency (Perrings 2014, 89), states often declare martial law, abandoning human rights and the freedom to choose in the interest of public safety. Because in such circumstances there is a huge fear of ensuing panic and chaos, orderly and uniform mass public responses are essential, without any room for idiosyncratic individual preferences or impulsive behavior impeding the functioning of emergency services. During such crises national governments may restrict human rights and freedoms, lowering their priority until the crisis seems to be successfully managed. Assuming that this human rights restriction is imposed during a widely recognized crisis by a political regime perceived as legitimate, the mass public usually accepts for at least a while the temporary curtailment of their right to free choice in favor of restoring order and repairing the damaged physical environment; but if the rights restrictions last too long or become permanent, significant public outcry is highly likely.

A worst-case scenario resulting from ignoring these trade-offs under resource scarcity involves intensified unending, anarchic, bloody conflict and instability within and across countries (see Klare 2002, 2012). Failing to safeguard basic freedoms can lead to violence, triggering intensifying action-reaction cycles of hostility that can make any form of resolution difficult. Failing to safeguard natural ecosystems can intensify violent resource-grabbing competition that can lead to unending cross-national tensions. In such circumstances, human rights and environmental protection advocates would be clashing constantly, as their opposing agendas vie for attention, often causing policy makers to skirt both agendas for fear of showing favoritism or to emphasize arbitrarily whichever one garners the greatest political gain. Already, "frustrated expectations have led to a backlash against conservation from some groups with human development and rights as their central focus, while fueling sentiment within certain corners of the conservation field to turn away from the plight of communities adjacent to protected areas and resume calls for a more protectionist approach" (McShane et al. 2011, 968). No compromise or consensus would easily emerge, and each side appears highly likely to feel that the other is getting an unfair advantage in its priority on the policy agenda. A widespread feeling of mutual futility and lack of control would easily emerge in such a situation. Escalating human rights abuses and physical environmental degradation could cause exchanges between the two sets of advocates to become even more heated, with no amicable resolution in sight.

Although both environment and human rights advocates suggest a combination of education and coercion to properly safeguard citizen protection, in such worst-case scenarios state coercion often becomes the dominant mode for attaining compliance, given the pressing needs of both physical environment and human rights protection. The occasional alignment of the environmental community with coercive repressive or authoritarian regimes to get their conservation agendas addressed has often backfired when local communities have risen up against state-sponsored, top-down approaches that lack consultation with citizen groups and citizen participation in the decision-making process, with the explicit concern that the community's right to a voice has been stifled. A crisis or violent conflict does not usually allow the time for cross-generational education, explanation of complex issues, input from citizens groups, or enlightened learning to take place. As a result, human rights advocates can become outraged by national governments' assumption that, to protect the mass public, their freedoms and choices could be taken away; and physical environment protection advocates can similarly angrily question the long-term ecological impact of quickly made coercive decisions by policy makers who are not environmentally aware.

Moreover, the use of coercion in any form to promote human rights seems inherently contradictory. For this reason, environmental activists are much more at home with—and are much more likely to promote—national governments undertaking restrictive coercive measures to achieve their protection goals than are human rights activists. While laws guaranteeing the protection of individuals and the punishment of those who disrupt others' lives are certainly supported by human rights activists, they generally oppose any coercive regulation of human activity that does not directly and immediately cause tangible physical or psychological harm to others. In contrast, many environmental advocates believe that activities that promote long-term indirect harm to the planet and to one's fellow human beings, not immediately or directly visible, merit coercive responses because these kinds of hidden destructive effects may ultimately be the most dangerous. Of course, extremist alarmists for both environmental and human rights causes may think coercion is the only way to get recalcitrant opponents to change.

A Concrete Illustration of Physical Environment–Human Rights Protection Trade-Offs

One of the most visible manifestations of unresolved tensions between human rights and environmental protection is the growing global conflict over water rights and access to fresh water (Barlow 2009). The different interests of those using water for sports recreation, energy, irrigation for agriculture, human drinking and bathing, fish harvesting, and transportation frequently clash (Mandel 1992), with no commonly accepted system for weighing human rights and development needs against environmental priorities. Cross-state water disputes pose even more obstacles than within-state disputes, particularly when a powerful upstream state pollutes a river and a weak downstream state has no recourse but to suffer the consequences. Although a few instances successfully navigate the balance between human rights and environmental protection to facilitate cooperation in water usage—such as the Mekong River delta management system in Southeast Asia—these are few and far between and are far less representative of the global pattern than the escalating bitter and violent rivalries over water access that many analysts think will become dangerously volatile in the future.

The Middle East and North Africa contain especially intense and enduring cross-national water conflicts, primarily in the Jordan River basin (affecting Israel, Jordan, Lebanon, and Syria), Nile River basin (primarily affecting

Egypt, Ethiopia, and Sudan), and Tigris-Euphrates River basin (primarily affecting Turkey, Syria, and Iraq) (Klare 2002, 161–189; see also Ward 2002). Regional water shortages are mainly caused by "decades of bad management and overuse" (Goldenberg 2014), and recently regional frictions have dramatically been exacerbated as a result of global warming (Morris 1997): "Western policy and military establishments, in particular, have expressed mounting concern that climate-change-related environmental changes may foment civil strife, undermine state capacities, exacerbate existing international security challenges, and increase migration flows to the Global North" (Selby and Hoffmann 2012, 997). Indeed, within the region "current disputes over borders, religion, and ethnicity may pale in comparison to potential water conflicts" (Morris 1997).

Within the Jordan River basin, depleted shared groundwater resources, greater variability in water availability, water pollution, and poor coordination among countries have caused reduced resiliency to floods and drought, degraded regional food security, and continuing regional tensions over water (Office of the Director of National Intelligence 2012, v). Behind these disturbing trends "the major issues are water flow and diversion and ownership of water sources" (Morris 1997). As a consequence, out-migration has ensued: "Unprecedented drought in Syria between 2006 and 2011, together with massive groundwater over-abstraction over decades, was having a catastrophic effect on local farmers, who were being forced to leave the land" (Iceland 2017). More specifically, "Jordan, which has the third lowest [water] reserves in the region, is struggling with an influx of Syrian refugees" and has undergone power cuts; and Prince Hassan, the uncle of King Abdullah, "warned that a war over water and energy could be even bloodier than the Arab spring" (Goldenberg 2014).

Within the Nile River basin, a decreasing amount of water available per capita, inadequate water agreements and management structure, greater variability in water available, water flow impeded as new dam reservoirs are filled, and delta erosion have led to degraded food security, reduced resiliency to floods and droughts, and increased regional tensions over water and use of water as leverage (Office of the Director of National Intelligence 2012, v). Underlying issues include flooding, siltation, water flow, diversion, pollution, "water borne disease, and soil degradation through irrigation and fertilization" (Morris 1997). In 1979, President Anwar Sadat of Egypt said, "The only matter that could take Egypt to war again is water," and in 1988 Foreign Minister Boutros Boutros-Ghali of Egypt (later UN secretary-general), predicted that "the next war in the Middle East would be fought over the waters of the Nile, not politics" (Kameri-Mbote 2007, 1). Such conflict "could fan existing conflicts in the Greater Horn of Africa, making them more complex and harder to address" (3). Recently, "Egypt has demanded Ethiopia stop construction of a mega-dam on the Nile, vowing to protect its historical rights to the river at 'any cost'" (Goldenberg 2014).

Within the Tigris-Euphrates River basin, there have been no multilateral water-sharing agreements, but there has been increased variability in water supply, reduced water flow, and altered sediment flows to downstream agricultural lands and marshlands, resulting in reduced resiliency to floods and droughts, reduced regional food security, and continued regional tensions over unilateral water-development projects and management undertaken by states without outside consultation or agreement (Office of the Director of National Intelligence 2012, v). For example, across time Turkish dams and power plants have been an irritant to Syria and Iraq, reducing the volume of water on which they almost totally depend. Overall, between 2003 and 2010, "parts of Turkey, Syria, Iraq and Iran along the Tigris and Euphrates rivers lost 144 cubic kilometres of stored freshwater—or about the same amount of water in the Dead Sea" (Goldenberg 2014).

Admittedly, these water disputes are extreme examples of trade-offs between environmental and human rights protection, revealing a relatively high potential to create instability, out-migration, and conflict, but their value is in suggesting the dire consequences likely if such trade-offs remain unmanaged in other areas. In each of the three cases, where human development needs were given precedence over the competing needs of environmental protection, the outcomes have been poor, promoting refugee outflows and raising the potential for future violent conflict. The environmental impact of overexploitation and pollution of water is well documented, accelerating environmental degradation, enhancing crop failure, spreading disease, endangering species, and critically reducing biodiversity and ecological resiliency (see, e.g., Elhance 1999). In regard to human rights, the UN has asserted that "water should be treated as a social and cultural good and not primarily as an economic good," as "the manner of the realization of the right to water must also be sustainable, ensuring that the right can be realized for present and future generations" (Biswas 2008, 5). Given that "already a billion people, or one in seven people on the planet, lack access to safe drinking water" (Goldenberg 2014), the negative human rights impact is getting progressively worse.

Remedial Steps Addressing Physical Environment–Human Rights Protection Trade-Offs

The similar roadblocks faced by human rights protection and physical environment protection facilitate joint ways to address both concerns. First, protection of both environmental and human rights faces comparable handicaps in terms of Western/non-Western differences of interpretation and generally low placement on states' security agendas. In recent decades, both issues have risen as international relations challenges: because many global activists "face the problem of environmental and human rights abuse" (exemplified by the March 2016 killing of an environmental activist in Honduras), there is an emerging "need to frame environmental rights as a significant component of human rights issues," where "environmental injustice and human rights violations are inextricably interwoven" (Adeola 2000, 687). Second, existing global levels of protection for both physical environments and human rights are unacceptably low, so advocates for both causes aspire to elevate their issue of concern on state policy agendas by claiming that each is absolutely fundamental to security. However, this mutual pressure can create huge rhetoric-reality gaps in which political leaders give bold speeches and sign promising treaties without enforcing state commitments or including vital civil-society groups; afterward, failure by signatories to live up to treaty commitments results only in weak "naming and shaming" rebukes (Clark 2013, 126; Wintle and Reeve 1994). Third, people tend to care most about current protection of citizens and ecosystems within their own societies rather than future protection of citizens and ecosystems around the world (Mandel 1988, 117), causing problems when attempting to address trade-offs within an integrated global system. For resolution of the important trade-offs to occur, there needs to be facilitation of a transformed focus that does not deal just with the here and now, particularly challenging given common priorities in today's world (as evidenced by the 2015 Paris Climate Change Conference).

Furthermore, despite the persistent skewed trade-offs, the interconnectedness of the two protection types—especially given globalization pressures—should be conducive to joint action. Reduced biodiversity has a significant impact on human well-being, especially by imposing costs on future generations, as nature "comprises assets of intrinsic value . . . that are direct sources of human wellbeing (the air we breathe and the water we drink), and many others that have indirect value as inputs in the production of goods and services (crops providing food, and trees providing timber and energy)" (Perrings 2014, xviii, 466, 481). A common consequence of resource scarcity is rationing these resources to the population, curtailing the ability of citizens to make personal choices about consumption:

> There is increasing recognition that resource scarcity exacerbated by climate change will lead to conflict, which could give rise to an influx of refugees, internally displaced people or migrants. In other words, climate change can threaten human security (and sustainable development) in many ways: it will lead to a violation of many of the

protected rights of people, including right to privacy and family life, the right not to be displaced, the right to a livelihood, right to health, and the right to food, water, and housing. (Atapattu 2015, 249)

Environmental degradation can reduce the habitability of some areas, causing poor people to have no choice but to live in physically contaminated and often toxic settings: "At the local, national, and cross-national levels, environmental burdens including locally undesirable land uses (LULUS), toxic chemicals, hazardous waste dumping, contamination of water, and other forms of environmental degradation are disproportionally placed in the habitats of powerless minority entities (e.g., Blacks, indigenous tribal groups, or Third World states)" (Adeola 2000, 701). European toxic waste dumping in West Africa exemplifies this tendency. Likewise, human rights breaches can hurt the environment:

> Environmental damage is often worse in countries and in areas where human rights abuses are greatest, particularly where outside forces are driving the exploitation of valuable natural resources—for example, gold or oil—over the objections of local communities. Repression is often the only way to force this type of "development," particularly when little or no benefit is obvious for the local community. Leading environmental activists such as Chico Mendes and Ken Saro Wiwa have been killed and many others have been beaten for raising their voices. In many of these instances, the international human rights movement offers the best hope for protection from internal oppression. (Hunter 1999)

So attempting to manage physical environment and human rights protection in a completely separate and isolated manner would be folly.

Often these common links between protection of physical environments and human rights are subsumed under the mantra of environmental justice. Today many diverse groups attempt to tightly connect ecology and justice: "People of color in cities throughout the United States are challenging the 'environmental racism' of concentrating toxic facilities in minority communities; rural women in India and elsewhere are protesting the impacts of deforestation and large-dam construction on their lives and communities; green activists in Europe are framing climate change as a matter of injustice against poor people, vulnerable communities, and future generations; indigenous peoples are organizing to reclaim their lands and their traditions as an alternative to the ecological onslaught of modernity" (Conca and Dabelko 2015, 313; see also Low and Gleeson 1998). The common ecological justice underlying themes includes "first, the close linkage between violence against nature and violence against human beings; second, the linkage between the power to control nature and the power to control people; third, the observation that not all people or groups are affected equally by environmental problems or by the responses to these problems; fourth, the pursuit of solutions that are both ecologically sound and socially just, because neither can endure in the absence of the other; and fifth, the need for a fundamental transformation of politics, economics, and society" (Conca and Dabelko 2015, 313).

With existing trade-offs between protection of the physical environment and human rights, the quest for improvement by both sets of advocates can be mutually undercutting, hurting both causes and indirectly and inadvertently elevating the importance of other protection needs. Remedying this difficulty requires finding ways to deepen understanding about when these trade-offs are most severe so that limited attention would have to be focused in such circumstances.

Effective and legitimate management of these protection trade-offs in a globalized world needs to properly balance the admittedly "hard choices" (McShane et al. 2011, 970) between environmental conservation and human well-being. Although those seeking this balance usually talk in generalities, suggesting, for example, that "investment must be directed to those technologies which can improve living standards without destroying the natural resource base" (Church 1992), more concrete and specific recommendations applicable to specified scenarios seem essential. While completely eliminating the trade-offs is impossible, new ideas could emerge about making trade-offs between environmental and human rights objectives "less stark" by learning how "to avoid either artificially inflating or exacerbating the trade-offs that exist between various stakeholders' interests" and how "to take diplomatic steps to ease the rigidity and the severity of the trade-offs" (Harris 2014, 93, 97).

One critical step to address these trade-offs would be a frank and open dialogue about their existence between environmental protection and human rights activist groups. For example, environmental groups such as Greenpeace, the National Audubon Society, the Nature Conservancy, the Sierra Club, and the World Wildlife Fund need to have a different kind of conversation with human rights organizations such as Amnesty International, Global Rights, the Human Rights Foundation, Human Rights Watch, and the International Federation for Human Rights. Such conversations would need to focus on explicit recognition (rather than the usual denial) of the trade-offs among both goals and strategies, mutual recognition of the legitimacy of the thrusts of both sets of advocates, and identification of ways to promote causes that minimize the potential for conflict.

A second important step to manage these trade-offs is properly determining under what conditions human rights protection should trump physical environment protection, and vice versa. Accomplishing this prioritizing end requires developing systematic valid and reliable assessment methods to gauge the relative magnitude, fungibility, and severity of physical environment and human rights dangers in different situations; thresholds for labeling a predicament as an environmental protection or a human rights crisis; security impacts deriving from physical environment and human rights abuses; and strategies protecting physical environments and human rights. Underlying this approach would be better monitoring and measurement of the impact of human rights protection on the environment and the impact of environmental protection on human rights. So much hype surrounds both that it is hard to evaluate objectively when each is truly most threatening locally, nationally, regionally, and internationally.

A third key step to address these trade-offs is to highlight practical actions that could be taken under the identified conditions to minimize the crossover effects of human rights protective measures on degrading physical environments and of physical environment protective measures interfering with human rights. Even though win-win scenarios where both are maximized simultaneously are highly unrealistic, political leaders could more carefully choose policies in each area—taking into account the circumstances when each should take priority—that have less significant negative impacts on the other area. For example, to protect the physical environment, in certain carefully identified circumstances, one could emphasize development of sustainable harvesting and replanting systems for renewable resources (rather than unrestricted mining of nonrenewable resources) that are sensitive enough to protect fragile ecosystems yet efficient enough to fulfill the needs and desires of burgeoning human populations; and to protect human rights, in certain carefully identified circumstances, one could focus on development of laws that secure and expand personal freedoms in those realms—including allowing oppressed exploited groups political expression of their concerns and frustrations (rather than allowing economic rights to exploit resources without limitation)—that cause the least direct detrimental environmental degradation.

Although in situations of globalization and resource scarcity these trade-off remedies are just preliminary tentative first steps, they point the way toward maximizing overall security while not doggedly standing pat with the unfounded and counterproductive belief that human and environmental rights can both be maximized without compromise. Safeguarding the human security concerns of physical environment and human rights protection necessitates a diverse and flexible combination of both bottom-up, private, mass public initiatives and transnational cross-country initiatives to play critical roles, so reliance on just national government public policies to manage these concerns—as is so often the case—makes little sense. Once officials of international organizations, leaders of transnational environment protection and human rights groups, national policy makers, and private citizens come to recognize more fully the unavoidable trade-offs between these noble protection objectives and the acute dangers of blind pursuit of both simultaneously, it is hoped that they will follow the path of coordinated, situationally qualified prioritization of dangers and minimization of undesired crossover effects. If this perceptual recognition and follow-up action occur, a type of harmony can then emerge between humans and nature as yet unseen in the modern world, with all species protected and flourishing synergistically together.

REFERENCES

Adeola, Francis O. 2000. "Cross-national Environmental Injustice and Human Rights Issues: A Review of Evidence in the Developing World." *American Behavioral Scientist* 43 (4): 686–706.

Anton, David K., and Dinah L. Shelton. 2011. *Environmental Protection and Human Rights.* New York: Cambridge University Press.

Atapattu, Sumudu. 2015. *Human Rights Approaches to Climate Change: Challenges and Opportunities.* New York: Routledge.

Barlow, Maude. 2009. *Blue Covenant: The Global Water Crisis and the Coming Battle for the Right to Water.* New York: New Press.

Behrouzi, Mahjid. 2006. *Democracy as the Political Empowerment of the Citizen.* 2nd ed. Lexington, MA: Lexington Books.

Biswas, Asit K. 2008. "Water as a Human Right in the MENA Region: Challenges and Opportunities." In *Water as a Human Right for the Middle East and North Africa*, edited by Asit K. Biswas, Eglal Rached, and Cecilia Tortajada, 1–18. New York: Routledge.

Church, Dennis. 1992. "The Economy versus the Environment: Is There a Conflict?" *Eco IQ*, April 17. Available at http://www.ecoiq.com/dc-products/prod_conflict.html.

Clark, Ann Marie. 2013. "The Normative Context of Human Rights Criticism: Treaty Ratification and UN Mechanisms." In *The Persistent Power of Human Rights: From Commitment to Compliance*, edited by Thomas Risse, Stephen C. Ropp, and Kathryn Sikkink, 125–144. New York: Cambridge University Press.

Conca, Ken, and Geoffrey D. Dabelko. 2015. *Green Planet Blues: Critical Perspectives on Global Environmental Politics.* 5th ed. New York: Westview Press.

Connelly, Matthew. 2010. *Fatal Misconception: The Struggle to Control World Population.* Cambridge, MA: Belknap Press.

Dewan, Shaila. 2009. "Extravagance Has Its Limits as Belt-Tightening Trickles Up." *New York Times*, March 9. Available at http://www.nytimes.com/2009/03/10/us/10reset .html.

El Amine, Loubna. 2016. "Are 'Democracy' and 'Human Rights' Western Colonial Exports? No; Here's Why." *Washington Post*, April 2. Available at https://www.washing tonpost.com/news/monkey-cage/wp/2016/04/02/are-democracy-andhuman-rights -western-colonial-exports-no-heres-why.

Elhance, Arun P. 1999. *Hydropolitics in the 3rd World: Conflict and Cooperation in International River Basins.* Washington, DC: United States Institute of Peace Press.

Engleman, Robert, Richard P. Cincotta, Amy Coen, and Kali-Ahset Amen. 2005. "The Future Is Not What It Used to Be: World Population Trends." In *From Resource Scarcity to Ecological Security: Exploring New Limits to Growth*, edited by Dennis Pirages and Ken Cousins, 21–38. Cambridge, MA: MIT Press.

Engler, Mark. 2012. "Hijacked Organic, Limited Local, Faulty Fair Trade." *Dissent*, Spring. Available at https://www.dissentmagazine.org/article/hijacked-organic -limited-local-faulty-fair-trade.

Feiock, Richard C., and Christopher Stream. 2001. "Environmental Protection versus Economic Development: A False Trade-Off?" *Public Administration Review* 61 (3): 313–321.

Goldenberg, Suzanne. 2014. "Why Global Water Shortages Pose Threat of Terror and War." *The Guardian*, February 8. Available at https://www.theguardian.com/en vironment/2014/feb/09/global-water-shortages-threat-terror-war.

Hardin, Garrett. 1986. *Filters against Folly: How to Survive despite Economists, Ecologists, and the Merely Eloquent*. New York: Penguin.

Harris, Peter. 2014. "A Political Trilemma? International Security, Environmental Protection and Human Rights in the British Indian Ocean Territory." *International Politics* 51 (1): 87–100.

Hirsch, Paul D., and J. Peter Brosius. 2013. "Navigating Complex Trade-Offs in Conservation and Development: An Integrative Framework." *Issues in Interdisciplinary Studies*, no. 31: 99–122.

Hunter, David. 1999. "Global Environmental Protection in the 21st Century." *Foreign Policy in Focus*, June 1. Available at http://fpif.org/global_environmental_protection _in_the_21st_century.

Iceland, Charles. 2017. "Water Stress Is Driving Conflict and Migration: How Should the Global Community Respond?" World Resources Institute, September 25. Available at http://www.wri.org/blog/2017/09/water-stress-driving-conflict-and-migra tion-how-should-global-community-respond.

Kameri-Mbote, Patricia. 2007. "Water, Conflict, and Cooperation: Lessons from the Nile River Basin." Wilson International Center for Scholars, January. Available at https:// www.wilsoncenter.org/sites/default/files/NavigatingPeaceIssuePKM.pdf.

Klare, Michael T. 2002. *Resource Wars: The New Landscape of Global Conflict*. New York: Henry Holt.

———. 2012. *The Race for What's Left: The Global Scramble for the World's Last Resources*. New York: Henry Holt.

Lin, Patrick, and Fritz Allhoff. 2008. "Against Unrestricted Human Enhancement." *Journal of Evolution and Technology* 18 (1): 35–41.

Low, Nicholas, and Brendan Gleeson. 1998. *Justice, Society, and Nature*. New York: Routledge.

Mandel, Robert. 1988. *Conflict over the World's Resources*. Westport, CT: Greenwood Press.

———. 1992. "Sources of International River Basin Disputes." *Conflict Quarterly* 12 (Fall): 25–56.

McShane, Thomas O., Paul D. Hirsch, Tran Chi Trung, Alexander N. Songorwa, Ann Kinzig, Bruno Monteferri, David Mutekanga, et al. 2011. "Hard Choices: Making Trade-Offs between Biodiversity Conservation and Human Well-Being." *Biological Conservation* 144 (3): 966–972.

Meadows, Donella H., Dennis L. Meadows, Jorgen Randers, and William W. Behrens III. 1972. *The Limits to Growth*. New York: Signet.

Meadows, Donella, Jorgen Randers, and Dennis Meadows. 2004. *Limits to Growth: The 30-Year Update*. White River Junction, VT: Chelsea Green.

"More Obese People in the World than Underweight, Says Study." 2016. *BBC News*, April 1. Available at http://www.bbc.com/news/health-35933691.

Morris, Mary E. 1997. "Water and Conflict in the Middle East: Threats and Opportunities." *Studies in Conflict and Terrorism* 20 (1). Available at http://web.macam.ac.il/~arnon/Int-ME/water/WATER%20AND%20CONFLICT%20IN%20THE%20MIDDLE%20EAST%20.htm.

Ngai, Catherine. 2010. "Replacing Oil Addiction with Metals Dependence?" *National Geographic*, October 1. Available at http://news.nationalgeographic.com/news/2010/10/101001-energy-rare-earth-metals.

Office of the Director of National Intelligence. 2012. "Global Water Security." Intelligence Community Assessment ICA 2012-08. Available at https://www.dni.gov/files/documents/Special%20Report_ICA%20Global%20Water%20Security.pdf.

Ophuls, William, and A. Stephen Boyan Jr. 1992. *Ecology and the Politics of Scarcity Revisited*. New York: W. H. Freeman.

Perrings, Charles. 2014. *Our Uncommon Heritage: Biodiversity Change, Ecosystem Services, and Human Wellbeing*. New York: Cambridge University Press.

"Rio + 20: CGIAR [Consultative Group for International Agricultural Research] Calls for Equal Sharing of Natural Resources." 2012. June 20. Previously available at http://www.cgiar.org/consortium-news/rio20-cgiar-calls-for-equal-sharing-of-natural-resources.

Roberts, James M. 2011. "How Western Environmental Policies Are Stunting Economic Growth in Developing Countries." Heritage Foundation, January 24. Available at http://www.heritage.org/research/reports/2011/01/how-western-environmental-policies-are-stunting-economic-growth-in-developing-countries.

Selby, Jan, and Clemens Hoffmann. 2012. "Water Scarcity, Conflict, and Migration: A Comparative Analysis and Reappraisal." *Environment and Planning* 30 (6): 997–1014.

Soroos, Marvin. 1977. "The Commons and Lifeboat as Guides for International Ecological Policy." *International Studies Quarterly* 21 (4): 647–674.

Stockholm Resilience Centre. 2016. "Why Protecting and Using Biodiversity Is a Human Rights Issue." Available at http://www.stockholmresilience.org/research/research-news/2016-10-06-why-protecting-and-using-biodiversity-is-a-human-rights-issue.html.

Stone, Christopher D. 2010. *Should Trees Have Standing?* 3rd ed. New York: Oxford University Press.

United Nations. 1948. "Universal Declaration of Human Rights." Available at http://www.un.org/en/universal-declaration-human-rights.

Ward, Diane Raines. 2002. *Water Wars*. New York: Riverhead Books.

Winship, Scott. 2013. "The Affluent Economy: Our Misleading Obsession with Growth Rates." Brookings, February 25. Available at http://www.brookings.edu/research/articles/2013/02/affluent-economy-winship.

Wintle, Michael, and Rachel Reeve. 1994. *Rhetoric and Reality in Environmental Policy*. Avebury, UK: Avebury Studies in Green Research.

World Nuclear Association. 2018. "World Energy Needs and Nuclear Power." Available at http://world-nuclear.org/information-library/current-and-future-generation/world-energy-needs-and-nuclear-power.aspx.

Zetland, David. 2011. *The End of Abundance*. Mission Viejo, CA: Aguanomics Press.

PART II VIOLENCE

Out of the Fire, into the Frying Pan?

Examining Violence against Forced Migrants in Africa

Kerstin Fisk

ccording to United Nations High Commissioner for Refugees (UNHCR) estimates, the number of refugees—individuals forced to flee their countries because of armed conflict and persecution—has increased by nearly 4.7 million, about 45 percent, over the past five years. In 2015, the worldwide refugee population reached 15.1 million, the highest level seen in twenty years. Although the vast majority of those newly displaced during the past five years fled the ongoing civil war in Syria, about half a million are known to have fled other violent conflicts, including those taking place in South Sudan, the Democratic Republic of the Congo, Somalia, Nigeria, and Burundi. These refugees have witnessed and/or experienced massive human rights abuses in the forms of forced recruitment, summary executions, deliberate and arbitrary killings, torture, and rape at the hands of their governments and other organized, armed actors, as well as generalized violence and economic and food insecurity. They are "survival migrants" outside their home countries because of existential threats to their most fundamental human rights, for which they have no real recourse (Betts 2013). Refugee populations also face extreme physical insecurity in sanctuary countries. Indeed, anti-refugee violence and refugee protection are two central human rights concerns of our time. The very foundation of the international refugee protection regime depends on the provision of security by host governments, yet many are failing to uphold this obligation.

Some 148 states around the world are party to the 1951 UN Convention relating to the Status of Refugees (Refugee Convention) and/or its 1967 Protocol, which legally obligate signatories to assist and protect refugees and asylum seekers.[1] The most fundamental aspect of such protection is the principle of nonrefoulement, which prohibits state parties from expelling or returning individuals to their home countries if they have a reasonable fear of being persecuted there. While every state party to the treaty and its protocols bears the responsibility of refugee protection, only ten—nearly all of them developing countries—host the vast majority. Overall, the developing countries host an estimated 86 percent of the world's refugees.[2] Industrialized countries, meanwhile, have backed away from their earlier pledges to take in greater numbers, despite direct UNHCR appeals for them to do so (UNHCR 2016). Governments have pledged to accept less than two-thirds of the number the UNHCR requested in 2015 (Sengupta 2016), and the number they eventually take in is likely to be far lower (Nebehay 2016; Wintour 2016). Because the refugee crisis and its effects are expected to worsen in coming years, it is imperative to find ways of ensuring these governments uphold their obligations under the Refugee Convention.

The UN's pleas for more countries to shoulder greater responsibility for refugee protection have been met with stiff opposition in a climate in which politicians increasingly associate refugees with threats to national security, including the spread of disease (Rettman 2015), terrorism, and crime (Thorpe 2015). U.S. politicians have made similar charges, with thirty governors calling for a ban on Syrian refugees entering the country (Fantz and Brumfield 2015). The Obama administration cited border-security concerns as justification for rounding up and deporting asylum seekers who fled violence and persecution in Central America (Johnson 2016). Other countries (including Hungary, Slovenia, Austria, and Macedonia) have brazenly disregarded human rights by constructing razor wire–lined fences along their borders to bar refugees and other migrants from entry (Baczynska and Ledwith 2016).

Countries that have accepted large refugee populations have become increasingly wary of them. In 2015 in response to "emergency security challenges," the Kenyan government attempted to round up some fifty thousand Somali refugees living in urban areas. Numerous abuses were documented as police attempted to force the refugees, often collectively referred to as terrorists, into already overcrowded camps (Human Rights Watch 2014).[3] In Turkey, authorities have forcibly expelled Syrian refugees on the basis of unfounded accusations that they have links to "criminal gangs" (Aslan 2015). It appears as though "threat and danger now dominates the refugee discourse" to the extent that "refugees are framed as threats to security rather than as a humanitarian issue" (Mogire 2011, 17).

Extant political science scholarship also focuses on how refugees can threaten state security. Several studies, for instance, consider the conditions under which refugee inflows may increase the risk that civil war diffuses from the refugees' country of origin to the host state, affect the likelihood of intrastate war, and contribute to terrorism. However, the amount of research on security threats to refugee populations is scant, despite evidence that refugees are often highly physically insecure in their host countries.

This chapter takes a less conventional approach by illuminating such threats to refugees' physical security. It examines two cases in sub-Saharan Africa, a region home to several of the largest refugee populations in the world. The first section lays out some of the existing literature on the relationship between forced migration and security in host states. The second examines instances of refugee insecurity based on these insights. The third introduces some alternative policy solutions for achieving better protection for refugee populations in light of some of the failures identified in the case studies. This chapter therefore speaks to what Alexander Betts aptly identifies as survival migration and shows how threats to survival migrants often persist in sanctuary countries. Though host governments often undermine refugee security through rights violations of both omission and commission, the chapter's conclusion reflects on how inter- and nongovernmental groups can help fill in the protection gaps states leave behind.

Whose Security? The Securitization of Forced Migration

Forced migration generally can be housed within one of two security frameworks. In the first, conventional framework, refugee populations are considered probable agents of conflict and violence within and among states and something from which the state needs to be secured. This "refugees-as-threat" conception stresses the security ramifications of refugee inflows for states, including the role of refugee populations in bringing war to their host countries. For instance, Aristide Zolberg, Astri Suhrke, and Sergio Aguayo (1989, 65) point out that refugee populations may contain rebel fighters, or "refugee-warriors," from the refugee-sending state, creating military states in exile that undermine the security of the host. Of particular concern here is refugee militarization, or the "storage and trafficking of arms, the presence of active and ex-combatants, recruitment, military training and the use of camps as military bases" (Mogire 2004, 20). A consequence of refugee militarization is increasing the probability of conflict between refugee-sending and refugee-receiving governments, as sending governments pursue refugee combatants into the host country's territory, violating its sovereignty (Salehyan 2008, 796). Civil war is also theorized to be more likely in receiving countries that neighbor the refugees' country of origin, based on the logic that refugees can expand cross-border social networks, extend the reach of rebel networks into neighboring host states, and create "negative externalities," including intensified economic competition and tension, demographic shifts, and the proliferation of weapons and subversive ideologies (Salehyan and Gleditsch 2006, 338; also see Fisk 2014). Other research emphasizes that hosting many refugees can increase the risk of experiencing both domestic and international terrorism, as militants are able to appropriate greater levels of humanitarian aid to finance conflict (Choi and Salehyan 2013; also see Milton, Spencer, and Findley 2013, who argue that lower opportunity costs related to poor conditions in refugee camps can increase the risk of transnational terrorism). More recently, Gina Lei Miller and Emily Hencken Ritter (2014, 52) underscore how migrant populations in general (including refugees) can make civil war in their countries of origin more likely by showcasing "rights gaps" that make individuals in the origin country more dissatisfied with the status quo and by sending remittances that can be used to fund a war economy.

By conceptualizing refugees in this way, the refugees-as-threat framework prioritizes the state as the referent object in need of securing, in line with traditional understandings of security. Yet the state-centric framework detracts from the reality that refugees are often the targets of violence, much of it state perpetrated or state sanctioned (Onoma 2013, 10; also see Fisk 2018). An alternative, less conventional framework for analyzing migration-related security prioritizes individuals rather than states as the referent objects to be secured. Human security is based on the normative assertion that each individual's security and rights ought to be prioritized. Unlike the traditional security framework (which focuses on military-related threats to states), human security recognizes that some of the most severe threats to individuals come not from external factors but from internal conflicts and their own governments. Situating forced migration within a human-security framework engenders the study of violence against refugee populations. The following section outlines some of the main theories in the literature on violence directed at refugee communities.

Theories on Violence against Refugees

Refugees have been known to face direct, intentional violence inside host states that is committed by a variety of state and nonstate actors, including sending- and host-government forces, state-sponsored militias, rebel groups, and local populations. This section outlines some of the factors thought to motivate government and government-supported violence against refugees. It considers proposed motivations of the refugee-sending state, as well as the conditions under which host-country actors (government forces and local populations) are likely to carry out this violence.

The occurrence of refugee militarization previously described is thought to result in refugee targeting by both sending- and host-country forces. Combatants may militarize refugee-hosting communities to take advantage of the "refugee resources" they offer, including cross-border sanctuaries in the form of refugee camps; pools of refugee recruits (forced or voluntary); and various forms of refugee aid such as food, supplies, and money (Lischer 2005; Terry 2002). Refugee militarization has previously been linked to intra- and interstate war; yet sending- and host-country forces may attack entire refugee communities to prevent rebels from appropriating capability-enhancing resources. In more severe cases, host-country forces may wage attacks on refugee communities because of concerns that the host state is being destabilized. Along these lines, Ato Kwamena Onoma notes that host governments are likely to "violently crack down on refugees with the goal of either expelling them altogether or suppressing their military activities" in an effort to stop attacks on their territory (2013, 36). The actions of what is generally a very small number of fighters relative to the civilian refugees can thereby affect the entire population (10).[4]

Others focus on the causes of government (or government-sanctioned) violence against refugee civilians. Some theorize that political entrepreneurs attempt to mobilize support by taking "xenophobic and anti-refugee" positions, which can eventually result in violence against refugee communities (e.g., Crisp 2002, 3). In this view, politicians instrumentally label individuals or entire groups "foreigners" as part of an overall strategy to discredit and disqualify the opposition and reduce political competition by limiting participation (Whitaker 2005, 113). The adoption of antiforeigner language enables politicians to strategically play into "a climate of growing xenophobia" related to concerns over refugees' impacts, which they use to rally voters and may use to both justify and encourage violence against refugees and other migrants (Whitaker 2005, 117–118).[5] Onoma also argues that the likelihood of violence "conducted openly and systematically by the local population against refugees" (2013, 4) increases when host governments portray refugees as threats (32). Yet he reasons that states "only withdraw protection from and promote attacks on refugees when sections of refugee populations are associated with groups that pose a real threat to the host government" itself (35). Where and when refugees join powerful opposition groups, incumbents portray opponents as "foreign invaders or the pawns of foreign refugees" and "seize on links between refugees and opposition groups to expel citizens belonging to opposition groups under the guise of expelling refugees" (35). Still, local populations are unlikely to carry out their own anti-refugee attacks unless the host community "privileges residence over indigeneity in the allocation of rights" (5). If locals privilege residency over indigeneity, Onoma expects that they will engage in anti-refugee violence because they are unlikely to know enough about the refugees to discern if the state's accusations against them are true or false (39). If this precondition does not hold, local civilian hosts are reluctant to follow the government's incitement toward violence and, in some cases, will attempt to protect the refugees (40).

Similar to these studies of anti-refugee violence, which focus on political motivations for refugee targeting by host governments and host populations, work by Claire Adida (2014) investigates the impacts economic factors have had on mass immigrant expulsions in Africa. In line with the "scapegoating" theory of xenophobia (e.g., Morris 1998, 1124), Adida argues that leaders are more likely to enforce immigration policy as well as blame foreigners for economic problems during times of crisis. She finds that the likelihood of targeted expulsion of foreigners significantly increases during an economic crisis; however, this occurs only when the leader's ethnic group share (as a proportion of the total population) is small. She reasons, "In their decision to expel immigrants, leaders facing a more fractionalized ethnic landscape are more sensitive to changes in their economy than are leaders facing a more homogenous ethnic landscape" (2014, 137). Although Adida's work does not focus on refugees exclusively, her findings suggest that economic and political vulnerability mutually produce anti-refugee violence.

This chapter next investigates the rhetoric and details surrounding violent attacks on refugee communities in a handful of country cases in sub-Saharan Africa. It relies on human rights reports, newspaper articles, politicians' official remarks, and data from Afrobarometer surveys. The goal is twofold: to highlight refugee insecurity and to discern some of the factors that contribute to refugee insecurity in host states.

Cases

Sending-Country Violence against Burundian Refugees

In April 2015, Burundi's president, Pierre Nkurinziza, announced that he would run for an unconstitutional third term. Large-scale protests broke out in Bujumbura in the months before the election, and members of the opposition attempted a coup in May. The Nkurinziza government, including members of his party's youth wing, the Imbonerakure, responded by brutally cracking down on opposition members and their known and suspected supporters. The violence worsened once Nkurinziza won reelection in July (Human Rights Watch 2016). An estimated 400 people were killed and 3,500 arrested between April and December 2015, while another 220,000 fled the country ("Burundi Violence" 2015).

The UNHCR estimated an outflow of more than 265,000 Burundian refugees by mid-2016. They mainly fled to neighboring states, including relatively stable Tanzania (131,834) and Rwanda (73,926) (Dobbs 2016). Yet the refugees are reportedly not safe from those loyal to Nkurinziza and his supporters in the National Council for the Defense of Democracy–Forces for the Defense of Democracy (CNDD-FDD). Nkurinziza's security forces have been accused of "hunting down" the refugees in Tanzania, who "live in fear of Burundian government militia [members] who are in the camp" ("Burundi Accused" 2016). According to a *Guardian* report, "Some say they are being targeted to prevent them from sharing their accounts of abuse . . . where thousands have been abducted, tortured, raped and killed. Others believe they are being singled out by people who want to punish family members active in the opposition. Almost all say the violence that followed them across the border is even more terrifying than what they endured at home, because now they have nowhere to run" (Graham-Harrison 2016). The refugees in Tanzania say they are being targeted to be punished, as well as to keep them from giving away information about what they witnessed in Burundi.

In Rwanda, where Paul Kagame's government is an adversary of Nkurunziza, both Rwandan and Burundian opposition groups have been accused of forcibly recruiting Burundian refugees, including teenagers, to go back and fight the regime (Boyce and Vigaud-Walsh 2015). Amid growing criticism from the international community over its complicity in refugee recruitment, the Rwandan government announced in February 2016 that the refugees would be moved to an unspecified third country. Representatives from the UNHCR have since expressed concern that Rwanda's plans will further erode host-government responsibility, as well as refugee protection (Aglietti 2016). Indeed, the Rwandan government has been accused of forcibly expelling Burundian refugees from its territory, reportedly citing the threat these refugees—who have been accused of spying for Burundi—pose to the country's security (Biryabarema 2016).

In the Democratic Republic of the Congo, refugees have reported seeing Nkurunziza's security forces near Lusenda camp, about forty miles from the border with Burundi ("Burundi Refugees" 2016). Refugees located much farther away from Burundi also claim that pro-government forces are in pursuit of them. The Coalition for Constitution Implementation in Kenya (CCI Kenya), a civil-society organization, recognizes that Burundian refugees are "now the target of a systematic campaign by Nkurunziza's regime to eliminate opponents" in Kenya (Buchanan 2016a). In one instance, refugees in Nairobi said they found the bloodstained identification cards of refugees along with the mutilated body of opposition member Jean de Dieu Kabura in a field. Another refugee in Nairobi admitted that he had been sent by the government with a list of people to kill, but he did not fulfill his orders after he saw that one name on the list was someone he knew ("Why Assassins"

2016). Kenyan human rights activists investigating these incidents also report they have received death threats referencing their work (Buchanan 2016b).[6]

The Burundi case highlights threats to refugees stemming from refugee-sending governments and their affiliated forces. It is not the first case in which the government responsible for refugee flight pursued them into sanctuary countries; Charles Taylor's security forces and government-sponsored rebels targeted Liberian refugees in Ghana, Guinea, and Sierra Leone in a similar manner (Amnesty International 2002). Today, Burundian refugees face a variety of threats in East and Central Africa, including targeted killing based on their known or suspected political allegiances. Nkurunziza appears undeterred by international criticism or about possible concerted action in response to his government's actions (Human Rights Watch 2016).

Theory linking refugee targeting to refugee militarization does not seem to explain refugee victimization in Tanzania, Kenya, and the Democratic Republic of the Congo, where the Imbonerakure reportedly targets refugees to silence any criticism of the Nkurunziza government and to eliminate opposition supporters. In Rwanda, however, militarization—primarily through refugee recruitment—appears to be central to the refugees' insecurity. Refugee civilians in Rwanda reportedly fear retribution from both Burundian and Rwandan forces. According to Martina Pomeroy of the UNHCR, the Rwandan government's negative framing of the refugees could profoundly affect tensions between the local population and the refugees, leading to violence. Given that most of the refugees are "living in families or the community where they have been dependent on the generosity and goodwill of Rwandans hosting them," she wonders, "What can happen if the population thinks that refugees have become undesirable for the government?" (Aglietti 2016). Indeed, the next case study indicates that refugee (in)security may be closely linked to the political calculations of host governments.

Anti-refugee Violence in South Africa

The population of refugees in South Africa quadrupled from around 28,000 in 2004 to approximately 112,000 in 2014 (UNHCR 2006, 2015). These refugees came from more than forty countries, although the vast majority fled conflicts in Somalia (approximately forty thousand), the Democratic Republic of the Congo (approximately thirty thousand), and Ethiopia (approximately nineteen thousand).[7] The country also hosts nearly five hundred thousand asylum seekers or those whose refugee status determination is pending (UNHCR 2015). Although refugees and asylum seekers are scattered throughout South Africa, the largest populations reside in cities, including Johannesburg, Cape Town, Pretoria, Durban, and Port Elizabeth.[8]

South Africa signed the 1951 Refugee Convention and its 1967 Protocol in 1996. It is often described as having generous asylum policies, since those with refugee and asylum-seeker permits have access to public resources, are able to work and move freely, and are not confined to camps (see, e.g., Wellman and Landau 2015). It is nevertheless clear that forced migrants have experienced severe insecurity over the past two decades. Twenty-one major attacks on migrant populations, including refugees, were documented between 1994 and April 2008 (Misago, Landau, and Monson 2009, 23–24). A single attack in Cape Town resulted in the deaths of twenty-nine Somali refugees (Le Roux 2006). The most deadly violence occurred in May 2008. In a two-week period, locals killed more than sixty foreigners and drove tens of thousands from their homes (Patel and Essa 2015). Judith Hayem describes the violence as systematic targeting that took the form of "national cleansing" (2013, 81), as it was "characterised by the brutalisation of people identified as foreigners by their neighbours" who "were beaten by South African assailants armed with sticks and machetes" (78). She argues, "The common denominator among all these people was their actual or assumed status of *makwerekwere* ('foreigners' in Johannesburg slang): as if some people 'belong' to the nation more than others; they were attacked because of their not being thought to be South African" (80). The government, however, dismissed the violence as conventional criminality.[9]

Physical assaults on refugees and other migrants have continued since 2008, leading to more than one hundred deaths and mass displacement in 2011, 2012, and 2013 (Landau 2014). In March and April 2015, large-scale violence against foreigners erupted after King Goodwill Zwelithini—the traditional leader of the Zulu, the country's largest ethnic group—reportedly told South Africans, "Let's take out the ants and leave them out in the sun. We ask that immigrants must pack their bags and go back to where they came from" (Allison 2015). The attacks that followed in Kwazulu Natal and Gauteng provinces left eight people dead and an estimated five thousand displaced.[10] Many of those who fled reportedly did so after receiving anonymous text messages alerting them of the impending attack, one of which read: "Wednesday, Zulu people are coming to town. . . . Their mission is to kill every foreigner on the road" (Dixon 2015). In response, then-president Jacob Zuma held that "millions of peace loving South Africans are in pain also because they are being accused of xenophobia, which is not true. South Africans are definitely not xenophobic" ("South Africa" 2015). Zuma's eldest son, however, not only backed Zwelithini's comments but further asserted that foreigners are "a ticking time bomb" and a "real security threat" ("Zuma's Son" 2015). The UNHCR reiterated that "those affected in these xenophobic attacks are refugees and asylum-seekers who were forced to leave their own countries due to war and persecution. They are in South Africa because they require protection" (de Gruijl 2015).

The government's claim that xenophobia does not play a role in the violence that targets refugees and asylum seekers is contradicted by the nature of the attacks, by the content and tone of migration-related media coverage (which has been shown to negatively portray foreigners; see, e.g., Danso and McDonald 2001), and by longitudinal survey research. Jonathan Crush and Wade Pendleton demonstrate that the majority of South Africans polled in 2001 and 2002 had negative attitudes toward foreigners, with these views "so pervasive and widespread that it is actually impossible to identify any kind of 'xenophobic profile'" (2004, 43). The 2011–2013 Round 5 of the Afrobarometer survey also found that a full 67 percent of respondents said they do not trust foreigners living in South Africa "at all," while 44 percent disagreed with the statement "People who are persecuted for political reasons in their own countries deserve protection in South Africa" (Afrobarometer 2011).

Accordingly, the Thabo Mbeki and Zuma governments did little to hold accountable those who have incited or directly participated in violence against refugees, asylum seekers, and other migrants. The Zuma government's most coordinated action following the more recent spate of attacks was Operation Fiela (sweep out the dirt). The government maintained that Operation Fiela was implemented to root out criminals. Critics, however, contend that it indiscriminately targeted foreigners, particularly asylum seekers the government considered "illegal" though they had been waiting—often for years—to receive refugee status determination because of a severely backlogged asylum application system (Wallis 2015; see Chapter 8 for discussion of how the uneven application of and delays in statelessness determination can increase migrants' vulnerability). In one raid, riot police and military swept a Johannesburg Methodist church that was home to approximately one thousand foreigners, many of them Zimbabwean refugees (Laing 2015). Amnesty International (2015) later reported that "the police and immigration officials detained all foreigners they encountered, including recognized refugees and asylum-seekers."

Some of the explanations presented in the literature on violence against refugees by host-country actors certainly apply in the South African case. First, there is clear evidence that antiforeigner rhetoric has been propagated at even the highest levels of leadership. While denying that attacks targeting refugees and other migrants are tied to xenophobia, the leadership has both implicitly and explicitly promoted the view that foreigners pose serious threats to host communities and the country. A 1998 Human Rights Watch report details a series of statements made by government and police officials, as well as by opposition politicians, linking foreigners to rising crime rates, poverty, unemployment, and other economic turmoil; barriers to basic service provision; and the spread of disease. Along these lines, Michael Neocosmos (2008) identifies a "state discourse of xenophobia" whereby "politicians of all shades of opinion [have] asserted their politics of fear" and "have pro-vided an environment wherein such xenophobic violence has appeared as legitimised by the state."

Second, political calculations appeared to play a role in national and lo-cal leaders' uncommunicativeness and inaction during both major rounds of violence. Hayem maintains that the sluggishness of national and local governments' responses to the 2008 attacks—and that there was no real "di-rective to actively oppose or prevent the violence"—was tied to the fact that national elections were being held the following year (2013, 88). Others inti-mate that Jacob Zuma's unwillingness to effectively address the violence or condemn King Zwelithini's incitement is partly rooted in Zuma's reliance on Zulu support (Magaziner and Jacobs 2015). However, there are no clear in-dications that the violence was a response to migrant support for the African National Congress's (ANC's) more powerful political opponents in either the Democratic Alliance or the Economic Freedom Fighters, as Onoma's (2013) logic anticipates; nor does there seem to be an attempt by the ANC to accuse its political opponents of being foreigners. Furthermore, whereas Claire Adida (2014) maintains that mass expulsions of migrants are more likely to occur when the country's leaders have a small ethnic group share, both Mbeki and Zuma come from relatively large groups (Xhosa and Zulu).

Another key factor to consider, based on previous literature, is how South Africa's conception of citizenship rights—whether it privileges resi-dency or indigeneity in determining who rightfully belongs—relates to a local population's propensity to attack refugee populations. In contrast to the conventional wisdom (which links indigeneity to violence), Onoma (2013) argues that societies that privilege indigeneity in the allocation of rights should be *less likely* to engage in violence against refugees. Since local leaders have more information about refugees residing in indigeneity-privileging societies, the local population is less likely to believe the leadership's at-tempts to demonize the refugees. Yet as Neocosmos (2008) notes, postapart-heid South Africa has "a conception of citizenship founded exclusively on indigeneity." "Indigeneity," he says, "implies an exclusive conception of na-tionality and citizenship, meaning that those conceived (in whatever way) to be outside territorial boundaries are excluded from rights and entitlements" (2010, 14). Accordingly, with regard to the 2008 violence, Hayem demon-strates that "one of the motives of the attackers when brutalising and looting foreign nationals was that they believed that they compete with citizens or, in their view, that they illegitimately access economic goods, facilities or rights *to which only those who are stereotypically seen as South African should be entitled*" (2013, 84, emphasis added). The key, she says, is that the provi-sion of basic services was "seen as a national privilege which can be refused to those who do not belong to the nation" (86; also see Chapter 9 for further discussion of how citizenship laws dictate the rights migrants are entitled to in receiving states). Hayem argues that the narrow construction of belonging based on nationality was apparent in how the government referred to victims, many of whom were permanent residents: "The ambivalence of Mbeki appears in his naming the victims 'foreigners.' . . . The president alternately used the notion of 'African brothers and sisters' and the term 'foreign guests' to designate the victims of the attacks" (85).

Conclusion

Conventional security research conceptualizes refugees as potential threats to governments and, in doing so, prioritizes the security of the state over that of individuals. This obscures the reality that refugees face anti-refugee sentiment and violence in countries of sanctuary. Substantial increases in refugee inflows accompanied by blanket allegations that refugees threaten national and regional security have been used to justify less generous and increasingly hostile refugee policies. These charges scapegoat refugees and make it easier for politicians to demand their repatriation, even if returning to their origin country is unsafe for them (Mogire 2011, 152). In Kenya, for instance, the former foreign minister made it clear that the government wants Somali refugees to leave: "We definitely want the refugees to go home. We want them out yesterday" (Ali 2012). The government subsequently announced its plans to close the Dadaab refugee camp and repatriate more than three hundred thousand Somali refugees, referencing security concerns (Yackley 2016).

This chapter looks into some of the challenges refugees encounter in host states, generating insights on some of the more recent failures of refugee protection. It advances the human-security framework to study individuals—refugees in this case—as the referent objects of security analysis. The case discussions demonstrate that refugee populations can face severe threats from both sending- and host-country actors. For instance, it is clear that forces loyal to the government in Burundi have targeted both militarized and nonmilitarized Burundian refugees in several countries.

These findings also are in line with past scholarship arguing that threats to refugees and other migrants are partly the result of political actors' incentives to advance exclusive notions of citizenship (Whitaker 2005). While rousing xenophobia against migrants may be part of a strategy intended to garner political support, it can have broader and more dangerous implications. Beth Elise Whitaker notes, "As people become mobilized along these lines and conflicts emerge over which groups should benefit from the rights of citizenship, social cleavages widen and the likelihood of instability increases. . . . The trigger for conflict comes from elite strategies that intensify the politics of exclusion" (2005, 122–123). The South African case demonstrates that the politics of exclusion have had clear, detrimental impacts on the security of forced migrants. Taken together, the case studies make it clear that further protections for refugees and asylum seekers in host communities are necessary; this includes protection from manipulation and abuse perpetrated by both sending-country and host-country actors.

Of central concern, therefore, is who can reliably protect refugees and asylum seekers. The case discussions give rise to several considerations regarding international efforts to protect forced migrants. The UNHCR has long insisted that refugee protection is fundamentally the host state's responsibility. Yet the vast majority of refugees and asylum seekers are located in relatively poor, developing countries, most of which have low state capacity and are unable to effectively administer or secure their full territories. Thus, as Mariano-Florentino Cuéllar argues, "The principled case for neglect here is almost impossible to make. . . . Host state responsibility does not extinguish UNHCR's role" (2006, 43). Potential strategies to protect refugees from violence committed by sending-state perpetrators could therefore include UN peacekeepers with civilian-protection mandates acting in the defense of refugee civilians, in line with the Responsibility to Protect (R2P). The CCI in Kenya is an important example of how nongovernmental organizations can play a key role in refugee protection. The organization has called on the government of Kenya to investigate the Burundian government's role in the violence and provide greater protections for refugees residing there (Buchanan 2016b).

When the perpetrator of violence against refugees and asylum seekers is the host government, or the host government is complicit in the abuse, the credibility of the refugee protection mandate is obviously in doubt. In these cases, international and nongovernmental organizations could increase their ability to effectively investigate, report, and promote the prosecution of those who perpetrate violence against refugees. In addition, as the director of the Africa Division of Human Rights Watch has argued, "The victims of these attacks must have adequate protection against threats of deportation to facilitate a credible justice process and to encourage their full participation in legal proceedings. . . . Such protection would enable undocumented foreign victims to testify in court, and would serve as a deterrent to their attackers, who believe their victims are legally defenseless" (Human Rights Watch 2008).

UNHCR and its partners could also work in concert with local organizations to actively counter public misconceptions and misinformation about refugees and asylum seekers. One example of an organization working to improve refugee rights in this way is the International Organization for Migration, which not only works to track and report on incidents of violence and forced repatriation in South Africa and elsewhere but also engages in public-outreach campaigns to draw attention to the positive contributions of migrant populations. As refugee crises are expected to worsen in the coming years, finding effective ways to counter xenophobia is increasingly vital for refugee protection.

A further solution is for more parties to the 1951 Refugee Convention to aid overburdened host governments in processing asylum applications more quickly. Currently, host governments are tasked with determination of refugee status unless they are unwilling or unable, in which case the UNHCR steps in. The UNHCR, however, is now facing a backlog of its own. Speeding up refugee-status determination for asylum seekers living in limbo could help increase host responsibility for the refugees (by clarifying violations of nonrefoulement) and thereby discourage the perpetration—or allowance—of attacks on refugee communities.

In general terms, the international community needs to broadly renew its commitment to refugee protection in the twenty-first century. This entails sharing the financial burden of refugee assistance and protection, as well as dramatically increasing commitments to resettle refugees in third countries. As scholars, practitioners, and politicians continue broader debates regarding the relative merits of rewriting the 1951 Refugee Convention (see, e.g., Ferracioli 2014), there are myriad ways inter- and nongovernmental organizations and citizens can work together to fill the fundamental protection gaps that deny refugees true sanctuary today.

NOTES

Portions of this chapter were previously published in Kerstin Fisk, "One-Sided Violence in Refugee-Hosting Areas," *Journal of Conflict Resolution* 62, no. 3 (2018): 529–556; and Kerstin Fisk, "Refugees: Out of the Fire, into the Frying Pan?" *World Policy*, February 18, 2016, available at https://worldpolicy.org/2016/02/18/refugees-out-of-the-fire-into-the-frying-pan.

1. The 1969 Organisation of African Unity (OAU) Convention Governing the Specific Aspects of the Refugee Problems in Africa expanded the definition of a refugee to include people compelled to leave their country as a result of events that have "seriously disturbed public order" (UNHCR 1969).

2. These include Turkey, Pakistan, Lebanon, Iran, Ethiopia, Jordan, Kenya, Uganda, Chad, and Sudan.

3. The Somali community also suffered several deadly attacks by al-Shabaab, the insurgent/terrorist group with which they were (and still are) accused of collaborating. See, e.g., Sperber 2015.

4. Civilians constitute the vast majority of refugees even where militarization has occurred. See, e.g., Onoma 2013, 10.

5. Sarah Dryden-Peterson and Lucy Hovil (2004, 33) also show how politicians in Uganda highlight inequities between nationals and self-settled refugees who have managed to become successful in business, which engenders xenophobia.

6. Burundian security forces are also accused of infiltrating and carrying out attacks on the refugee community in Kampala, Uganda (Reporters without Borders 2016).

7. UNHCR Population Statistics Database, available at http://popstats.unhcr.org/en/overview.

8. UNHCR demographic and location data, 2005, in the author's possession.

9. Then-president Thabo Mbeki responded, "When I heard some accuse my people of xenophobia, of hatred of foreigners, I wondered what the accusers knew about my people, which I did not know. . . . I will not hesitate to assert that my people are not diseased by the terrible affliction of xenophobia" (Patel and Essa 2015).

10. Zwelithini, however, maintains that he was misquoted. See Smith 2015.

REFERENCES

Adida, Claire. 2014. *Immigrant Exclusion and Insecurity in Africa*. Cambridge: Cambridge University Press.

Afrobarometer. 2011. "Summary of Results: Afrobarometer Round 5 Survey in South Africa." Available at http://afrobarometer.org/sites/default/files/publications/Summary%20of%20results/saf_r5_sor.pdf.

Aglietti, Stephanie. 2016. "Burundi Refugees Fearful after Rwanda Expulsion Threat." *Zululand Observer*, February 15. Available at https://zululandobserver.co.za/afp/145777/burundi-refugees-fearful-after-rwanda-expulsion-threat.

Ali, Noor. 2012. "Life Grim in Somali Camps That Kenya Wants to Shut." *Reuters*, February 23. Available at http://www.reuters.com/article/us-kenya-somalia-refugees-id USTRE81M1QR20120223.

Allison, Simon. 2015. "South Africa: Attacks on Migrants Show Failure to Stem Racial Tension." *The Guardian*, November 9. Available at https://www.theguardian.com/world/2015/nov/09/south-africa-attacks-migrants-show-failure-stem-racial -tension.

Amnesty International. 2002. "Liberia: Civilians Face Human Rights Abuses at Home and across Borders." October 1. Available at http://www.refworld.org/docid/3dc 2903c4.html.

———. 2015. "South Africa: Authorities Must Uphold Refugee and Migrant Rights and Respect the Rule of Law." May 14. Available at http://www.amnesty.ca/news/news -releases/south-africa-authorities-must-uphold-refugee-and-migrant-rights-and -respect-the.

Aslan, Melih. 2015. "Migrants Fleeing Syria Encounter a Life of Detention in Turkey." *Washington Post*, December 27. https://www.washingtonpost.com/world/migrants -fleeing-syria-encounter-a-life-of-detention-in-turkey/2015/12/27/3f63ce4c-acdb -11e5-9ab0-884d1cc4b33e_story.html.

Baczynska, Gabriela, and Sara Ledwith. 2016. "How Europe Built Fences to Keep People Out." *Reuters*, April 4. Available at http://www.reuters.com/article/us-europe -migrants-fences-insight-idUSKCN0X10U7.

Betts, Alexander. 2013. *Survival Migration: Failed Governance and the Crisis of Displacement*. Ithaca, NY: Cornell University Press.

Biryabarema, Elias. 2016. "Rwanda Expels Burundians Who Say They Were Accused of Spying." *Reuters*, June 12. Available at http://www.reuters.com/article/us-burundi -politics-idUSKCN0YY0OH.

Boyce, Michael, and Francisca Vigaud-Walsh. 2015. "Asylum Betrayed: Recruitment of Burundian Refugees in Rwanda." Refugees International, December 14. Available at http://www.refugeesinternational.org/reports/2015/12/14/rwanda.

Buchanan, Elsa. 2016a. "Kenya: Burundian Opposition Refugees Plea for Protection from Pro-regime 'Hit Squads.'" *International Business Times*, January 13. Available at http://www.ibtimes.co.uk/kenya-burundian-opposition-refugees-plea-protection-nkurunziza-hit-squads-1537431.

———. 2016b. "Kenya: Human-Rights Defenders Investigating Violations in Burundi Have Received Death Threats." *International Business Times*, February 5. Available at http://www.ibtimes.co.uk/kenya-human-rights-defenders-investigating-violations-burundi-have-received-death-threats-1542122.

"Burundi Accused of Hunting Refugees in Tanzania Camps." 2016. *Al Jazeera*, February 5. Available at http://www.aljazeera.com/news/2016/02/burundi-militias-hunting-refugees-tanzania-160205141830846.html.

"Burundi Refugees in DR Congo Border Camp Still Live in Fear." 2016. *New Vision*, January 23. Available at https://www.newvision.co.ug/new_vision/news/1415484/burundi-refugees-dr-congo-border-camp-live-fear.

"Burundi Violence: Africa 'Will Not Allow Genocide.'" 2015. *Al Jazeera*, December 17. Available at http://www.aljazeera.com/news/2015/12/burundi-deploy-experts-monitor-violence-151217142631031.html.

Choi, Seung-Whan, and Idean Salehyan. 2013. "No Good Deed Goes Unpunished: Refugees, Humanitarian Aid, and Terrorism." *Conflict Management and Peace Science* 30 (1): 53–75.

Crisp, Jeff. 2002. "No Solutions in Sight: The Problem of Protracted Refugee Situations in Africa." Center for Comparative Immigration Studies Working Paper No. 68. Available at https://escholarship.org/uc/item/89d8r34q.

Crush, Jonathan, and Wade Pendleton. 2004. "Regionalizing Xenophobia? Citizen Attitudes to Immigration and Refugee Policy in Southern Africa." Southern African Migration Programme Migration Policy Series No. 30. Available at https://scholars.wlu.ca/cgi/viewcontent.cgi?referer=https://www.google.com/&httpsredir=1&article=1126&context=samp.

Cuéllar, Mariano-Florentino. 2006. "Refugee Security and the Organizational Logic of Legal Mandates." *Georgetown Journal of International Law* 37:583.

Danso, Ransford, and David A. McDonald. 2001. "Writing Xenophobia: Immigration and the Print Media in Post-apartheid South Africa." *Africa Today* 48 (3): 115–137.

de Gruijl, Karin. 2015. "UNHCR Concern at Xenophobic Violence in South Africa." UNHCR, April 17. Available at http://www.unhcr.org/en-us/news/latest/2015/4/5530cdaa9/unhcr-concern-xenophobic-violence-south-africa.html.

Dixon, Robyn. 2015. "South Africa Grapples with Outbreak of Anti-immigrant Violence." *Los Angeles Times*, April 15. Available at http://www.latimes.com/world/africa/la-fg-south-africa-immigrant-violence-20150415-story.html.

Dobbs, Leo. 2016. "Number of Burundian Refugees Tops 250,000 since April." UNHCR, March 4. Available at http://www.unhcr.org/en-us/news/latest/2016/3/56d97f2d9/number-burundian-refugees-tops-250000-since-april.html.

Dryden-Peterson, Sarah, and Lucy Hovil. 2004. "A Remaining Hope for Durable Solutions: Local Integration of Refugees and Their Hosts in the Case of Uganda." *Refuge* 22 (1): 26–38.

Fantz, Ashley, and Ben Brumfield. 2015. "More than Half the Nation's Governors Say Syrian Refugees Not Welcome." *CNN*, November 19. Available at http://www.cnn.com/2015/11/16/world/paris-attacks-syrian-refugees-backlash.

Ferracioli, Luara. 2014. "The Appeal and Danger of a New Refugee Convention." *Social Theory and Practice* 40 (1): 123–144.

Fisk, Kerstin. 2014. "Refugee Geography and the Diffusion of Armed Conflict in Africa." *Civil Wars* 16 (3): 255–275.

———. 2018. "One-Sided Violence in Refugee-Hosting Areas." *Journal of Conflict Resolution* 62 (3): 529–556.

Graham-Harrison, Emma. 2016. "Nowhere to Run: Burundi Violence Follows Escapees across Borders." *The Guardian*, April 15. Available at http://www.theguardian.com/global-development/2016/apr/15/nowhere-to-run-burundi-violence-follows-escapees-across-borders.

Hayem, Judith. 2013. "From May 2008 to 2011: Xenophobic Violence and National Subjectivity in South Africa." *Journal of Southern African Studies* 39 (1): 77–97.

Human Rights Watch. 1998. *"Prohibited Persons": Abuse of Undocumented Migrants, Asylum-Seekers, and Refugees in South Africa*. New York: Human Rights Watch.

———. 2008. "South Africa: Punish Attackers in Xenophobic Violence." May 22. Available at https://www.hrw.org/news/2008/05/22/south-africa-punish-attackers-xenophobic-violence.

———. 2014. "Kenya: Plan to Force 50,000 Refugees into Camps." March 26. Available at https://www.hrw.org/news/2014/03/26/kenya-plan-force-50000-refugees-camps.

———. 2016. "Burundi: Abductions, Killings, Spread Fear." February 25. Available at https://www.hrw.org/news/2016/02/25/burundi-abductions-killings-spread-fear.

Johnson, Jeh C. 2016. "Statement by Secretary Jeh C. Johnson on Southwest Border Security." U.S. Department of Homeland Security, January 4. Available at https://www.dhs.gov/news/2016/01/04/statement-secretary-jeh-c-johnson-southwest-border-security.

Laing, Aislinn. 2015. "South African Church Sanctuary for Refugees Targeted in Police Raid." *The Telegraph*, May 8. Available at http://www.telegraph.co.uk/news/worldnews/africaandindianocean/southafrica/11593301/South-African-church-sanctuary-for-refugees-targeted-in-police-raid.html.

Landau, Loren B. 2014. "Xenophobia, a Backtrack on Promise of Tolerance." *Saturday Star*, March 1. Available at https://www.pressreader.com/south-africa/saturday-star/20140301/281998965377868.

Le Roux, Mariette. 2006. "Somali Refugees Fear Deadly Violence in Cape Town." *Mail and Guardian*, September 17. Available at http://mg.co.za/article/2006-09-17-somali-refugees-fear-deadly-violence-in-cape-town.

Lischer, Sarah Kenyon. 2005. *Dangerous Sanctuaries: Refugee Camps, Civil War and the Dilemma of Humanitarian Aid*. Ithaca, NY: Cornell University Press.

Magaziner, Daniel, and Sean Jacobs. 2015. "South Africa Turns on Its Immigrants." *New York Times*, April 24. Available at http://www.nytimes.com/2015/04/25/opinion/south-africa-turns-on-its-immigrants.html.

Miller, Gina Lei, and Emily Hencken Ritter. 2014. "Emigrants and the Onset of Civil War." *Journal of Peace Research* 51 (1): 51–64.

Milton, Daniel, Megan Spencer, and Michael Findley. 2013. "Radicalism of the Hopeless: Refugee Flows and Transnational Terrorism." *International Interactions* 39:621–645.

Misago, Jean Pierre, Loren B. Landau, and Tamlyn Monson. 2009. "Towards Tolerance, Law, and Dignity: Addressing Violence against Foreign Nationals in South Africa." International Organization for Migration, February. Available at http://www .atlanticphilanthropies.org/app/uploads/2015/09/IOM_Addressing_Violence _Against_Foreign_Nationals.pdf.

Mogire, Edward. 2004. "A Preliminary Exploration of the Links between Refugees and Small Arms." Bonn International Center for Conversion Paper 35. Available at https://www.bicc.de/uploads/tx_bicctools/paper35.pdf.

———. 2011. *Victims as Security Threats: Refugee Impact on Host State Security in Africa.* Burlington, VT: Ashgate.

Morris, Alan. 1998. "'Our Fellow Africans Make Our Lives Hell': The Lives of Congolese and Nigerians Living in Johannesburg." *Ethnic and Racial Studies* 21 (6): 1116–1136.

Nebehay, Stephanie. 2016. "Few New Pledges at U.N. Talks to Resettle Syrian Refugees." *Reuters*, March 30. Available at http://www.reuters.com/article/us-mideast-crisis -syria-refugees-idUSKCN0WW0L4.

Neocosmos, Michael. 2008. "The Politics of Fear and the Fear of Politics." *Abahlali baseMjondolo*, June 8. Available at http://abahlali.org/node/3616.

———. 2010. *From "Foreign Natives" to "Native Foreigners": Explaining Xenophobia in Post-apartheid South Africa.* Dakar, Senegal: CODESRIA.

Onoma, Ato Kwamena. 2013. *Anti-refugee Violence and African Politics.* Cambridge: Cambridge University Press.

Patel, Khadija, and Azad Essa. 2015. "No Place like Home." *Al Jazeera.* Available at http://interactive.aljazeera.com/aje/2015/xenophobiasouthafrica.

Reporters without Borders. 2016. "Burundi: Regime a Threat to Journalists, Even Those Who Have Fled Abroad." August 3. Available at https://rsf.org/en/news/burundi -regime-threat-journalists-even-those-who-have-fled-abroad.

Rettman, Andrew. 2015. "Poland: Election Talk on Migrant 'Protozoas' Gets Ugly." *EU Observer*, October 14. Available at https://euobserver.com/political/130672.

Salehyan, Idean. 2008. "The Externalities of Civil Strife: Refugees as a Source of International Conflict." *American Journal of Political Science* 52 (4): 787–801.

Salehyan, Idean, and Kristian Skrede Gleditsch. 2006. "Refugees and the Spread of Civil War." *International Organization* 60 (2): 335–366.

Sengupta, Somini. 2016. "U.S. Has Taken In Less than a Fifth of Pledged Syrian Refugees." *New York Times*, May 10. Available at http://www.nytimes.com/2016/05/11/ world/middleeast/us-has-taken-in-less-than-a-fifth-of-pledged-syrian-refugees .html.

Smith, David. 2015. "Zulu Leader Suggests Media to Blame for South Africa's Xenophobic Violence." *The Guardian*, April 20. Available at https://www.theguardian.com/ world/2015/apr/20/south-africa-xenophobic-violence-zulu-king-goodwill -zwelithini.

"'South Africa Is Not a Xenophobic Nation': A Letter from Jacob Zuma." *The Guardian*, April 28. Available at https://www.theguardian.com/world/2015/apr/28/south -africa-is-not-a-xenophobic-nation-a-letter-from-jacob-zuma.

Sperber, Amanda. 2015. "Little Mogadishu, under Siege." *Foreign Policy*, April 14. Available at http://foreignpolicy.com/2015/04/14/kenya-shabab-somalia-garissa-ken yatta.

Terry, Fiona. 2002. *Condemned to Repeat? The Paradox of Humanitarian Action.* Ithaca, NY: Cornell University Press.

Thorpe, Nick. 2015. "Migrant Crisis: Hungary Denies Fuelling Intolerance in Media." *BBC News*, December 22. Available at http://www.bbc.com/news/world-europe -35162515.

UNHCR (United Nations High Commissioner for Refugees). 1969. "OAU Convention Governing the Specific Aspects of the Refugee Problems in Africa." September 10. Available at http://www.unhcr.org/en-us/about-us/background/45dc1a682/oau -convention-governing-specific-aspects-refugee-problems-africa-adopted.html.

———. 2006. *Statistical Yearbook, 2004: Trends in Displacement, Protection and Solutions*. Geneva: UNHCR. Available at http://www.unhcr.org/statistics/country/ 44e96c842/unhcr-statistical-yearbook-2004.html.

———. 2015. *UNHCR Statistical Yearbook, 2014*." Geneva: UNHCR. Available at http:// www.unhcr.org/en-us/statistics/country/566584fc9/unhcr-statistical-yearbook -2014-14th-edition.html.

———. 2016. "Resettlement and Other Admission Pathways for Syrian Refugees." April 29. Available at https://www.ecre.org/wp-content/uploads/2014/12/www.unhcr.org _52b2febafc5.pdf.

Wallis, Lara. 2015. "South Africa: Operation Fiela—Sweeping Dignity Aside." *All Africa*, May 18. Available at http://allafrica.com/stories/201505181057.html.

Wellman, Elizabeth Iams, and Loren B. Landau. 2015. "South Africa's Tough Lessons on Migrant Policy." *Foreign Policy*, October 13. Available at https://foreignpolicy .com/2015/10/13/south-africas-tough-lessons-on-migrant-policy.

Whitaker, Beth Elise. 2005. "Citizens and Foreigners: Democratization and the Politics of Exclusion in Africa." *African Studies Review* 48 (1): 109–126.

"Why Assassins Are Hunting These Burundian Refugees in Kenya." 2016. *PBS News-Hour*, April 26. Available at http://www.pbs.org/newshour/bb/why-assassins-are -hunting-these-burundian-refugees-in-kenya.

Wintour, Patrick. 2016. "Countries Not Fulfilling Pledges to Help Refugees, Report Finds." *The Guardian*, May 20. Available at https://www.theguardian.com/world/ 2016/may/20/countries-who-pledged-to-help-syrian-refugees-not-doing-it-report -finds.

Yackley, Ayla Jean. 2016. "Kenya Will Close World's Biggest Refugee Camp This Year." *Reuters*, May 23. Available at https://www.reuters.com/article/us-humanitarian -summit-kenya-somalia-idUSKCN0YE2E8.

Zolberg, Aristide, Astri Suhrke, and Sergio Aguayo. 1989. *Escape from Violence: Conflict and Refugee Crisis in the Developing World*. New York: Oxford University Press.

"Zuma's Son Wants Foreigners out of the Country." 2015. *Mail and Guardian*, April 1. Available at http://mg.co.za/article/2015-04-01-zumas-son-wants-foreigners-out-of -the-country.

Human Security and the Perils of (Partial) Peace

Human Rights after Cease-Fires

Neil A. Englehart

ivil war is bad for human rights: Hobbes opines that nothing can be worse than "the miseries, and horrible calamities, that accompany a Civill Warre," with the worst calamity of all being the "continual Feare, and danger of violent death" it presents (1958, 238, 186). Armed combatants seek not only to kill each other but also to intimidate or destroy each other's supporters or simply use the chaos to prey on civilians and settle old grudges. Numerous studies confirm that the violence unleashed by civil war harms respect for human rights. Thus, if conflict promotes human rights abuses, its cessation should decrease them, so cease-fires should improve the human rights situation even if they do not fully resolve the problems that fed the conflict.

Unfortunately, cease-fires rarely have this palliative effect. Unlike peace agreements, cease-fires typically do not require rebels to disband or disarm. Combatants may refrain from violence against each other, but that does not mean they will necessarily refrain from violence against civilians. Practices and patterns of interaction with civilians developed during wartime persist on both the government and rebel sides. From the perspective of civilians, security and human rights may not be much improved by cease-fires.

Armed groups may persist in abusive behavior following cease-fires out of habit or financial necessity. At least one influential study of nonstate armed groups explicitly assumes that the behavior of groups is fixed at birth, with their origins determining their future activities (Weinstein 2007). Governments may be reluctant to insist on disarmament and the end of abuses for fear of pushing groups back into insurgency.

Groups with better human rights records are not necessarily more likely to seek cease-fires. It could be that groups prone to terrorize civilians are also more likely to agree to cease-fires because they are more willing to accept government support and that governments may be more eager to recruit them because of their perceived benefits as proxies or force multipliers. If so, we would not expect the cease-fires to improve the behavior of these groups, since their behavior predisposed them to negotiate cease-fires in the first place.

The behavior of groups that do change after cease-fires might actually get worse. Insurgent groups that depend on civilian support may have incentives to restrain abuses against civilian supporters, following Mao's (2000) dictum that the guerrilla should swim like a fish in the sea of the peasantry. The behavior of groups with government support differs from that of groups without such support, at least partly because government-supported groups need to maintain official support (Carey, Mitchell, and Lowe 2013; Englehart 2016). We might therefore expect groups that accept government support following cease-fire agreements to start behaving in ways similar to those of other government-supported groups.

There are at least two sets of questions to explore with respect to the behavior of cease-fire groups. One is whether more abusive or less abusive groups are more likely to make cease-fire agreements with governments. The other is whether their behavior changes after cease-fires and, if so, whether it tends to change for better or worse. To address these questions, I begin with case studies of cease-fire agreements in Burma/Myanmar and Northeast India. I then explore whether these examples can be generalized by examining human rights after cease-fires using new data on nonstate armed groups from twenty-three Asian countries. The conclusion is that cease-fire groups do tend to be more abusive than non-cease-fire groups even prior to the cease-fire. After cease-fires, they tend to remain abusive, but there is some change in their behavior so that the pattern of abuses they commit begins to resemble that of government-supported groups more than that of antigovernment groups.

Case Study: Myanmar

Myanmar has suffered the world's longest-running civil war, beginning with the Karen and Communist rebellions launched at independence in 1948 (Lintner 1994; Smith 1999). The grievances behind these insurrections included the ambiguous citizenship status of many of the country's ethnic minority groups. Insurgency was feasible because of natural resources and minerals, such as timber and gems, which led to severe environmental consequences. The conflict has involved serious abuse of the human rights of civilians, in particular causing enormous suffering to minority groups in combat zones. These abuses include the persecution of hill peoples and the Rohingya, both provoking refugee flows into neighboring countries.

There has been a decades-long string of cease-fire agreements between rebels and the government. Table 5.1 shows the major agreements that followed the watershed 1988 crackdown on democracy activists; if extended back to 1948, it would show a lengthy history of cease-fires made and broken, with some groups shifting back and forth between supporting and opposing the government multiple times. Recent negotiations between the government and the country's oldest and most consistently antigovernment insurgent group, the Karen National Union (KNU), suggest that the country's civil strife may be nearing an end. However, fighting continues between some other groups and the government, and as Heather Smith-Cannoy discusses in Chapter 7, renewed violence against the Rohingya minority in Rakhine State has led to the creation of at least one new insurgent group.

The history of the previous cease-fire agreements between the government and armed groups is sobering. The cease-fires have actually done little to reduce the number or size of armed groups. The current practice of cease-fires in Myanmar does tend to change the incentives and behavior of armed groups, but not necessarily in ways that make them less violent or more respectful of human rights.

Armed groups in Myanmar can be divided roughly into three types. When we think of nonstate armed groups, we typically picture antigovernment insurgents: rebels who fight government forces and claim to protect local populations. However, as in many other conflicts, there are also a large number of pro-government groups in Myanmar, which are used by the government as force multipliers or foils against opposition groups (Carey, Mitchell, and Lowe 2013). Many groups in this category started out in opposition to the government but switched sides after negotiating cease-fire arrangements. The third type are neutral groups, consisting largely of local forces raised to protect criminal operations such as drug smuggling. Although such groups commonly collude with or pay off government officials, they tend not to act as proxies for the government against other armed groups. These categories are not fixed, and groups shift between them over time.

The government has actively sought cease-fire agreements with insurgent groups at various times, both to reduce the size of opposition forces and to recruit groups to act as auxiliary forces. Most cease-fires in Myanmar have been unwritten, informal agreements, which have created a patchwork of different arrangements in different areas (Callahan 2007; Kramer 2007).

TABLE 5.1 MAIN MYANMAR CEASE-FIRE GROUPS

Group	Size	Year of cease-fire
Myanmar National Democratic Alliance Army	1,000	1989
National Democratic Alliance Army–Eastern Shan State	3,500	1989
New Democratic Army–Kachin	400	1989
Shan State Army–North	10,000	1989
United Wa State Party/Army	20,000	1989/2011
Kachin Defense Army	2,000	1991
Palaung State Liberation Party	700	1991
Pao National Organization	300	1991
Kachin Independence Organisation	4,000	1994
Shan Nationalities People's Liberation Organisation	250	1994
Democratic Karen Buddhist Army	6,000	1995
New Mon State Party	700	1995
Shan State National Army	3,500	1995
Mong Tai Army	3,000	1996
Karen National Liberation Army Peace Council	300	2007/2012
Arakan Liberation Party	80	2012
Chin National Army	200	2012
Democratic Karen Buddhist Army Brigade 5	1,500	2012
Karen National Union	7,500	2012
Karenni National Progressive Party	600	2012
National Democratic Alliance Army–Eastern Shan State	3,000	2012
National Mon State Party	770	2012
National Socialist Council of Nagaland–Khaplang	500	2012
Pa-O National Organiszation	900	2012
Shan State Army	3,000	2012
Shan State Army–South	5,000	2012
Total armed strength, cease-fire groups	78,700	

Note: Lists are not exhaustive. The government lists several very small cease-fire groups that are not reported here because no size estimates are available. Several smaller non-cease-fire groups also operate, but information about them is also limited. The Mong Tai Army was formally dissolved in 1996, but elements still operate in support of the government. The Myanmar National Democratic Alliance Army was attacked by the government in August 2009; its continued operation is unclear. The Karenni National Progressive Party reached a cease-fire agreement with the government in 1995, but it rapidly broke down, and the group went back into insurgency.

Relatively few groups have actually disarmed or disbanded, although in the 2000s the government began to actively press many groups to become a Border Guard Force (BGF) under the command of officers from the Myanmar military. As a result, the cease-fires have sometimes reduced the number or size of antigovernment groups but have multiplied the number and size of pro-government and neutral groups. At the same time, disgruntled splinter groups often emerge to challenge the cease-fire leaders, so the reduction in the number of antigovernment groups is less than one might expect.

The 1988 collapse of the Burma Socialist Programme Party (BSPP), the accompanying demonstrations, and subsequent military crackdown sparked a wave of cease-fires.[1] The military junta that replaced the BSPP was afraid it would be caught between Burman opposition groups and the ethnic insurgencies. It had good reasons for concern, as one effect of the 1988 crackdown was a short-term increase in the number and size of opposition armed groups. Democracy activists fleeing the government swelled the ranks of existing groups and created their own, including the highly durable All Burma Student's Democratic Front (ABSDF). The KNU helped the ABSDF and other nascent groups with arms and training, seeking allies and antigovernment proxy forces.

At the same time, the number of pro-government armed groups also increased as part of a steady trend involving the recruitment of government militias to act as spoilers and force multipliers. As Figure 5.1 shows, the number of antigovernment armed groups jumped between 1988 and 1989.

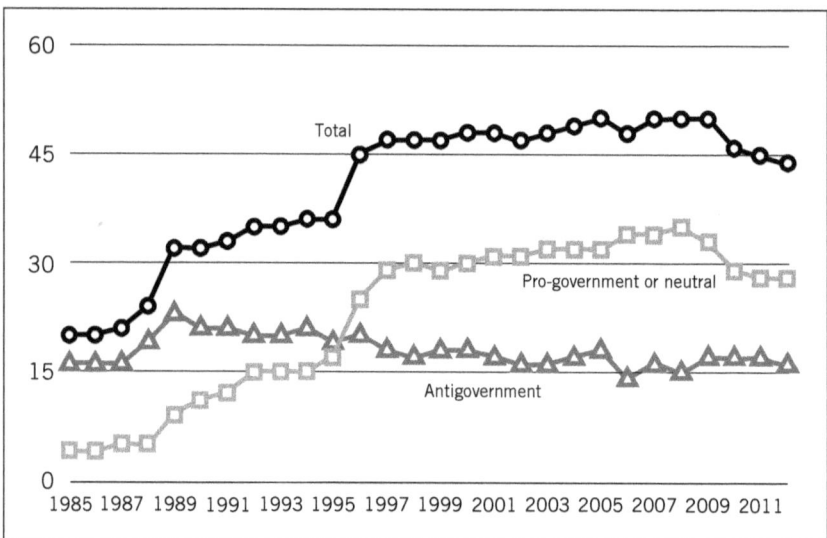

Figure 5.1 Number of armed groups in Burma/Myanmar, 1985–2012

The upward trend in pro-government and neutral groups continued after 1989, as the government actively sought cease-fire agreements to neutralize antigovernment groups.

The government experienced an extraordinary stroke of luck in 1989, when the largest and most powerful armed opposition group, the Communist Party of Burma (CPB), disintegrated because of the loss of Chinese patronage and internal dissension (Lintner 1990; Smith 1999). The CPB's armed forces split into several successor groups, many with an ethnic basis. Four of these negotiated cease-fire agreements with the government almost immediately: the Myanmar National Democratic Alliance Army (MNDAA), the New Democratic Army (NDA), the United Wa State Army (UWSA), and the National Democratic Alliance Army (NDAA). Three of the four had an ethnic basis: the MNDAA was Kokang Chinese, the NDA was Kachin, and the UWSA was Wa. The long-standing Shan insurgent group the Shan State Army (SSA; sometimes known as the Shan State Army–North) also negotiated a cease-fire with the government in 1989. Another three groups negotiated cease-fires with the government in 1991. Figure 5.1 shows the resulting decline in the number of antigovernment groups and a corresponding increase in the number of pro-government or neutral groups. After 1989 the number of pro-government and neutral groups drives the trend in the data on the total number of groups.

The size of nonstate forces also increased over this period as well, as seen in Figure 5.2. The size of antigovernment forces jumped in 1989 but then

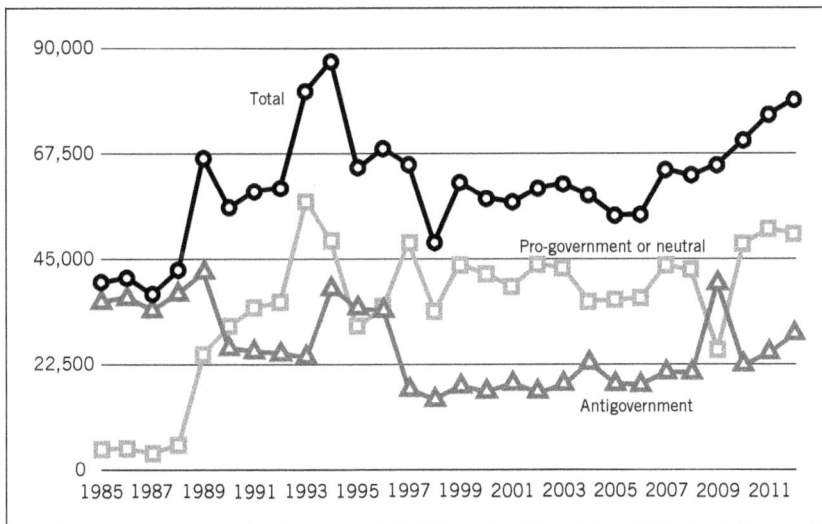

Figure 5.2 Total size of armed groups in Burma/Myanmar, 1985–2012

immediately began to drop as cease-fire agreements switched groups into the pro-government/neutral category. The pro-government/neutral trend is sharply upward and accounts for most of the increase in the total size of nonstate forces in Myanmar that continued into the mid-1990s.

The military government continued to seek cease-fire agreements with armed groups through the mid-1990s. Between 1994 and 1996 a further six major groups agreed to cease-fires. This resulted in a gradual reduction in the number of antigovernment groups and a corresponding increase in the number of pro-government and neutral groups.

The cease-fire agreements of the 1990s did lead to a decline in the total number of and size of armed nonstate groups. However, both the number and size of groups began to increase again in the 2000s, in direct response to cease-fire agreements. Disgruntled leaders from cease-fire groups sometimes break away to form splinter groups. They may be ideologically opposed to the cease-fire or dissatisfied with their share of the government benefits offered to the leaders of the cease-fire groups. In addition, there is often popular support for splinter groups by local people seeking protection from the depredations of the Burmese military and its allied nonstate armed groups.

One might assume that the cease-fires would at least reduce the size of the forces opposed to the government. As Figure 5.2 shows, this is not really the case. As cease-fire groups begin to draw on government resources to maintain their forces, it appears that non-cease-fire groups are able to take advantage of the popular support and economic resources formerly exploited by the original opposition group. This permits them to field forces similar in size to those of the original group. Thus, a cease-fire can increase not only the number of groups, because of the splinter effect, but also the total size of nonstate forces, because of recruiting by the new splinter organizations.

Only in the late 2000s and early 2010s was there a substantial drop in the total number of groups, primarily the result of the government forcing a number of cease-fire groups to reform as a BGF under military officers. The government successfully pressured six of the groups included in these data, mainly smaller groups completely dependent on government support.

However, the BGF process had the unintended consequence of increasing the size of both pro-government and antigovernment armed groups. The leaders of cease-fire groups began to expand their forces and seek new resources to resist government pressure to become a BGF. Antigovernment groups, meanwhile, also responded by increasing in size because they were concerned about the government's strengthening position, increased influence, and improved access to their bases of operation. The armed strength of both pro- and antigovernment forces increased in the late 2000s as a consequence.

The mistrust between the government and cease-fire groups came to a head in 2009, when the government sought to compel one of the CPB successor groups, the MNDAA, to become a BGF. MNDAA forces resisted, leading to a major outbreak of violence. This episode alarmed other cease-fire groups and led to additional clashes between government forces and the UWSA, another CPB successor group and the largest of the cease-fire groups. The abrupt decrease in pro-government/neutral forces in 2009 and the equivalent increase in the size of antigovernment forces seen in Figure 5.2 result from the temporary breakdown of these cease-fire agreements. Some of these agreements were subsequently renewed, but both pro- and antigovernment forces have increased in size as a result of the increased tension. The mean size for all kinds of groups decreased from a high of 2,041 in 1989 to a low of 1,080 in 1998, but it increased to 2,023 in 2014.

The constitutional process that culminated in the 2010 election included a renewed effort by the government to develop cease-fire agreements (Burma News International 2014), and a large number of additional cease-fires have been negotiated since the election (see Table 5.1). Many of these are cease-fires in name only, as hostilities have continued. In such cases the group is still coded as antigovernment based on its behavior.

One of the recent agreements has been especially important: in 2012 the KNU, one of the larger groups still fighting the government, agreed to a cease-fire. It is the oldest surviving insurgent group in Myanmar, having started fighting the government in 1948. Even more important, the KNU had helped nurture many other insurgent groups. The KNU cease-fire thus has had symbolic effects that outweigh its military significance.

The cease-fires have not reduced the size of Myanmar's nonstate armed groups; nor have they improved the human rights behavior of groups. Both pro- and antigovernment forces have engaged in well-documented abuses against civilians (see, e.g., SHRF and SWAN 2002; Human Rights Watch 2002, 2009, 2012; Network for Human Rights Documentation–Burma 2010).

Some cease-fire groups are particularly notorious, for instance, the Democratic Karen Buddhist Army (DKBA), which recently renamed itself the Democratic Karen Benevolent Army. The DKBA split from the KNU in 1994, at least in part over differences between Buddhists in the KNU rank and file and its predominantly Christian leadership. It rapidly negotiated a cease-fire agreement with the government and began operating regularly with military units. The DKBA now engages in many of the same abuses as the military units with which it operates, including sexual assaults, murder of civilians, theft, destruction of property, and forced movement of civilians.

Some other groups maintain fairly constant patterns of behavior after cease-fires. The KNU, for instance, has been quite consistent in its human rights behavior since the early 2000s. The group's record is hardly perfect: It engages in extortion and forcible conscription, including the recruitment of child soldiers. However, this behavior has not changed significantly since the 2012 cease-fire. Similarly, the Karenni National Progressive Party has had a relatively clean human rights record since the mid-2000s, which has not changed significantly since it renewed its cease-fire agreement with the government in 2012.

Negotiating a cease-fire can change the incentives of leaders of armed groups, however. Cease-fire groups usually receive financial incentives from the government, including natural resource concessions; import-export licenses; lucrative business opportunities; and in some cases direct transfers of food, supplies, and cash. This relieves cease-fire groups from the need to finance themselves, reducing incentives to engage in fund-raising activities such as theft, extortion, and kidnapping for ransom. However, they are also often expected to cooperate with the military against non-cease-fire groups and their civilian supporters. This can lead to an increase in abuses aimed at terrorizing civilians, including rape and torture, which are more commonly associated with government-supported groups. Because they can no longer claim to be protecting civilian coethnics from the government, they may have more difficulty recruiting, leading to an increase in forcible conscription.

The government of Myanmar has already begun to lift the financial burdens of the recent cease-fire groups. For instance, it has distributed automobile import licenses to the groups' leaders. The government's chief negotiator, Aung Min, reportedly passed envelopes containing the permits personally to armed group leaders attending a 2014 Union Day ceremony. Because of import restrictions and high tariffs, these licenses are extremely valuable (Saw Yan Naing 2014). Some groups have also been permitted to open lucrative businesses and awarded government natural resource concessions (Saw Yan Naing 2013b, 2014). Such concessions weaken the reliance of armed groups on civilian supporters and increase their dependence on the government, potentially setting in motion the transformation common to the earlier cease-fire groups.

The political context in which the newer cease-fires have occurred might be described as one of optimism tempered by experience. Myanmar's process of political reform has been halting and partial. Despite criticism by activists that current and former military officers remain too important in the government, there have been significant structural changes in the way political power is distributed that have had the effect of increasing political pluralism (Englehart 2012). However, increasing violence against Rohingya has accompanied improvements in toleration for the political opposition. Furthermore, there has been no effort to address the continued dominance of the ethnic Burman population over minority ethnic groups or resolve the country's ongoing problems of state capacity and poor governance (Englehart 2005). In the absence of a robust and independent judiciary, police who enjoy the confidence of citizens, a tax system that can support the military so that soldiers are not encouraged to steal land and food from local populations, and a military effectively constrained by civilian leadership, it is not surprising that Myanmar's armed groups are reluctant to disarm.

Over the past three years the government and cease-fire groups have engaged in lengthy negotiations about a comprehensive national cease-fire agreement, which presumably would pave the way for a more permanent peace agreement, the integration of some nonstate forces into the military, and the disarmament of the remainder (Nyein Nyein 2013; Saw Yan Naing 2013a, 2014, 2016). The danger of a nationwide cease-fire is that it will create a situation in which both former rebels and government forces can collude to commit abuses against civilians. This is not a theoretical worry: as shown previously, such collusion has been common in the ad hoc cease-fire arrangements negotiated over the last twenty-five years.

Myanmar's long history of abuse related to the civil war has been hard on the civilian population. The potential for a national cease-fire is enticing, but it must be carefully constructed to satisfy not only the interests of the parties negotiating it: the military, the central government, and the insurgent groups. To be successful at promoting peace and stability in the long run, it must also protect the interests of the civilian population. The cessation of hostilities alone will not achieve this, any more than the earlier cease-fire agreements did. A well-crafted nationwide cease-fire must protect civilians from both government and antigovernment forces, and this will require a break from past practice, not just of war but also of cease-fires.

The case of Myanmar thus suggests that cease-fire agreements are not necessarily good for human rights. Although the cessation of conflict should in theory be associated with fewer abuses, in practice governments and groups often reach cease-fires to accommodate mutual interests, which may not include the security and well-being of civilians. This not only is a feature of authoritarian government but has persisted throughout Myanmar's gradual process of democratization, which began in 2008, and is also found in the much more democratic context of Northeast India.

Case Study: United Liberation Front of Assam and Surrendered United Liberation Front of Assam in Northeast India

The dynamics described in Myanmar can be found in a slightly different form in India's equally conflict-prone northeastern region, where multiple interconnected insurgencies have complex and close relations with state governments and political parties that may collude in the victimization of civilians (Baruah 2005; Lacina 2009). An example is the case of the United Liberation Front of Assam (ULFA) and its factions that have entered into cease-fires with the government, known as surrendered ULFA or SULFA.

ULFA is an insurgent group founded in 1979 to resist "colonial" rule in the region by the Indian government. The founding ceremony was held in the former palace of the kings of Assam, symbolically emphasizing the region's independence prior to the British conquest. ULFA's cadres regard the independent Indian state not as a liberating force but as a continuation of the British colonial regime. The issues that fuel the movement involve multiple interconnected problems: immigration into the region from other parts of India, domination of the economy by nonlocals, high unemployment among the Assamese, and government and police corruption. Through the 1980s the group enjoyed considerable local support, especially after the Indian military launched a series of repressive campaigns in Assam that did not distinguish too carefully between insurgents and ordinary Assamese (Baruah 2005; Mahanta 2012; Human Rights Watch 1993). The group also enjoyed some support from the Pakistani and Bangladeshi intelligence agencies and was able to establish safe base areas in Bhutan and Myanmar. It paid for training from the Kachin Independence Army in Myanmar as well. By the mid-1980s it controlled a substantial zone within Assam, running a parallel government that included public services such as policing, a court system, education, and some infrastructure development (Mahanta 2013).

ULFA came under increasing military pressure in the 1990s when the Indian army launched a series of brutal campaigns against them. The liberated zone began to shrink, and foreign allies began to abandon the group. The military was guilty of significant human rights abuses in Assam. However, the pattern of ULFA abuses also began to shift in response to the crackdown. These changes were closely connected to changes the group was forced to make in its financing strategy.

Financing for ULFA was primarily local and initially included donations from sympathizers and taxation of communities within the liberated zone. However, much of the financing also came from illicit activities, including extortion from businesses and nonsupporters, drug smuggling, and robberies. As government counterinsurgency campaigns took their toll on the group and the liberated zone began to shrink, these illicit forms of financing became more important. In response, from the early 1990s ULFA became increasingly predatory on the local population, in particular adding kidnapping for ransom to its resource strategy.

As a consequence of the military campaign, beginning in 1992 significant numbers of ULFA cadres began to surrender to the government, some-

times in whole units. These cadres were permitted to retain their arms, ostensibly as protection against ULFA revenge attacks. As a result of the
surrenders, the government obtained a ready-made counterinsurgency force,
the so-called SULFA, already armed and trained and well versed in ULFA's
strategic objectives and tactics.

SULFA is not a tightly organized group. It is factionalized around leaders
who surrendered at different times, with an especially strong tension between those who surrendered between 1992 and 1996, who tend to be aligned
with the Congress Party, and those who surrendered in 1998, who tend to be
associated with the Assamese party Asom Gana Parishad. These differences
can, however, be useful, as some faction of the group will be allied with
whichever party holds power in the Assam state government. In practice, the
different factions are not ideological and cooperate on issues of mutual interest (Sahni and Routray 2001).

Despite these alliances with political parties, support for the demobiliza-
tion of surrendered ULFA cadres never matched the government's promises.
As a result, many SULFA cadres never disarmed and continue the financing
behavior they engaged in before surrendering: extortion, drug smuggling,
robbery, and kidnapping for ransom. Members operating legitimate businesses also coerce and intimidate competitors as a way to improve their market position and obtain government contracts. SULFA leaders are typically
never held accountable for crimes committed before or after their surrender.
Their behavior is tolerated so they will not return to insurgency and so the
government can continue to employ them as a counterinsurgency force
(Sahni and Routray 2001; Prakash 2008).

In other words, the Indian government has treated SULFA in ways that
are very similar to the ways in which the Myanmar military has treated its
cease-fire groups. Both the Myanmar and Indian governments actively seek
to use cease-fire groups as counterinsurgency forces. Governments therefore
do not have an interest in disarming them or in curbing their abuses; indeed,
they may intend that cease-fire groups commit abuses against civilian supporters of insurgents. In Assam, however, abuses have not reached the critical threshold that would prompt large-scale refugee movements.

The next section examines a broader array of groups in other countries
to determine whether the changing pattern of abuse is common to many
cease-fires or a peculiarity of these two cases.

Data and Methods

The human rights consequences of cease-fires are examined here using data
on 236 armed groups from twenty-three Asian countries (Bangladesh, Bhutan, Brunei, Burma/Myanmar, Cambodia, China, Fiji, India, Indonesia,

Japan, Laos, Malaysia, Nepal, New Zealand, Pakistan, Papua New Guinea, the Philippines, Singapore, Sri Lanka, Taiwan, Thailand, Timor-Leste, and Vietnam). The time period covered by the data is 1985–2014.[2] Because some groups operate across borders, it is most productive to investigate neighboring countries in turn. This group of Asian countries constitutes an extremely diverse set in terms of economic development, level of democracy, conflict history, culture, colonial legacies, size, population, terrain, and religious and ethnic diversity.

These data were collected to reflect a broad range of nonstate armed groups. The goal was to include all groups that could reasonably be construed as representing a threat to the state's monopoly of the use of force, defined as exhibiting certain minimal characteristics: groups must have an armed strength of at least one hundred at some point in their existence, be armed with firearms or explosives, persist at least one year, and have an identifiable command structure. Government-supported groups are included, but only if they do not come under the command structure of state security forces, for example, by being commanded by serving military officers.[3] Group behavior per se was not a criterion for inclusion, because that is the subject under investigation.

Groups change over time along many dimensions, and many of the most interesting questions about them involve the causes, consequences, and dynamics of change. To capture change, the data are in a group-year format similar to the country-year format used in cross-national time-series analyses, widely employed to analyze the dynamics of state behavior over time. Each line of data represents one year for each group, with a total of 4,058 lines or group-years of data. This structure means that groups do not need to be characterized according to their behavior at a single point in time as insurgent, pro-government, terrorist, or some other category. Instead, group behavior and resources can be analyzed as they change over time.

The results of a crude first cut comparing the incidence of human rights abuse for all group-years in which there were cease-fires with those in which they were not shows that the incidence of abuse is only slightly less among cease-fire groups: they commit abuses of some kind in 72.1 percent of group-years, as opposed to 75.4 percent for non-cease-fire groups. This is not a statistically significant difference.

Table 5.2 breaks down the data in more detail, examining changes over time and separating abuses by type. When we confine the analysis to only cease-fire groups, the number of cases drops dramatically. In total the data include 433 group-years of cease-fires. Most of the cease-fires are concentrated in three countries: Myanmar (154 group-years), India (120 group-years), and the Philippines (96 group-years). All occur in the context of longstanding insurgencies, and some persist for long periods of time. There are

TABLE 5.2 INCIDENCE OF ABUSE BY CEASE-FIRE AND NON-CEASE-FIRE GROUPS

	All groups (%)	Before cease-fire (%)	One-year change (%)	Three-year change (%)	Government-supported groups (%)
No abuse	25	16	0	0	–19***
Kill civilians	41	50	–9**	–16*	–14***
Kidnapping	27	48	–2	–9*	–20***
Forcible conscription	8	7	–2	–3	+2**
Kill government officials	11	11	0	–3	–9***
Property damage	25	30	0	–6	–17***
Theft	11	11	+4	–3	–3***
Rape	4	5	0	0	+5***
Forced labor	5	5	0	0	–3***
Forced movement	3	7	+2	0	+2***
Child soldiers	26	25	+2	0	–7***
Extortion	46	66	0	+3	–31***
Religious freedom	12	9	0	+3	–9***
Torture	7	9	0	+3	+9***
Freedom of movement	5	5	+2	+3	+4***
Civil rights	20	2	+6	+9*	+7***
N	4,058	57	54	32	4,058

Note: "All groups" and "Before ceasefire" columns show mean values; "One-year change" and "Three-year change" columns show mean change over time; and "Government support" column shows mean difference between government-supported and non-government-supported groups, where a positive number indicates abuse committed more often by government-supported groups and a negative number indicates abuse committed more often by non-government-supported groups. *significant at the .10 level; **significant at the .05 level; ***significant at the .01 level.

only fifty-seven separate cease-fires in the data, with fifty-four persisting one year, and only thirty-two persisting three years. This makes meaningful multivariate analysis impossible. Even bivariate compare means tests require major differences to achieve statistical significance. With these caveats in mind, the results do show some interesting patterns.

It is notable that cease-fire groups tend to be more abusive than non-cease-fire groups even prior to agreeing to the cease-fire. The mean value for "no abuse" is 24.6 percent across all country-years. However, the groups that agree to cease-fires tend to be more abusive, committing no abuses in the year prior to the cease-fire in only 16 percent of cases. Furthermore, there is no change in the "no abuse" category after one or three years of a cease-fire. In fact, the close values for abuses by cease-fire and non-cease-fire groups across all country-years (see Table 5.2) result from a handful of long-running cease-fires with groups that have relatively good human rights records. The typical cease-fire group is actually more prone to abuse than the average nonstate armed group even before agreeing to the cease-fire.

Things become more complicated when we look at individual abuses. Some abuses do decline after cease-fires, including killing civilians, kidnapping, and forcible recruitment. All of these remain at a lower level after three years. Property damage and killing government officials also drop off after three years, despite not changing after only one year.

Theft displays a paradoxical pattern, increasing after one year but then declining after three years. Forced movement and use of child soldiers increase after one year but then decline to pre-cease-fire levels at three years. Some abuses show no impact at all from cease-fires. Rape and forced labor remain at their pre-cease-fire levels after one and three years.

Other abuses increase after cease-fires. Extortion, torture, and abuses of religious freedom are unchanged after one year but increase by the third year. Restrictions on freedom of movement and civil rights increase in the first year and increase even more by the third year.

Forced movement here indicates that the group directly compelled people to leave their homes. In some cases these refugees crossed borders, while in others they became internally displaced. Conversely, violations of freedom of movement indicate that groups prevented people from moving, meaning that some groups actually forcibly block refugee movements. Indirect drivers of movement, such as fear of being caught between warring factions, are not captured in the data. Notably, both forced movement and freedom of movement violations increase substantially after cease-fires, although they are relatively rare forms of abuse overall.

The net effect of cease-fires thus appears to be minimal: There is no change in the overall incidence of abuses. However, there are clearly changes to the pattern of abuses. To some degree these differences parallel the differences between government-supported and non-government-supported groups more broadly, as shown in the last column of Table 5.2. Abuses on average committed more often by government-supported groups are marked with a plus sign (+), while those more often committed by non-government-supported groups are marked with a minus sign (–). In general, government-supported groups tend to terrorize civilians, and antigovernment groups are more likely to commit abuses that raise funds and extract resources from civilians. The logic of this is fairly straightforward: Groups that are not funded and supplied by the government need to raise their own funds. At the same time, they typically need to be more concerned with civilian support and therefore often avoid terrorizing civilian populations. Conversely, government-supported groups typically do not need to worry about funding and supplies so have less need to commit economically motivated abuses

(Englehart 2016). However, they are often used as proxies or force multipliers by governments and are expected to commit abuses to terrorize the enemies of the government, something Bruce B. Campbell and Arthur D. Brenner (2002) characterize as "murder with deniability" (see also Hangzo and Kaur 2011; Carey, Mitchell, and Lowe 2013).

Many of the abuses that decline after cease-fires, including killing civilians, killing government officials, kidnapping, and property damage, are those associated with groups not supported by governments. However, forcible conscription, which is more associated with government-supported groups, also decreases. Conversely, for the seven abuses that increase after cease-fires, four are associated with government-supported groups: forced movement, torture, restrictions on freedom of movement, and abuses of civil rights. However, three abuses more commonly associated with non-government-supported groups are also found in this category: use of child soldiers, extortion, and abuse of religious freedom.

Forced movement and restrictions on freedom of movement are both increased by government support, suggesting again these abuses increase as a consequence of government influence over armed-group behavior. In both cases government support nearly doubles their incidence from the baseline value for all groups, although it should be borne mind that these are relatively uncommon abuses to begin with.

It appears, therefore, that not only are cease-fire groups more abusive to begin with, but they tend to become somewhat more like government-supported groups over time and less like independent groups. Seven types of abuses move in that direction, and four move in the opposite direction. Two show no change, and one (theft) displays paradoxical change over time. Clearly, other factors are involved, but the general trend seems to be for cease-fire groups to migrate toward abusive behavior more characteristic of government-supported groups.

Conclusion

Even with these limited data we can begin to offer tentative answers to our questions. The overall level of abusiveness of groups does not change significantly after cease-fires, but the behavior of the groups that conclude cease-fires is, on average, worse to begin with than that of the "typical" non-state armed group.

There is, however, a change in the pattern of abuses groups commit before and after cease-fires. The behavior of cease-fire groups does on balance come to resemble that of government-supported groups more than that of non-government-supported groups. This makes sense, because many cease-fire groups begin to receive government support, which alters their incentives. Whether they contribute to forced migration, for instance, appears to depend on government policy. In Myanmar, where the government sought to displace minority populations perceived as supporting insurgents, cease-fire groups participated in that activity. In Assam, where the government never sought to displace civilians as a matter of policy, cease-fire group activities never passed the threshold of abuse that would prompt large-scale migration.

Cease-fires thus do not appear to have the effect of alleviating suffering and reducing human rights abuse. They may shift the types of abuses groups engage in. However, by their nature they do not result in the disarmament or disbandment of groups, which remain in the field with their arms, ready and able to commit abuses.

Full-fledged peace agreements are likely to have different dynamics. They more often involve the disbandment of armed groups, disarmament, and the reintegration of fighters into civilian life. As a consequence, armed groups that conclude peace agreements lose their corporate capacity for violent abuses. Even where peace agreements do not entail disarmament, they generally encourage greater accountability by integrating nonstate armed groups into the apparatus of government. The agreement between the Moro National Liberation Front (MNLF) and the government of the Philippines, for instance, created an autonomous region initially governed by the rebels. Such arrangements create greater responsibility and accountability for insurgent groups, which may tend to reduce abuses. The MNLF, for instance, did significantly moderate its behavior after the peace agreement, despite retaining its armed forces. It has maintained this improved record despite its leaders being subsequently voted out of office.

Other problems may ensue from peace agreements, including revenge attacks by both ex-insurgents and government security forces and renewed government repression of minority groups. As Chapter 6 argues, the quality of transitional justice is likely to have an important effect on human rights protections after conflict. Transitional justice mechanisms that leave past abuses unpunished may encourage revenge attacks by ex-combatants, for instance. There are too few peace agreements in the data for a more substantial analysis, but it is clear that peace agreements are far from being problem-free. The MNLF's behavior after the Mindanao peace agreement has been better but not spotless. Violence and abuses have also continued in Nepal following the peace agreement between the government and the Communist Party (Human Rights Watch 2010).

However, cease-fires are worse. The core problem with cease-fire agreements is that they leave groups armed and organized, providing nonstate armed groups and governments opportunities to collude to commit abuses.

In effect, they multiply the number of government-supported nonstate armed groups, and such groups are a major threat to human rights (Carey, Mitchell, and Lowe 2013; Englehart 2016). Peace, whatever problems it may bring, is clearly better than either war or cease-fire. Partial measures to resolve conflict, such as cease-fires, tend not to provide relief for those suffering from human rights abuses.

NOTES

1. Note that the data begin in 1985, so earlier waves of cease-fires are not recorded.

2. The data-collection window does not predate 1985 because of budgetary constraints.

3. There are a handful of cases in which officers still nominally in the security services have broken away to command nonstate armed groups, often in opposition to the government. The so-called Lost Commands in the Philippines are an example. If the group is effectively outside government control, it is included. Conversely, groups that are folded into government-controlled forces and accept government officers exit the data at that point, as has happened with several cease-fire groups in Myanmar.

REFERENCES

Baruah, Sanjib. 2005. *Durable Disorder: Understanding the Politics of Northeast India.* New York: Oxford University Press.

Burma News International. 2014. *Deciphering Myanmar's Peace Process: A Reference Guide, 2014.* Chiang Mai, Thailand: Burma News International. Available at https://www.bnionline.net/sites/bnionline.net/files/publication_docs/deciphering_myanmar_peace_process_2014.pdf.

Callahan, Mary P. 2007. *Political Authority in Burma's Minority States: Devolution, Occupation, and Coexistence.* Washington, DC: East-West Center/ISEA.

Campbell, Bruce B., and Arthur D. Brenner. 2002. *Death Squads in Global Perspective: Murder with Deniability.* New York: Palgrave Macmillan.

Carey, Sabine C., Neil J. Mitchell, and Will Lowe. 2013. "States, the Security Sector, and the Monopoly of Violence: A New Database on Pro-government Militias." *Journal of Peace Research* 50 (2): 249–258.

Englehart, Neil A. 2005. "Is Regime Change Enough for Burma? The Problem of State Capacity." *Asian Survey* 45 (4): 622–644.

———. 2012. "Two Cheers for Burma's Rigged Election." *Asian Survey* 52 (4): 666–686.

———. 2016. "Non-state Armed Groups as a Threat to Global Security: What Threat, Whose Security?" *Journal of Global Security Studies* 1 (2): 171–183.

Hangzo, Paul Khan Khup, and Manpavan Kaur. 2011. *Pro-government Armed Groups: A Source of Peace or Multipliers of Conflict?* Singapore: Consortium for Nontraditional Security Studies.

Hobbes, Thomas. 1958. *Leviathan.* Edited by C. P. Macpherson. New York: Penguin Books.

Human Rights Watch. 1993. "No End in Sight: Human Rights Violations in Assam." Available at https://www.hrw.org/legacy/reports/pdfs/i/indonesa/indones2934.pdf.

———. 2002. *"My Gun Was as Tall as Me": Child Soldiers in Burma.* New York: Human Rights Watch.

———. 2009. "'We Are like Forgotten People': The Chin People of Burma; Unsafe in Burma, Unprotected in India." Available at https://www.hrw.org/report/2009/01/27/we-are-forgotten-people/chin-people-burma-unsafe-burma-unprotected-india.

———. 2010. "Indifference to Duty: Impunity for Crimes Committed in Nepal." Available at https://www.hrw.org/report/2010/12/14/indifference-duty/impunity-crimes-committed-nepal.

———. 2012. "'Untold Miseries': Wartime Abuses and Forced Displacement in Burma's Kachin State." Available at https://www.hrw.org/report/2012/03/20/untold-miseries/wartime-abuses-and-forced-displacement-burmas-kachin-state.

Kramer, Tom. 2007. *The United Wa State Party: Narco-Army or Ethnic Nationalist Party?* Washington, DC: East-West Center/ISEA.

Lacina, Bethany. 2009. "The Problem of Political Stability in Northeast India: Local Ethnic Autocracy and the Rule of Law." *Asian Survey* 49 (6): 998–1020.

Lintner, Bertil. 1990. *The Rise and Fall of the Communist Party of Burma.* Ithaca, NY: Cornell University Southeast Asia Program.

———. 1994. *Burma in Revolt: Opium and Insurgency since 1948.* Bangkok: White Lotus.

Mahanta, Nani Gopal. 2012. "The United Liberation Front of Asom (ULFA): Liberating Force or to Be Liberated?" In *Non-state Armed Groups in South Asia: A Preliminary Structured Focused Comparison,* edited by Anant Arpita, 105–117. New Delhi: Institute for Defense Studies and Analyses.

———. 2013. *Confronting the State: ULFA's Quest for Sovereignty.* Thousand Oaks, CA: Sage.

Mao Zedong. 2000. *On Guerrilla Warfare.* Translated by Samuel B. Griffith. Urbana: University of Illinois Press.

Network for Human Rights Documentation–Burma. 2010. *"We Have to Give Them So Much That Our Stomachs Are Empty of Food": The Hidden Impact of Burma's Arbitrary and Corrupt Taxation.* Chiang Mai, Thailand: Network for Human Rights Documentation–Burma.

Nyein Nyein. 2013. "Peace Talks Turn to Future Federal Army Structure." *The Irrawaddy,* November 22. Available at https://www.irrawaddy.com/news/burma/peace-talks-turn-future-federal-army-structure.html.

Prakash, Ved. 2008. *Terrorism in India's Northeast: A Gathering Storm.* Thousand Oaks, CA: Sage.

Sahni, Ajai, and Bibhu Prasad Routray. 2001. "SULFA: Terror by Another Name." *Faultlines* 9. Available at http://www.satp.org/satporgtp/publication/faultlines/volume9/Article1.htm.

Saw Yan Naing. 2013a. "Govt, Armed Rebels Look Headed for Clash on Federal Army Issue." *The Irrawaddy,* November 28. Available at https://www.irrawaddy.com/news/burma/govt-armed-rebels-look-headed-clash-federal-army-issue.html.

———. 2013b. "'Peace Permit' Bonanza Puts Ethnic Groups on Defensive." *The Irrawaddy,* December 20. Available at https://www.irrawaddy.com/news/burma/peace-permit-bonanza-puts-ethnic-groups-defensive.html.

———. 2014. "Peace Drive." *The Irrawaddy,* August 2. Available at https://www.irrawaddy.com/business/peace-drive.html.

———. 2016. "Suu Kyi's Rushed Peace Conference Worries Ethnic Leaders." *The Irrawaddy,* August 11. Available at https://www.irrawaddy.com/news/burma/suu-kyis-rushed-peace-conference-worries-ethnic-leaders.html.

SHRF (Shan Human Rights Federation) and SWAN (Shan Women's Action Network). 2002. "License to Rape." Available at https://www.shanwomen.org/reports/36 -license-to-rape.

Smith, Martin. 1999. *Burma: Insurgency and the Politics of Ethnicity.* New York: Zed Books.

Weinstein, Jeremy. 2007. *Inside Rebellion: The Politics of Insurgent Violence.* New York: Cambridge University Press.

6

Transitional Justice Mechanisms and Human Rights

BRIAN FREDERKING AND
MAXIMILIAN AVILES

S tates in democratic transitions often struggle with the legacy of human rights atrocities. How should states deal with human rights violators from the previous regime? One approach is for states to use transitional justice mechanisms (TJMs), including truth commissions and tribunals. A consistent theme in the literature on transitional justice is an expectation that TJMs will increase future levels of human rights.[1] Advocates offer a variety of reasons why TJMs should facilitate respect for human rights: (1) they help establish the truth about past human rights abuses; (2) they provide validation, closure, and justice for victims; (3) they hold human rights abusers accountable and potentially deter future abuse; (4) they contribute to the development of the rule of law; and (5) they help reconcile competing groups and establish a durable peace.

In this chapter, we review two important arguments within the transitional justice literature and then present cross-national empirical evidence regarding levels of human rights in countries that have used TJMs. One argument is the peace-versus-justice debate: Should TJMs emphasize political reconciliation among postconflict groups or legal punishment for past human rights violations? What is the more effective and appropriate path for countries in democratic transitions? A second argument is whether TJMs are part of an overall Western liberal project that is likely to fail because they presume universality and ignore local factors. Should we expect Western assumptions and institutions to be effective in non-Western contexts?

Our empirical analysis asks two questions that address these arguments. Do countries in democratic transitions that use TJMs end up with higher levels of human rights in the future than countries in democratic transitions that do not use TJMs? Our analysis suggests that the answer is yes, but only marginally so. While some may consider TJMs part of Western cultural imperialism, the countries that embrace them end up with higher levels of human rights than countries that do not. Are "peace" or "justice" TJMs more effective at raising future levels of human rights? Our analysis suggests that the justice approach is much more effective than the peace approach. Countries that have pursued legal punishment or compensation in the form of tribunals and reparations have higher future levels of human rights than countries that have pursued the peace mechanisms of truth commissions and amnesty.

Transitional Justice Mechanisms: Peace or Justice?

Four central types of TJMs are tribunals, truth commissions, amnesties, and reparations. Tribunals are trials for alleged human rights violators to determine guilt or innocence. Truth commissions are state-sanctioned, temporary bodies that investigate patterns of abuse and make recommendations to prevent future abuses. Amnesties are a promise by the ruling party, sometimes in the form of legislation, not to prosecute or punish past violators. Reparations are compensation given by the state to an individual or group to redress past human rights violations. Truth commissions and amnesties are considered peace TJMs: they emphasize the goals of reconciliation and political stability during democratic transitions. Tribunals and reparations are considered justice TJMs: they emphasize the goals of accountability and deterrence during democratic transitions.

An important part of the TJM literature is the peace-versus-justice debate (Skaar 1999; Sriram 2004). One side advocates the peace TJMs: the perpetrators admit what happened, the victims accept the public apology, no one goes to jail, and the society heals and moves forward with its democratization. The other side advocates the justice TJMs: human rights violators are punished, victims are compensated, and the rule of law is established as a necessary component of any democratic transition. The sides differ on the more viable logic that drives a successful democratic transition—social peace or legal justice?

Advocates of pursuing peace through truth commissions argue that they are more likely to facilitate the necessary political and cultural change for reconciliation by focusing on underlying causes of conflict and human rights abuses rather than on prosecuting individuals (Minow 1998, 2008; Chapman and Ball 2001; Amstutz 2005). Truth-commission advocates fear that the adversarial nature of trials makes reconciliation less likely and may instead promote future violence; that trials focus on a few individuals and are less effective in dealing with systematic abuses; that trials may be unfair if the abuses occurred many years ago or if only lower-level perpetrators rather than the leadership are tried; and that trials may be either impractical or a farce if the perpetrators remain too influential during the transition. Even the prospect of trials may undermine negotiations and present obstacles to ending conflict (Guercio 2015; Grono and O'Brien 2008). Why should leaders agree to a negotiated cease-fire and/or a peaceful transition if part of that process means they will go on trial for past atrocities?

Advocates argue that truth commissions give a voice to the victims of abuse and help a society understand and acknowledge its past. Truth commissions also reconstruct the reasons that led vast numbers of people to forsake basic morality and enable citizens to regain their capacity to determine right and wrong (Dimitrijevic 2006). They reinterpret the past in a way that undermines the official truth of the previous regime. Advocates also cite the therapeutic value for victims of truth telling and receiving the state's acknowledgment of their suffering. Truth commissions incorporate a greater range of victims than tribunals and take a broad view of society that enables them to recommend institutional changes to prevent future atrocities. Overall, the argument is that truth commissions bring accountability to political institutions, increase future support for human rights, restore trust in post-conflict societies, and help create the conditions for future democratization (Valiñas and Vanspauwen 2009).

The successful truth commission in postapartheid South Africa is a major warrant of this argument. James Gibson (2004, 2006) generalizes from his research on South Africa and argues that truth commissions can lead to reconciliation, democratization, and respect for human rights. He points to "macro" factors contributing to reconciliation: a rule-of-law culture, political pluralism (competing centers of power), amnesty, and the extent of injuries perpetrated by the previous regime. Gibson also cites "micro" factors contributing to reconciliation: even-handedness (assigning blame to all sides), leadership, and societal penetration of the process (2006, 421). Such factors can facilitate certain components of reconciliation, including the reduction of political intolerance, support for human rights, institutional legitimacy, and a collective national memory.

Some case studies of other truth commissions support Gibson's arguments. Mark Ensalaco (1994) argues that the truth commissions in Chile and El Salvador were successful precisely because they focused on reconciliation and truth rather than justice and punishment. Christian Tomuschat (2001) argues that the truth commission in Guatemala helped propel the country toward peace by recognizing the acts committed by all sides. Robert

Kwame Ameh (2006) similarly argues that the truth commission in Ghana, despite the difficulties in offering an authoritative account of the truth, will succeed because it did not try to place blame and create a basis for future trials.

Accounts of unsuccessful truth commissions also offer support for the peace approach. Gberie Lansana (2008) argues that the truth commission in Liberia was unsuccessful because it placed blame on only one side and the current political leadership did not support the process—two factors highlighted by Gibson. Martha Nevins (2007) and David Webster (2007) both argue that the reconciliation process in East Timor was unsuccessful because it did not grant amnesty and tried to prosecute offenders who had fled to Indonesia. Without extradition agreements from Indonesia, East Timor was unable to prosecute the alleged offenders, and public support for that approach waned. Elizabeth Evenson (2004) argues that the process in Sierra Leone failed because it included the use of truth commissions and tribunals concurrently, which encouraged conflict in the population rather than reconciliation.

The competing justice argument is that tribunals are often more effective than truth commissions (Stensrud 2009; Tepperman 2002). Tribunals emphasize deterrence, accountability, punishment, and the rule of law. Advocates for tribunals argue that they are the only way to guarantee accountability because not all truth commissions trigger processes that lead to consequences for human rights violators. Similarly, amnesty programs are unacceptable to those who emphasize punishing the guilty (Sadat 2007). For example, Geoff Dancy and Eric Wiebelhaus-Brahm (2015) argue that trials were a necessary condition for successful democratization in Latin America.

In this view, truth commissions are "compromise justice"—inferior alternatives used when the legal system is too weak to prosecute human rights violations (Grodsky 2008, 285; 2009). From this perspective truth commissions are considered weak because they generally have time limits, restrictions on access to evidence, no enforcement powers, and a poor record of implementing recommendations. Advocates argue that only tribunals hold perpetrators accountable for their crimes, affirm that the victims do indeed have fundamental rights, and deter those who might consider such actions in the future.

Some take these tensions so seriously that they argue that TJMs are ultimately counterproductive. Jack Snyder and Leslie Vinjamuri (2004) argue that even truth commissions—if they reveal individual responsibility for crimes—can potentially upset long-term peace because they can foster divergent interpretations of history and generate insecurity for the alleged perpetrators. David Mendeloff (2004) argues that there is little empirical evidence that tribunals or truth commissions provide psychological or emotional benefits to victims. W. James Booth (2001) contends that sometimes the truth causes more suffering than a forced amnesia because it removes the incentive for the elites of the old regime to obstruct the process. Janine Natalya Clark (2011) argues that truth commissions cannot deal with the issue of denial; for example, many Serbian leaders simply do not view their actions as harmful or criminal. Obiora Chinedu Okafor and Uchechukwu Ngwaba (2015) criticize both the use of truth commissions in the Democratic Republic of the Congo and the International Criminal Court in Africa more broadly as unable to promote peace processes in postconflict African nations.

This debate shows the tensions between emphasizing peace or justice during democratic transitions (Vandeginste and Sriram 2011). Pursuing peace rather than justice may seem inadequate to many if the process does not include the punishment of those responsible. To avoid impunity, many human rights advocates cite the necessity of trials. Yet pursuing justice through trials can often hinder the long-term goal of peace by alienating the supporters of the previous regime and preventing the development of future power-sharing arrangements. Similar dynamics result from the policy options to grant amnesty or seek reparations. Combining truth commissions and amnesty risks a situation in which victims do not feel that justice was done. Combining trials and reparations may lead to resentment and animosity among the social groups privileged by the previous regime and prevent the reconciliation necessary for long-term peace. The official UN position recognizes these tensions and also attempts to walk a fine line—it discourages both trials and blanket amnesties for serious crimes prior to forming new governments (United Nations 2010).

Transitional Justice as Western Cultural Imperialism

An important part of the transitional justice literature is a critique that TJMs are likely to fail because, as part of the overall Western project, they presume universality and ignore local factors. In this view, TJMs are consistent with the Western project of globalization and liberal state building. They are part of a hegemonic discourse that sees liberal democracy as its end point. Paul Gready and Simon Robins argue that TJMs are likely to fail because the Western project prioritizes abstract goals of "liberal peace" over the concrete needs of people (2014, 345). The liberal peace emphasizes political and civil rights over social and economic rights. It emphasizes procedural goals like elections, constitutionalism, and the rule of law over substantive goals like providing basic human needs and reducing unequal social relations. The Western project equates peace with liberal institutions, and the critique is that such a project often fails in fragile states.

Like the overall Western project, TJMs focus on individual acts of violence rather than the structural violence of unequal social relations. Tribunals explicitly put individuals on trial for specific human rights violations. Truth commissions often establish factual accounts of brutality without the larger context that made such violence possible. Reparations go to individuals to compensate specific harms. The overall critique is that while such mechanisms may respond to individual actions, they do not address socioeconomic rights or challenge unequal power structures. A specific critique is that TJMs should put individual human rights violations into a larger cultural context. They should document resistance and promote solidarity and encourage agency rather than victimhood.

Critics like Gready and Robins (2014) prefer "transformative justice" over "transitional justice." Transformative justice emphasizes local agency and resources, prioritizes process rather than preconceived outcomes, and challenges power relationships and structures of exclusion. It shifts focus from the legal to the social and political and from state institutions to local communities. Unlike transitional justice, it addresses the root causes of conflict: grievances over land and natural resources, economic and social rights, and structural inequalities. Wendy Lambourne (2009) advocates a model of transformative justice that supports sustainable peace building through civil-society participation in the design and implementation of TJMs. Transformative justice includes truth and acknowledgment (factual, narrative, social, and restorative truth); socioeconomic justice (reparation, restitution, compensation, distributive justice); and political justice (political reform, governance, democratization). Lambourne also argues that transformative justice requires a synthesis of the peace and justice approaches, and she provides examples of this combined approach in field research in Rwanda and East Timor.

While case studies in the literature may not explicitly embrace this radical critique, many highlight examples of cultural mismatches between TJMs and the local context where the international search for justice has hindered domestic political stability. For example, Michael Humphrey argues that the Lebanon tribunal for the Hariri assassination is in tension with the traditional Lebanese use of "amnesty and amnesia" as a mechanism for peace (2011, 12), and many groups easily politicized and manipulated the domestic political meaning of the trial. Cyrus Samii similarly argues that people in Burundi overwhelmingly prefer a "forgive-and-forget" approach because they fear political instability (2013, 221). Many believe that the political gains enjoyed by victimized groups after the conflict was sufficient compensation rather than seek justice in the form of indictments and prosecutions. Friederike Mieth (2013) contends that most people in Africa prefer restorative justice (compensating the victims) to retributive justice (punishing the perpetrators). Pursuing punishment will not seem like justice to most citizens, particularly when tribunals target only high-ranking individuals, as was the case in Sierra Leone. Eric Wiebelhaus-Brahm (2016) argues that TJMs in the Middle East are intentionally used to exact revenge on the previous regime and concludes that retributive measures have negative consequences in unstable conditions or in contexts where real political transition does not occur.

Many other case studies make similar arguments about the use of courts created by the West without an adequate understanding of the perceptions of local people. Elizabeth Andersen (2015) advocates for the importance of locality in the effectiveness of TJMs. When tribunals are far away at the Hague, citizens are less likely to feel as if their voices are heard and justice is attainable. James Meernik and Jose Raul Guerrero (2014) argue that the Yugoslavia tribunal established by the UN Security Council did not include outreach toward the local population and thus failed to increase national reconciliation in Serbia because many simply ignored the truths established by the tribunals. Marlene Spoerri (2011) contends that the international use of sanctions to compel Serbia to hand over indicted individuals also drastically reduced local support for the Yugoslavia tribunal. Justice requires the citizenry to wrestle with the moral necessity of the situation, not comply with outside material leverage. Michal Ben-Josef Hirsch, Megan MacKenzie, and Mohamed Sesay (2012) summarize this overall position, arguing that local conceptions of justice and reconciliation may differ from Western approaches, and they advocate more community-based approaches to determining the implementation and goals of truth and reconciliation commissions.

TJMs and Human Rights

Scholars analyzing whether TJMs increase human rights run into methodological issues about what counts as an example of the concept. When analyzing tribunals, should one include domestic, hybrid, and international tribunals? Should one include trials in absentia? Should one somehow exclude show trials that involve breaches of justice? Regarding truth commissions, should one distinguish between sincere and insincere government efforts? Truth commissions in sub-Saharan Africa prior to the seminal one in South Africa, for example, were generally used as political cover for repressive regimes (Roper and Barria 2009). Also, the scope and processes of truth commissions vary widely (e.g., subpoena powers, the authority to grant amnesty, a publicly released report). Should analysts include weaker forms of truth commissions when evaluating their effectiveness (Heine and Turcotte 2015)? The concept of a democratic transition is also fuzzy. Should the concept include both postauthoritarian examples and post–civil war examples? What criteria for civil war or authoritarianism should one use? When comparing countries in democratic transitions that have and have not used TJMs, what is the universe of cases?[2]

Given these methodological difficulties, scholars attempting cross-national analyses often look at a different universe of cases, and it is difficult to compare results and generate cumulative knowledge.[3] There are also few empirical cross-national studies testing the claims that TJMs facilitate democratic transitions (Arenhovel 2008; Arthur 2009; Mendeloff 2009; Thoms, Ron, and Paris 2010). As expected in such a situation, the few studies that do exist show mixed results. Eric Brahm (2006, 2007) finds no difference in the levels of democracy between transitioning countries that have used truth commissions and those that have not. Tricia D. Olsen, Leigh A. Payne, and Andrew G. Reiter (2010a) studied countries in democratic transitions and found that no single mechanism when used alone improved human rights. Indeed, they argued that truth commissions, when used alone, had a negative impact on human rights. Only when TJMs were used in combination did they have a positive impact. Wiebelhaus-Brahm (2010), who included all countries in the analysis, found a negative correlation between truth commissions and human rights.

Other studies have more optimistic conclusions. Kathryn Sikkink and Carrie Booth Walling (2007) created an original data set of truth commissions and trials in Latin America and concluded that human rights trials have a positive effect on human rights, conflict resolution, democracy, and rule of law. Hunjoon Kim and Kathryn Sikkink (2010) studied one hundred democratic transitions and also found that trials lead to improvements in human rights. They argue that trials have more influence than truth commissions because trials combine normative pressures and material punishment while truth commissions do not include material punishment. Laura K. Taylor and Alexander Dukalskis (2012) created the Truth Commission Publicness Dataset and conclude that countries using truth commissions with public hearings, public reports, and publicly named perpetrators have higher levels of democracy than countries with truth commissions that are less public. Brian K. Frederking (2015) analyzed post–civil war countries and found that those using a TJM have higher levels of democratization and human rights than those that did not.

Our analysis is also in this more optimistic category. We rely heavily on the data in the Transitional Justice Database Project (TJDP) (Olsen, Payne, and Reiter 2010b). The TJDP includes 255 cases of democratic transitions from 1970 to 2007 and identifies the use of TJMs in these cases. The democratic-transition cases include both postauthoritarian societies and post–civil war societies. We include the same ninety-one cases of postauthoritarian societies identified by TJDP (which is based on the "regime transition" variable in the Polity IV data set). We do not, however, use all 164 civil wars identified by TJDP (which is based on the conflicts identified in the Uppsala/ PRIO Armed Conflict Database). The PRIO coding rule has a relatively low threshold (twenty-five battle deaths) and counts geographically disparate and/or recurring conflicts separately. Since our interest is the use of TJMs in a national context in post–civil war societies, we collapse such cases. For example, while the TJDP includes seven different civil wars in Ethiopia during this time period, we include only one case for Ethiopia. As a result, our data set includes 93 cases of civil wars, not the 164 identified by TJDP. The following analysis results from a data set of 184 cases of democratic transitions from 1970 to 2007 that includes the following variables:

- Type indicates whether the case is a postauthoritarian or post–civil war society.
- Year is the year of democratic transition (for postauthoritarian cases) or the year the civil war ended, as identified in the TJDP.
- Tribunal is a dummy variable indicating whether or not the state prosecuted individuals for human rights violations, as identified in the TJDP.
- Truth Commission is a dummy variable indicating whether or not the state issued a truth-commission report, as identified in the TJDP.
- Amnesty is a dummy variable indicating whether or not the state issued amnesty to human rights violators, as identified in the TJDP.
- Reparations is a dummy variable indicating whether or not the state issued monetary compensation to victims of human rights violations, as identified in the TJDP.
- CIRI+5 is the CIRI Physical Integrity Index from the CIRI Human Rights Data Set. This index measures the rights not to be tortured, executed, or imprisoned for one's political beliefs. It ranges from 0 (no government respect for these rights) to 14 (full government respect for these rights). This variable is the CIRI score either five years after the transition year or five years after the civil war ended.
- CIRI+10 is the CIRI score either ten years after the transition year or ten years after the civil war ended. If CIRI+5 was the most recent score available, then this variable was coded as missing.
- CIRI current is the most recent CIRI score available. If CIRI+5 or CIRI+10 was the most recent score available, then this variable was coded as missing.

- PTS+5 is the Political Terror Scale, which measures levels of political violence on a scale from 1 (no political violence) to 5 (high levels of political violence). This variable is the PTS score either five years after the transition year or five years after the civil war ended.
- PTS+10 is the PTS score either ten years after the transition year or ten years after the civil war ended. If PTS+5 was the most recent score available, then this variable was coded as missing.
- PTS current is the most recent PTS score available. If PTS+5 or PTS+10 was the most recent score available, then this variable was coded as missing.
- FH+5 is the Freedom House ranking for civil liberties, which includes freedom of expression and belief, rights of association, rule of law, and personal autonomy rights. It ranges from 1 (highest level) to 7 (lowest level). This variable is the FH ranking either five years after the transition year or five years after the civil war ended.
- FH+10 is the FH ranking either ten years after the transition year or ten years after the civil war ended. If FH+5 was the most recent score available, then this variable was coded as missing.
- FH current is the most recent FH ranking available. If FH+5 or FH+10 was the most recent score available, then this variable was coded as missing.

We use this data set to analyze whether the use of TJMs influences a variety of human rights measures. CIRI and PTS focus on a narrow range of physical-integrity rights (extrajudicial killings, disappearances, torture, and political imprisonment) that are more likely to be associated with the work of tribunals and truth commissions. These are the most severe violations, they are clearly the responsibility of the government to prevent, and their narrow focus enables these measures to be distinct from other measures of democracy or economic opportunity. Both CIRI and PTS rely on reports from Amnesty International and the U.S. State Department. The FH ranking is a broader measure of human rights, including rights of expression and association beyond physical-integrity rights. We also include all three human rights measures at three different time intervals (five years after the transition, ten years after, and the most recent measures) to determine varying amounts of influence over time.

The data set illustrates the increasing use of TJMs by states undergoing democratic transitions. The descriptive statistics in Table 6.1 show that more than 57 percent of the cases used at least one TJM. Using more than one, however, was less frequent—only 16.8 percent used two TJMs, and only 8.2 percent used three. (Argentina was the only case to use all four TJMs.) Table 6.1 also shows that countries were more likely to use the peace TJMs. More

TABLE 6.1 DESCRIPTIVE STATISTICS

Number and types of cases	Percentage
Cases using each type of TJM	
75 cases used amnesty	40.8
40 cases used truth commissions	21.7
37 cases used tribunals	20.1
18 cases used reparations	9.8
Cases using any type of TJM	
78 cases used no TJMs	42.4
106 cases used at least one TJM	57.6
Cases using multiple types of TJM	
31 cases used two TJMs	16.8
15 cases used three TJMs	8.2
1 case used all four TJMs	0.5
Cases using justice TJMs (tribunals and reparations)	
136 used no justice TJMs	73.9
48 used at least one TJM	26.1
Cases using peace TJMs (truth commissions and amnesty)	
93 used no peace TJMs	50.5
91 used at least one TJM	49.5

Note: Total cases of democratic transitions = 184.

than 40 percent of the cases used amnesty, and more than 21 percent of the cases used a truth commission. However, countries were much less likely to use the justice TJMs. Around 20 percent of the cases used tribunals, and less than 10 percent used reparations. While nearly half of the cases used at least one peace TJM, only a quarter of the cases used at least one justice TJM.

The first question is whether TJMs matter: Do countries that have used TJMs achieve higher levels of human rights than countries that did not? We created a dummy variable with 0 representing the countries that used no TJMs and 1 representing the countries that used one or more TJMs. The results of an independent samples hypothesis test (*t*-test) comparing the average human rights levels of the countries coded 0 with the countries coded 1 are shown in Table 6.2. The results offer only limited support for the effectiveness of TJMs. All of the CIRI and FH measures are in the right direction—countries that used a TJM have a better human rights record than countries that do not. However, none of those six measures are statistically significant, and none of the three PTS measures show any meaningful difference.

TABLE 6.2 AVERAGE HUMAN RIGHTS LEVELS FOR
COUNTRIES WITH AND WITHOUT TJMS

	Mean
CIRI+5	(.212)
TJM	8.95
No TJM	8.23
CIRI+10	(.068)
TJM	9.32
No TJM	8.34
CIRI current	(.341)
TJM	7.75
No TJM	7.25
FH+5	(.136)
TJM	3.94
No TJM	4.24
FH+10	(.122)
TJM	3.65
No TJM	3.97
FH current	(.630)
TJM	3.78
No TJM	3.90
PTS+5	(.781)
TJM	2.96
No TJM	2.91
PTS+10	(.405)
TJM	2.73
No TJM	2.86
PTS current	(.929)
TJM	2.75
No TJM	2.73

A related question is whether using multiple types of TJMs is more effective than using none or only one type. Perhaps there is a cumulative effect from using multiple TJMs. We created an additive index with a scale of 0–4 from the four TJM variables: 0 for countries that used no TJMs, 1 for countries that used one TJM, 2 for countries that used two TJMs, and so on. Table 6.3 shows the results of simple correlations between this TJM additive index and the human rights measures. These results are more promising. Six of the

TABLE 6.3 CORRELATION BETWEEN USE OF TJMS
AND HUMAN RIGHTS

	Mean
CIRI+5	.211*
	(.010)
CIRI+10	.218*
	(.008)
CIRI current	.189*
	(.011)
FH+5	−.216*
	(.003)
FH+10	−.207*
	(.008)
FH current	−.162*
	(.029)
PTS+5	−.069
	(.372)
PTS+10	−.141
	(.100)
PTS current	−.103
	(.175)

*significant at the .05 level.

nine measures are statistically significant. Once again, the CIRI and FH measures show more of an effect than the PTS measures.

One possible explanation for these mixed results is that some TJMs are more effective than others, which is within the parameters of the peace-versus-justice debate. Table 6.4 shows the average human rights levels for countries that used each individual TJM and those that did not use that particular TJM. The results show that the average differences for the justice TJMs are much higher than those for the peace TJMs. The average scores for the tribunal variable are significantly different in the right direction for all nine human rights measures, including the PTS measures that were not significant in previous tests. Importantly, the most significant differences are with the three current human rights measures, suggesting that the influence may not be temporary. The average scores for reparations, the other justice TJM, are significantly different in the right direction for five of the nine measures, and a sixth (FH+10) barely missed that status. Once again the three PTS variables are not significant.

The two peace TJMs do not show the same results. The average scores for the truth commission variable go in the right direction but are significantly different in only one of the nine measures (CIRI current)—and that one only

TABLE 6.4 AVERAGE HUMAN RIGHTS MEASURES AND THE USE OF INDIVIDUAL TJMS

	Amnesty	Reparations	Tribunals	Truth commissions
CIRI current	(.116)	(.008)*	(.000)**	(.043)*
Yes	7.10	9.61	9.56	8.53
No	7.83	7.31	7.03	7.26
CIRI+5	(.404)	(.001)*	(.003)*	(.081)
Yes	8.28	11.25	10.34	9.55
No	8.79	8.3	8.19	8.35
CIRI+10	(.745)	(.005)*	(.002)*	(.116)
Yes	8.9	11.07	10.38	9.69
No	8.71	8.59	8.41	8.63
FH current	(.050)*	(.003)*	(.000)**	(.213)
Yes	4.11	2.78	2.81	3.55
No	3.64	3.95	4.08	3.91
FH+5	(.190)	(.001)*	(.000)**	(.087)
Yes	4.23	3.06	3.14	3.75
No	3.96	4.18	4.29	4.16
FH+10	(.927)	(.053)	(.001)*	(.095)
Yes	3.81	3.19	3.12	3.45
No	3.79	3.87	3.98	3.89
PTS current	(.039)*	(.225)	(.000)**	(.880)
Yes	2.94	2.44	1.97	2.72
No	2.6	2.78	2.94	2.75
PTS+5	(.288)	(.454)	(.013)*	(.647)
Yes	3.04	2.75	2.54	2.87
No	2.86	2.96	3.05	2.96
PTS+10	(.629)	(.226)	(.008)*	(.830)
Yes	2.74	2.53	2.41	2.82
No	2.82	2.82	2.89	2.78

*significant at the .05 level; **significant at the .001 level.

marginally so. The amnesty variable, however, fares very poorly. Seven of the nine averages go in the wrong direction; that is, the countries that used amnesty have worse human rights levels than countries that did not, and two of those results are significantly different. These results suggest that while truth commissions may have marginally positive effects, the use of amnesty clearly does not.

The correlations in Table 6.5 show similar results. We combined the TJM variables to create a Justice TJM index and a Peace TJM index. Both use scales from 0 to 2, measuring whether a country used zero, one, or two of the relevant justice or peace TJMs. The correlations with the human rights measures are consistent: the justice index is significantly correlated with all nine measures, and the peace index is significantly correlated with none of them. Indeed, while seven of the nine justice TJM correlations are highly significant, meeting the .000 threshold, none of the peace TJM correlations are close to the .05 threshold, and three measures go in the wrong direction.[4]

These results address two important debates within the transitional justice literature. One debate is whether or not TJMs help facilitate the development of human rights in states going through a democratic transition. Critics assert the radical argument that TJMs are consistent with the Western hegemonic project and unlikely to be effective in a wide variety of non-Western contexts. These empirical results generally support the advocates: democratic transition states that used TJMs have higher levels of human

TABLE 6.5 CORRELATIONS BETWEEN JUSTICE TJMS, PEACE TJMS, AND HUMAN RIGHTS

	Justice (trials plus reparations)	Peace (truth commissions plus amnesty)
CIRI current	.325**	.017
	(.000)	(.824)
CIRI+5	.325**	.039
	(.000)	(.634)
CIRI+10	.312**	.060
	(.000)	(.475)
FH current	−.356**	.045
	(.000)	(.546)
FH+5	−.390**	−.007
	(.000)	(.929)
FH+10	−.281**	−.074
	(.000)	(.353)
PTS current	−.320**	.103
	(.000)	(.178)
PTS+5	−.175*	.036
	(.023)	(.642)
PTS+10	−.224*	−.018
	(.008)	(.833)

*significant at the .05 level; **significant at the .001 level.

rights than states that did not. We do not expect these results to persuade radical critics of TJMs. The human rights measures we used in this study are consistent with Western, individualist assumptions about human rights. They do not capture critical arguments about the importance of social inequality or structural violence, but we are not aware of any measures that do.

These results also address a second debate in the transitional justice literature. Which TJMs are more effective in facilitating the development of human rights: the TJMs that prioritize peace (truth commissions and amnesty) or the TJMs that prioritize justice (tribunals and reparations)? The advocates of peace TJMs argue that they promote reconciliation because of their more inclusive and wide-ranging agendas, give a larger voice to the victims, and establish a healthier political landscape to allow for future democratization. The advocates of justice TJMs argue that they prevent feelings of impunity, establish the rule of law, and deter future violations of human rights. Our results, across multiple measures of human rights and across multiple time frames, suggest that justice TJMs are much more effective than peace TJMs.

However, these results must be considered tentative. They are limited to bivariate relationships between TJMs and human rights. We do not include alternative explanations as control variables within more sophisticated regression models. Other variables may have significant influences on both the use of TJMs and human rights levels. Standard control variables include, among others, economic wealth, ethnic fractionalization, colonial history, scope of previous conflicts, population, and religion. Another limitation, which applies to the entire literature, is that we lack a causal theory to explain why TJMs work in this way. More important, we lack a theoretical understanding about when different types of TJMs are more likely to be effective.

Conclusion

The overall theme of this book focuses on migration, refugees, and cross-border flight. Despite obvious connections between the repatriation of refugees and postconflict democratic transitions, there is very little in the transitional justice literature regarding refugees (Rimmer 2010). Consistent with the radical critique, the transitional justice literature focuses on the liberal project of building institutions within national borders rather than directly addresses the concrete needs of those displaced by conflict. Few truth commissions explicitly include refugees to focus on how forced displacement and cross-border flight influenced their lives (Liberia is an important exception). Occasionally tribunals hold perpetrators accountable for the forced displacement of fellow citizens; an important example is the International Criminal Tribunal for Yugoslavia prosecuting Bosnian Serbs for ethnic cleansing. In general, few transitional justice processes have consciously attempted to address the needs of refugee populations as they return to their country during the postconflict democratic transition.

This is perplexing because the repatriation of refugees plays an important symbolic role in a democratic transition process (Fresia 2014). Repatriation itself is an act of transitional justice in two ways. First, it reverses the past human rights violations of displacement simply by coming home. Second, it is a prerequisite for additional transitional justice measures. It represents a new beginning for postconflict societies—a first step toward an end to discrimination and a possible return to both peace and justice. Susan Harris Rimmer (2010) argues that the conceptual exclusion of refugees from the transitional justice literature harms democratic transitions, stating that we should interpret refugees as "transitional justice actors" and that a more effective process would explicitly include refugees in all democratic transition decisions: constitution drafting, legislative agendas, security-sector reform, national development plans, and so on.

Refugees could play a more central role in both peace and justice mechanisms in postconflict societies. Refugees would benefit from both reparation programs like the restitution of land and financial compensation for lost property and the prosecution of past human rights violations. Refugees would be a tremendous source for peace mechanisms like truth commissions. Refugees often play a role in building narratives about the meaning of past human rights violations. Refugee camps are extremely politicized spaces in which inhabitants are preoccupied with making sense of past injustices and asserting claims for what constitutes a just order. The roles played by refugees may help explain why some societies pursue justice mechanisms and others pursue peace mechanisms.

The few studies we have suggest that refugees may skew national conversations toward justice mechanisms. Marion Fresia (2014) studied the repatriation of refugees from Senegal back into Mauritania, and these groups strongly advocated for justice mechanisms. They asserted an intention to return home, reacquire recognition of citizenship, restore lost dignity, gain restitution of land and compensation for lost property, and demand trials for those responsible for human rights violations and their resulting displacement. The dominant narrative among these refugees was a "logic of exception": since refugees were people with an exceptional status, exceptional measures were required to atone for this humiliation and regain dignity (Fresia 2014, 443). Rimmer's (2010) study of refugees from East Timor also hinted at this trend. The Timorese emphasis on peace and reconciliation often contradicted the goal of protecting refugees. The postconflict East Timor government, emphasizing peace over justice, refused to prosecute former militia leaders for sexual violence in refugee camps because they wanted to encourage those leaders to return from West Timor. Even when we analyze transitional justice through the prism of refugees, the tensions between peace and justice approaches remain.

NOTES

1. We make no effort to comprehensively summarize the vast transitional justice literature. Reviews can be found in Kritz 1995; Hayner 2011; Roht-Arriaza and Mariecurrena 2006; Van der Merwe, Baxter, and Chapman 2008; Fletcher, Weinstein, and Rowen 2009; Backer 2008; and Buckley-Zistel et al. 2014.

2. Recent studies vary greatly on this issue. Olsen, Payne, and Reiter (2010a) include both post–civil war and postauthoritarian societies and list 255 cases. Kim and Sikkink (2010) use more restrictive criteria for "civil war" and list 102 cases. Hun Joon Kim (2012) does not include civil wars and lists 71 cases.

3. Regarding tribunals, for example, Olsen, Payne, and Reiter (2010a) include eighty-one; Kim and Sikkink (2010) include forty-eight; Kim (2012) includes thirty-three; and Helga Malmin Binningsbø et al. (2012) include seventy-eight. Regarding truth commissions, Olsen, Payne, and Reiter (2010a) include fifty-three; Priscilla Hayner (2011) includes forty; Geoff Dancy, Hunjoon Kim, and Eric Wiebelhaus-Brahm (2010) include thirty-seven; Kim and Sikkink (2010) include twenty-eight; and Binningsbø et al. (2012) include only nine (because of a coding rule that the truth commission must occur within five years after the start of the democratic transition).

4. These overall results were similar when we split the data set into civil war cases only and postauthoritarian cases only. Again the justice TJMs were often significantly correlated with human rights, and peace TJMs, rarely so. These results diverged from the overall results in one important way: the justice TJMS were much more strongly correlated with human rights in the postauthoritarian cases than the civil war cases. Civil wars are the hard cases within the democratic transition literature.

REFERENCES

Ameh, Robert Kwame. 2006. "Uncovering Truth: Ghana's National Reconciliation Commission Excavation of Past Human Rights Abuse." *Contemporary Justice Review* 9 (4): 345–368.

Amstutz, Mark R. 2005. *The Healing of Nations: The Promise and Limits of Political Forgiveness*. Lanham, MD: Rowman and Littlefield.

Andersen, Elizabeth. 2015. "Transitional Justice and the Rule of Law: Lessons from the Field." *Case Western Reserve Journal of International Law* 47 (3): 305–317.

Arenhovel, Mark. 2008. "Democratization and Transitional Justice." *Democratization* 15 (3): 570–587.

Arthur, Paige. 2009. "How 'Transitions' Reshaped Human Rights: A Conceptual History of Transitional Justice." *Human Rights Quarterly* 31 (2): 321–367.

Backer, David. 2008. "Cross-national Comparative Analysis." In *Assessing the Impact of Transitional Justice*, edited by Hugo Van der Merwe, Victoria Baxter, and Audrey R. Chapman, 23–90. Washington, DC: U.S. Institute of Peace Press.

Binningsbø, Helga Malmin, Cyanne E. Loyle, Scott Gates, and Jon Ester. 2012. "Armed Conflict and Post-conflict Justice, 1946–2006." *Journal of Peace Research* 49 (5): 731–740.

Booth, W. James. 2001. "The Unforgotten: Memories of Justice." *American Political Science Review* 95 (4): 777–791.

Brahm, Eric. 2006. "Truth and Consequences: The Impact of Truth Commissions in Transitional Societies." Ph.D. diss., University of Colorado at Boulder.

———. 2007. "Uncovering the Truth: Examining Truth Commission Success and Impact." *International Studies Perspectives* 8 (1): 16–35.

Buckley-Zistel, Susanne, Teresa Koloma Beck, Christian Braun, and Friederike Mieth. 2014. *Transitional Justice Theories*. New York: Routledge.

Chapman, Audrey R., and Patrick Ball. 2001. "The Truth of Truth Commissions: Comparative Lessons from Haiti, South Africa and Guatemala." *Human Rights Quarterly* 23 (1): 1–43.

Clark, Janine Natalya. 2011. "Transitional Justice, Truth and Reconciliation: An Underexplored Relationship." *International Criminal Law Review* 11 (2): 241–261.

Dancy, Geoff, Hunjoon Kim, and Eric Wiebelhaus-Brahm. 2010. "The Turn to Truth: Trends in Truth Commission Experimentation." *Journal of Human Rights* 9 (1): 45–64.

Dancy, Geoff, and Eric Wiebelhaus-Brahm. 2015. "Timing, Sequencing, and Transitional Justice Impact: A Qualitative Comparative Analysis of Latin America." *Human Rights Review* 16 (4): 321–342.

Dimitrijevic, Nenad. 2006. "Justice beyond Blame: Moral Justification of (the Idea of) a Truth Commission." *Journal of Conflict Resolution* 50 (3): 368–382.

Ensalaco, Mark. 1994. "Truth Commissions for Chile and El Salvador." *Human Rights Quarterly* 26 (1): 409–429.

Evenson, Elizabeth M. 2004. "Truth and Justice in Sierra Leone: Coordination between Commission and Court." *Columbia Law Review* 104 (3): 730–767.

Fletcher, Laurel E., Harvey M. Weinstein, and Jamie Rowen. 2009. "Context, Timing, and the Dynamics of Transitional Justice: A Historical Perspective." *Human Rights Quarterly* 31 (1): 163–220.

Frederking, Brian K. 2015. "Putting Transitional Justice on Trial: Democracy and Human Rights in Post–Civil War Societies." *International Social Science Review* 91 (1). Available at https://digitalcommons.northgeorgia.edu/issr/vol91/iss1/3.

Fresia, Marion. 2014. "Performing Repatriation? The Role of Refugee Aid in Shaping New Beginnings in Mauritania." *Development and Change* 45 (3): 434–457.

Gibson, James. 2004. *Overcoming Apartheid: Can Truth Reconcile a Divided Nation?* New York: Russell Sage Foundation.

———. 2006. "The Contribution of Truth to Reconciliation: Lessons from South Africa." *Journal of Conflict Resolution* 50 (3): 409–432.

Gready, Paul, and Simon Robins. 2014. "From Transitional to Transformative Justice: A New Agenda for Practice." *International Journal of Transitional Justice* 8 (2): 339–361.

Grodsky, Brian. 2008. "Justice without Transition: Truth Commissions in the Context of Repressive Rule." *Human Rights Review* 23 (2): 281–297.

———. 2009. "International Prosecutions and Domestic Politics: The Use of Truth Commissions as Compromise Justice in Serbia and Croatia." *International Studies Review* 11 (4): 687–706.

Grono, Nick, and Adam O'Brien. 2008. "Justice in Conflict? The ICC and Peace Processes." In *Courting Conflict? Justice, Peace and the ICC in Africa*, edited by Nicholas Waddell and Phil Clark, 13–20. London: Royal African Society.

Guercio, Laura. 2015. "International Justice and Politics in Libya: A Lost Opportunity for the International Criminal Court and for a Lasting Peace in Libya." *Juridical Current* 18 (1): 94–116.

Hayner, Priscilla. 2011. *Unspeakable Truths: Transitional Justice and the Challenge of Truth Commissions*. New York: Routledge.

Heine, Jorge, and Joseph F. Turcotte. 2015. "Panaceas after Pandemonium? Truth Commissions in the Wake of Protracted Conflicts." *Global Governance* 21 (2): 343–350.

Hirsch, Michal Ben-Josef, Megan MacKenzie, and Mohamed Sesay. 2012. "Measuring the Impacts of Truth and Reconciliation Commissions: Placing the Global 'Success' of TRCs in Local Perspective." *Cooperation and Conflict* 47 (3): 386–403.

Humphrey, Michael. 2011. "The Special Tribunal for Lebanon: Emergency Law, Trauma and Justice." *Arab Studies Quarterly* 33 (1): 4–22.

Kim, Hun Joon. 2012. "Structural Determinants of Human Rights Prosecutions after Democratic Transitions." *Journal of Peace Research* 49 (2): 305–320.

Kim, Hunjoon, and Kathryn Sikkink. 2010. "Explaining the Deterrence Effect of Human Rights Prosecutions for Transitional Countries." *International Studies Quarterly* 54 (4): 939–963.

Kritz, Neil, ed. 1995. *Transitional Justice: How Emerging Democracies Reckon with Former Regimes*. Washington, DC: United States Institute of Peace.

Lambourne, Wendy. 2009. "Transitional Justice and Peacebuilding after Mass Violence." *International Journal of Transitional Justice* 3 (1): 28–48.

Lansana, Gberie. 2008. "Truth and Justice on Trial in Liberia." *African Affairs* 107 (3): 455–465.

Meernik, James, and Jose Raul Guerrero. 2014. "Can International Criminal Justice Advance Ethnic Reconciliation? The ICTY and Ethnic Relations in Bosnia-Herzegovina." *Journal of Southeast European and Black Sea Studies* 14 (3): 383–407.

Mendeloff, David. 2004. "Truth-Seeking, Truth-Telling, and Post-conflict Peacebuilding: Curb the Enthusiasm?" *International Studies Review* 6 (3): 355–380.

———. 2009. "Trauma and Vengeance: Assessing the Psychological and Emotional Effects of Post-conflict Justice." *Human Rights Quarterly* 31 (3): 592–623.

Mieth, Friederike. 2013. "Bringing Justice and Enforcing Peace? An Ethnographic Perspective on the Impact of the Special Court for Sierra Leone." *International Journal of Conflict and Violence* 7 (1): 10–22.

Minow, Martha. 1998. *Between Vengeance and Forgiveness: Facing History after Genocide and Mass Violence*. Boston: Beacon Press.

———. 2008. "Making History or Making Peace: When Prosecutions Should Give Way to Truth Commissions and Peace Negotiations." *Journal of Human Rights* 7 (2): 174–185.

Nevins, Joseph. 2007. "The CAVR: Justice and Reconciliation in a Time of 'Impoverished Political Possibilities.'" *Pacific Affairs* 80 (4): 593–602.

Okafor, Obiora Chinedu, and Uchechukwu Ngwaba. 2015. "The International Criminal Court as a 'Transitional Justice' Mechanism in Africa: Some Critical Reflections." *International Journal of Transitional Justice* 9 (1): 90–108.

Olsen, Tricia D., Leigh A. Payne, and Andrew G. Reiter. 2010a. "The Justice Balance: When Transitional Justice Improves Human Rights and Democracy." *Human Rights Quarterly* 32 (4): 980–1007.

———. 2010b. "Transitional Justice in the World, 1970–2007: Insights from a New Dataset." *Journal of Peace Research* 47 (6): 803–809.

Rimmer, Susan Harris. 2010. "Reconceiving Refugees and Internally Displaced Persons as Transitional Justice Actors." *Contemporary Readings in Law and Social Justice* 2 (2): 163–180.

Roht-Arriaza, Naomi, and Javier Mariecurrena, eds. 2006. *Transitional Justice in the Twenty-First Century: Beyond Truth versus Justice.* Cambridge: Cambridge University Press.

Roper, Steven, and Lilian Barria. 2009. "Why Do States Commission the Truth? Political Considerations in the Establishment of African Truth and Reconciliation Commissions." *Human Rights Review* 10 (3): 373–391.

Sadat, Leila Nadya. 2007. "The Effect of Amnesties before Domestic and International Tribunals: Morality, Law and Politics." In *Atrocities and International Accountability,* edited by Edel Hughes, William A. Schabas, and Ramesh Thakur, 225–245. New York: United Nations Press.

Samii, Cyrus. 2013. "Who Wants to Forgive and Forget? Transitional Justice Preferences in Postwar Burundi." *Journal of Peace Research* 50 (2): 219–233.

Sikkink, Kathryn, and Carrie Booth Walling. 2007. "The Impact of Human Rights Trials in Latin America." *Journal of Peace Research* 44 (3): 427–445.

Skaar, Elin. 1999. "Truth Commissions, Trials—or Nothing? Policy Options in Democratic Transitions." *Third World Quarterly* 20 (6): 1109–1128.

Snyder, Jack, and Leslie Vinjamuri. 2004. "Trials and Errors: Principle and Pragmatism in Strategies of International Justice." *International Security* 28 (3): 5–44.

Spoerri, Marlene. 2011. "Justice Imposed: How Policies of Conditionality Effect Transitional Justice in the Former Yugoslavia." *Europe-Asia Studies* 63 (1): 1827–1851.

Sriram, Chandra Lekha. 2004. *Confronting Past Human Rights Violations: Justice vs. Peace in Times of Transition.* London: Routledge.

Stensrud, Ellen. 2009. "New Dilemmas in Transitional Justice: Lessons from the Mixed Courts in Sierra Leone and Cambodia." *Journal of Peace Research* 46 (1): 5–15.

Taylor, Laura K., and Alexander Dukalskis. 2012. "Old Truths and New Politics: Does Truth Commission 'Publicness' Impact Democratization?" *Journal of Peace Research* 49 (5): 671–684.

Tepperman, Jonathan D. 2002. "Truth and Consequences." *Foreign Affairs* 81 (1): 128–145.

Thoms, Oskar N. T., James Ron, and Roland Paris. 2010. "State-Level Effects of Transitional Justice: What Do We Know?" *International Journal of Transitional Justice* 4 (3): 329–354.

Tomuschat, Christian. 2001. "Clarification Commission in Guatemala." *Human Rights Quarterly* 23 (2): 233–258.

United Nations. 2010. "Guidance Note of the Secretary-General: United Nations Approach to Transitional Justice." Available at https://www.un.org/ruleoflaw/files/TJ_Guidance_Note_March_2010FINAL.pdf.

Valiñas, Marta, and Kris Vanspauwen. 2009. "Truth-Seeking after Violent Conflict: Experiences from South Africa and Bosnia and Herzegovina." *Contemporary Justice Review* 12 (3): 269–287.

Vandeginste, Stef, and Chandra Lekha Sriram. 2011. "Power Sharing and Transitional Justice: A Clash of Paradigms?" *Global Governance* 17 (4): 489–505.

Van der Merwe, Hugo, Victoria Baxter, and Audrey R. Chapman, eds. 2008. *Assessing the Impact of Transitional Justice.* Washington, DC: U.S. Institute of Peace Press.

Webster, David. 2007. "History, Nation and Narrative in East Timor's Truth Commission Report." *Pacific Affairs* 80 (4): 581–591.

Wiebelhaus-Brahm, Eric. 2010. *Truth Commissions and Transitional Societies: The Impact on Human Rights and Democracy.* New York: Routledge.

———. 2016. "Goals and Processes: The Arab World and the Transitional Justice Impact Literature." *International Journal of Human Rights* 20 (3): 426–443.

PART III CITIZENSHIP

Deprivation of Citizenship

An Examination of the Rohingya Refugee Crisis

HEATHER SMITH-CANNOY

n May 2015 the *Alpha*,[1] a large passenger ship was carrying 820 people, approximately half Rohingya (a Muslim minority persecuted in Burma) and half Bangladeshi, 60 of them women and 217 of them children (UNHCR 2015), all hoping to reach sanctuary in Malaysia. But after more than one hundred days at sea, their food and water rations began to run out. The crew abandoned the *Alpha*, leaving the passengers stranded in the Andaman Sea, halfway between Malaysia and Indonesia with no provisions. Eventually, the *Alpha* was permitted to land on the coast of Indonesia. The *Alpha* was but one of many large ships carrying Rohingya and Bangladeshi migrants seeking asylum in Malaysia and Thailand that were abandoned by crews in the summer of 2015. The UNHCR reports that at least seventy people died at sea when crews abandoned their passengers. And the people on board these ships experienced dehydration, hunger, and violence at the hands of traffickers (UNHCR 2015). In all, more than five thousand migrants, at least half of them Rohingya fleeing persecution, were stranded at sea when both Thailand and Malaysia refused to allow the ships to dock.

For the long-persecuted Rohingya, whose citizenship in Burma was slowly dissolved through a series of discriminatory government policies, the 2015 crisis at sea was the culmination of years of repression. This chapter makes three arguments that focus on the human rights consequences of statelessness. First, it illustrates the ways in which statelessness, in this case the deprivation of Burmese citizenship for the Rohingya, undermines their enjoyment of social, economic, and political rights. Second, it argues that this deprivation of rights serves as a driver of cross-border flight. Finally, because of their need to find safety abroad, Rohingya often seek out traffickers and smugglers, which can contribute to further deterioration of rights.

This chapter is part of a larger project to identify the most pressing human rights violations confronting our world today and to illustrate the extent to which these violations contribute to cross-border migration. We use Alexander Betts's (2013) concept of survival migration to examine the relationship between human rights violations in the country of origin and the likelihood of cross-border flight. The term "survival migrant" describes people who flee their country of origin or residence in response to an existential threat, such as environmental degradation, generalized violence, or state failure. Technically, these threats fall short of the requirements for obtaining refugee status contained in the 1951 Convention on the Status of Refugees (Refugee Convention). The convention requires that asylum seekers demonstrate a well-founded fear of persecution from their government. But as other chapters in this book demonstrate, there are many reasons for people to flee their country of residence—climate change (see Chapter 1) and lack of access to clean water (see Chapter 3)—that fall outside the Refugee Convention's narrow requirements for refugee status.

In the case of the Rohingya in Burma, Betts's concept is especially helpful in clarifying the relationship between human rights violations and the propensity for cross-border flight. The Rohingya are among the most persecuted minority in the world today in large part because of their stateless status. The Rohingya case illustrates just how valuable citizenship is as a means for securing human rights. Once Burmese citizenship became definitively out of reach for the Rohingya, the Burmese government slowly rescinded virtually all of their civil, political, and social and economic rights; in western Burma today, those Rohingya who remain live in camps and are unable to travel, work, attend school, or seek medical care. The cascade of human rights violations against the Rohingya that has followed in Burma serves as a test of Betts's concept of survival migration—the Rohingya face an existential threat to their existence that has caused many to flee their country of habitual residence in droves.

I examine this case not because it is typical of the relationship between statelessness and cross-border flight but because it represents an extreme case that allows us to examine the worst-case scenario: a government persecutes a minority by withdrawing their citizenship status. Withdrawing the citizenship of a group for an immutable characteristic is also referred to as the discriminatory deprivation of nationality (van Waas 2008). Other instances of discriminatory deprivation of nationality have affected relatively smaller numbers of people—for example, the denationalization of 120,000 Kurds by the Syrian government in 1962 (Human Rights Watch 1996). The UNHCR (2017) estimates that between August and November 2017 approximately 620,000 Rohingya deprived of citizenship in Burma have fled. This chapter argues that deprivation of citizenship serves as a driver of cross-border migration by diminishing human rights standards to intolerable levels.

Causes of Statelessness

In a global system composed of sovereign nation-states an individual's nationality might seem relatively uncomplicated. If one is born in country X to parents who are citizens of country X and plans to live and work in country X, the right to be a national of that state would seem to follow rather simply. Indeed, a multitude of international human rights treaties enshrine the right to nationality,[2] a child's right "to acquire a nationality,"[3] and a woman's right to "acquire and change" her nationality and that of her children.[4]

As early as 1954, before the emergence of most of the core UN Human Rights Treaties,[5] the international community established the Convention relating to the Status of Stateless Persons (Statelessness Convention), which defines stateless persons in Article 1 as those who "are not recognized as a national by any state under the operation of its law." Though the convention does not use the term, this definition is typically referred to as "de jure statelessness" because a person who is not recognized by any state as a citizen is legally stateless. A person who is a citizen of a state that ceases to exist is also rendered de jure stateless. De facto statelessness is implied in the 1951 convention and referenced explicitly in the Final Act of the 1961 Convention on the Reduction of Statelessness (UNHCR 2014a). The concept of de facto statelessness means that even though a person possesses a "legally meritorious claim for citizenship," that person is nevertheless "precluded from asserting it because of practical considerations" (Milbrandt 2011, 82). Civil war, fear of persecution, loss of documentation, and prohibitive expense are reasons to avail oneself of the protections of nationality. Alex Paxon explains, "In short, a *de jure* stateless person lacks a legal nationality and a *de facto* stateless person lacks meaningful nationality" (2012, 627). The 1961 Convention on the Reduction of Statelessness aims to reduce statelessness by pressing states to incorporate provisions into their nationality laws that provide for the obtainment of nationality at birth, if nationality will not be obtained any other way. The treaty also establishes that states must limit situations that deprive people of citizenship without providing for an alternative citizenship (Weissbrodt and Collins 2006, 247).

Despite this attention to statelessness within international law, for the approximately ten million stateless people in the world today, the right to a nationality is denied (UNHCR 2018). To be deprived of nationality or citizenship inhibits the ability to travel outside the country of residence.[6] Without proper documentation, it is virtually impossible to return home. In some parts of Asia, the stateless are not allowed to travel between villages within their country without prior approval from the government, making them prisoners in their own villages (Fortify Rights 2014). Obtaining access to education, employment, medical care, and even housing can and often is contingent on citizenship status, meaning that to deprive people of this right undermines the most basic human rights protections in existence. To understand how nationality can be withdrawn or denied, it is necessary to first establish how nationality is typically acquired.

Methods of Acquiring Nationality

Determining who is a citizen and who may become one is a foundational element of state sovereignty. States determine how citizenship is granted, typically using one or a combination of three methods: (1) jus sanguinis (law of blood), the conferral of citizenship by descent or parentage; (2) jus soli (law of territory), the conferral of citizenship through birth on the territory; and (3) naturalization, a long residence on the territory (Edwards 2015). Underlying these principles is the notion that nationality is indicative of a "bond of attachment" (Liechtenstein v. Guatemala 1955) between the individual and the state that can be established by the fact of one's birth to parents of that state, through birth on the territory, or through a long period of residence within the state. Many states use a combination of these methods to confer citizenship, which can leave gaping holes in the right to nationality for many.

For example, Article 15 of the Malaysian Federal Constitution stipulates that a child born in Malaysia can be granted citizenship only if one parent is a citizen or permanent resident at the time of the child's birth.[7] Such a rule renders stateless the children born to undocumented migrants in Malaysia. Additionally, the Malaysian government has historically held that children born out of wedlock to foreign mothers in Malaysia should be granted citizenship in their mother's country. Malaysian citizenship is granted to children in these cases only when the mother can produce evidence of her citizenship, which is often not possible. The result has been that many children of foreign parents born in Malaysia are rendered stateless—at least ten thousand children born in Malaysia to parents who are Filipino Muslim refugees in the state of Sabah have neither Philippine nor Malaysian citizenship (U.S. Department of State 2017).

Becoming Stateless

Statelessness can occur in a variety of ways. Laura van Waas (2008) names four categories of causes: (1) technical causes, (2) state succession or war and irregular migration, (3) deficiencies in birth or marriage registration, and (4) discriminatory deprivation of nationality. Technical causes can occur through the manner in which states implement their nationality laws. Jus sanguinis dictates that citizenship should be granted based on family heritage. But the exact ways in which states interpret "family" can contribute to statelessness. For example, in Jordan citizenship is passed down only through the father. If a child is born in Jordan to a Jordanian mother and a foreign father, that child will not receive Jordanian citizenship (Whitman 2013). In the twenty-nine countries with patrilineal descent laws, if a female citizen gives birth to the child of a foreign or stateless man, then the child will also be stateless (see Weissbrodt and Collins 2006, 254).[8]

War and state dissolution are also major drivers of statelessness. When the Soviet Union broke apart in 1991, more than three hundred million people were left to sort out their new nationalities. For some, it is merely a bureaucratic inconvenience to obtain new citizenship status following state dissolution, but in other cases certain groups are intentionally left out. For example, when Czechoslovakia broke apart, neither the Czech Republic nor Slovakia was keen to offer citizenship to the Roma (Fullerton 2015). New successor states need time to create citizenship laws and ratify human rights agreements, both of which serve to increase the likelihood of statelessness following succession. War and ethnic conflict that lead to state dissolution may also engender statelessness. The war between the now independent states of the former Yugoslav Republics between 1991 and 1995, as well as the war in Kosovo in 1999, created population shifts, dislocation, and statelessness that endures today. During the Yugoslav conflict, for example, birth registries for Serbia, Montenegro, and Macedonia were destroyed. During the conflict in Kosovo, registry books for Serbian residents of Kosovo were destroyed or went missing. In both cases the destruction of these registry books led to statelessness, particularly among the Roma, Egyptian, and Ashkali minorities (UNHCR 2011).

Statelessness also occurs through deficiencies in birth and marriage certification. Laws that inhibit birth registration for noncitizen parents can render their children stateless. In the Dominican Republic, children born to undocumented parents of Haitian descent are routinely denied birth registration, preventing them from obtaining citizenship.[9] When refugees have children in an asylum country, they often must have their own official documents to register their children's birth. In Lebanon, Syrian refugees who give birth must have their own identity documents to ensure that their Syrian nationality is passed on to their children. Yet with the exigencies of war, many simply do not have their documentation: the UNHCR (2014b) found that 78 percent of surveyed Syrian refugees in Lebanon had been unable to register their child's birth, rendering their children stateless. In some countries, when women get married, their nationality is linked to or dependent on that of their spouse (Weissbrodt and Collins 2006). Referred to as dependent nationality laws, these antiquated rules can render women stateless if their husband dies or they are divorced.

Finally, the discriminatory deprivation of nationality covers nationality that is either withdrawn or withheld entirely from a certain group (van Waas 2008, 95). These policies are particularly nefarious because at their core they use the revocation or denial of nationality as a means to punish and discriminate against groups for immutable characteristics. A government can pass policies to withdraw nationality, also known as "discriminatory denationalization," from a group that previously held that nationality. In 1962 Syria denationalized all Kurds residing in Syria, depriving them of their previously held Syrian citizenship and rendering them stateless (Human Rights Watch 1996). Discriminatory denationalization is the means through which the Rohingya, who have resided in Burma for centuries, were rendered stateless by the passage of a law withdrawing their citizenship in 1982.

A Case Study of the Human Rights Consequences of Statelessness: The Rohingya

As the previous section clearly demonstrates, laws and policies governing who may become a citizen and the method through which citizenship is acquired can be fraught with complications and in some cases lead to discriminatory deprivation of nationality. This section is concerned with one particular case of discriminatory deprivation of nationality, the Rohingya, who today reside throughout the Greater Mekong Subregion but lack citizenship in any country. This group has endured some of the most severe human rights consequences of their statelessness, which has led to precisely the sort of existential threat that Betts connects to survival migration.

The Rohingya are an ethnic, linguistic, and religious minority in Burma. They are Sunni Muslim and have historically resided in the Arakan state of Burma, situated on the west coast of the country. Unlike the majority of the Burmese population, who are of East Asian descent, the Rohingya are related to the Chittagong Bengalis in Bangladesh (Lewa 2009). The Rohingya have a very long history in Arakan, having resided there since approximately the eighteenth century (Staples 2012). In spite of their long-term residence in

Burma, they have not had access to Burmese citizenship. Chris Lewa (2009) explains that since the Burmese obtained independence from the British in 1948, the Rohingya have gradually been "excluded from the process of nation-building." Following Human Rights Watch (2012), I use the official names of the country "Burma" and the state "Arakan" that were in place before the military seized control of the country in 1989. The government now refers to the country as Myanmar and the state as Rakhine. Burmese authorities have long argued that the term "Rohingya" is fiction, made up to conceal the fact that this group actually consists of undocumented economic migrants from the Bengal region (Rakhine Inquiry Commission 2013, 53–56). Again, I use the term "Rohingya," which is how the group describes itself, while Burmese authorities refer to them as "Bengali."

Though the Rohingya endured intense discrimination in Burma for many years, they did not face explicit group-based persecution in the form of deprivation of nationality until 1974, when the Burmese government passed the Emergency Immigration Act, requiring all citizens to carry identity cards (national registration certificates). The Rohingya were issued foreign registration cards (Human Rights Watch 2000). In 1982 the Burmese government passed a new citizenship law, which recognized 135 different ethnic groups, but the Rohingya were excluded from the list. Exclusion from this list in 1982 meant that in the 1983 census, the Rohingya would not be counted (Human Rights Watch 2000). Beginning in 1994, the Burmese government also refused to issue birth certificates to Rohingya babies (Green, MacManus, and Venning 2015).

In 1977 Operation Nagamin was launched by immigration officials and designed to crack down on "foreigners" in border regions in advance of the coming census. Approximately 200,000 Rohingya fled from Burma to Bangladesh when they were chased out of their homes for failure to possess proper identification. Though Bangladesh set up refugee camps, with the assistance of the International Committee of the Red Cross, eventually the Bangladeshi government negotiated the repatriation of the Rohingya with the Burmese government. Of the original 200,000 Rohingya that had fled, 180,000 were sent back to Burma between 1978 and 1979 (Abrar 1995).

By 1992 nearly 250,000 Rohingya had fled from Burma, this time specifically from Arakan to Bangladesh because of forced labor, rape, mass detentions, and religious persecution, all at the hands of the Burmese army (Human Rights Watch 2000). In April 1992 the Bangladeshi government sought the assistance of the UNHCR and signed a memorandum of understanding with the Burmese government to once again repatriate the Rohingya. When Bangladesh began to block UNHCR access to Rohingya refugee camps in October 1992, the UNHCR responded by withdrawing from the repatriation program in December (Abrar 1995). Between 1992 and 1997 nearly 230,000 Rohingya were forcibly repatriated to Burma (Human Rights Watch 2000; UN General Assembly 1997). By the summer of 1997 the Burmese authorities determined that they would no longer allow Rohingya to be repatriated after July 15, which prompted the government of Bangladesh to push as many remaining Rohingya refugees across the Naf River as possible in advance of the deadline (Human Rights Watch 2000).

During the summer of 2012 violence erupted between Rakhine Buddhists and the Rohingya in Arakan. Throughout Arakan state, entire villages and parts of towns were burned. Satellite images showed that hundreds of buildings were destroyed by violence in Kyaukpyu ("Burma Violence" 2012). Between June and October 2012 approximately 140,000 people were displaced from their homes in Arakan state (UN Human Rights Council 2016). Research conducted by the International State Crime Initiative (ISCI) provides compelling evidence that the massacre of Rohingya beginning in June 2012, centered in Sittwe, was carefully planned and organized by Arakanese activists with the explicit cooperation and support of the Burmese government and Arakan state administrators (Green, MacManus, and Venning 2015, 74–78). The Arakanese activists arranged for the transportation of Arakanese from other parts of the country to join them to participate in the violence in Sittwe, helped coordinate the attacks on the Rohingya, and even provided refreshments to those participating in the violence (74). Arakanese activists and leaders displayed a startling degree of preparation for the attacks on Rohingya in Arakan state. Penny Green, Thomas MacManus, and Alicia de la Cour Venning suggest:

> Some days before the violence erupted, Rakhine [Arakanese] activists sent letters to administrators of Rakhine village tracts in the Sittwe hinterland. The letters urged each household to send at least one man between the ages of 20 and 40 to participate in the planned attacks on Rohingya neighborhoods, while others were to remain behind in order to defend their village in case of retaliatory attack. The men were to be ready on the morning of 8 June to be collected and bussed in to Sittwe. They were informed that it was their duty as Rakhine to participate in an attack on the Muslim population. (2015, 74)

Across the Arakan townships of Maungdaw, Sittwe, Buthidaung, and Rathedaung violence erupted between angry mobs of both Arakanese and Rohingya. Mobs attacked places of worship and stormed homes and shops. Arakanese were enraged about the murder and rape of an ethnic Arakanese Buddhist woman, Thida Htwe, on May 28, allegedly by three Muslim men. In retaliation an Arakanese mob boarded a bus and killed ten Muslim men on June 3, though the men accused of the crime had already been detained (Human Rights Watch 2012, 18). Human Rights Watch reports that on June 8, thousands of Muslims rioted in the town of Maungdaw and destroyed Arakanese property. By June 10, President Thein Sein declared a state of emergency in these four townships.

Between 2012 and 2014 violent clashes broke out between these groups in Meiktila and Kanbalu in Central Burma, in Arakan state, and in Mandalay ("Why Is There Communal Violence" 2014). In all there have been three recent waves of Rohingya fleeing Burma in the wake of this violence: the first following the violence in June 2012, the second following a new outbreak of violence in the fall of 2012, and one more wave of irregular migration beginning in 2014, largely in response to ongoing repression and human rights violations (UN Human Rights Council 2016). Yet in none of these cases have other states in the region welcomed Rohingya asylum seekers.

Rohingya Rights Violations

In this section I evaluate how Burmese deprivation of Rohingya citizenship has contributed to civil and political, as well as economic, social, and cultural, rights violations. I note where these rights violations intersect with trafficking push factors and causes of migration. Importantly, many well-respected international human rights organizations have published reports illustrating the extent to which the violence that engulfed Burma in the summer of 2012 was truly sectarian in nature—with initial attacks by one group and counterattacks by the other (see, e.g., Human Rights Watch 2012, 21–24).[10] My analysis focuses on the extent to which violence and rights deprivation targeted at the Rohingya may have encouraged them to flee Burma. For this reason, the following discussion consciously pays more attention to the violations suffered by rather than perpetrated by the Rohingya in Burma.

Civil and Political Rights Violations

Lack of Freedom of Movement and Forced Relocation

Rohingya living in Burma are not allowed to travel between villages, leave their home villages for major cities, or travel outside the country. These travel restrictions have been in place for decades, ostensibly to provide security, but they are directed exclusively at Muslim communities (UN Human Rights Council 2016, 8). Since 2012, many of the travel restrictions imposed by security forces have become so onerous that Rohingya simply cannot leave their homes, even to gather food from local markets, for fear of arrest and hostility from local Rakhine people. In an interview with Human Rights

Watch, a Rohingya man living in Sittwe, after the initiation of violence there, explained that he had been trapped in his house for two weeks and surreptitiously went to a local market to buy food for his family so that they would not starve (Human Rights Watch 2012, 40).

To legally leave one's home requires prior, written approval from the government, and if a Rohingya fails to return home by the specified time, the person risks being removed from the village register (Staples 2012). If someone travels to a destination other than that marked on the certificate and fails to report to immigration, then the person has committed a criminal act (Fortify Rights 2014, 33) The Rohingyas' noncitizen status is a critical tool used by Burmese security services to arrest and detain Rohingya for traveling without a permit (Irish Centre for Human Rights 2010).

Because Rohingya Muslims are mostly clustered in northern Arakan state, it has been easy for authorities to limit their movement by simply invoking Section 144(1) of the Myanmar Code of Criminal Procedure, permitting temporary curfews in the name of public order (UN Human Rights Council 2016). Following the violence in the summer of 2012, many Rohingya tried to flee and were instead herded through the streets of Sittwe into a massive detention complex known as Bumay Junction (Green, MacManus, and Venning 2015, 80). Others who tried to escape the violence were forcibly relocated to one of thirty-nine other internally displaced people (IDP) camps throughout Burma. The camps severely restrict residents' movement, again in the name of security. Some 138,000 Rohingya who sought to flee the violence ended up in this detention complex or in one of the IDP camps (UN Human Rights Council 2016, 8).

The presence of a large population of internally displaced people has been linked to a greater probability of trafficking (Akee et al. 2010). IDPs, like refugees, are acutely vulnerable to traffickers because they face particularly poor living conditions in the camps. Limited economic opportunities for large, concentrated groups create openings for traffickers, who can lure these populations easily with the promise of better prospects abroad. Such severe restrictions on movement can be considered a migration push factor because Rohingya have exceptionally limited abilities to leave their homes to earn a living or acquire basic provisions.

Restrictions on Voting and Holding Public Office

In 2011 the military junta initiated the process of political liberalization by instituting wide-ranging democratic reform. This process culminated in democratic elections in November 2015 that resulted in the election of a civilian government in Burma. Yet in the run-up to these elections the military junta rescinded the temporary identity cards held by approximately

seven hundred thousand stateless people throughout Burma, disenfranchis-
ing them with the stroke of a pen in May 2015 (UN Human Rights Council
2016, 11). Of those, approximately five hundred thousand are Rohingya
Muslims (Minority Rights Group International 2015, 151). Muslim candidates were not allowed to run for election, and the current Burmese parliament lacks even a single Muslim member. For the Rohingya, whom Burmese
authorities have long considered "Bengali" and therefore foreign, this was
one of the final strikes at undermining whatever remaining legal status they
had previously possessed in Burma. Up until 2015 those with temporary
identity cards had been permitted to vote but were generally discouraged
from participating in civic life.

When the military junta disenfranchised minority populations and excluded them from holding public office in 2015, they undercut the core rights
we typically attribute to democracies. Voting and holding public office are
key attributes of democratic regimes, typically differentiating them from
autocratic regimes in practice. The extent to which Burmese authorities sev-
ered this form of political participation for repressed Muslim communities
may contribute to Rohingya eagerness to flee. The literature on trafficking
points to low levels of democracy as one of many push factors that could
explain cross-border flight (Jac-Kusharski 2012; Frank 2011).

Mass Arrests and Systematic Extortion

In the period immediately following the sectarian violence in the summer of
2012, state security forces (Burmese army, Lon Thein [riot police], and Nasaka [border police]) swept through northern Arakan state and engaged in
mass arrests of Rohingya (Human Rights Watch 2012). Security forces held
lists as they went door to door through Maungdaw Township seeking out
those they thought responsible for participating in the violence. Human
Rights Watch also reported mass arrests of Rohingya in remote villages
south of Maungdaw between June 12 and 24 (2012, 28). Determining where
the arrested individuals were taken by state security services was challenging
because the arrested were not given the opportunity to call their families.
Some were reportedly taken to Buthidaung Prison, while others were taken
to local police stations (29).

Even before the 2012 violence, the Rohingya experienced systematic arrest and extortion at the hands of the state security services. In a 2010 study,
the Irish Centre for Human Rights conducted a field mission in Burma that
highlighted the arbitrary nature of arrest and detention of Rohingya. The
police, army, or Nasaka regularly arrested Rohingya on completely fabri-
cated charges (lack of proper travel documentation or forgery, for example) and then demanded a bribe in exchange for the detainee's release (Irish

Centre for Human Rights 2010, 120–121). Even more troubling were the numerous instances in which third-party brokers, working informally for the Nasaka, identified Rohingya to be targeted for a bribe. Once the Nasaka agrees, the broker speaks to the Rohingya in question, explaining that the person faces arrest unless the individual pays the amount designated by the Nasaka. A broker's fee is also added to the Rohingya's expense. As the Irish Centre for Human Rights explains, the Rohingya "are essentially paying a fee for their liberty and in order to stay the inevitable infliction of violence on their person. The security forces profit by obtaining guaranteed bribes with a minimum of effort" (2010, 121).

Threats to integrity of person, virtually identical to those described previously, are identified in the migration literature as a driver of flight (Davenport, Moore, and Poe 2003). Being the target of extortion is not identified anywhere in the trafficking literature as a trafficking push factor; corruption and a low level of law enforcement, however, have been clearly linked to a greater probability of trafficking (Akee et al. 2014). In Burma, Rohingya are the targets of this systematic extortion, which can contribute to the economic hardship that trafficking victims frequently cite as motivation for their willingness to be trafficked. The economic burden associated with retaining the Rohingya's liberty in Burma may simply become prohibitive and force them to make the difficult choice to flee, possibly with the assistance of a trafficker.

Targeted Violence and Deprivation of Life

The Arakan coordination of attacks on Rohingya towns, centering in Maungdaw Township, in the summer of 2012 has already been described. There is no question that at least since the initiation of this conflict Rohingya have endured targeted violence. But here I focus on the role of state security forces in coordinating with Arakanese civilians to perpetuate the violence against the Rohingya. Early in that summer interviews conducted by Amnesty International and Equal Rights Trust of Rohingya, which had fled Burma, suggested that members of the Burmese army and the Nasaka accompanied and assisted mobs of Arakanese civilians as they opened fire on Rohingya villagers in Maungdaw on June 24. Witnesses also suggested that state security forces participated in the torching of entire Rohingya villages and rape of Rohingya women and girls (Equal Rights Trust 2012, 11–12). According to an interview conducted by Human Rights Watch, members of the Lon Thein and Nasaka walked the streets with machete-wielding Arakanese villagers:

> I saw some young Arakan with long swords and machetes walking together with law enforcement—the Nasaka and the police. You

could see them traveling on the same truck, young Arakan with police on the same truck, some with homemade instruments. You
wouldn't see any Muslims in the street at that time, and during the
night you wouldn't see any Muslims either. Instead we saw many
Nasaka and young Arakan, and we heard many shootings. Apparently it was them pushing the Muslims back. Arakan said the village
was attacked by a group of Muslims, and Nasaka was armed. . . . We
saw four or five young guys walking with machetes alongside four or
five [Nasaka soldiers]. We could see villages burning. We could see
smoke. We could hear shooting. We didn't know who was shooting
at whom. The shooting was not long. It would last a minute or two.
Mostly it wouldn't be intensive. It would be one shot, another shot,
and at other times it was rapid firing. (2012, 25)

As Arakanese civilians swept through Rohingya villages, burning homes
and violently killing Rohingya, the police who were not assisting the Arakanese in the attacks refused to protect Rohingya. One Rohingya woman in
Sittwe told Human Rights Watch that her home was surrounded by an Arakanese mob (2012, 23). When her brother-in-law tried to jump out a back
window to escape the violence, he was caught by the mob, and his throat was
cut. The mob yelled to the rest of the remaining residents of the house that
they could come out and be killed or stay in the house and burn to death.
Throughout the ordeal the family phoned the police, begging for protection,
but the police did not come. Another Rohingya man explained that the police watched as a his two brothers-in-law were stabbed to death in Sittwe (25).
    Security forces (police, Lon Thein, Nasaka, and the military) did more
than support angry Arakanese mobs or watch idly as Rohingya were murdered; they themselves were engaged directly in the killings of Rohingya
villagers. Interviews conducted by the Equal Rights Trust and Human Rights
Watch with Rohingya who managed to escape the violence suggest that security forces shot at Rohingya as they tried to extinguish the fires set by
Arakanese villagers (Human Rights Watch 2012, 26; Equal Rights Trust
2012, 9). The Nasaka, Lon Thein, and police from Maungdaw fired on Rohingya trying to flee the violence (Human Rights Watch 2012, 27). Obtaining reliable information on the number of Rohingya murdered in Burma
since 2012 is very difficult because much of the existing information is obtained from eyewitness interviews. Human Rights Watch reports that the
deadliest incident for Rohingya occurred on October 23 in Yan Thei village
in Mrauk-U Township, where "at least" seventy Rohingya were killed
(2013, 4).
    The relationship between violence at home and out-migration is well es-
tablished in the migration literature (Davenport, Moore, and Poe 2003;

Schmeidel 1997; Melander and Oberg 2007). Rohingya experienced extreme violence at the hands of both the government and a hostile majority population. There is no question that the threat of violence and death can increase the likelihood of trafficking. The Rohingya who have experienced their villages being razed to the ground, their homes destroyed, and family members murdered are much like refugees from a war zone. We know from the trafficking literature that war, human rights violations, and violence can compel victims to use any means necessary to flee in search of safety (Akee et al. 2010; Clawson, Layne, and Small 2006). But religious and ethnic fragmentation is also identified as a trafficking push factor in the trafficking literature (Akee et al. 2010). The Rohingya face a sort of double vulnerability to trafficking because they are persecuted by both state authorities and a hostile ethnic and religious majority population.[11]

Economic, Social, and Cultural Rights

Access to Health Care and Food

Access to health care and food is a particularly acute problem for Rohingya in Burma today, because the population is mostly confined to IDP camps or their villages. Since the 2012 violence, the Burmese government has severely restricted even the very limited access to health-care services that Rohingya had enjoyed earlier. For example, an interview conducted by Penny Green, Thomas MacManus, and Alicia de la Cour Venning (2015) with a resident of Mrauk-U explained that villagers used to be able to pay between fifty thousand and seventy thousand kyat (between thirty-nine and fifty-four U.S. dollars) to apply for a travel permit to visit a hospital in Minbya, Kyauk Taw, or Sittwe. But following the events of 2012, Rohingya were no longer permitted to leave the village to seek medical treatment (2015, 94). The Muslims able to get out of their villages or the camps to receive medical care are treated in segregated and substandard hospital wards (UN Human Rights Council 2016, 10). The villages and camps have very limited medical supplies and health-care providers. Without access to even basic health care the villages and camps have endured widespread, preventable illness and death. Included among the common medical conditions are infant malnutrition, tuberculosis, and diarrhea (Green, MacManus, and Venning 2015, 93). In 2014, after treating twenty-two Rohingya who had been attacked by Arakanese in Chee Yar Tan, the Burmese government expelled Medicins Sans Frontieres for treating Rohingya victims of an alleged Buddhist massacre that the government said did not happen (93; see also "Medecins" 2014).

Rohingya in Burmese IDP camps and in unofficial Bangladeshi camps also have very limited access to food.[12] Within Burma, the travel restrictions in place make it impossible for Rohingya to work and buy food, so they are dependent on food aid from the government and foreign organizations. Since 2010 the UN's World Food Programme has been active in the state of Arakan (as well other poor states in Burma), but the rations supplied are not sufficient to stave off malnutrition (Green, MacManus, and Venning 2015, 96).[13] When the ISCI conducted interviews with Rohingya in villages and IDP camps throughout Burma in 2015, their research found "evidence of a hunger crisis within all Rohingya camps and communities. Researchers observed the signs of malnutrition on a daily basis in the camps, including children with distended abdomens and discolored hair" (2015, 95). The economic isolation that leads to food deprivation is carried out by both Buddhist monks and the Rakhine Nationalities Development Party (RNDP). In June 2012 the monks circulated a pamphlet in Sittwe instructing Buddhist residents not to buy from or sell to Muslims for any reason and said they must not be "friendly" to Muslims (Human Rights Watch 2013, 15). Similar pamphlets were eventually circulated throughout the state of Arakan. The RNDP went a step further and issued threats to any Buddhists who supported Muslims (16).

For the Rohingya living in unofficial Bangladeshi refugee camps there are no food rations, and since they are illegally residing in Bangladesh, they cannot work. The result has been widespread hunger and death by starvation. In the unofficial Bangladeshi refugee camp for Rohingya, Kutupalong, the Global Acute Malnutrition rate, which measures the percentage of children who are malnourished, is 18.2 percent. In a healthy country less than 5 percent of children should meet this threshold, and even in countries we tend to think of as food insecure, the Global Acute Malnutrition rate is much lower—in Haiti it is 6 percent (Physicians for Human Rights 2010, 19).

Deprivation of Work and Forced Labor

Paradoxically, Rohingya are both deprived of the ability to work legally for pay and then forced into unpaid labor. Being forced to remain inside a camp or a village without provisions makes it impossible to run any sort of business or find a job. Rohingya villagers report that following the violence in the summer of 2012, all of their businesses were lost (Green, MacManus, and Venning 2015, 97). Across the many reports used to conduct this research, there are countless references to Rohingya begging for rice and money in the streets as their only means for survival. Frequently, Rohingya in unofficial camps beg or borrow money at exorbitant rates from the relatively better-off Rohingya in official camps (Physicians for Human Rights 2010).

The army, Nasaka, and police all use the Rohingya for forced labor. Rohingya village administrators are given a quota for the number of laborers that these groups will need and must then fill the quota with Rohingya workers (Arakan Project 2012). Rohingya are selected by village administrators on a rotating system, but better-off community members can pay to avoid working. Rohingya laborers are used in a variety of fields—construction, animal husbandry, paddy cultivation, and log and bamboo collection; and they are also used as workers to maintain Nasaka camps, porters in remote areas, and sentries in townships that border Bangladesh (3–5). The burden of these demands for forced labor are so great that families are often left with little choice but to send children so that breadwinners can try to eke out resources for the rest of the family. In the spring of 2012, just before the violence broke out in Rakhine state, the Arakan Project documented the use of Rohingya child laborers between the ages of nine and twelve, suggesting that as much as 20 percent of forced labor is done by children (6).

Deprivation of work and forced labor without pay create dramatic income inequality between Rohingya and the rest of the Burmese population. Income inequality is frequently cited (Clawson, Layne, and Small 2006; JacKucharski 2012) as a statistical predictor of trafficking (Cho 2015).

Right to Freely Establish Family Life

Rohingya in Burma are subject to a series of restrictions of their right to marry and make family-planning decisions. Fortify Rights documented official Arakan state policies as early as 2005 that limited Rohingya families to no more than two children (2014, 25). Debates in the national parliament and comments from national politicians also suggest that there is widespread knowledge and support beyond Arakan state for these discriminatory policies.[14] Regional authorities defend the two-child policy as necessary "family planning" for Rohingya families, who may practice polygamy and have more children than Buddhist families do.[15] The two-child policy has dramatic effects on Rohingya human rights generally and Rohingya women's health specifically. To avoid violating the policy, Rohingya women and girls often opt for unsafe and unsanitary abortions. Fortify Rights explains that abortions are performed using the "stick method," wherein a stick is inserted into the uterus to terminate the pregnancy (28). This method leads to infection, complications, and sometimes death. The lack of access to reliable health-care services and the stringent two-child policy put Rohingya in a very difficult and dangerous position.

Rohingya also face tremendous bureaucratic hurdles if they want to obtain a certificate of marriage. To obtain a legal marriage certificate, Rohingya couples must meet ten separate requirements, which include presenting themselves to the authorities on multiple occasions and providing pictures of themselves (for men, without a beard, and for women, without a hijab).

Authorities typically demand bribes that can be as high as one hundred thousand kyat (one hundred U.S. dollars), and the wait time for approval can be two years (Fortify Rights 2014, 30–31). State authorities go out of their way to punish those who live together without getting married and engage in "spot checking"—visiting Rohingya homes unannounced to determine whether an unmarried couple appears to be living together. Those found to be living together "illegally" can be punished by up to ten years in prison (31).[16] But marriage can function as a double-edged sword in regard to human rights. While some Rohingya may flee in the hope of freely marrying, those who arrive in Bangladesh face yet another marriage ban. Since 2014 Rohingya in Bangladesh have been prohibited from marrying each other or marrying Bangladeshi nationals (Blumberg 2014). And for those Rohingya who have successfully fled Burma and arrived in Malaysia, troubling reports beginning in 2016 suggest that young Rohingya girls are being forced into marriage with Malaysian nationals.[17]

Statelessness, Trafficking, and Migration: The 2015 Rohingya Refugee Crisis

Each of these individual human rights violations alone might be enough to reasonably compel Rohingya in Burma to make the difficult choice to flee, perhaps with the help of a trafficker, in search of better living conditions. Yet it is the cumulative effect of these human rights violations that seems to coalesce to make escaping from the repressive conditions a necessity. For those without citizenship or proper documentation, there is little choice but to use illicit means to escape abusive conditions. Their desperate need to flee Burma to alleviate the very real threats to their lives has rendered the Rohingya acutely susceptible to traffickers and very likely to flee Burma. In early 2013, following the waves of violence against Rohingya in Burma in the summer and fall of 2012, those Rohingya who crossed the southern Burmese border into Thailand were frequently detained by Thai immigration officials. In a candid interview with Reuters reporters, the Thai Royal Police acknowledged that once detained by immigration officials, Rohingya migrants were subject to a covert policy they called "option two": Thai immigration officials transporting and selling Rohingya to traffickers waiting on ships in the Bay of Bengal. Once at sea, the ships take Rohingya to jungle camps on the Malaysia-Thai border, where they are held for ransom by traffickers (Szep and Marshall 2013). Those who could not find a benefactor to pay the ransom of about two thousand U.S. dollars were detained indefinitely in the camps.

The UN Office on Drugs and Crime (2016) reports that between 2012 and 2014, the number of migrants escaping Burma and Bangladesh tripled, with Rohingya constituting the largest population in this group. The UN Human Rights Council reports that between early 2014 and early 2016, more than ninety-four thousand Rohingya and Bangladeshi migrants left their countries by boat en route to Thailand and Malaysia with the assistance of traffickers and smugglers (2016, 3). By 2015 the mass exodus of Rohingya from Burma was labeled "the Rohingya refugee crisis." In early 2015 these flows peaked with thirty-one thousand people attempting to escape through maritime routes in the Bay of Bengal (3).

When the Thai and Malaysian governments cracked down on the international smuggling and trafficking networks that were facilitating these flows in May 2015, five thousand migrants were abandoned at sea. The UNHCR (2015) documented the stories of ships like the *Alpha*. Other ships, such as the *Charlie*, were abandoned in the Andaman Sea for twenty days with 409 passengers, 341 of which were Rohingya and 184, children.[18] Malaysia, Thailand, and Indonesia were unwilling to grant the ship landing, and both Malay and Thai authorities turned the ship away as it approached their coasts. Ultimately an Indonesian fishing crew came to the rescue of the starving, dehydrated passengers aboard the *Charlie*.

Conclusion

This book examines emerging threats to human rights and evaluates the extent to which these threats drive cross-border migration. The Rohingya crisis illustrates how deprivation of citizenship can contribute to cascading human rights violations and, ultimately, cross-border flight. Betts suggests that survival migrants are those who face existential threats in their country of habitual residence but for whom refugee status is out of reach. Since the campaign to eliminate their citizenship rights began in Burma in 1974, hundreds of thousands of Rohingya have fled in search of safety. In 2017, before the most recent wave of violence in August, the Inter Sector Coordination Group of the International Organization for Migration estimated that 300,000 Rohingya were already living in Bangladesh. Following the August 2017 violence another 604,000 Rohingya have fled Burma to Bangladesh, placing the approximate number of displaced Rohingya migrants near one million (Inter Sector Coordination Group 2017). This analysis strongly supports Betts's findings that when human rights drop below a certain level, people become more willing to escape by any means necessary. This chapter documents the extent to which diminished human rights protections also create openings for traffickers, who take advantage of migrants fleeing for their lives.

As recently as 2016, Foreign Minister Aung San Suu Kyi was being celebrated by President Barack Obama for Burma's democratic progress. These accolades were accompanied by the withdrawal of long-held American sanctions on the Burmese government. Lost amid this celebration was the plight of the Rohingya, whose human rights have been decimated by the perpetuation of discriminatory Burmese policies. But as Chapter 8 demonstrates, democracy is no guarantee that the rights of stateless populations will be protected. Even the European Union, often celebrated as a beacon of human rights protections, has yet to harmonize its stateless determination procedures, leading to a patchwork approach to the rights of this community across Europe.

The Rohingya case tragically shows that indeed "where those who seek refuge end up matters" in terms of the quality of refugee and specter of human rights protections (see Chapter 9). In Bangladesh today Rohingya are prohibited from marrying each other or Bangladeshi nationals, and as of fall 2017 they were being rounded up and confined in a refugee camp in Cox's Bazaar. The camp is the largest refugee camp in existence today, holding approximately eight hundred thousand people (Arora and Westcott 2017). Even in Malaysia, frequently regarded by Rohingya as a safer place to reside, Rohingya girls are being increasingly sold into marriage. Rohingya have endured unspeakable rights violations, virtually all of which have been permitted because Rohingya have no access to nationality. This study shows that without citizenship, stateless populations are vulnerable to a multitude of civil, political, economic, and social rights violations. When these violations rise to severe levels, as they have in the case of the Rohingya in Burma, escape is the natural response. The experiences of the Rohingya provide a tragic and cautionary tale: when large populations are deprived of citizenship and flee to escape violence, they become easy targets for traffickers, further diminishing their human rights.

NOTES

Acknowledgments: I gratefully acknowledge the support of the American Philosophical Society for this research. I am also indebted to my two excellent research assistants, Laurel Olden and Maya Anthony-Crosby.

1. The UNHCR has dubbed this ship the *Alpha* because its true name is unknown. See UNHRC 2015.

2. Universal Declaration of Human Rights, Article 15.

3. International Covenant on Civil and Political Rights, Article 24 (3) and Convention on the Rights of the Child, Article 7.

4. Convention on the Elimination of All Forms of Discrimination against Women, Article 9.

5. The UN General Assembly had already passed the Universal Declaration of Human Rights by this time, although it is not a treaty.

6. I use the terms "nationality" and "citizenship" interchangeably throughout this chapter per convention in this field.

7. Malaysian Federal Constitution, Article 15.

8. Of the twenty-nine states that apply jus sanguinis nationality laws unequally between men and women, fourteen are in the Middle East and North Africa (Women's Refugee Commission 2013).

9. This practice has become so pervasive in the Dominican Republic that it was taken to the Inter-American Court of Human Rights in 1998 in the case of *Yean and Bosico v. Dominican Republic* (see Open Society Foundations 2009).

10. The Human Rights Watch report details Arakanese violence against Rohingya and Rohingya violence against Arakanese.

11. I am intentionally excluding internal conflict as a cause of human trafficking because the few studies that test this relationship suggest that while external conflict acts as a trafficking push factor, paradoxically, internal conflict does not. See Akee et al. 2014.

12. Rohingya live within two tiers of camps in Bangladesh. Official refugee camps in Bangladesh face their own set of problems but tend to have relatively better conditions than the unofficial Rohingya refugee camps. For more distinctions between the two, see Physicians for Human Rights 2010.

13. For more on the UN World Food Programme's activities in Burma, see World Food Programme 2018.

14. For example, in 2012 Burma's minister of home affairs, Lieutenant-General Ko Ko, told the Burmese parliament that he would work to strengthen restrictions on Rohingya birth, marriage, migration, and so on (Fortify Rights 2014, 26).

15. For many examples of this justification, see Fortify Rights 2014, 25–27.

16. UN Special Rapporteur Tomas Ojea Quintana suggested that a majority of the prison population in Buthidaung were Muslim men imprisoned for marriage and immigration violations (UN Human Rights Council 2010, 22, para. 89).

17. In 2015 the UNHCR suggested that there had been 120 Rohingya child brides. Since 2015 there have been growing reports that many more Rohingya girls are fleeing violence in Burma only to be caught by traffickers and sold as brides in Malaysia. For details on these growing rates of child trafficking and marriage, see Latiff and Harris 2017.

18. The UNHCR (2015) dubbed this ship *Charlie* because its real name could not be determined.

REFERENCES

Abrar, Chowdhury R. 1995. "Repatriation of Rohingya Refugees." *Forced Migration Online.* Available at http://repository.forcedmigration.org/show_metadata.jsp?pid= fmo:50.

Akee, Randall, Arnab Basu, Arjun Bedi, and Nancy Chau. 2014. "Transnational Trafficking, Law Enforcement, and Victim Protection: A Middleman Trafficker's Perspective." *Journal of Law and Economics* 57 (2): 249–286.

Akee, Randall, Arnab Basu, Nancy Chau, and Melanie Khamis. 2010. "Ethnic Fragmentation, Conflict, Displaced Persons and Human Trafficking: An Empirical Analysis." In *Migration and Culture: Frontiers of Economics and Globalization*, edited by Gil Epstein and Ira Gang, 691–716. Bingley, UK: Emerald Group.

Arakan Project. 2012. "Forced Labour against the Rohingya Persists in the Aftermath of the June 2012 Communal Violence in the North Arakan/Rakhine State." Burma Partnership, September 13. Available at http://www.burmapartnership.org/2012/09/

forced-labour-against-the-rohingya-persists-in-the-aftermath-of-the-communal
-violence.

Arora, Medhavi, and Ben Westcott. 2017. "Bangladesh to Move 800,000 Rohingya into
Single Enormous Camp." *CNN*, October 23. Available at http://www.cnn.com/2017/
10/06/asia/bangladesh-rohingya-new-camp/index.html.

Betts, Alexander. 2013. *Survival Migration: Failed Governance and the Crisis of Displacement*. Ithaca, NY: Cornell University Press.

Blumberg, Antonia. 2014. "Rohingya Muslim Refugees Can No Longer Wed in Bangladesh under New Marriage Ban." *Huffington Post*, July 10. Available at https://www
.huffingtonpost.com/2014/07/10/rohingya-muslims-bangladesh_n_5574415.html.

"Burma Violence: 20,000 Displaced in Rakhine State." 2012. *BBC*, October 28. Available
at http://www.bbc.com/news/world-asia-20114326.

Cho, Seo-Young. 2015. "Modeling for Determinants of Human Trafficking: An Empirical Analysis." *Social Inclusion* 3 (1): 2–21.

Clawson, Heather J., Mary Layne, and Kevonne Small. 2006. "Estimating Human Trafficking into the United States: Development of a Methodology." Available at https://
www.ncjrs.gov/pdffiles1/nij/grants/215475.pdf.

Davenport, Christian, Will Moore, and Steven Poe. 2003. "Sometimes You Just Have to
Leave: Domestic Threats and Forced Migration." *International Interactions* 29 (1):
27–55.

Edwards, Alice. 2015. "The Meaning of Nationality." In *Nationality and Statelessness
under International Law*, edited by Alice Edwards and Laura van Waas, 11–43.
Cambridge: Cambridge University Press.

Equal Rights Trust. 2012. "Burning Homes, Sinking Lives: A Situation Report on Violence against Stateless Rohingya in Myanmar and Their *Refoulement* from Bangladesh." June. Available at http://www.equalrightstrust.org/ertdocumentbank/The
%20Equal%20Rights%20Trust%20-%20Burning%20Homes%20Sinking%20Lives
.pdf.

Fortify Rights. 2014. "Policies of Persecution: Ending Abusive State Policies against
Rohingya Muslims in Myanmar." February. Available at http://www.fortifyrights
.org/downloads/Policies_of_Persecution_Feb_25_Fortify_Rights.pdf.

Frank, Richard. 2011. "The Political Economy of Human Trafficking." Unpublished
paper. In the author's possession.

Fullerton, Maryellen. 2015. "Comparative Perspectives on Statelessness and Persecution." *Kansas Law Review* 63 (4): 863–902.

Green, Penny, Thomas MacManus, and Alicia de la Cour Venning. 2015. *Countdown to
Annihilation: Genocide in Myanmar*. London: International State Crime Initiative.

Human Rights Watch. 1996. "Syria: The Silenced Kurds." *Human Rights Watch Reports*
8 (4). Available at https://www.hrw.org/reports/1996/Syria.htm.

———. 2000. "Burma/Bangladesh: Burmese Refugees in Bangladesh; Still No Durable
Solution." *Human Rights Watch Reports* 12 (3). Available at https://www.hrw.org/
reports/2000/burma/index.htm.

———. 2012. "'The Government Could Have Stopped This': Sectarian Violence and
Ensuing Abuses in Burma's Arakan State." Available at https://www.hrw.org/sites/
default/files/reports/burma0812webwcover_0.pdf.

Inter Sector Coordination Group. 2017. "Situation Update: Rohingya Refugee Crisis."
October 24. Available at https://reliefweb.int/sites/reliefweb.int/files/resources/
171024_iscg_sitrep_one_pager_final_0.pdf.

Irish Centre for Human Rights. 2010. "Crimes against Humanity in Western Burma: The Situation of the Rohingyas." Available at http://burmacampaign.org.uk/images/uploads/ICHR_Rohingya_Report_2010.pdf.

Jac-Kucharski, Alicja. 2012. "The Determinants of Human Trafficking: A US Case Study." *International Migration* 50 (6): 150–165.

Latiff, Rozanna, and Ebrahim Harris. 2017. "Sold into Marriage—How Rohingya Girls Become Child Brides in Malaysia." *Reuters*, February 15. Available at https://www.reuters.com/article/uk-myanmar-rohingya-childbrides-insight/sold-into-marriage-how-rohingya-girls-become-child-brides-in-malaysia-idUSKBN15U009.

Lewa, Chris. 2009. "North Arakan: An Open Prison for the Rohingya in Burma." *Forced Migration Review* 32. Available at https://www.fmreview.org/sites/fmr/files/FMRdownloads/en/statelessness/lewa.pdf.

Liechtenstein v. Guatemala. 1955. Second Phase. 1955 I.C.J. 4 (April 6). Available at https://www.refworld.org/cases,ICJ,3ae6b7248.html.

"Medecins Sans Frontieres' Shock at Myanmar Suspension." 2014. *BBC News*, February 28. Available at http://www.bbc.com/news/world-asia-26379804.

Melander, Erik, and Magnus Oberg. 2007. "The Threat of Violence and Forced Migration: Geographical Scope Trumps Intensity of Fighting." *Civil Wars* 9 (2): 156–173.

Milbrandt, Jay. 2011. "Statelessness." *Cardozo Journal of International and Comparative Law* 20 (75): 75–103.

Minority Rights Group International. 2015. *State of the World's Minorities and Indigenous Peoples, 2015: Events of 2014*. London: Minority Rights Group International. Available at http://minorityrights.org/wp-content/uploads/2015/07/MRG-state-of-the-worlds-minorities-2015-FULL-TEXT.pdf.

Open Society Foundations. 2009. "Litigation: Yean and Bosico v. Dominican Republic." Available at https://www.opensocietyfoundations.org/litigation/yean-and-bosico-v-dominican-republic.

Paxon, Alex. 2012. "Finding a Country to Call Home: A Framework for Evaluating Legislation to Reduce Statelessness in Southeast Asia." *Pacific Rim Law and Policy Journal* 21 (3): 623–653.

Physicians for Human Rights. 2010. "Stateless and Starving: Persecuted Rohingya Flee Burma and Starve in Bangladesh." March. Available at https://s3.amazonaws.com/PHR_Reports/stateless-and-starving.pdf.

Rakhine Inquiry Commission. 2013. "Final Report of Inquiry Commission on Sectarian Violence in Rakhine State." July 8. Available at http://www.burmalibrary.org/docs15/Rakhine_Commission_Report-en-red.pdf.

Schmeidel, Susanne. 1997. "Exploring the Causes of Forced Migration: A Pooled Time-Series Analysis." *Social Science Quarterly* 78 (2): 284–308.

Staples, Kelly. 2012. *Retheorising Statelessness: A Background Theory of Membership in World Politics*. Edinburgh: Edinburgh University Press.

Szep, Jason, and Andrew R. C. Marshall. 2013. "Special Report: Thailand Secretly Supplies Myanmar Refugees to Trafficking Rings." *Reuters*, December 4. Available at https://www.reuters.com/article/us-thailand-rohingya-special-report/special-report-thailand-secretly-supplies-myanmar-refugees-to-trafficking-rings-idUSBRE9B400320131205.

UN General Assembly. 1997. "Interim Report on the Situation of Human Rights in Myanmar." October 16. Available at http://www.refworld.org/docid/3b00f2e70.html.

UNHCR (United Nations High Commissioner for Refugees). 2011. "Report on Stateless-ness in South Eastern Europe." September. Available at http://www.refworld.org/pdfid/514d715f2.pdf.
———. 2014a. *Handbook on Protection of Stateless Persons*. Geneva: UNHCR. Available at http://www.unhcr.org/en-us/protection/statelessness/53b698ab9/handbook -protection-stateless-persons.html.
———. 2014b. "A Special Report: Ending Statelessness within 10 Years." Available at http://www.unhcr.org/en-us/protection/statelessness/546217229/special-report -ending-statelessness-10-years.html.
———. 2015. "Abandoned at Sea." August 26. Available at http://tracks.unhcr.org/2015/ 08/abandoned-at-sea.
———. 2017. "Desperate Rohingyas Flee to Bangladesh in Flimsy Rafts." November 17. Available at http://www.unhcr.org/en-au/news/latest/2017/11/5a0ef0af4.html.
———. 2018. "Figures at a Glance." Available at http://www.unhcr.org/en-us/figures-at -a-glance.html.
UN Human Rights Council. 2010. "Human Rights Situations That Require the Council's Attention: Progress Report of the Special Rapporteur on the Situation of Human Rights in Myanmar." March 10. Available at http://www2.ohchr.org/english/bodies/ hrcouncil/docs/13session/A-HRC-13-48.pdf.
———. 2016. "Situation of Human Rights of Rohingya Muslims and Other Minorities in Myanmar." June 28. Available at http://burmacampaign.org.uk/media/A_HRC _32_18_AEV.pdf.
UN Office on Drugs and Crime. 2016. "Protecting Peace and Prosperity in Southeast Asia: Synchronizing Economic and Security Agendas." February. Available at http:// www.globalsecurity.org/military/library/report/2016/protecting_peace_and_pros perity_in_sea.pdf.
U.S. Department of State. 2017. "Country Reports on Human Rights Practices for 2017: Malaysia." Available at https://www.state.gov/j/drl/rls/hrrpt/humanrightsreport/ index.htm?year=2017&dlid=277095#wrapper.
van Waas, Laura. 2008. *Nationality Matters: Statelessness under International Law*. Cambridge, UK: Intersentia Press.
Weissbrodt, David, and Clay Collins. 2006. "The Human Rights of Stateless Persons." *Human Rights Quarterly* 28 (1): 245–276.
Whitman, Elizabeth. 2013. "Jordan's Second-Class Citizens." *Boston Review*, October 14. Available at http://bostonreview.net/world/whitman-jordan-citizenship.
"Why Is There Communal Violence in Myanmar?" 2014. *BBC*, July 3. Available at http:// www.bbc.com/news/world-asia-18395788.
Women's Refugee Commission. 2013. "Our Motherland, Our Country: Gender Dis-crimination in the Middle East and North Africa." June. Available at https://www .womensrefugeecommission.org/images/zdocs/Our_Motherland,_Our_Country _final_for_web.pdf.
World Food Programme. 2018. "WFP Myanmar Country Brief." Available at https:// www.wfp.org/countries/myanmar/food-security/reports-and-bulletins.

8

Challenges in Protection

Stateless Refugees and Victims of Human Trafficking
in the European Union

PATRICIA C. RODDA AND
CHARLES ANTHONY SMITH

nternational and human rights laws both assume a system of sovereign
states that includes a core foundational premise that every individual belongs to a particular state. However, we know this assumption is not reflected in reality. Stateless persons—individuals without citizenship or who,
in other words, do not belong to any state—reside around the world. These
individuals fall outside the established international system and, therefore,
find themselves without many of the traditional protections associated with
citizenship. When stateless persons become survival migrants, as refugees
or victims of human trafficking, for example, their standing in the world
becomes even more precarious. In this chapter, we focus on the challenges
survival migrants face in the second half of their journey—after they have
fled their country of origin and are seeking protection and security from
other states and the international community.

In the European Union (EU), member states have pledged to offer protection to individuals facing persecution and exploitation, implementing
legal regimes to combat statelessness, offer asylum to refugees, and assist
victims of human trafficking. However, these legal regimes and the good
intentions behind them often come into conflict with states' immigration
agendas (Hepburn and Simon 2013). As Europe faces its greatest migration
crisis since World War II, this clash of agendas has moved to the front of
many national domestic debates. Indeed, England's vote in 2016 to exit the
EU, the so-called Brexit vote, is largely thought to be the result of domestic

dissatisfaction with immigration policies and dramatic increases in the number of migrants seeking sanctuary each year. These challenges for the EU illuminate one of the paradoxes of human rights. Any movement toward fulfilling the human rights of migrants may come at the cost of domestic political support and shift public opinion away from open-immigration policies. The conflict between human rights and immigration policies has created and, in many places, institutionalized wide disparities in the protections available to different categories of survival migrants. Stateless persons, in particular, face significant obstacles to protection; these obstacles only intensify for stateless persons who are also refugees or victims of human trafficking.

The EU and its member states have taken relatively clear policy positions in relation to asylum protection for refugees and the fight against human trafficking. The EU has also implemented agreements and put forth guidelines to address statelessness (De Groot, Swider, and Vonk 2015; van Waas 2014; Vukas 1972; UNHCR 2014a). However, there remain important challenges for stateless persons seeking protection in Europe, especially when they also identify as refugees or victims of human trafficking. Two primary sources of these challenges are examined in this chapter: the European approach to statelessness and the disparity between laws and their implementation within the asylum and trafficking protection regimes.

We first deconstruct the idea of statelessness and outline the complications in analyzing the concept in practice. Then we summarize international and European efforts to address existing instances of statelessness and offer protection to stateless persons. We conclude by examining the gaps in the available protections for stateless persons, paying particular attention to the obstacles faced by individuals seeking protection via the asylum and anti-trafficking regimes.

Statelessness Deconstructed

Statelessness, on its face, is a simple concept. It occurs when an individual lacks a recognized nationality or citizenship. However, in practice statelessness is much more complicated. To shed light on the nuances of statelessness, we first deconstruct the definition of statelessness into its relevant components. We then outline the roles of nationality in domestic and international human rights law.

De Jure Statelessness

Stateless persons fall into one of two groups: de jure stateless and de facto stateless. Although both groups are considered to be part of the larger stateless population, each is addressed differently in international law, and, thus, they deserve separate consideration (Blackman 1998). The first group fits most closely with the simple definition for statelessness. De jure stateless persons have no nationality in any legal sense.[1] One of the core concerns about this traditional form of statelessness is that it often starts at birth and is passed on from generation to generation. This traditional form of statelessness results largely from differences in how nationality is conferred.

Nationality laws can be divided into two traditions: jus soli and jus sanguinis. Laws of nationality determined by jus soli are based on a person's birthplace, generally speaking; being born in the territory of a country with jus soli laws is often enough to receive nationality in that state (Weil 2001). Children born in states with these types of nationality laws, therefore, are usually conferred some type of citizenship status regardless of whether or not their parents are stateless, thus ending the cycle of statelessness. Jus soli nationality laws are common in the Americas, which explains, in part, why this region has the lowest rates of statelessness in the world (UNHCR 2014c; van Waas, de Chickera, and Albarazi 2014).

However, most states in Europe have nationality laws based primarily on the jus sanguinis principle, which relies on bloodlines to determine nationality.[2] In most European member states "citizenship [is] the result of [the] nationality of one parent or other more distant ancestors" (Weil 2001, 17). Under this category of nationality law, statelessness can be inherited, which often results in the creation of entire communities of stateless persons. According to the United Nations High Commissioner of Refugees (UNHCR), Europe hosts the third-largest regional population of stateless persons, behind Asia and the Pacific and Africa (UNHCR 2014c). In 2013, of the nearly 3.5 million stateless persons under the UNHCR's statelessness mandate, 670,828 were reported as residing in Europe (UNHCR 2014c).[3] However, advocates have raised serious concerns about how individual states report these statistics. In particular, European states often report individuals of "unknown nationality," which the European Network on Statelessness (ENS) contends is a way to mask the true number of stateless persons in a country (van Waas, de Chickera, and Albarazi 2014).

Additionally, in Europe many states officially provide for the conferral of nationality at birth to stateless persons in their territory. However, because of the stigma often associated with statelessness, parents may not know of or be willing to take advantage of the national laws providing citizenship to their children for fear of facing repercussions themselves. Further, the European Union Democracy Observatory on Citizenship (EUDO) has highlighted the inconsistent conferral of citizenship to various ethnic groups, especially the Roma (see, e.g., Krasniqi 2012; Kusá 2013). These two factors may indicate there are substantially higher numbers of stateless persons in Europe than reported.

De Facto Statelessness

Before the end of World War II, a form of statelessness that did not fit the traditional definition came to the attention of the international community: de facto statelessness. In particular, the experience of the German Jews driven out by the Third Reich demonstrated that having a nationality on paper does not mean it comes with the "usual attributes of nationality, including effective protection" of the state (Batchelor 1995, 233; Deng 2001). This experience has since been repeated for many other populations, including black Mauritanians in the late 1980s, black South Africans under apartheid, and the Rohingya in Burma (Sironi 2016; see also Chapter 7 for a discussion on the Rohingya). Faced with existence as "nationals *and* non-citizens," individuals or even entire populations in this situation may choose or be forced to flee their country of citizenship, creating, by default, instances of statelessness (Batchelor 1995, 233; Arendt 1945).

For the de facto stateless, the definition of statelessness itself presents a key challenge in seeking protection. The recognized definition of statelessness—found in the 1954 Convention Relating to the Status of Stateless Persons (hereafter Statelessness Convention)—is a legal one, as are the concepts of citizenship and nationality in this context. Such a legal definition does not take into account the nuances of lived realities for stateless populations. The experiences of de facto statelessness, in particular, highlight the problematic nature of an exclusively legal definition of nationality. The legal approach does not take into account the quality of the citizenship or the myriad ways in which it can be slowly eroded over time. Although these complications can affect de jure stateless persons, it does so less severely since de jure statelessness most often starts at birth. For the de facto stateless, the transition into statelessness can happen at any point in life. These variations in how statelessness is manifested in different countries and among various communities, therefore, can make determining the point at which statelessness occurs difficult, if not impossible (Batchelor 1995; Settlage 1997).

Nationality in Domestic and International Law

Even in the EU, where supranational laws and directives have taken precedence in several areas of law, decisions regarding how and when to confer nationality still lie with individual states (Aleinikoff and Klusmeyer 2001; Blackman 1998; Deng 2001; Weil 2001). Nationality is "a legal relationship between an individual and the state, 'conferring mutual rights and duties on both'" (Blackman 1998, 1147–1148). It is through this relationship that individuals have access to the system of rights and protections available through the state (Blackman 1998; Blitz and Otero-Iglesias 2011). In fact, Hannah Arendt characterized the right to nationality as the right to have rights (1945; see also Blitz and Ortero-Iglesias 2011). To be without a nationality, therefore, deprives a person of "the prerequisite for the realization of other fundamental rights" (Blackman 1998, 1148).

At the international level, nationality is viewed as "the mechanism by which states designate individuals to themselves in dealing with other states" (Blackman 1998, 1148–1149). In international law, nationality plays an important role in several areas of law, including human rights law. Just as nationality gives the individual access to rights at the state level, nationality operates as the "individual's primary link to the operation of international law" (1150). So in the same way that statelessness deprives an individual of access to rights from a state, it also puts him or her outside the normal mechanisms by which an individual seeks international rights or protection, including the rights to asylum or protection against human trafficking.

Human Rights Protections and International Law

The history of stateless persons and refugees is a long and strongly intertwined one. The international legal approaches to both were influenced particularly by the migrant flows during the two world wars and the problematic nationality shifts caused by the fall of various European empires during the interwar period. At the end of World War II, dignitaries gathered to address the dual challenges of refugees and stateless persons. These delegations built on previous agreements, standard practices, and definitions developed by the League of Nations and refugee organizations. Refugees came to be seen as a broader population, encompassing several groups without protection from their states of origin. They were also seen as the more serious and immediate problem for states in the postwar period, many of which were still hosting or trying to facilitate the repatriation of refugees (Batchelor 1995). The 1951 Convention relating to the Status of Refugees (hereafter Refugee Convention) established the international definition of refugee as an individual who,

> owing to a well-founded fear of persecution for reasons of race, religion, nationality, membership of a particular social group or political opinion, is outside the country of his nationality and is unable, or owing to such fear, is unwilling to avail himself of the protection of that country. (UNHCR 2010)

The convention also obligates signatories to offer asylum protections to individuals meeting this definition.

A concern for all refugees, especially stateless refugees, is documentation, which is often essential both for verifying asylum claims and for making a life while waiting for a decision on their case. Many refugees were not able to bring identification documents with them as they fled their states of origin, had them invalidated by their governments, or lost them along the way. Stateless persons may never have had such documents in the first place. Articles 27 and 28 of the Refugee Convention state that signatories will provide documentation for refugees residing in their territories whether or not they are in the country legally (UNHCR 1984). Unfortunately, the convention does not directly address the issues a lack of documentation causes before refugee status is determined, an issue of particular salience for stateless persons. However, the Executive Committee of the UNHCR has recommended that applicants for asylum be supplied with some form of identity document while waiting for the decision on their case, and according to the UNHCR (1984) most states with formal refugee determination procedures do provide applicants with such documentation.

The pressure to deal with the issue of refugee populations and to deal with it quickly meant the 1951 conference was dominated by discussions of refugees and the issue of statelessness was tabled for later debate. It was also felt that statelessness was too poorly understood and in need of more study before any international agreement could be reached (Batchelor 1995). Although the same concerns plagued a conference held three years later to address the protection of stateless persons and the reduction of statelessness worldwide, the delegates in attendance did reach an international agreement to address some concerns related to stateless populations. In particular, the 1954 Statelessness Convention provides the definition of stateless individuals as persons "not considered as a national by any State under the operation of its law" (UNHCR 2014b). Also, like the Refugee Convention, the Statelessness Convention provides a minimum standard of treatment for individuals meeting the definition of stateless persons.

However, neither the 1954 conference nor the Statelessness Convention led to development of an independent advisory body charged with assisting stateless persons akin to the UNHCR's role with refugees, and initiatives to reduce or prevent statelessness were again tabled for future consideration. These specific concerns, championed by the United Nations (UN) and human rights organizations, were thought too controversial; they would "compel the members of the Conference to consult their Governments and might give rise to endless debate" (Batchelor 1995, 245). Instead, stateless persons were added as another population of concern under the UNHCR's mandate.

It would take nearly another decade before the 1961 Convention on the Reduction of Statelessness would be negotiated and enter into force.

The international protections against human trafficking have a more recent history and one largely separated from the concerns of refugees and stateless persons. The primary international instrument related to trafficking is the 2003 Protocol to Prevent, Suppress and Punish Trafficking in Persons, Especially Women and Children (also known as the Palermo Protocol), supplementing the UN Convention against Transnational Organized Crime, which came into force earlier the same year. Although the Palermo Protocol also clearly falls within the remit of international human rights law, the international—and European—laws on human trafficking are unique among these protection regimes for their simultaneous focus on the criminal nature of trafficking. To that end, the Palermo Protocol lays out the definition of trafficking as well as the expected rights for victims of trafficking and the requirements for the prosecution of their traffickers (OHCHR 2000).

European Protection Regimes

The conventions relating to refugees and stateless persons that emerged in the wake of World War II were a response, in part, to larger ongoing concerns about immigration—especially survival migration—into and across Europe. Starting with these conventions, a hierarchy of protection agendas emerged in the region and became clearer over time, with concerns about controlling immigration often dominating all three of the protection schemes examined here. The preference given to each of these areas of protection can be seen, for example, in the rates and speed with which EU member states have ratified the relevant treaties and the importance given to harmonizing the policy area within the EU.

The protection available to refugees has emerged as the strongest regime in Europe, and the EU has taken the lead in this area of law among its member states. The fight against human trafficking is a close second in this protection hierarchy, falling behind the asylum protection regime only because of the conflict between the regional-level focus on human rights and the focus among many individual member states on the criminalization and prosecution of trafficking. Preventing and addressing statelessness have received the least amount of attention and coordinated effort in the EU.

The pride of place given to refugees and victims of human trafficking in protection schemes has remained evident despite the entry into force of the two statelessness conventions. In Europe, for example, all of the EU member states are signatories to the Geneva Convention. Thirteen of the current member states signed the convention within ten years. All current EU member states had signed the convention by 1997 (UNHCR 2015). The response to the Palermo Protocol was just as strong across the EU. All member states signed the protocol within two years of its entry into force—the vast majority within one month. Further, all of the member states have taken the necessary steps to ratify the protocol, with the Czech Republic's ratification at the end of 2014 the most recent (United Nations 2019c).

Twenty-four of the twenty-eight member states have signed the Statelessness Convention, and only twenty have signed the Convention on the Reduction of Statelessness. Four member states—Cyprus, Estonia, Malta, and Poland—are party to neither convention (United Nations 2019a, 2019b). Most accessions to the conventions have been quite recent—half of the EU member states that are parties to the Statelessness Convention signed after 1990, thirty-six years after it was introduced, and more than half signed the 1961 Convention on the Reduction of Statelessness after 2000. The lack of dedication to the statelessness conventions among European member states has persisted despite the EU's promise that all member states would sign the 1954 convention by 2014 and "consider" signing the 1961 convention soon thereafter (Council of the European Union 2015).

Beyond international legal concerns, the EU and individual member states have addressed refugees, human trafficking victims, and stateless persons differently in practice. Every member state has some form of asylum determination procedure, and the EU has taken the lead in harmonizing asylum policies across Europe (Blockmans and Wessel 2009; Collett 2016; Tolley 2012). Determination of refugee status is strongly supported by the international convention and four key EU directives: the Reception Conditions Directive, the Dublin II Regulation, the Qualifications Directive, and the Asylum Procedures Directive. There is, of course, a great deal of debate over the nuances of refugee law in Europe, especially during the current migrant crisis, but there are, at least, an ongoing discussion and action to address individuals qualifying as refugees (Collett 2016; Kanter 2016).

The EU's efforts to address human trafficking are newer than those for refugee determination and protection, largely because the international protocol is relatively new. The EU acted swiftly to implement the elements of the Palermo Protocol. Two key pieces of law are important for the regional efforts against trafficking. The first is the 2005 Council of Europe Convention on Action against Trafficking in Human Beings, which codifies elements of the Palermo Protocol and lays out regional efforts for the fight against trafficking. This convention also establishes an evaluation mechanism through the Group of Experts on Action against Trafficking in Human Beings (GRETA) for monitoring the progress and compliance of member states of the Council of Europe. The second regulation is specific to the EU. The 2011 directive on preventing and combating trafficking in human beings establishes the plan for an "integrated, holistic, and human rights approach to fight against trafficking in human beings" within the EU (European Parliament 2011). Additionally, the directive expands the definition of human trafficking to reaffirm the focus on both labor and sexual exploitation and to specifically include forced begging, trafficking for human organs, illegal adoption, and forced marriage.

European Statelessness Policies and Protection Regimes

There has also been a great deal of discussion in the EU about addressing statelessness. The EU has even gone as far as to publicly acknowledge that "several Member States violate the international and European standards regarding protection against statelessness" (De Groot, Swider, and Vonk 2015, 9). There has been discussion but very little action to address the gaps in the protection of stateless persons or to reduce their numbers within Europe. A set of "conclusions" adopted by the European Council in 2015 highlighted several promises and directives it had tried to implement to address statelessness. The items fall into four general categories: the right to nationality, asylum and immigration policy, statelessness in non-EU countries, and procedures for determining statelessness. The issues related to asylum policy are discussed later. To our knowledge, the EU has not directly addressed statelessness within the context of human trafficking.

Right to Nationality

The right to nationality is enshrined in the Universal Declaration of Human Rights and is cited as one of the "basic principles" of the 1997 European Convention on Nationality (Council of the European Union 2015). However, decisions regarding nationality law remain under the authority of individual member states. The lack of leadership at the supranational level has prevented stateless populations that exist in multiple EU member states, such as the various Romani communities, from having effective remedy to their stateless status. No state wishes to take on the responsibility for these communities, and, given their dispersion across Central and Eastern Europe in particular, it is possible for states to claim that these communities are in fact nationals of other states and thus ineligible for international or supranational protection (Sardelić 2013). There has been some effort, however, made by various nongovernmental organizations (NGOs) and the UNHCR in conjunction with the Council of Europe to address statelessness in this part of Europe, especially in response to the disintegration of the Soviet Union and Yugoslavia (Sawyer 2011). Interestingly, in contrast to the effect the deprivation of citizenship has in other cases, the existence of the EU seems to have alleviated the push to flee for European stateless populations. Even without citizenship from a specific state, these populations are afforded certain levels of rights at the supranational level and freedom of movement that stateless persons living in countries outside the EU do not enjoy.

External Statelessness

The EU has been most active in addressing stateless populations outside Europe. In 2012, the EU agreed on the Strategic Framework on Human Rights and Democracy and two action plans, which, among other things, proposed "the establishment of a joint framework to tackle statelessness issues with non-EU countries." These action plans are part of the EU's foreign policy initiatives to promote democracy (Council of the European Union 2015).

This approach to statelessness might ultimately benefit European states by addressing the causes of stateless persons who become survival migrants seeking protection or assistance in Europe. Côte d'Ivoire serves as a potential example of how these two initiatives can be linked. The country has a long history of encouraging regional migration, especially of labor migrants, reaching back to the colonial era. Nationality laws changed over time, especially in the postcolonial era, but in general many of these immigrant communities were integrated into Ivorian society and at least offered the option for nationality for themselves or for children born in Côte d'Ivoire. However, beginning in the mid-1990s, the Ivorian government introduced increasingly discriminatory policies that targeted individuals with migrant backgrounds whom the government saw as foreigners. The stripping of rights and nationality from these communities created thousands of stateless persons, contributed directly to the outbreak of civil war in 2002, and forced individuals out of the country to seek safety across the region and in Europe. In response to the crisis, the EU helped facilitate peace talks to bring an end to the war, was a major donor in addressing the humanitarian crisis caused by the violence, and is working to support new government policies and laws that are restoring nationality to those made stateless before the war (van Waas 2014).

Dealing with statelessness in crisis situations like the civil war in Côte d'Ivoire and its aftermath is certainly important in preventing the violence and deprivation of rights that lead to the flight of certain categories of survival migrants to Europe. However, despite the role the EU is choosing to play externally, its framework does not address the problem of statelessness within Europe; nor does it directly give guidance to states in Europe on how to assist stateless persons who flee to Europe but do not qualify as refugees. Further, despite the external focus of efforts to reduce statelessness, serious concerns have been raised by researchers about how to address the causes of survival migration in the territories of EU member states. This is especially true in addressing factors such as statelessness that contribute to an individual's vulnerability to becoming a victim of human trafficking. Heather M. Smith-Cannoy and Charles Anthony Smith (2012), for example, show that despite being a leader in the antitrafficking movement in Europe, the Netherlands carefully excluded its Caribbean territories from its treaty commitments. However, as territories of an EU member state, these islands also fall outside the external efforts of the EU to combat both statelessness and human trafficking.

Determination Procedures

The final category of pledges made by the EU relates to the formal determination of an individual's status as stateless. Recognition of stateless status, like refugee status, generally requires an official process to determine whether an individual meets the legal definition of statelessness. Also like the refugee process and, in some ways, antitrafficking programs, an individual's official recognition as being stateless plays a part in whether he or she would be eligible for protection. Unlike the EU's leadership role in developing and harmonizing asylum procedures and refugee status determination mechanisms as well as the regulations for fighting trafficking and assisting victims, there is no supranational requirement to implement determination procedures or offer any form of protection for stateless migrants.

There are two potential foundations from which such a requirement could develop. First, Article 14 of the European Convention on Human Rights (ECHR) prohibits discrimination based on "national . . . origin" or "association with a national minority." The asylum legal regime in the EU draws heavily on Articles 3 and 8, the prohibition against torture and the right for private and family life. Similarly, the antitrafficking law in Europe relies in part on Article 4 prohibiting both slavery and forced labor, Article 5 providing for the right to liberty and the security of one's person, and most recently, Article 12 arguing that forced marriage contravenes the right to marry (Council of Europe 1950). It would not be unprecedented, therefore, for the European Parliament to draw on the ECHR as a foundation to justify regional directives to respond to statelessness.

Second, the EU has "invited the [European] Commission to launch exchanges of good practices among member states" interested in developing procedures to determine an individual's stateless status (Council of the European Union 2015). There have been some efforts to share common practices and lessons learned, but these efforts are few and far between. This lack of shared knowledge is largely due to the relative dearth of determination procedures for statelessness among EU member states. According to the

TABLE 8.1 STATELESSNESS DETERMINATION PROCEDURES

	First generation	Second generation	Third generation
Specific rules in law, clear or relatively clear procedural framework		Spain (2001) Latvia (2004) Hungary (2007)	Moldova (2012) Georgia (2012) Philippines (2012) UK (2013)
Clear protection ground but no detailed rules in law yet functioning procedural framework	France (1952) Italy (1970s)	Mexico (2007)	
Clear protection ground yet incomplete procedural framework			Slovakia (2012) Turkey (2013)

Source: Gyulai 2013.

ENS, only twelve states worldwide have statelessness determination procedures, seven of which are in the EU: France, Hungary, Italy, Latvia, Slovakia, Spain, and the United Kingdom (Gyulai 2013).[4] The ENS rates these determination procedures by clarity and strength relative to the law as well as the time at which the state adopted the procedure. Table 8.1 shows the twelve states with determination procedures for stateless status by these two criteria.

Although there are only a few European states with statelessness determination procedures, there is a clear trend toward incorporating more specific approaches to determining statelessness when such a mechanism is put in place. This trend is reinforced by recent developments in France, which updated its procedure from the one analyzed by the ENS in its 2013 guidelines. The French authorities replaced the original procedure, which according to ENS recognized statelessness as grounds for protection only in its administrative process, with one "regulated by law" (Cosgrave 2016). This change means that all of the European statelessness determination procedures, except that in Slovakia, have enshrined protection on the grounds of statelessness in domestic law.

The ENS guide on good practices emphasizes that none of the models in place for determining stateless status constitutes a good model on its own (Gyulai 2013). Indeed, each of the European procedures has strengths and weaknesses that can positively or negatively affect the protections received by stateless persons. All of the member states with determination procedures, except Hungary, for example, do not require an individual to be in the state legally to apply for stateless-status determination. Additionally, all of the states with a determination mechanism have established a right to residency to anyone whose statelessness is recognized. However, there is a great deal of variation in access to education, health care, and, most important, naturalization procedures for individuals with recognized stateless status (Gyulai 2013).

More striking than the differences between states with determination procedures, however, are the pitfalls stateless persons face in states without explicit determination procedures. Earlier this year, the European Migration Network (EMN) Ireland and UNHCR Ireland together hosted a seminar with representatives from Ireland, the United Kingdom, and France. The seminar was developed to follow the recommendation of the EU to share good practices in addressing statelessness, focusing on improving these practices in Ireland. The seminar highlighted some of the positive steps the Irish have taken to address the needs of stateless persons, including "potentially faster access to citizenship and waiver of the fees that are usually required of naturalisation applicants" (Cosgrave 2016). However, since Ireland does not have a specific determination procedure, it has been dealing with applications for consideration of statelessness status on an ad hoc basis. Catherine Cosgrave (2016) argues that this approach not only has been unsatisfactory for applicants, whose access to the few rights outlined in Irish law is not always guaranteed, but is not cost effective or efficient for the state.

Representatives from the United Kingdom and France were invited to offer advice from their own experiences with determining stateless status. Irish courts and administrators often look to British institutions for precedents, and the French have the oldest statelessness determination procedure in Europe, making them natural sources for guidance. The British offered several suggestions for the Irish procedures, but the discussion also underlined weaknesses in the British approach to determining statelessness, including high refusal rates and the lack of judicial review. Recent improvements in the French system, however, through its 2015 reforms, offered a view into a system attempting to implement lessons learned over decades. For example, under its original statelessness determination procedure, an individual identified as stateless was not necessarily guaranteed residency or the rights afforded to legal French residents. Under the 2015 reforms, an official determination of statelessness now "always results in the grant of residence permits, including family reunification rights" for the recognized individual (Cosgrave 2016).

Statelessness and the Asylum-Protection Regime

There are two ways in which asylum protection intersects with issues of statelessness in Europe. The first is through the explicit delegation of statelessness determination to the state's asylum authorities. The second, and far more common, takes place when stateless persons seek protection as refugees in states where there is no other official mechanism through which they can receive assistance. Both options present unique challenges for stateless people that often reflect the historical conflation of stateless populations with refugees.

Three of the seven EU member states with statelessness determination procedures—France, Spain, and the United Kingdom—have delegated the responsibility for this procedure to the state authority that is also charged with asylum determination (Gyulai 2013). In France and Spain these authorities are specialized for asylum; in France the authorities are also specialized in dealing with statelessness. In the United Kingdom, however, the asylum authority falls under the immigration authorities of the Home Office (Asylum Information Database 2016). According to the EMN, this approach is acceptable in situations where the stateless population in the country is primarily migratory rather than a domestic stateless population. By focusing on migratory stateless populations, the asylum and statelessness determination procedures face similar challenges, including an applicant's lack of documentation; fear of contacting or interacting with the state of origin; and need for translation, legal, and other basic services.

Thus, placing statelessness determination procedures under the control of asylum authorities makes sense because the expertise of these preexisting asylum institutions is believed to be effectively transferable. Even in states without determination procedures, the ENS argues that utilizing asylum or immigration procedures can be an effective option until an official determination procedure for statelessness can be put in place. These authorities "have long standing experience in dealing with nationality," and they generally have "the necessary human . . . and infrastructural resources to effectively conduct statelessness determination procedures" (Gyulai 2013). Indeed, some research shows that being stateless may increase the likelihood of receiving protection through asylum procedures (Rodda 2015). The asylum authorities in European states also have a certain level of established legitimacy in respecting international and regional standards since they are also expected to meet minimum criteria set by supranational authorities.

Challenges to Seeking Protection via Asylum Procedures

Despite the benefits of using asylum or immigration authorities to conduct statelessness determinations, there are several serious challenges to this approach. The assumption that expertise with nationality in the context of immigration or asylum is necessarily transferable to issues of statelessness could be problematic. The differences between statelessness concerns and those regarding less controversial types of migrants, even survival migrants, are particularly problematic. There are different issues at stake for stateless persons than for other migrants, who still have the legal protection of their state of origin to fall back on if the immigration procedure goes against them. It may not be an ideal economic solution for the migrant, but as a national of some state, he or she at least has the potential to access domestic and international legal protections should the need arise; this possibility does not exist for stateless migrants.

Statelessness and refugee determination procedures are perhaps more similar in the obstacles involved in seeking protection. However, subsuming statelessness determination under asylum authorities—either officially or on an ad hoc basis—still raises several concerns. First, delegating the stateless-ness determination procedure to asylum authorities perpetuates the confla-tion of stateless persons and refugees. It creates a situation in which stateless persons who do not meet the requirements of the international refugee defi-nition may still struggle to secure protection, even when statelessness mech-anisms exist, because they are seen as less worthy of or eligible for protection (Deng 2001; Sawyer 2011).

A second concern stems from EU law. According to Article 67.2 of the Treaty on the Functioning of the European Union, "Stateless persons shall be treated as third-country nationals when devising and implementing a common policy on asylum, immigration and external border control" (Council of the European Union 2015). This provision works to the benefit of stateless persons seeking asylum protection and, implicitly, protection based on statelessness because they are not required to prove their national-ity to seek official recognition of either status. However, treating stateless persons as third-country nationals does not address two problems caused by a lack of nationality. First, Article 67.2 does not address the core issue of statelessness: not having a nationality. It simply places the stateless person in a short-term category for the purposes of asylum determination or immigra-tion proceedings. Once that process is over, the individual still lacks a na-tionality. In addition, it is not clear how and whether individual applicants will be told that admitting statelessness will not harm their asylum applica-tion. The stigmas connected with statelessness may make an applicant un-willing to admit he or she lacks a nationality (van Waas, de Chickera, and Albarazi 2014). Further, the applicant may not even be aware that he or she would be considered stateless. These complications often lead to questions about an applicant's credibility when the asylum authority is unable to verify the applicant's stated nationality.

A third challenge for stateless individuals seeking protection via asylum authorities is proving their claims. In most asylum systems, the burden of proof falls largely on the applicant. This is especially the case in applications where the asylum seeker was a resident of or passed through a "safe third country": a state passed through by the applicant before arriving in the state of application that is deemed safe enough to alleviate the applicant's well-founded fear of persecution in the state of origin (Costello 2005). As discussed previously, EU-level regulations direct member states to treat stateless persons as third-country nationals in asylum determination procedures. This means that if the stateless applicant had been a resident of a state considered to be a safe third country, the individual could be denied asylum protection and deported. Further, if the statelessness determination procedure is under the control of the asylum authorities, especially when there is no official statelessness determination procedure, this same principle may be applied to requests for stateless status, making the individual ineligible for any protection.

In instances where safe third countries are not at issue, the burden of proof for asylum applications or statelessness determinations can still be exceedingly difficult, perhaps impossible, for a stateless applicant to meet. Getting information from embassies and consulates can be costly in terms of time, money, and effort, especially if the state of potential nationality refuses to recognize or assist the applicant (Gyulai 2013). Further, if the stateless person has reason to fear his or her state of origin or last residence—regardless of whether he or she qualifies as a refugee—then contacting the state of origin to acquire documentation may be an unreasonable requirement for the individual. As the case studies in Chapter 4 make clear, even after leaving the state of origin, refugees, stateless persons, and other migrants often continue to face discrimination and violence. In many cases, the act of fleeing itself makes individuals targets for retribution. To alleviate some of this danger, some states, such as France, take on the task of contacting states of origin and more equitably share the burden of proof with the applicant in determination procedures (Cosgrave 2016). This may also be the direction EU-level standards are heading in asylum determination, which could also be a good sign for determinations of stateless status (Costello 2005).

Finally, an important critique of subsuming statelessness determination procedures under asylum structures is that asylum determination procedures do not always provide durable solutions to statelessness. Asylum seekers who are granted asylum protection or another protection status are granted protection only in the short term. Ultimately, if the situation in the state of origin improves, the protection is lifted and the refugee is repatriated. Asylum protection can lead to opportunities to apply for permanent residency or even nationality, but these opportunities are not guaranteed. So even when granted asylum protection, a stateless refugee would still be without a long-term solution to his or her lack of nationality.

If an individual does not receive asylum protection or is not eligible to apply in the first place, he or she has other protection options only if the state recognizes statelessness as a protected status. If the individual claimed statelessness at the beginning of the status determination process, he or she could, depending on the national system, seek orders to stop deportation, to grant temporary residence permits, or to provide other protections. However, this is still a problematic process in most of the EU, and the options open to individuals in such situations vary across member states.

Risk of Statelessness and Failed Asylum Claims

An interesting obstacle related to the durability of statelessness that is new to the literature occurs when applications for asylum protection are denied. In particular, when individual applicants who were not considered stateless at the beginning of the application process are denied protection as refugees, they can become de facto stateless. When individuals flee a state of origin and seek asylum, several events can take place that affect their nationality. The situation in the state of origin that caused them to flee can worsen, resulting in administrative breakdowns, the destruction of records, or the refusal of migrants to report important identity information to government agencies; migrants fleeing the ongoing violence in Syria are already facing these obstacles and will likely continue to do so the longer the war continues (van Waas 2014). State authorities may also choose to retaliate against refugees or take ongoing persecution of groups a step further by stripping individuals or groups of their nationality (Blitz and Otero-Iglesias 2011). When these refugees are denied asylum protection, they enter into the legal limbo of statelessness. In this case, the statelessness of the individual is created not only by the state of origin but also by the state that has denied the asylum claim. As Chapter 7 describes, the deprivation of nationality can serve as a cause of survival migration for the Rohingya in Southeast Asia. For individuals made stateless by European asylum procedures, however, migration—other than human trafficking—is often no longer an option. The limited resources used to flee initially are gone, and European directives prohibit individuals from seeking asylum protection in more than one European state. In this instance the same deprivation of rights that causes flight in one case instead traps individuals in another.

Brad K. Blitz and Miguel Otero-Iglesias (2011) show that the asylum procedure in the United Kingdom, for example, can result in statelessness for individuals denied asylum. Although the United Kingdom now has a statelessness determination procedure, statelessness caused by a denied asylum claim appears to remain a potential risk for stateless migrants. Perhaps more important, the introduction of the statelessness determination procedure has now put these two protection regimes in conflict with each other. Individuals who think they may qualify as a refugee cannot seek statelessness determination until after they have applied for and been refused refugee status. At that time, they may apply to be allowed to stay in the United Kingdom as a stateless person. However, it is unclear whether individuals who receive refugee status but are later deemed eligible for repatriation after conditions in the state of origin have improved may apply for stateless status at that point. The focus of this protection is still on the short term. The average length of stay granted is 2.5 years, with possibilities to renew but no clear path to securing a nationality (Government of the United Kingdom, n.d.).

Statelessness and the Antitrafficking Regime

There is surprisingly little research available on the intersection of statelessness and human trafficking. Some of the literature does identify statelessness as increasing a potential victim's vulnerability to traffickers (see, e.g., Smith-Cannoy, Smith, and Rodda, forthcoming); therefore, addressing statelessness has also been discussed as a way to prevent human trafficking (Blitz 2011). However, there is not much information available on how stateless trafficking victims fare in antitrafficking protection regimes; the only text we have found to date that examines this directly is by Stephanie Hepburn and Rita J. Simon (2013), and their case studies on trafficking and statelessness come from outside Europe.

The EU's policies also do not directly address the intersection of statelessness and human trafficking. Further, to our knowledge, no European state has combined trafficking and statelessness determination procedures in any way, though trafficking victims are often able to seek protection via asylum procedures. However, there are several important ways in which the fight against human trafficking affects stateless persons and challenges to protection for such victims. The challenges for stateless persons within the trafficking context fall into two broad categories: the conflict between human rights and criminalization frames and the conflict between immigration and antitrafficking regimes.

The fight against human trafficking is unique among the protection regimes examined in this chapter because it is a hybrid between the human rights regime and international efforts to combat transnational organized crime. The international and regional agreements regarding trafficking focus on protection, prevention, and prosecution (Hepburn and Simon 2013, 344). The combination of efforts to penalize traffickers and assist trafficking victims sounds like an effective way to combat the practice and its effects, but the two approaches do not always fit well together. States are faced with practical challenges to addressing both the human rights and criminal aspects of trafficking—including finances, human resources, and intelligence. When faced with such challenges, many states focus their efforts on prosecution of traffickers in an effort to improve human rights in the long run by making trafficking a more difficult and costly enterprise, often at the expense of the short-term needs of victims (Belser 2005; Chang and Kim 2007; Gallagher and Holmes 2008; Surtees 2008). For example, in several European states, access to immigration relief and other services for victims is contingent on victims assisting the investigation and prosecution of their traffickers. Unfortunately, the emphasis on prosecution contrasts sharply with the relatively light sentences for traffickers and consistent barriers to prosecution in many cases. In the United Kingdom, for example, prosecutors must prove two elements of intent in human trafficking cases: the intent to both move the victims and to exploit them, which makes cases of internal trafficking particularly difficult to prosecute (Hepburn and Simon 2013). While criminal proceedings are often given precedence in terms of resources and attention, it does not always result in preventing trafficking. So the trade-off between providing services and protection to victims and prosecuting traffickers is an unequal one that, as yet, seems to have limited benefit to victims of trafficking or anti–human trafficking efforts (Gallagher 2001; Gallagher and Holmes 2008; Smith-Cannoy, Smith, and Rodda, forthcoming).

Further, the focus on the criminalization approach is detrimental to the human rights needs of victims in the long run. Making assistance contingent on assisting the authorities is problematic for trafficking victims who have been told they will be deported or detained if they go to the police (Hepburn and Simon 2013). Stateless victims, in particular, are likely to have no other immigration options without relief from the state to which they were trafficked. Indeed, they may be barred from returning to their original state of residence. Thailand, a major source nation for trafficking victims that also has a large stateless population, has been known to deny the reentry of residents without proof of Thai citizenship (Hepburn and Simon 2013). Such a situation leaves stateless individuals in a perpetual state of limbo, where they cannot remain and they cannot return. All the while, they have lost access to the services and assistance they desperately need to begin healing after the trafficking experience and limit their vulnerability to being retrafficked.

Just as occurs in the asylum protection regime, there is a persistent conflict between member states' immigration concerns and their efforts at combating human trafficking. This materializes particularly in the under- and nonidentification of trafficking victims. Despite the knowledge that human trafficking is an enormous global enterprise, few victims are actually identified. The European Commission (2016) released a report assessing the EU's progress in combating human trafficking. This report stated that in 2013–2014 there were 15,846 people registered as victims of human trafficking; however, in other EU publications, the leadership recognizes that it is likely that hundreds of thousands of trafficking victims are moved through Europe each year (European Parliamentary Research Service 2014).

In many cases the disparity in reported and suspected rates of trafficking is due to underidentification of victims, which results from several factors, including an overemphasis on sex trafficking; poor training on the signs of human trafficking; and the lack of attention paid to internal trafficking, forced labor, and male victims (Hepburn and Simon 2013; Laczko and Gramegna 2003; Macy and Graham 2012; Smith-Cannoy, Smith, and Rodda, forthcoming; Warria, Nel, and Triegaardt 2015). The results of underidentification can be devastating for the victims of trafficking. Often these individuals are detained along with other illegal migrants because they have no proof of their legal status. Even if the victims had legitimate visas, identification documents are most often seized by traffickers, leaving the victims with no way to identify themselves or prove their legal right to be in the country (Hepburn and Simon 2013; Smith-Cannoy, Smith, and Rodda, forthcoming; Surtees 2008). Stateless victims of trafficking would be even less able to fight this detention without even the possibility of proving citizenship elsewhere. Stateless trafficking victims also may be more likely to be underidentified as trafficking victims because of the stigma of statelessness and fears of deportation to the country where their vulnerability put them at risk of trafficking in the first place. The systematic deportation of resident stateless peoples, as France did with stateless and Romanian Roma populations, is unlikely to increase stateless trafficking victims' trust in state authorities (Hepburn and Simon 2013).

For victims of human trafficking, underidentification is certainly problematic, but nonidentification—where no attempt is made to assess the situation of the individual—is clearly a more serious obstacle to protection. In some states, the emphasis on immigration concerns leads to a "deport first and ask questions later"—or never—approach (Geddes 2005; Hepburn and Simon 2013). Hepburn and Simon (2013) use Italy as an example of this approach to immigration control; individuals believed to be illegal migrants are often deported before Italian law enforcement officials can determine their status. This affects illegal and legal migrants, refugees, stateless persons, and trafficking victims alike. The Italian government even went as far as to make an "agreement with the government of Libya in 2008 that allows Italy to forcibly return and reroute boat migrants back to Libya" (Hepburn and Simon 2013, 182). Although the Italians suspended the agreement in 2010, it was reinitiated in 2011. This is particularly problematic in light of conditions in Libya. The country continues to suffer from ongoing violence and civil unrest as well as an economy teetering on collapse (World Bank 2017). Libya is also a major transit nation for migrants moving between Africa, the Middle East, and Europe. Libya is currently a perfect storm for driving survival migration, but agreements like the one with Italy significantly reduce the options these migrants have for seeking security and protection elsewhere.

European states with statelessness determination procedures allow a stateless victim of human trafficking to seek protection if made aware of and given access to the procedure. Similarly, if the trafficking victim is able to make a claim for refugee status, that may at least stay his or her deportation, depending on the particular asylum process and applicability of the nonrefoulement principle. However, the nonrefoulement principle is not generally applicable outside the asylum context; so barring access to these other two protection regimes, trafficking victims can be and often are forced to leave the country in which they are discovered. Some European states seek to ease the burden of this deportation; Germany, for example, offers to pay the costs of repatriation. However, for stateless persons this is complicated by their lack of citizenship. To which country should they be returned? What happens if the individual's country of last residence refuses to allow him or her reentry after being trafficked?

Risk of Retrafficking and Statelessness

Perhaps the largest obstacle for stateless victims of human trafficking is that, like the asylum protection regime, the antitrafficking regime does not address the element at the core of what makes stateless persons most vulnerable to traffickers: their lack of nationality. However, within the EU's antitrafficking regime, temporary resident visas are supposed to be available for identified victims of human trafficking, though individual states have some control over the conditions and rights these visas confer. The visas potentially allow trafficking victims to seek permanent residency, and in the long run, this could lead to citizenship options for stateless victims.

As noted previously, however, these temporary visas are often contingent on assisting authorities in the prosecution of traffickers. If the victim chooses not to cooperate with the authorities, this visa may not be offered or renewed. The individual may then be deported or repatriated. For most victims of human trafficking, this simply returns them to the environment that initially made them susceptible to traffickers. For stateless persons, these conditions are exacerbated by their status, which limits their access to education, the labor market, government services, and other opportunities that might enable them to resist the enticing offers of employment made by traffickers (Adams 2011; Hepburn and Simon 2013).

If the victim remains in the host-EU country, with or without a visa, the individual is still at risk for being retrafficked. Victims without legal status, including stateless persons and individuals in EU states that do not allow holders of the temporary visas for trafficking victims to seek employment, have limited or no access to the legal labor market. These victims must find other ways to support themselves, making them susceptible to human traffickers who prey on their desperation to find work to support themselves and their families. In this scenario, the freedoms of the EU can work to perpetuate survival migration more broadly and human trafficking networks in particular. If the victim is already inside the EU, especially if he or she is inside the Schengen Area (the twenty-six EU countries where free movement across borders is guaranteed), then transportation within the EU host country or to other member states is relatively easy (Boswell 2005; Hepburn and Simon 2013).

Finally, as does being denied asylum protection, the realities of human trafficking and the disparities in the protections offered to victims across Europe can create instances of statelessness among trafficking victims. These types of victims often have their identification documents confiscated or destroyed by their traffickers. If the country of origin were unwilling or unable to recognize the victim's nationality, he or she would become de facto stateless. Similarly, victims are often moved from place to place during the trafficking process, creating problems in determining an individual's status. The current crises in Iraq and Syria highlight this problem. Many of the refugees fleeing violence in Iraq found their way to Syria. However, many of them were unable to find work or not permitted to work because of their refugee status, making them targets for traffickers. When the civil war began in Syria, many of these refugees were then forced to flee again (Hepburn and Simon 2013; van Waas 2014). This scenario has created several opportunities for personal identification and state records to become lost or destroyed. The victim of trafficking may then be unable to prove either his or her citizenship or refugee status or to substantiate applications for refugee, stateless, or trafficking victim status in the EU.

Conclusion and Future Research

A primary goal of this book is to explore innovative solutions to human rights problems. However, the most durable and perhaps most practical solution to statelessness is to confer citizenship to stateless people and change nationality laws to prevent the perpetuation of statelessness to successive generations. The UNHCR, as well as several regional and local NGOs, such as the ENS, work hard to raise awareness about stateless populations, provide access to legal and other necessary services to stateless persons, and engage states on the issue. However, as long as nationality policies remain under the authority of states, it will be up to lawmakers to decide whether and how to address the problem of statelessness.

This is not to say that there has been no progress in addressing statelessness in the EU. As this analysis shows, various states have, on their own, implemented statelessness determination procedures and are offering good practices and lessons learned to fellow member states. States with such determination procedures still face challenges and will need to closely examine their procedures to assess whether they actually assist the populations they were put in place to help. The recent reforms in France give good cause to hope for a better and stronger statelessness determination approach in Europe moving forward.

The right to nationality is the foundation on which access to all other rights is granted. If states are serious about addressing human rights concerns in the long run—both for the individuals in need of protection and for states that would like to eliminate the need for such protection—tackling statelessness must become a priority. This will likely mean challenging core ideas about state sovereignty and determination of nationality. The EU has a unique opportunity to take the lead in this area, building on other areas of policy harmonization and protection structures. In a time and area of immense migration flows and protection crises, more efficient protection regimes can benefit both states and individuals.

NOTES

1. Nationality has taken on a different meaning within international relations over the last several decades. In particular, it is now often tied to ideas of identity and community belonging rather than a legal relationship to a political entity (Smith 2010). However, we use "nationality" here in line with the definition for the term given by the International Court of Justice (ICJ): "Nationality is a legal bond having as its basis a social fact of attachment, a genuine connection of existence, interests and sentiments, together with the existence of reciprocal rights and duties" (Blackman 1998, 1147).

2. Several European states also include laws based on jus soli, but they are often very constrained. For example, in France, birthplace nationality is a possibility only beginning with the third generation (Weil 2001).

3. The UNHCR's Europe bureau includes the EU member states as well as the other states within the geographic area of Europe.

4. In April 2016, the Greek parliament passed an initiative that sets the country on the path to institute a statelessness determination procedure of its own. However, the initiative does not give a deadline by which this procedure needs to be in place, so it is not included in the table (Kalantzi 2016).

REFERENCES

Adams, Cherish. 2011. "Re-trafficked Victims: How a Human Rights Approach Can Stop the Cycle of Re-victimization of Sex Trafficking Victims." *George Washington International Law Review* 43:201–234.

Aleinikoff, T. Alexander, and Douglas Klusmeyer. 2001. "Plural Nationality: Facing the Future in a Migratory World." In *Citizenship Today: Global Perspectives and Practices*, edited by T. Alexander Aleinikoff and Douglas Klusmeyer, 63–88. Washington, DC: Brookings Institution Press.

Arendt, Hannah. 1945. "The Stateless People." *Contemporary Jewish Record* 8:137–153.

Asylum Information Database. 2016. "Country Report." Available at http://www.asy
    lumineurope.org/reports.

Batchelor, Carol A. 1995. "Stateless Persons: Some Gaps in International Protection."
    International Journal of Refugee Law 7:232–259.

Belser, Patrick. 2005. "Forced Labour and Human Trafficking: Estimating the Profits."
    Social Science Research Network, March 1. Available at http://ssrn.com/abstract=
    1838403.

Blackman, Jeffrey L. 1998. "State Successions and Statelessness: The Emerging Right to
    an Effective Nationality under International Law." *Michigan Journal of International
    Law* 19:1141–1194.

Blitz, Brad K. 2011. "Policy Responses and Global Discourses on the Rights of Non-
    citizens and Stateless People." In *Statelessness in the European Union: Displaced,
    Undocumented, and Unwanted*, edited by Caroline Sawyer and Brad K. Blitz,
    108–137. Cambridge: Cambridge University Press.

Blitz, Brad K., and Miguel Otero-Iglesias. 2011. "Stateless by Any Other Name: Refused
    Asylum-Seekers in the United Kingdom." *Journal of Ethnic and Migration Studies*
    37:657–573.

Blockmans, Steve, and Ramses A. Wessel. 2009. "The European Union and Crisis Man-
    agement: Will the Lisbon Treaty Make the EU More Effective?" *Journal of Conflict
    and Security Law* 14:1–44.

Boswell, Christina. 2005. "Migration in Europe." Global Commission on International
    Migration, September. Available at http://citeseerx.ist.psu.edu/viewdoc/download
    ?doi=10.1.1.612.3249&rep=rep1&type=pdf.

Chang, Grace, and Kathleen Kim. 2007. "Reconceptualizing Approaches to Human
    Trafficking: New Directions and Perspectives from the Field(s)." *Stanford Journal
    of Civil Rights and Civil Liberties* 3 (2): 317–344.

Collett, Elizabeth. 2016. "The Paradox of the EU-Turkey Refugee Deal." Migration
    Policy Institute, March. Available at https://www.migrationpolicy.org/news/para
    dox-eu-turkey-refugee-deal.

Cosgrave, Catherine. 2016. "Ireland's Ad-Hoc Approach Is Failing Stateless Persons:
    Dublin Seminar Highlights Shortfalls and Need for Formal Procedures." European
    Network on Statelessness, May 6. Available at http://www.statelessness.eu/blog/ire
    land-ad-hoc-approach-failing-stateless-persons-dublin-seminar-highlights-short
    falls-and.

Costello, Cathryn. 2005. "The Asylum Procedures Directive and the Proliferation of Safe
    Country Practices: Deterrence, Deflection and the Dismantling of International
    Protection?" *European Journal of Migration and Law* 7:35–69.

Council of Europe. 1950. "European Convention on Human Rights, as Amended by
    Protocols Nos. 11 and 14." Available at http://www.refworld.org/docid/3ae6b3b04
    .html.

Council of the European Union. 2015. "Council Adopts Conclusions on Statelessness."
    April 12. Available at https://www.consilium.europa.eu/en/press/press-releases/
    2015/12/04/council-adopts-conclusions-on-statelessness.

De Groot, Gerard-René, Katja Swider, and Olivier Vonk. 2015. "Practices and Ap-
    proaches in EU Member States to Prevent and End Statelessness." European Parlia-
    ment. Available at http://www.europarl.europa.eu/RegData/etudes/STUD/2015/
    536476/IPOL_STU(2015)536476_EN.pdf.

Deng, Francis M. 2001. "Ethnic Marginalization as Statelessness: Lessons from the Great
    Lakes Region of Africa." In *Citizenship Today: Global Perspectives and Practices*,

edited by T. Alexander Aleinikoff and Douglas Klusmeyer, 183–208. Washington, DC: Brookings Institution Press.

European Commission. 2016. "First Report on the Progress Made in the Fight against Trafficking in Human Beings." May 19. Available at https://ec.europa.eu/anti -trafficking/eu-policy/first-report-progress-made-fight-against-trafficking-human -beings-2016_en.

European Parliament. 2011. "Directive 2011/36/EU of the European Parliament and of the Council of 5 April 2011 on Preventing and Combating Trafficking in Human Beings and Protecting Its Victims, and Replacing Council Framework Decision 2002/629/JHA." *Official Journal of the European Union* 15:101/1–101/11.

European Parliamentary Research Service. 2014. "The Problem of Human Trafficking in the European Union." Briefing, September 4. Available at http://www.europarl .europa.eu/RegData/bibliotheque/briefing/2014/140780/LDM_BRI(2014)140780 _REV1_EN.pdf.

Gallagher, Anne. 2001. "Human Rights and the New UN Protocols on Trafficking and Migrant Smuggling: A Preliminary Analysis." *Human Rights Quarterly* 23:975–1004.

Gallagher, Anne, and Paul Holmes. 2008. "Developing an Effective Criminal Justice Response to Human Trafficking: Lessons from the Front Line." *International Criminal Justice Review* 18:318–343.

Geddes, Andrew. 2005. "Chronicle of a Crisis Foretold: The Politics of Irregular Migration, Human Trafficking and People Smuggling in the UK." *British Journal of Politics and International Relations* 7:324–339.

Government of the United Kingdom. n.d. "Apply to Stay in the UK as a Stateless Person." Available at https://www.gov.uk/stay-in-uk-stateless (accessed January 4, 2019).

Gyulai, Gabor. 2013. "Statelessness: Determination and the Protection of Stateless Persons." European Network on Statelessness. Available at http://www.statelessness.eu/ sites/www.statelessness.eu/files/attachments/resources/Statelessness%20determina tion%20and%20the%20protection%20status%20of%20stateless%20persons%20 ENG.pdf.

Hepburn, Stephanie, and Rita J. Simon. 2013. *Human Trafficking around the World: Hidden in Plain Sight.* New York: Columbia University Press.

Kalantzi, Erika. 2016. "Greece Moves One Step Closer to Introducing an Effective Statelessness Procedure." European Network on Statelessness, April 14. http://www.state lessness.eu/blog/greece-moves-one-step-closer-introducing-effective-statelessness -determination-procedure.

Kanter, James. 2016. "European Union Reaches Deal with Turkey to Return New Asylum Seekers." *New York Times,* March 18. Available at www.nytimes.com/2016/03/19/ world/europe/european-union-turkey-refugees-migrants.html.

Krasniqi, Gëzim. 2012. "Country Report: Albania." EUDO Citizenship Observatory, November. Available at http://eudo-citizenship.eu/admin/?p=file&appl=country Profiles&f=Albania.pdf.

Kusá, Dagmar. 2013. "Country Report: Slovakia." EUDO Citizenship Observatory, January. Available at http://eudo-citizenship.eu/admin/?p=file&appl=country Profiles&f=Slovakia.pdf.

Laczko, Frank, and Marco A. Gramegna. 2003. "Developing Better Indicators of Human Trafficking." *Brown Journal of World Affairs* 10:179–194.

Macy, Rebecca J., and Laurie M. Graham. 2012. "Identifying Domestic and International Sex Trafficking Victims during Human Service Provision." *Trauma, Violence, and Abuse* 13:59–76.

OHCHR (Office of the High Commissioner for Human Rights). 2000. "Protocol to Prevent, Suppress and Punish Trafficking in Persons Especially Women and Children, Supplementing the United Nations Convention against Transnational Organized Crime." Available at http://www.ohchr.org/EN/ProfessionalInterest/Pages/ProtocolTraffickingInPersons.aspx.

Rodda, Patricia C. 2015. "Decision-Making Processes and Asylum Claims in Europe: An Empirical Analysis of Refugee Characteristics and Asylum Application Outcomes." *Decisions* 23:23–46.

Sardelić, Julija. 2013. "Romani Minorities Caught In-Between: Impeded Access to Citizenship and De Facto Statelessness in the Post-Yugoslav Space." European Network on Statelessness, September 20. Available at http://www.statelessness.eu/blog/romani-minorities-caught-between-impeded-access-citizenship-and-de-facto-statelessness-post.

Sawyer, Caroline. 2011. "Statelessness in Europe: Legal Aspects of *De Jure* and *De Facto* Statelessness in the European Union." In *Statelessness in the European Union: Displaced, Undocumented, and Unwanted*, edited by Caroline Sawyer and Brad K. Blitz, 69–107. Cambridge: Cambridge University Press.

Settlage, Rachel. 1997. "No Place to Call Home: Stateless Vietnamese Asylum-Seekers in Hong Kong." *Georgetown Immigration Law Journal* 12:187–202.

Sironi, Alice. 2016. "The Double Plight of Stateless Migrants." European Network on Statelessness, May 13. Available at http://www.statelessness.eu/blog/double-plight-stateless-migrants.

Smith, Anthony D. 2010. *Nationalism: Theory, Ideology, and History*. Cambridge, UK: Polity Press.

Smith-Cannoy, Heather M., and Charles Anthony Smith. 2012. "Human Trafficking and International Cheap Talk: the Dutch Government and the Island Territories." *Journal of Human Rights* 11:51–65.

Smith-Cannoy, Heather M., Charles Anthony Smith, and Patricia C. Rodda. Forthcoming. *Sex Trafficking: From the Local to the Global*. Washington, DC: Georgetown University Press.

Surtees, Rebecca. 2008. "Traffickers and Trafficking in Southern and Eastern Europe: Considering the Other Side of Human Trafficking." *European Journal of Criminology* 5:39–68.

Tolley, Michael. 2012. "Judicialization of Politics in Europe: Keeping Pace with Strasbourg." *Journal of Human Rights* 11:66–84.

UNHCR (United Nations High Commissioner for Refugees). 1984. "Identity Documents for Refugees: EC/SCP/33." July 20. Available at https://www.unhcr.org/en-us/excom/scip/3ae68cce4/identity-documents-refugees.html.

———. 2010. "Convention and Protocol Relating to the Status of Refugees." Available at http://www.unhcr.org/3b66c2aa10.html.

———. 2014a. "Convention on the Reduction of Statelessness." Available at http://www.unhcr.org/3bbb286d8.html.

———. 2014b. "Convention Relating to the Status of Stateless Persons." Available at https://www.unhcr.org/protection/statelessness/3bbb25729/convention-relating-status-stateless-persons.html.

———. 2014c. "War's Human Cost: Global Trends, 2013." Available at https://www.unhcr.org/en-us/statistics/country/5399a14f9/unhcr-global-trends-2013.html.

———. 2015. "States Parties to the 1951 Convention relating to the Status of Refugees and the 1967 Protocol." Available at http://www.unhcr.org/3b73b0d63.html.

United Nations. 2019a. "Chapter V: Refugees and Stateless Persons; 3. Convention Relating to the Status of Stateless Persons." Available at https://treaties.un.org/pages/
ViewDetailsII.aspx?src=TREATY&mtdsg_no=V-3&chapter=5&Temp=mtdsg2&
lang=en.
———. 2019b. "Chapter V: Refugees and Stateless Persons; 4. Convention on the Reduction of Statelessness." Available at https://treaties.un.org/pages/ViewDetails.aspx
?src=TREATY&mtdsg_no=V-4&chapter=5&lang=en.
———. 2019c. "Chapter XVIII: Penal Matters; 12. A Protocol to Prevent, Suppress and
Punish Trafficking in Persons, Especially Women and Children, Supplementing the
United Nations Convention against Transnational Organized Crime." Available at
https://treaties.un.org/Pages/ViewDetails.aspx?src=TREATY&mtdsg_no=XVIII-12
-a&chapter=18&lang=en.
van Waas, Laura. 2014. "Addressing the Human Rights Impact of Statelessness in the
EU's External Action." European Parliament, November. Available at www.europarl
.europa.eu/RegData/etudes/STUD/2014/534983/IPOL_STU(2014)534983_EN.pdf.
van Waas, Laura, Amal de Chickera, and Zahra Albarazi. 2014. "The World's Stateless:
A New Report on Why Size Does and Doesn't Matter." European Network on Statelessness, December 15. Available at http://www.statelessness.eu/blog/world's-state
less-new-report-why-size-does-and-doesn't-matter.
Vukas, Budislav. 1972. "International Instruments Dealing with the Status of Stateless
Persons and of Refugees." *Belgian Review of International Law* 8:143–175.
Warria, Ajwang', Hanna Nel, and Jean Triegaardt. 2015. "Challenges of Identification of
Child Victims of Transnational Trafficking." *Practice: Social Work in Action*
27:315–333.
Weil, Patrick. 2001. "Access to Citizenship: A Comparison of Twenty-Five Nationality
Laws." In *Citizenship Today: Global Perspectives and Practices*, edited by T. Alexan-
der Aleinikoff and Douglas Klusmeyer, 17–35. Washington, DC: Brookings Institu-
tion Press.
World Bank. 2017. "Libya's Economic Outlook—April 2017." Available at http://www
.worldbank.org/en/country/libya/publication/economic-outlook-april-2017.

The Fates of Survival Migrants

The Quality of Refuge

JEANNETTE MONEY AND
SHAINA WESTERN

This book outlines emerging threats to human rights and points to potential solutions. One possible solution is fleeing the source of the human rights abuse to find refuge in another state. The European migrant crisis, just like the Rohingya refugee crisis that preceded it, is a vivid reminder that individuals have the agency and, more frequently than ever, the resources to move across international borders to improve their conditions. Moreover, the factors that lead individuals to move are likely to intensify in the future. Many of those who move do not qualify for refugee status under the narrow UN definition of refugee: persecution based on "race, religion, nationality, membership of a particular social group or political opinion" (UNHCR 1951, 14). Yet, as Chapters 3 and 7 effectively illustrate, many of these migrants cannot be considered "voluntary economic migrants" because their survival is at stake as a result of poverty, environmental degradation, threats of violence, or statelessness. Alexander Betts (2013) has suggested a new terminology to capture the status of all international migrants who face an existential threat: "survival migrant." Survival migrants leave their homes in response to poor governance that threatens individual lives because of factors such as civil conflict, political instability, or environmental degradation.[1] Because migration represents a potential remedy to these emerging threats to human rights, it is critical to understand the rights and protections that survival migrants receive in their countries of refuge.

In this chapter, we describe the hierarchy of rights among survival migrants based on international treaties, a critical determinant of an individual's ability to find refuge. We connect this hierarchy of rights to the quality of refuge, the characteristics of countries that best permit new arrivals to thrive. A fundamental component of this picture is the mismatch between the countries where many of these people arrive and the conditions necessary for them to thrive. Although the human rights of these individuals are ostensibly universal, in reality these rights are limited by the location where individuals find themselves (Stern and Straus 2014).

Researchers, policy makers, and practitioners are aware of the problem of "burden sharing" in the global refugee regime (Inder 2017, 523). Refugee protection is undersupplied as a public good because of free riding (Betts 2003). We, too, sketch the maldistribution of those seeking protection in poor countries that can ill afford it. However, we make a second point that is equally important. Even when wealthy countries contribute to the Office of the UN High Commissioner for Refugees (UNHCR) to help poor countries shoulder the burden of providing refuge, the conditions that refugees and others fleeing catastrophe encounter are often quite poor, so their vulnerability continues. Both the quality and quantity of refuge are important; states may accept many survival migrants but be unable to provide adequate resources, or states may provide sufficient resources but accept only a limited number. Thus, in determining the fate of these individuals, it is necessary to adopt a holistic perspective rather than focus solely on their nominal rights as described in international instruments.

Those seeking refuge leave their own country because it is unable to protect their rights, including access to the basic necessities of life. Individuals who meet the refugee criteria established in the 1951 UN Convention relating to the Status of Refugees (Refugee Convention) are generally accepted by the destination country; others may be granted "complementary forms of protection" if they can demonstrate that they are fleeing indiscriminate violence (UNHCR 2001, 1). Yet those who do not fall within current accepted international definitions are left in limbo:[2] they need protection and, according to many ethical standards, should have some access to human rights law more broadly (Bustamante 2002; Dembour and Kelley 2011; Mattila 2000), yet no country is required to accept them. This is the crux of the problem regarding contemporary international law on migrants and refugees. Both the UN Charter and the International Covenant on Political and Civil Rights establish that individuals are free to leave any country, including their own; yet only their own states are required to admit them.

Moreover, even when those who seek protection are admitted, their access to rights and resources is conditioned by the resources and governance structures in the destination country. Some who seek protection may end up in countries with resources to provide the basic necessities of life as well as opportunities to settle, learn the language, develop job skills, work, and integrate into the community. Such migrants are able to lead more productive lives and, indeed, may thrive in the new country. Others may find themselves in refugee camps with minimal basic necessities and where they are forbidden to work while their lives are put on hold. Still others may find themselves excluded entirely and detained and deported back to their country of origin. There is a wide variety of outcomes among those seeking protection. Just as individuals exercise their agency in moving, a critical determinant of their well-being depends on the degree to which the state where they settle facilitates such agency. In this chapter, we explore the characteristics of countries that improve the life chances of these migrants: the quality of refuge. We focus on the level of human development; the quality of governance, including physical security; and access to citizenship. These state-level characteristics are not the entire story for migrants. Nonetheless, we argue that the combination of these three factors allows migrants to use their agency to improve their lives. Where these characteristics are missing, those in need of protection remain vulnerable.

We begin by outlining the rights and responsibilities of refugees defined under the 1951 Refugee Convention and 1967 Protocol and distinguish those rights from other types of complementary protection. This creates a "hierarchy of rights." We describe the three state characteristics we believe are crucial to the quality of refuge. Each, alone, is insufficient to provide refuge. The three combined provide a basic level of opportunity that makes it possible for those who seek refuge to thrive. Finally, we address the issue of equity.

The Hierarchy of Protection

The Refugee Convention, created in the wake of World War II, established the principle of nonrefoulement: individuals whose state cannot or will not protect them from persecution cannot be returned to their country of origin. Moreover, individuals who claim asylum may not be punished for their illegal entry into the country, provided that they declare themselves to public officials on arrival. Although this convention seems to protect refugee rights, several problems make it an increasingly archaic instrument.

First, refugee status itself is narrow and difficult to establish, as it is founded on the principle of individual persecution for reasons of "race, religion, nationality, membership of a particular social group or political opinion" (UNHCR 1951, 14). Many individuals in need of protection do not meet this narrow definition because they are not individually persecuted by the regime or by forces the regime is unwilling to protect them from (Hathaway 1991). Rather, many individuals migrate for complex reasons, including indiscriminate violence, human rights violations, environmental degradation, economic turmoil, and/or natural disaster, as this book details. When the Refugee Convention was drafted, the definition adopted reflected the contemporaneous events of the era, the atrocities associated with the Nazi regime in Germany, and the persecution of specific groups of individuals. Although the 1967 Protocol removed the time and geographic limitations on the designation "refugee," the underlying definition has remained the same since 1951. It does not provide refuge to those fleeing natural or human-made disasters, such as earthquakes, floods, environmental degradation, or, in many cases, civil war. Although these individuals are promised human rights, these rights are threatened because states are unable to provide the necessary protection.

Second, the convention relies on the principle that the "first safe country" is obligated to provide protection. Yet many who seek protection do not stop at the first safe country; instead, they seek asylum in a country where there are greater opportunities, where there are familial ties, or where they speak the language. Although such decisions are rational from the migrant's point of view, state reactions to this autonomy threaten the rights regime. A clear example is the European migrant crisis that arose in 2015 as Syrian refugees traveled from their first country of refuge adjacent to Syria to Europe, and even within Europe to their preferred country. Yet in many cases they were not granted refugee status because (theoretically) they had already found refuge in the first country of asylum.

Finally, the current refugee system does not provide for adequate burden sharing, so the responsibility to provide for those who seek protection often falls on those who can least afford it. In the international refugee system refugees tend to flee to neighboring countries. States adjacent to the crisis are those most affected by large influxes of people seeking protection, whether or not they have adequate resources for the task.

Some countries and regions have recognized that the convention definition excludes others in harm's way who may need protection.[3] The European Union (2004), via EU Directive 2004/83/EC, provides for "subsidiary protection," which may be granted when there are "substantial grounds" that the person faces "a real risk of suffering serious harm." Article 15 of the directive defines serious harm as "(a) death penalty or execution; or (b) torture or inhumane or degrading treatment or punishment of an applicant in the country of origin; or (c) serious and individual threat to a civilian's life or person by reason of indiscriminate violence in situations of international or internal armed conflict" (3, 8). The United States offers a similar protection under the guise of temporary protected status (TPS). The United States makes a determination that conditions in a specific country are a threat to their citizens' human rights; nationals of that country who find themselves on U.S. territory may then apply for TPS.

A third category of refugee is "prima facie" refugee, a status granted by individual countries as well as the UNHCR when confronted with a "mass influx" of individuals in need of protection. Because the states' systems of asylum determination become overloaded when inundated with large numbers of individuals seeking protection, prima facie status is granted on a group basis, with provisions for exclusion if subsequent individual evaluation determines that the individual does not meet the conditions for refuge (Rutinwa 2002). Prima facie refugee status is granted on a temporary basis only, so that the security of status associated with individual determination is not available to prima facie refugees.

Entry under other legal auspices may also be available to those seeking protection, for example, as high-skilled workers or, more frequently, as a family member of someone already established in the country of refuge. Finally, when it appears that some type of legal entry may be denied, individuals seeking protection may resort to legal entry but overstay the terms of their visa or may seek to evade border controls and enter illegally.

The distinction between refugee status, prima facie status, subsidiary protection, and other methods of entry is important because the rights granted to each category of individual vary. The Refugee Convention not only defines the characteristics of "refugee"; it also outlines both the rights of refugees that convention signatories agree to provide as well as the refugee's responsibilities to his or her host state. In defining refugee rights, the convention requires treatment as a national for certain rights and treatment as least as good as the treatment available to alien residents for other rights. National courts have interpreted these clauses in varying ways, but the basic grant of rights based on these two criteria is summarized in Table 9.1.

A cursory review of these rights indicates that those with a refugee status have access to resources that meet their basic needs in the short term and that refugees gain rights over time, especially unequivocal access to the local labor market. Whatever the country provides its nationals in terms of welfare and primary education is available to the refugee. Freedom of movement is guaranteed, as well as access to travel documents. In general, access to the labor market is available, although in the first three years, states may privilege the employment of citizens over that of refugees.

Family reunion and access to citizenship are not guaranteed, even for individuals with the convention designation "refugee." Article 34 addresses access to citizenship in a nonmandatory fashion: "The Contracting States shall as far as possible facilitate the assimilation and naturalization of refugees. They shall in particular make every effort to expedite naturalization proceedings and to reduce as far as possible the charges and costs of such proceedings" (UNHCR 1951, 30). The principle of family unity and the ability of the family to reunite in the country of refuge take the form of a

TABLE 9.1 UN REFUGEE CONVENTION

Treatment of refugee "at least as favourable as that accorded to their nationals"	Treatment of refugee "the same treatment as is accorded to aliens generally"
Freedom of religion (Article 4)	
Intellectual property (Article 14)	Movable and immovable property (Article 13)
Access to courts (Article 16)	Rights of association (Article 15)
Employment after three years' residence (or when spouse or children are nationals of country of refuge) (Article 17)	Employment (in first three years) (Article 17) Self-employment (Article 18) Practicing liberal professions (Article 19)
Public elementary education (Article 22)	Public education beyond primary education (Article 22)
Public relief and assistance (Article 23)	Housing (Article 21)
Labor legislation and social security (family allowances, old age benefits, etc.) (Article 24)	
Travel documents (Article 28)	Internal freedom of movement (Article 26)
Fiscal charges (Article 29)	

Source: UN Convention Relating to the Status of Refugees (1951).

recommendation. Specifically, Recommendation B urges that contracting states ensure "the unity of the refugee's family is maintained particularly in cases where the head of the family has fulfilled the necessary conditions for admission to a particular country" (11). Nonetheless, these are recommendations rather than requirements, although many countries facilitate both family reunion and access to nationality. For example, the EU permits both refugees and legal migrants to be united with their nuclear families, although specific conditions may be attached. And many countries reduce the residence requirement for naturalization for refugees.

Those seeking refuge who do not meet the definition of "refugee" have access to fewer rights than those with the "refugee" designation. In those regions or states that have adopted principles of complementary protection, protections are fewer than those granted refugees. According to UNHCR experts, prima facie refugees should receive all the rights of convention refugees, although it is widely acknowledged that states frequently abridge the rights of these refugees, placing them in camps, sometimes remote, and preventing freedom of movement, because the refugees are seen as temporary (Hyndman and Nylund 1998; Rutinwa 2002). The Dadaab refugee camps in northeastern Kenya are an example (Hyndman and Nylund 1998). Those who enter legally under other guises are treated in the same fashion as legal resident aliens, and those who enter without documents have access to the fewest rights.

This brief summary indicates that there is a hierarchy of rights. Although the rights granted refugees via the convention are not equal to those of citizens in all cases, in many instances refugees are treated as nationals and, over time, obtain additional rights. Therefore, at the top of the hierarchy come formally designed "refugees," governed by the UN Refugee Convention, whose rights in contracting states are guaranteed through the convention. However, even treatment as a national does not guarantee the flourishing of human life. Rather, this is determined by the characteristics of the country itself. We now turn to those indicators central to the well-being of those seeking refuge.

Access to Resources

Definition. The Human Development Index (HDI) has now become a standard way of measuring the basic living conditions in a country for both citizens and residents. Developed by the United Nations Development Programme (UNDP) and initially published in 1990, the HDI is a multidimensional indicator that incorporates three country characteristics: wealth, longevity, and education.[4] It is a measure of the wealth produced by a country and the use of that wealth in sustaining the lives and livelihoods of its residents. Longevity is measured by life expectancy at birth; life expectancy is a snapshot of the residents' ability to feed and clothe themselves as well as the sufficiency of their access to health care. Education combines current enrollments as well as the expected enrollments of future students. Education opens opportunities to those who have access; it provides the knowledge to enhance human choice. Wealth also enters the equation as gross national income per capita adjusted for purchasing-power parity. A minimum of wealth is necessary to provide both private and public goods to the country's residents. However, wealth is incorporated into the HDI by taking the natural log of gross national income per capita. This transformation suggests that one additional unit of currency is worth more when you are poor than when you are wealthy. One hundred additional dollars increases well-being more when an individual earns one thousand dollars than when an individual earns forty thousand dollars. The absolute level of wealth alone is an insufficient measure of well-being. This multidimensional indicator is an improvement over the reliance on wealth alone, as it captures the distribution of resources in terms of population welfare.

Implications for protection seekers. Refugees need access to sufficient levels of resources to feed, clothe, and educate themselves and to ensure health. Admission into a state with high HDI means that those seeking protection are in a state where their basic needs and the needs of their children can be met. Consequently, protection seekers are better able to invest their resources in ways that make them able to succeed in the destination country. Additionally, research demonstrates that states with higher levels of HDI have an easier time incorporating migrants without suffering a drop in their overall HDI, whereas states with low HDI experience a small dip in their overall HDI with an influx of migrants because states with high HDI have economies and institutions that are more resilient to increased demands from migration (Sanderson 2010). Thus, when migrants enter a state with a lower HDI, their overall well-being is unlikely to improve to the same extent that it would were they to enter a country with higher HDI.

Of course, the UNHCR, tasked with facilitating the protection of displaced persons, usually supplements the host country's resources available to refugees based on contributions from convention signatories. This is an invaluable aid to refugees that in many cases permits refugees in poor countries to have access to minimum resources. Nonetheless, the country's HDI is a more accurate indicator of its ability to host refugees effectively and provide access to the basic amenities of life to those seeking protection. The HDI is an imperfect measure of the quality of life in individual countries. It does not incorporate many different facets of residents' experience and is only an average. However, countries with sufficient levels of human development are a necessary, if not sufficient, condition for those seeking refuge. Entering a country with low levels of human development means that those who seek refuge are, like citizens, unlikely to have access to sufficient resources to thrive.

Variation. The HDI takes on a range of values between 0 and 1; it can be interpreted as the level of human development in the country on a scale of lowest to highest values based on the three indicators. In 2012, the HDI varies from 0.304 (Niger) to 0.955 (Norway). The variation among regions is telling: sub-Saharan African countries have an average HDI score of 0.475; South Asia, 0.558; Arab states, 0.652; East Asia and the Pacific, 0.683; Latin America and the Caribbean, 0.741; and Europe and Central Asia, 0.771 (UNDP 2012).

Access to Good Governance

Definition. Good governance is another characteristic of states that affects the ability of those seeking refuge to thrive. There are two different ways to capture institutional quality. The first focuses on democracy. Democracies are institutions that provide a number of beneficial traits: electoral representation, the provision of public goods (Bueno de Mesquita et al. 2003), rule of law, and protection of human rights. One might think that this criterion matters most. However, one problem in evaluating democracy is that it can be a double-edged sword for migrants. Although democratic governments tend to protect human rights more fully than autocracies do, when there is a political backlash against migrants, democracies have incentives to respond in ways that could curtail migrant rights (Stasiulis 1997). Thus, we argue that a second dimension of governance is actually more useful for understanding the situation that survival migrants face: the quality of governance.

We focus on good governance rather than democracy because a central characteristic of good governance is the rule of law, a state characteristic that allows noncitizen residents to seek redress if their rights are violated. However, good governance also provides other protections for noncitizen residents. To measure the quality of governance, we adopt an aggregate measure of governance based on the World Bank Worldwide Governance Indicators (WGI) project (World Bank, n.d.). This project evaluates governments on six dimensions: voice and accountability, political stability and absence of violence, government effectiveness, regulatory quality, rule of law, and control of corruption. For each of these indicators, the index is normalized so that it has a standard deviation of 1 and a mean of 0. Thus, in each of these categories, states range from –2.5 to 2.5, where higher values indicate better governance. We create an index by summing across all of these indicators to have a snapshot of governance in each state.

Implications for protection seekers. Migration is an expression of agency when people leave their home state for protection abroad. The opportunities that migrants have to express their agency in their destination country depend on the ability of migrants to function in their country of destination with as little friction as possible and on their ability to seek redress if their rights are violated. Thus, our argument does not require governments to behave perfectly toward these migrants; rather, it depends on the ability of migrants, and those who advocate on their behalf, to have access to good governance. Good governance is a multidimensional state characteristic; the dimensions include protection of human rights such as physical security, access to redress, predictability, lack of corruption, and economic resilience. Each of these elements provides benefits to survival migrants. We argue that such conditions need not be perfect as long as the destination state provides migrants the basic ability to express their agency and thrive.

Most important, good governance provides the absence of violence and contributes to the survival migrants' physical security. As Chapter 4 describes, refugees fleeing violence in their home country often encounter violence in their country of refuge. The violence may be perpetrated by the home government, which extends its persecution abroad, or by opposition groups that may forcibly recruit the migrants to continue the battle in the homeland. Alternatively, the host government may scapegoat the new arrivals, allowing the host population to attack the refugees as competitors for scarce resources. States with good governance are able to quell violence and protect both citizens and residents from external and internal violence.

Good governance provides additional protections of survival migrants' human rights. In one sense, ours can be labeled "the age of human rights." Spurred by the atrocities committed during World War II, the states of the world resurrected international cooperation via the creation of the UN, with the Universal Declaration of Human Rights as a cornerstone document (United Nations 1948). In the intervening years, nine treaties dealing with human rights have been negotiated and adopted, followed by relatively widespread ratification by countries around the world.[5] These agreements form the basis of an international human rights regime (Donnelly 1986). These treaties promise protection based on an individual's status as a human being rather than as a citizen of a specific state. Thus, such rights should theoretically provide considerable protection to all individuals, including those who seek refuge. Unfortunately, there is a disconnect between rhetoric and reality, as states may profess their commitment to human rights but, in practice, violate these rights (Hafner-Burton and Tsutsui 2007; Dai 2013).

Although some rights violations may occur in all regimes, the key factor in influencing the overall well-being of survival migrants and citizens is the day-to-day practices of the regime. A number of components of good governance contribute to human rights protection. Voice and accountability mean that the government reflects, to a greater or lesser extent, the preferences of its citizens, which contributes to political stability. In turn, political stability and the absence of violence enhance the probability that the new arrivals will not confront threats to their physical security either from the government or from members of society. The rule of law ensures that all residents—citizens and noncitizens—are treated equally. And government effectiveness ensures that the society functions in providing public services such as access to clean water, education, and health services. The central component of human rights is the right to physical security; this is the main reason that survival migrants fled their country of origin in the first place. States with good governance help ensure the physical integrity of those who seek protection.

Moreover, human rights practices have positive effects beyond the direct effects on individuals. Good human rights practices tend to attract more foreign direct investment and, thus, more economic opportunities (Blanton and Blanton 2007). Poor states with good human rights practices are also more likely to receive more foreign aid (Lebovic and Voeten 2009). Thus, those who seek protection in countries with strong human rights records are more likely to find it.

Good governance decreases corruption, which can be considered a tax on many dimensions of human activity. In the economic arena, corruption decreases productivity of both citizens and migrants. If migrants enter a state with a high quality of governance, they can more easily enter into productive activities that allow them to provide for themselves economically and to become contributing members of the host society. In dealings with the state, the access to residence permits, travel documents, and so on, corruption creates higher costs for survival migrants. Good governance reduces instances of corruption and allows migrants to employ their resources in more efficient ways to integrate into the host society.

Good governance provides survival migrants with a predictable environment. Stable institutions allow migrants to more easily learn the "rules of the game" in their host state. If institutions promote good governance, migrants can easily learn where they can go for help and what steps they can take if their rights are violated.

Societies characterized by good governance constrain the government through the rule of law. This criterion is perhaps the most crucial because so much of survival migrants' well-being depends on their ability to access legal status, the right to work, and benefits that the state provides. In contrast, if survival migrants end up in states with poor institutions, they may very well go from the frying pan into the fire. If governance is poor, then migrants face considerably more uncertainty about their legal status, their access to resources, and the necessity of paying bribes to government officials. Given that in many cases poor governance is the cause of their need to move in the first place (Betts 2013), these migrants may remain in a situation where their survival is endangered. All told, good governance works to help guarantee that survival migrants' physical security is protected and that they have access to sufficient resources to contribute to their own well-being.

Finally, good governance creates a society with economic resilience. Research indicates that domestic institutions play a central role in shaping the political and economic outcomes of states (Acemoglu, Johnson, and Robinson 2001; North 1990). States with rule of law constrain the executive and promote economic growth, thus connecting to the level of human development and the ability of states to incorporate survival migrants into their economies (Sanderson 2010). States with resilient institutions can incorporate migrants into their societies in a more cohesive manner (Ireland 2004).

Variation. Theoretically, our index ranges from –15 to +15, with higher scores indicating better governance. However, empirically, we observe scores in the range of –15 to +10. Not surprisingly, members of the Organisation for Economic Cooperation and Development (OECD), a club of wealthy democracies, score the best on this indicator, although there are pockets of good governance in various regions around the world.

Access to Citizenship

Definition. Naturalization is a method of transforming a resident alien into a citizen of a country. However, states vary substantially in the conditions they put on access to citizenship, and citizenship often affects the rights and privileges that are extended to survival migrants. There are two separate dimensions of access: children's access to citizenship and adult access to citizenship (naturalization).[6] In each dimension, the burden posed varies.

When evaluating nationality legislation for children, often jus soli citizenship and jus sanguinis citizenship are juxtaposed. The former adopts a rule providing citizenship to those born on the territory of the state, while the latter grants nationality to children based on the nationality of the parent(s). However, the dichotomy is overdrawn, and a continuum better represents the ease of children's access to nationality. In some cases, children who arrive before a certain age and who are educated in the country of refuge have privileged access to citizenship; Germany after the nationality reforms of 1999 provides one example. The United States is well known for the unconditional jus soli it provides to any child born on its territory, regardless of the status of the parent. Countries such as the United Kingdom and Australia offer conditional access to jus soli to parents who are legal resident aliens, which incorporates the children of recognized refugees born in the host country. France provides that children born in France to alien parents automatically become citizens upon reaching majority if they have resided in France in the interim. And some countries treat these children the same as adult foreigners, requiring them to naturalize on reaching majority.

The second dimension of nationality law is the process of naturalization. Countries vary considerably on the requirements for naturalization. In almost all cases, legal residence is required, although the length of residence varies between three and fifteen years or more. States may also ask that prospective citizens know the language, culture, and history of their adopted country; that they live exemplary lives (no criminal convictions); and that they be able to support themselves financially.

Implications for protection seekers. The third component of our index of the quality of protection is often overlooked when evaluating the quality of refuge: access to citizenship. Citizenship, especially in countries with good governance, is the mechanism that allows migrants to better control their own destiny. It allows them to speak for themselves, to organize politically, and to become full members of the society. Moreover, many states limit certain rights and benefits to citizens (Morris 2001); when migrants naturalize, they are provided access to these resources, again enhancing their ability to thrive.

The issue of access to citizenship has become more visible in the debates that rage over immigration, especially in wealthy Western democracies. However, much less is known about the rights and responsibilities that citizenship provides. It is important to note which protections citizenship brings to migrants if they are able to naturalize. The human rights regime, put painstakingly into place after World War II, suggests that protection of human rights should be available to everyone. And many wealthy Western democracies have offered substantial portions of the welfare state to their new residents. However, there are rights that continue to be reserved for citizens.

In the contemporary era, there are three basic rights that are reserved exclusively for citizens almost everywhere: protection from deportation; the ability to enter and leave the country; and participation in national politics.[7] These rights are significant. Under current international law, even long-term residents can be deported at the will of the government; arbitrary deportations are avoided mostly through the requirement for individual adjudication. However, not just large infractions, such as felony criminal activity, are deportable offenses; small mistakes, such as traffic violations, can trigger deportation to home countries of which the migrant and/or his or her offspring may no longer have ties and knowledge.

International human rights law guarantees the right to leave and enter one's country of citizenship. No such absolute right is available to foreign residents of a host country. Individuals who leave a country of refuge may not be able to reenter that country. Finally, citizens may vote in national elections, but noncitizens are unable to voice their political preferences.[8] Depending on the citizenship laws in place, this can affect the ability to participate in the political process for generations. And participation in the political process is the mechanism that allows those who seek protection to make demands of the political system and to act as a counterweight to anti-immigrant activities (Money 1999a, 1999b). It is not surprising that politicians confront political incentives to "play the immigrant card" if their constituents confront the short-term costs of adjustment to a population surge. The result can turn into nasty, race- or ethnicity-based baiting and anti-immigrant policies. Migrants themselves, if politically empowered, can act as an electoral counterweight, providing the political support for politicians to avoid anti-immigrant policies and the ability to concentrate on offering the services necessary to diminish the dislocation that may be caused by rapid immigrant inflows. The rights that citizenship brings are thus important for immigrants.

Access to citizenship is especially important for stateless individuals. As Chapter 7 points out, statelessness itself may generate conditions that place individuals at risk and lead them to seek refuge outside their country of residence. And, as Chapter 8 describes, stateless individuals may have difficulty obtaining entry into a country of refuge, as the process of determination is often governed by asylum procedures rather than procedures specifically designed for statelessness. Nonetheless, if entry is granted, access to citizenship for both children and adults may resolve the issue of statelessness permanently for qualified individuals. Statelessness is not a bar to naturalization, and some states provide privileged access to citizenship for stateless children (Money, Western, and Yuh, forthcoming). This reinforces the importance of access to citizenship as a central attribute of the quality of refuge. Where access to citizenship is easy, stateless persons may transform themselves into citizens; where it is difficult, their status remains vulnerable.

Variation. For our nationality variables, we have created ordinal scales for both children's access to citizenship and adult access to naturalization. The scale for children runs from 1 to 14, where 1 represents countries that permit children of aliens, even those not born in the host country, to register for citizenship. Jus soli access to citizenship is a 3 on the scale, and 14 indicates that there are no provisions for children of aliens per se. They must wait until their majority and apply for naturalization as an adult. In much of the Western Hemisphere naturalization is given to all children born within the territory; however, in the rest of the world there is considerably more variation. For naturalization, we add the required years of residence to the various additional requirements that countries impose on resident aliens wishing to become citizens, including such items as language acquisition, cultural knowledge, and clean criminal record. Our scale ranges from 3 to 35 on required years of residence and from 3 to 45 on overall requirements.

Regions of Refuge

Putting the three components of refuge together, we can paint a picture of the quality of refuge around the world. This is not to say that countries' hospitality always reflects the underlying quality of refuge. Nonetheless, these are clear markers for individuals seeking protection, provided they have sufficient resources to reach their desired destination. To understand the plight of survival migrants, it is critical to understand where they come from and where they go. Current data on migrants and migration divide international population movement into the categories constructed by the refugee regime: refugees and "voluntary migrants," making it difficult to ascertain the fate of those in need of protection. This book suggests that this dichotomy fails to adequately capture the number of individuals who are fleeing for their lives. That said, the data do provide insights about which states are most likely to be generating such movement and which states are more likely to receive such people. To capture the picture of where these migrants are located, we use three sources of data from the World Bank.

The first is to simply look at net migration flows to see which countries are net receivers of migrants and which states are net senders. These data are from 2012, the most recent year available at the time of writing (World Bank 2017a). Obviously one problem with this picture is that it groups both forced and voluntary migrants together, and there are certainly individuals who move from one state to another for nonsurvival reasons. However, these data provide a snapshot of countries generating and countries receiving large flows of migrants. Figure 9.1 plots a global map with the net migration levels. This map reveals several interesting patterns: Although the largest migrant-receiving state is the United States, the next two largest recipient states are Turkey and Lebanon. The flow into the latter two states is largely explained by the fact that they border Syria, the country with the largest negative net migration. India, Bangladesh, and China have the next largest migrant outflows; one explanation is that these states have large populations, but the movement is a small fraction of the total population. Figure 9.2 plots the map with net migration figures divided by total population to put these statistics in perspective. In terms of number of migrants relative to that of the total population, four of the five largest net receiving states are in the Middle East: Oman, Lebanon, Qatar, and Kuwait. Syria, Libya, Micronesia, Georgia, and Tonga are the largest migrant-sending states as a fraction of the population. According to these estimates, in 2012 Syria lost approximately 20 percent of its population, whereas Libya, the next closest, lost almost 8 percent of its population. Based on these figures and the conflict in Syria and Libya, it is fair to say that a significant number of those fleeing Syria and Libya would be classified broadly under the category "survival migrants" if not also under the category of "refugee."

We can also observe the source and destination of refugees, those who meet the Refugee Convention criteria. Figure 9.3 plots the number of refugees by their country of origin as a function of the size of the overall population in the country of origin and shows that most refugees originate in sub-Saharan Africa and the Middle East. These data are from 2015, the most recent year available at the time of writing (World Bank 2017c). The largest refugee-generating states are Syria, Somalia, Central African Republic, Afghanistan, and South Sudan, all of which have more than 6 percent of their population classified as refugees. Indeed, 22 percent of the Syrian population consists of refugees. This figure shows, however, that these regions are not monolithic in terms of refugee generation. Some states in sub-Saharan

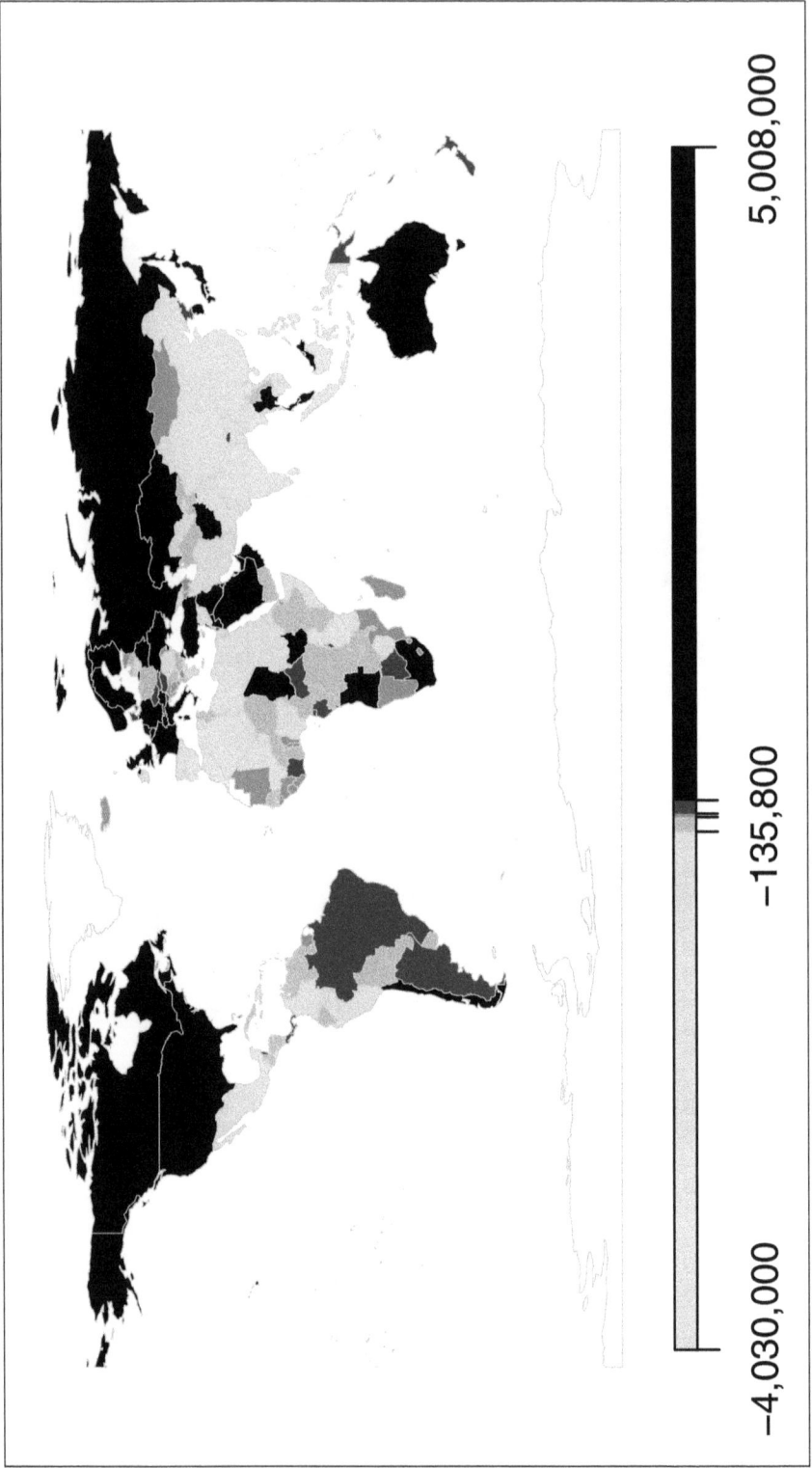

Figure 9.1 Net migration flows

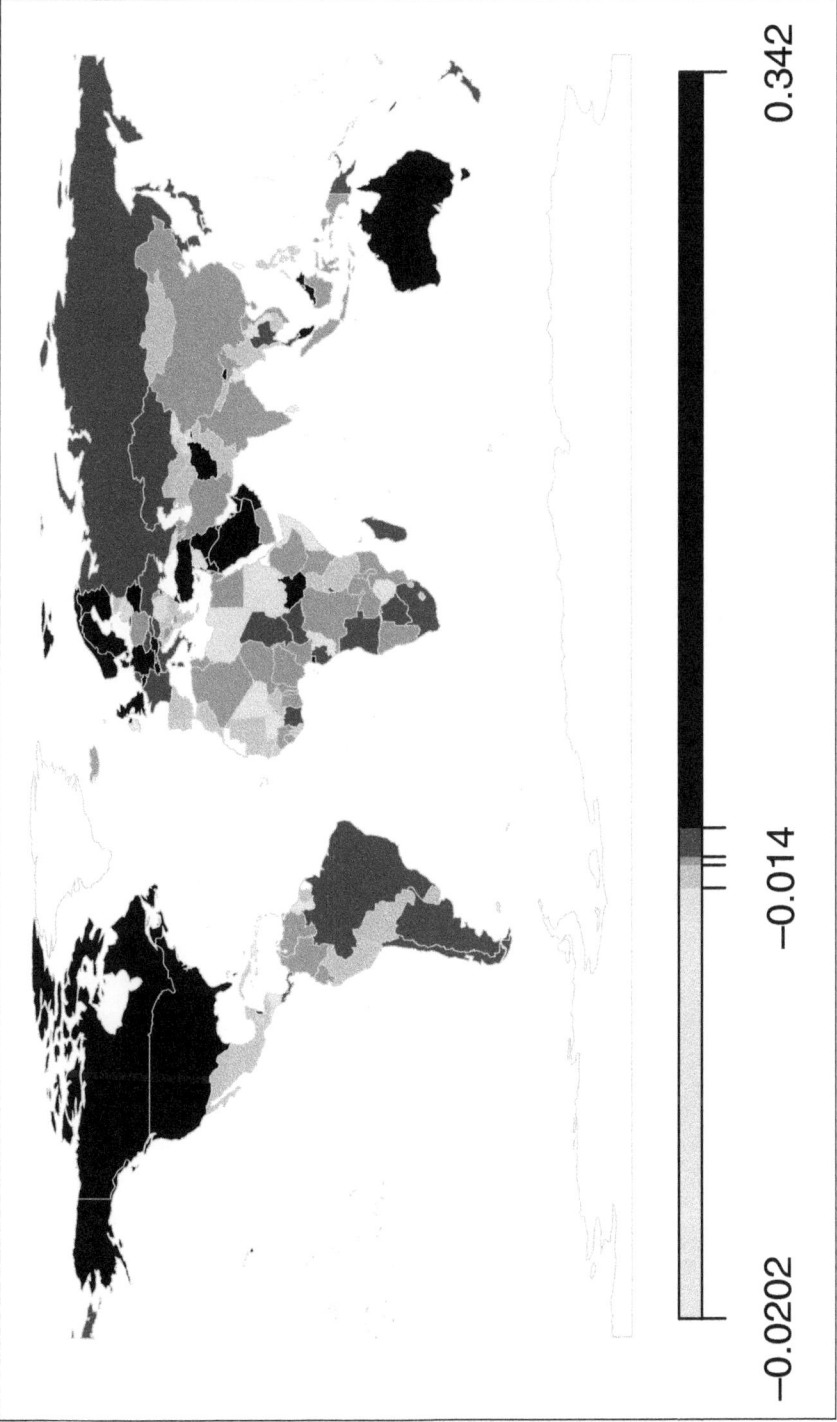

Figure 9.2 Net migration flows as a percentage of total population

-0.0202   -0.014   0.342

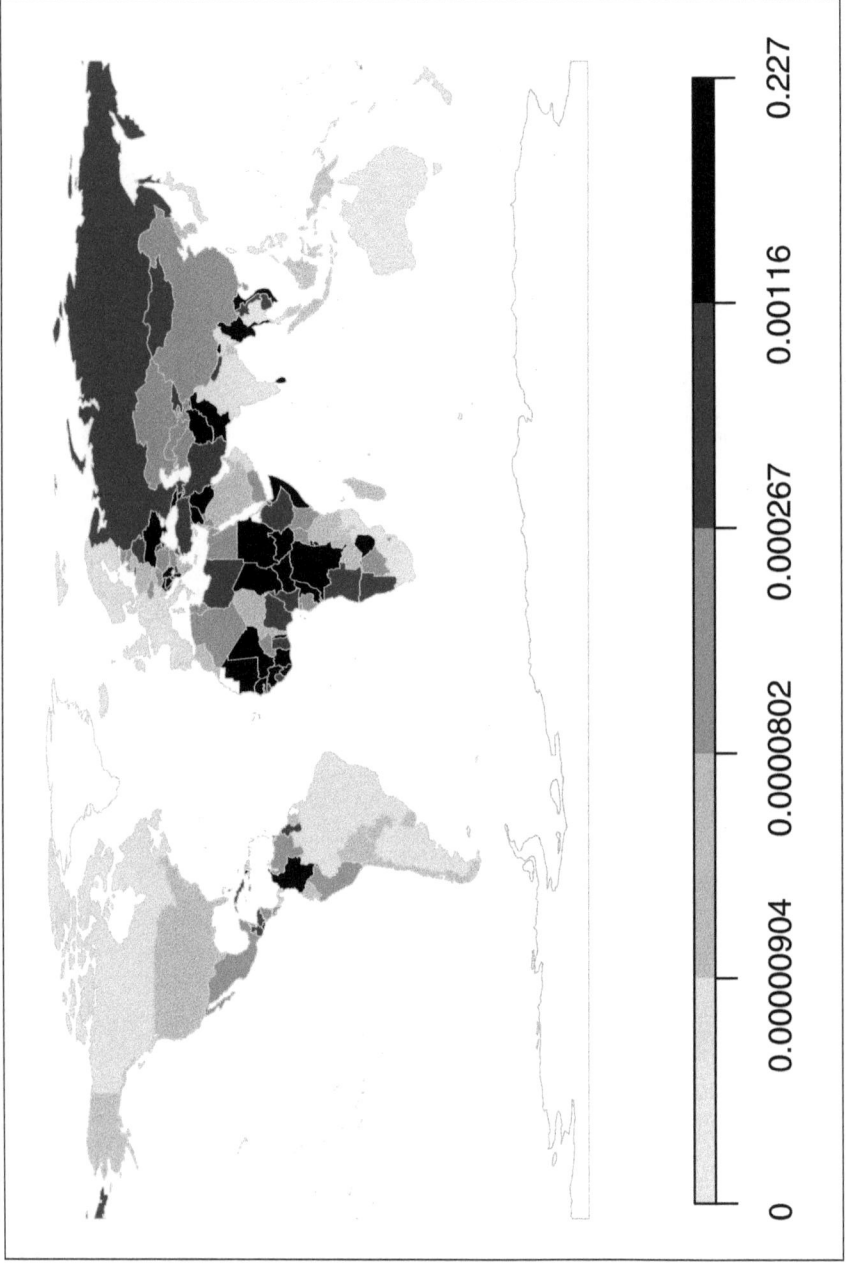

Figure 9.3 Refugees by country of origin

Africa have very low rates of refugee generation. Mozambique is comparable to Germany and Switzerland, and Algeria and Niger are comparable to states in Eastern Europe, in terms of generating refugees. Thus, it is simply not possible to classify regions by whether or not they generate refugees; this would risk masking important variation in the data.

Finally, there is the issue of where these refugees go, central in this chapter. Again, although we do not evaluate patterns of movement at the bilateral level, country-level data do provide interesting variation. The most recent data on refugee stocks at the time of writing were from 2014 (World Bank 2017b). Figure 9.4, which plots by country the number of refugees received as a portion of the population, makes it clear that many refugees end up in neighboring countries. Most refugees are concentrated in the Middle East and sub-Saharan Africa, the very same regions that have generated the largest number of refugees. Many states in Western Europe and Canada also accept a significant number of refugees as a portion of the total population. The number of refugees in Australia, the United States, and Russia is somewhat lower. However, the proportion of these refugees relative to the overall population is relatively small. As a proportion of the domestic population, in 2014, Sweden took the most refugees of any Western country; yet this amounts to only 1.5 percent of the population, whereas Jordan accommodates 37 percent of its population in refugees, and Lebanon takes in almost 29 percent of its population in refugees. Another contrast can be drawn with South Sudan and Syria. At the same time that they produce large numbers of refugees, they provide refuge for 2 percent and 3 percent of their population, respectively. It is not widely understood that countries that produce refugees can themselves be countries of refuge for others. Very few refugees end up in Latin America, as only Ecuador and Costa Rica have large numbers of refugees relative to their overall population. Similarly, there are relatively low rates of refugees in Oceania and many parts of Southeast Asia. These findings show that most migrants move to neighboring countries or to states that have resettlement programs. These data are not surprising, but they provide us with some indication about where those who seek protection settle. Thus, the fate of a survival migrant who ends up in Sweden is likely quite different from that of one who ends up in Syria.

Combined, these data reveal an interesting picture of the world that is necessary to grasp the nature of the issues. Most individuals seeking refuge move to countries within their region where they can seek safe havens. Wealthy Western countries, too, have accepted considerable numbers of refugees, but because these countries tend to be farther away from the conflicts and catastrophes that cause people to flee, they also can be more selective and can accept few refugees relative to their own population.

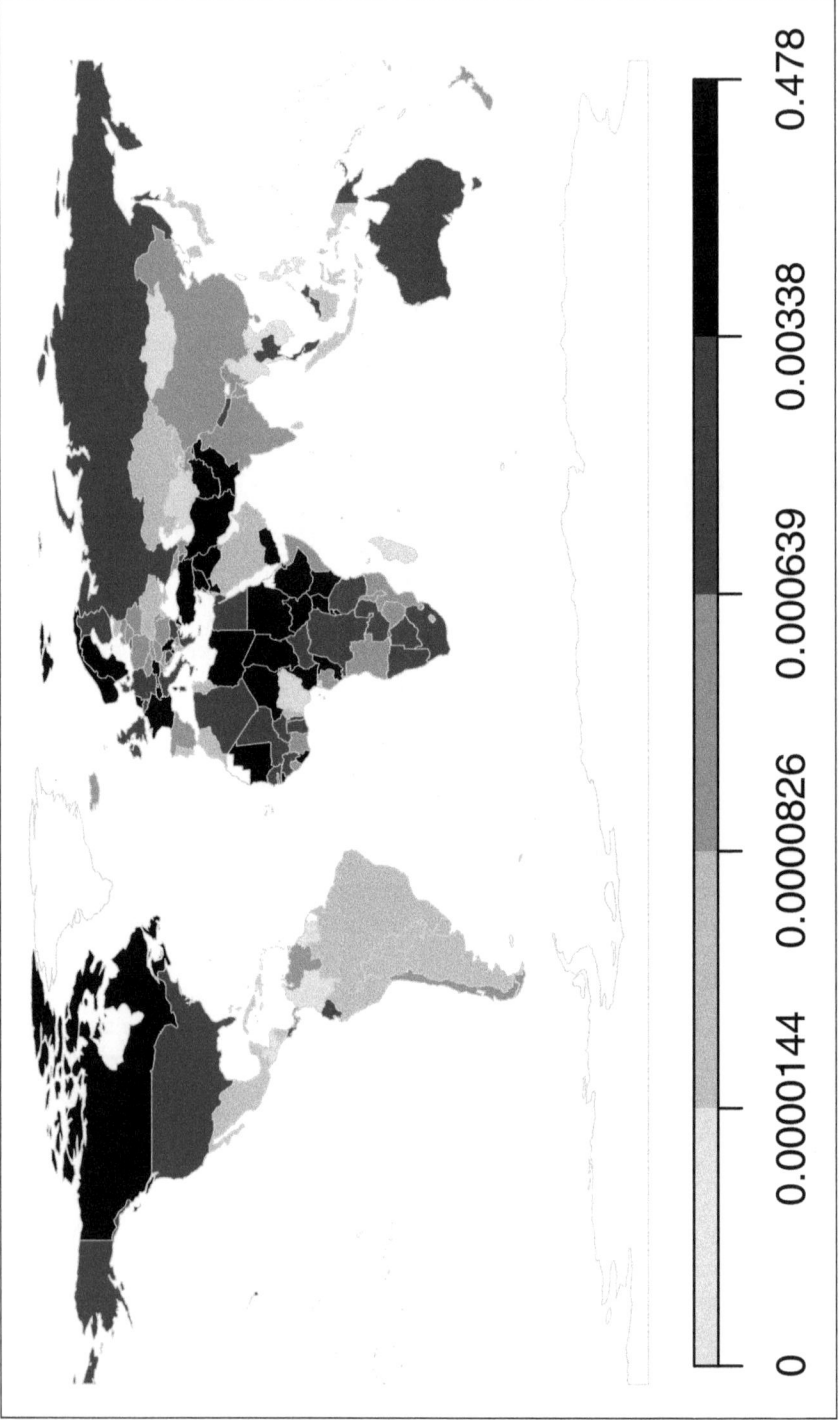

Figure 9.4 Refugees by country of asylum

Human development indicators. Figure 9.5 plots the levels of human development worldwide. The darkest countries depicted have the best outcomes in terms of human development. The worst levels of human development are found in sub-Saharan Africa. Additionally, Afghanistan and Pakistan have comparatively low levels of human development. These countries also tend to be both destinations and sources of refugees. In comparison, South American countries have levels of human development similar to those of Russia and China, and in a few cases are comparable to those of Eastern Europe, but host very few refugees. The states with the best human development, unsurprisingly, are those in Western Europe, North America, Australia, and Japan. Although many states in these regions accept a considerable number of refugees, they tend to have fewer refugees per capita than countries with lower levels of development.

Governance. Figure 9.6 plots levels of governance at the global level. States that are colored darker have better forms of governance. This figure shows that the highest levels of governance are found in Western Europe, the United States, Canada, Australia, and Japan. Those seeking protection who arrive in these countries are guaranteed some level of redress. The quality of governance is also relatively high in the Americas and in southern Africa, on average. However, Costa Rica and Ecuador, countries that host the highest number of refugees, actually do not have high quality of governance for their region. Looking at where most refugees actually receive asylum, it is clear that many migrants live in countries with relatively poor governance. Thus, many refugees move from the proverbial frying pan into the fire.

Citizenship. Figures 9.7, 9.8, and 9.9 map access to citizenship. Although there are missing data, the maps illustrate the opportunities for migrants to receive citizenship. Darker colors indicate that it is more difficult to obtain citizenship. Figure 9.7 maps access to citizenship for the children of aliens. The lightest colors represent countries that extend nationality to children of aliens with some residence requirement even if they were not born within the country. In the Americas the most common policy is to extend access to citizenship for all children of aliens at birth. However, in some states, such as the United Kingdom and Ireland, nationality is provided at birth only to the children of legal permanent residents. In many other cases nationality is not extended to children except when their parents naturalize or when they themselves request naturalization as an adult. There is considerable variation in the ease with which nationality is extended; however, it is interesting that countries in sub-Saharan Africa and the Middle East, where most of the individuals seeking protection are located, make access to citizenship difficult.

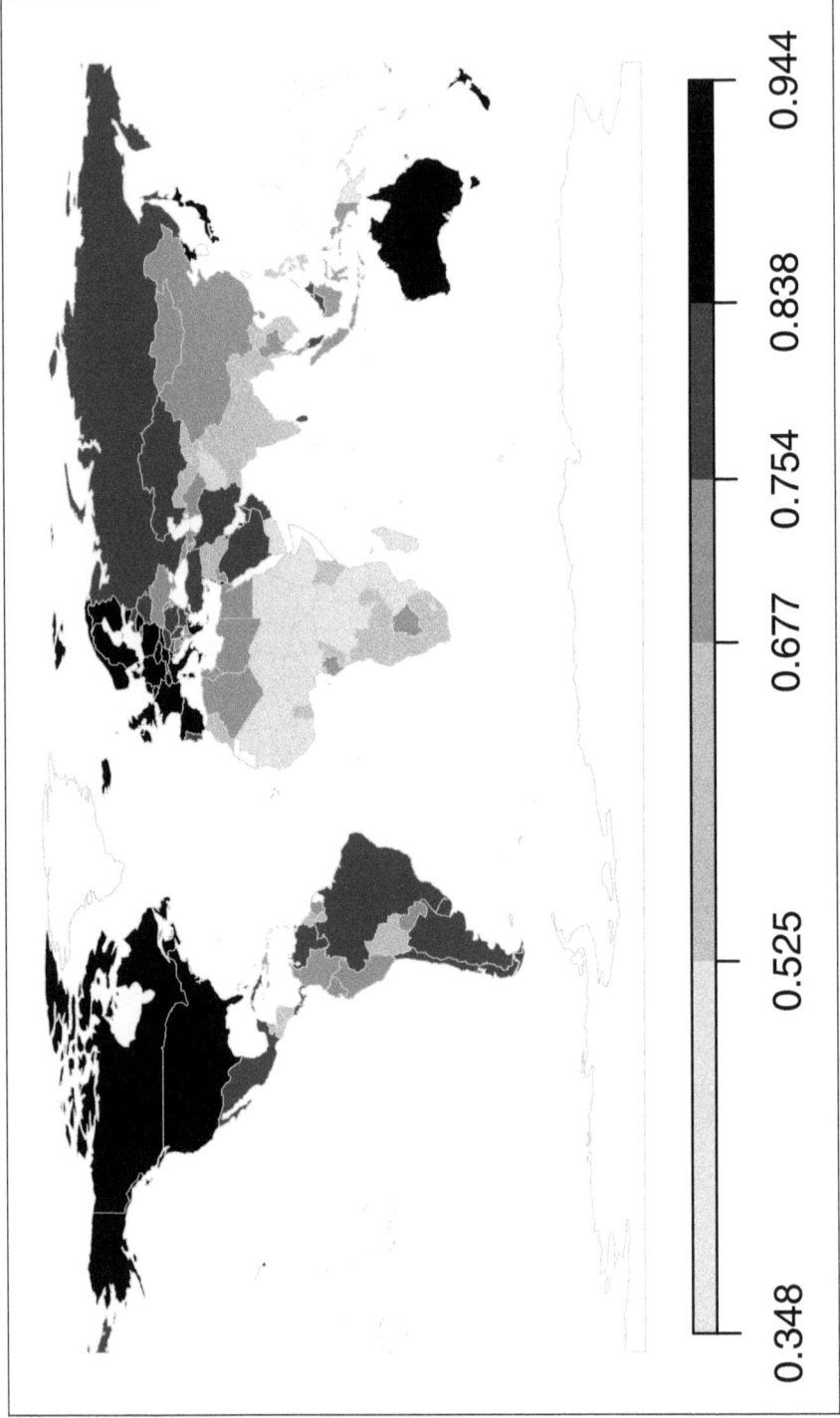

Figure 9.5 Human Development Index

Scale legend: 0.348 — 0.525 — 0.677 — 0.754 — 0.838 — 0.944

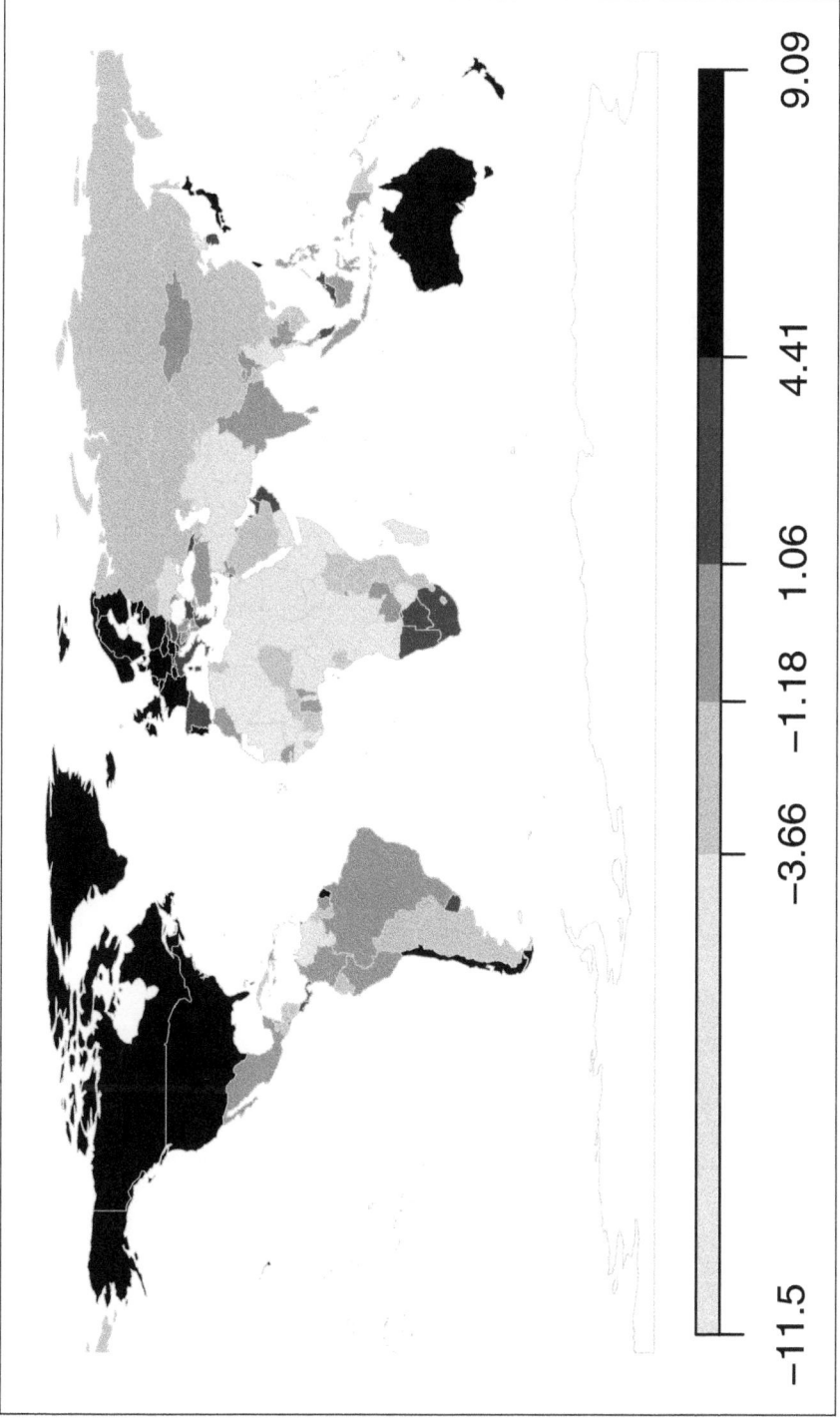

Figure 9.6 Governance

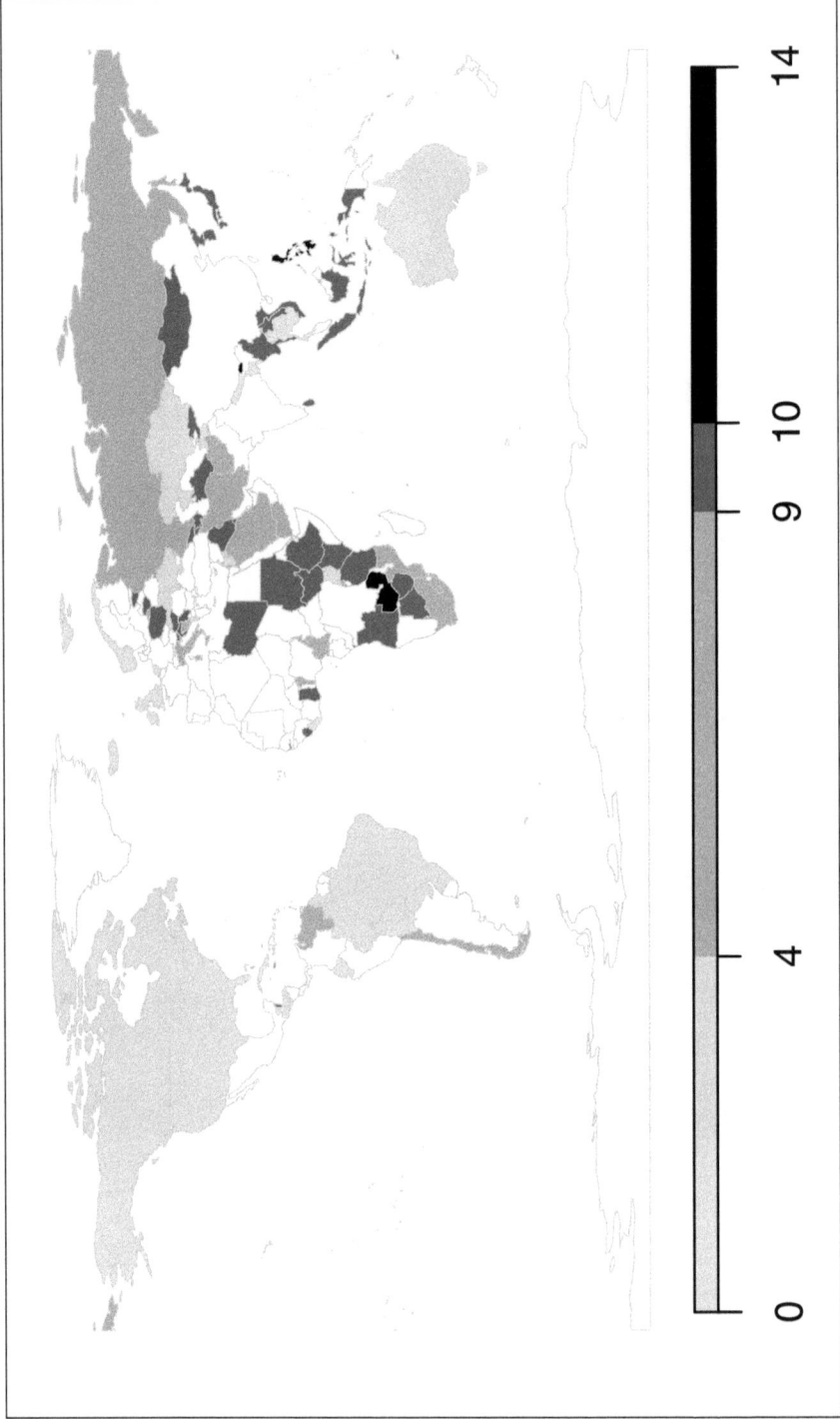

Figure 9.7 Children of aliens born in the country

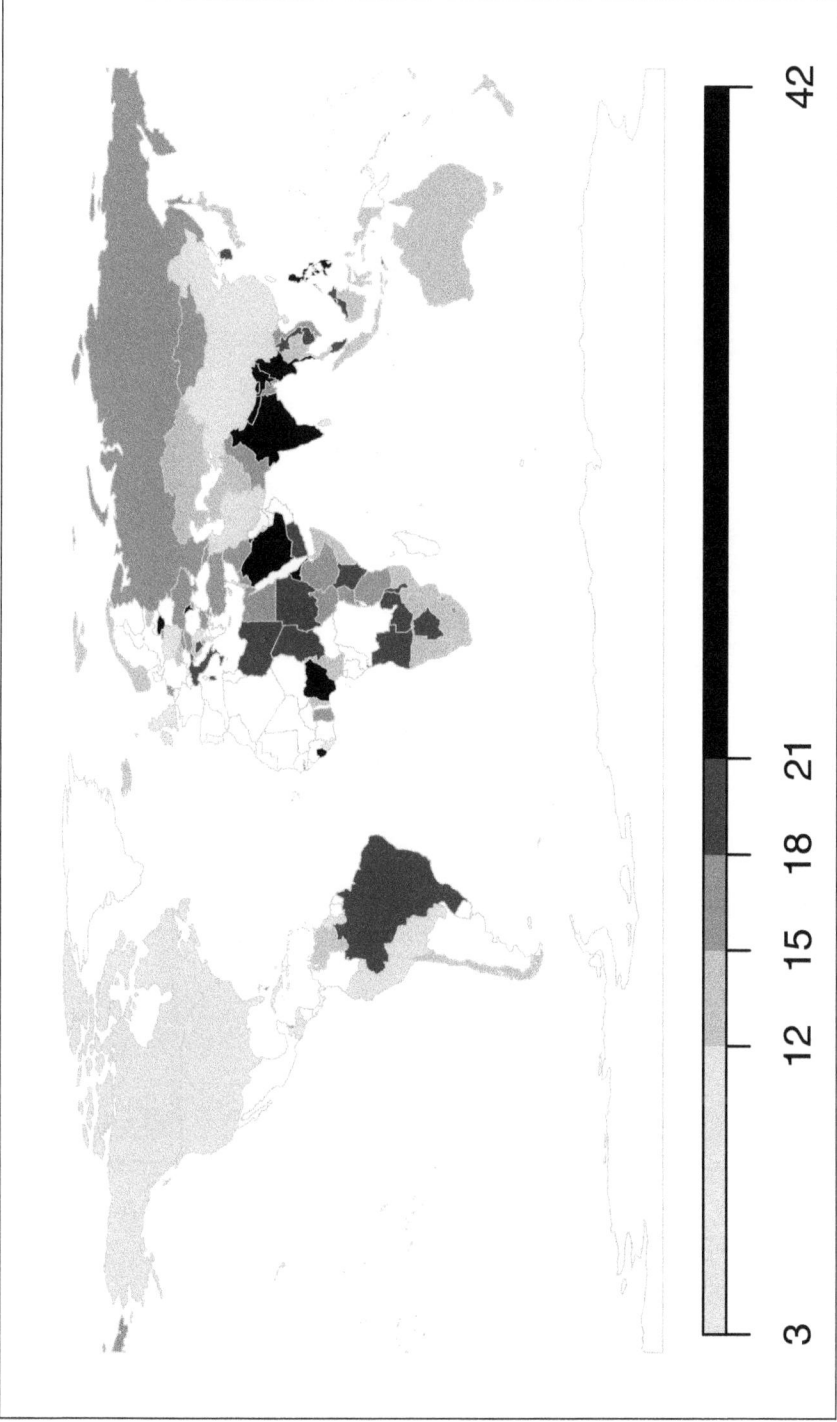

Figure 9.8 Adult naturalization

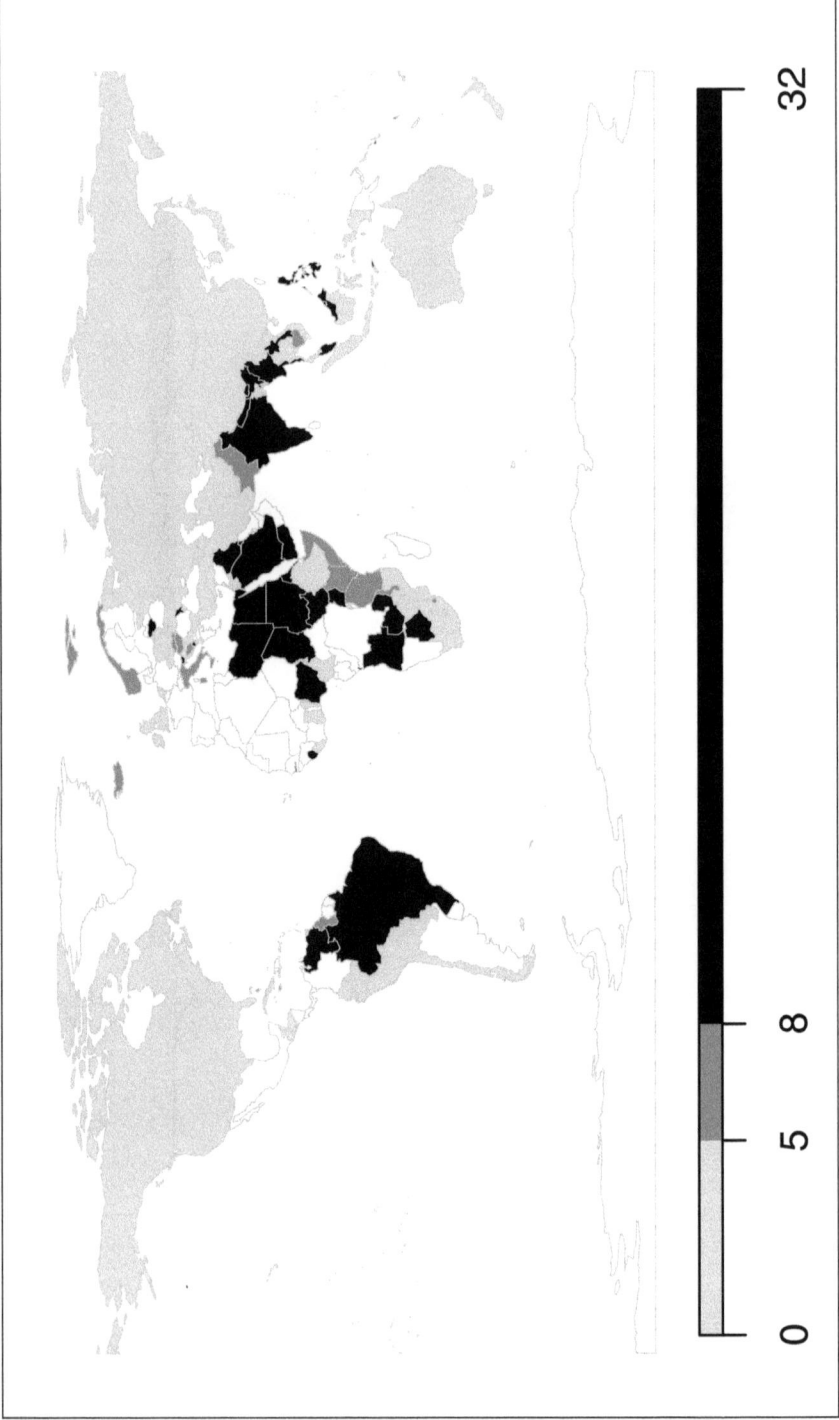

Figure 9.9 Period of residence

This, of course, is in contrast to the Western Hemisphere, where citizenship is extended to all those born in the territory.

Figure 9.8 maps the difficulty for adults to obtain citizenship. Again there are significant differences in the hurdles that adults have to overcome to naturalize. In some countries naturalization is relatively easy, and there are few hurdles to citizenship for migrants, while in other cases there are many hurdles. One of the most significant factors in this index is the period of residence required before migrants are eligible to apply for naturalization. In most states migrants must live in the country for five years. However, this period can be much longer. The waiting period is crucial because, until migrants naturalize, they lack many legal rights and may risk deportation. Thus, Figure 9.9 maps just the component for the period of residence. Again this figure is interesting, as most countries in the Americas have five-year residency periods. In contrast, there is considerable variation in Africa and Asia, as some states require fifteen years or more before aliens are permitted to naturalize. Given the requirements for children's naturalization that prohibit the extension of nationality until a parent naturalizes, such policies have far-reaching implications and potentially affect the rights of those individuals for generations, particularly if those individuals are stateless.

Conclusion. The conditions in countries of refuge vary considerably. This variation is a challenge for human rights in the twenty-first century; the protections survival migrants receive are contingent on where they end up rather than based on universal rights (Stern and Straus 2014). If survival migrants arrive in Sweden, they find a country with strong governance and high human development. Moreover, it is likely that their children will be able to receive access to a Swedish nationality relatively easily, and parents can apply for nationality after seven years of residence. Consequently, it is likely that the rights of such migrants will be protected by the rule of law and that these rights can be used to enhance these individuals' agency. In contrast, survival migrants who end up in Chad find a government with relatively low-quality governance and low levels of human development, and they may have difficulty obtaining citizenship because of restrictions and long residency requirements. These survival migrants are unlikely to have their rights protected, and their opportunities are likely to be limited. Although these structural characteristics do not always go hand in hand, there are several points to be taken from this evidence.

The first point is that those who seek protection, in many cases, are thrown from a bad situation into a worse one when neighboring states to which they flee have poor governance and few resources to share. Consequently, it is difficult for these individuals to thrive in their country of asylum because it is difficult for them to meet their basic needs and to advocate for their rights. The second point is that, although some individuals in search of refuge make it to Western Europe, the United States, Canada, or Australia and face a comparatively better fate, relatively few migrants reach such far-flung destinations. We should also offer a word of caution. What our maps do not reveal is the domestic political backlash in these countries toward both migrants and asylum seekers. Governments in these democracies may respond by abridging the rights of those who seek refuge in a manner that diminishes their ability to integrate into the host society. Examples of this are rife and are evident in the refugee camps such as Australia's camps in Nauru and those in Calais, France. Finally, these figures show that there are many countries in the world, particularly in Latin America, where those seeking protection would face relatively good circumstances if they were able to reach these countries. However, there are very few refugees, asylum seekers, or even migrants who are actually settled in such countries.

Where those who seek refuge end up matters. The mismatch between the demand for protection and the supply of countries with adequate resources to provide a decent refuge is significant. There are two political challenges (global and local) for overcoming this mismatch. At the global level, providing refuge can be understood as a public good that is generally undersupplied because of free riding (Betts 2003). The global community needs to think of incentives to encourage contributions. One solution might be moral or legal obligations as discussed in this book (see Chapters 1 and 2, for example), but doing so may be difficult for the citizens of such countries, particularly given the recent resurgence of nationalism. At the local level, contributions to providing global public goods generate political and economic liabilities that must be taken into account by national leadership. Therefore, it is necessary to strike the right balance between the two so that remedial actions are taken.

Equity and Refuge

The UNHCR (n.d.) privileges three solutions to the problems of refugees: voluntary repatriation, resettlement in a third country, or integration in the host community. Individuals and families seek protection abroad because their country of origin cannot or will not protect their rights. These survival migrants—whether or not they are classified as convention refugees, have a subordinate protected status or merely survive on the margins of the host society without any assurances or rights—need conditions of reception that allow them to reestablish their lives. We have argued that three characteristics of states are necessary for this to occur: good governance, adequate resources as represented by the HDI, and access to nationality. Our mapping exercise has shown what is widely known, that countries with the fewest resources are often the ones that provide the most refuge. We do not minimize the contributions of these countries; rather, we suggest that there are significant limits that these countries confront in providing human rights for survival migrants, as they often are dealing with securing their own survival in addition to development and governance issues.

As this book illustrates, these facts are problematic for individuals confronting emerging threats to human rights, as those states that are least able to bear the costs are often those shouldering the highest burden (see also Chapter 3). The UNHCR facilitates the reception of refugees in these countries, financed in part through donations of primarily wealthy Western democracies. However, real refuge is more than protection from physical harm; it entails access to the resources that promote human development. Thus, the possibilities for integration in many host countries are abbreviated. Those who seek protection are well aware of the distribution of resources worldwide and, with greater and greater frequency, have the information and the resources to travel to more attractive countries of refuge. The migrant crises that make international headlines are like the canaries in the coal mines: lack of governance and resources elsewhere is driving the movement of populations across international borders, and many individuals are not stopping at the country of first refuge. Therefore, resettlement should be more widely considered as a proactive and cost-effective response to migrant agency. But, ultimately, the only long-term solution to the breach of ethical norms associated with the global human rights regime is to shore up the provision of rights and resources around the world so that repatriation becomes a viable option.

NOTES

1. Betts's exact definition is "persons who are outside their country of origin because of an existential threat for which they have no access to a domestic remedy or resolution" (2013, 23). Thus, the term "survival migrant" is inclusive of both those who meet the criteria of the UN Refugee Convention and those who do not. The definition does make a distinction between survival migrant and the "economic" or "voluntary" migrant who moves without the prompt of an existential threat.

2. There is also the issue of adjudication: even if the individual qualifies, that individual must provide sufficient evidence to convince the adjudicator of the merits of his or her case.

3. Countries have employed different vocabulary to refer to similar categories of individuals. The United Kingdom uses "exceptional leave to remain." In EU legislation, "subsidiary protection" is the terminology. The UN prefers to refer to "complementary protection" (UNHCR 2008). In each case, protection is provided to those in harm's way who would not be eligible under the convention definition.

4. The particular indicators and methods of calculation have changed over time, but the underlying concepts remain constant. For index data, see http://hdr.undp.org/en/data.

5. The nine core human rights treaties, designated as such by the UN, are the International Convention on the Elimination of All Forms of Racial Discrimination (CERD), 1965; the International Covenant on Civil and Political Rights (ICCPR), 1966; the International Covenant on Economic, Social and Cultural Rights (ICESCR), 1966; the Convention on the Elimination of all Forms of Discrimination against Women (CEDAW), 1979; the Convention on Torture and Other Cruel, Inhuman or Degrading Treatment or Punishment (CAT), 1984; the Convention on the Rights of the Child (CRC), 1989; the International Convention on the Protection of the Rights of All Migrant Workers and Members of Their Families (ICRMW), 1990; the International Convention for the Protection of All Persons from Enforced Disappearance (CPED), 2006; and the Convention on the Rights of Persons with Disabilities (CRPD), 2006.

6. A third dimension is familial access to citizenship through marriage and adoption. We do not address this dimension here.

7. New Zealand permits legal resident aliens to vote in national elections after a year's residence, and other some countries provide noncitizens with the ability to participate at the local level, but in most states electoral participation is reserved only for citizens.

8. Some countries provide institutional mechanisms to allow or encourage those who seek refuge to provide input into policy making. Some countries also allow resident aliens to participate in local, but not national, politics (Groenendijk 2008).

REFERENCES

Acemoglu, Daron, Simon Johnson, and James A. Robinson. 2001. "The Colonial Origins of Comparative Development: An Empirical Investigation." *American Economic Review* 91 (5): 1369–1401.

Betts, Alexander. 2003. "Public Goods Theory and the Provision of Refugee Protection: The Role of the Joint-Product Model in Burden-Sharing Theory." *Journal of Refugee Studies* 16 (3): 274–296.

———. 2013. *Survival Migration: Failed Governance and the Crisis of Displacement.* Ithaca, NY: Cornell University Press.

Blanton, Shannon L., and Robert G. Blanton. 2007. "What Attracts Foreign Investors? An Examination of Human Rights and Foreign Direct Investment." *Journal of Politics* 69 (1): 143–155.

Bueno de Mesquita, Bruce, James D. Morrow, Randolph M. Siverson, and Alastair Smith. 2003. *The Logic of Political Survival.* Cambridge, MA: MIT Press.

Bustamante, Jorge. 2002. "Immigrants' Vulnerability as Subjects of Human Rights." *International Migration Review* 36 (2): 333–354.

Dai, Xinyuan. 2013. "The 'Compliance Gap' and the Efficacy of International Human Rights Institutions." In *From Commitment to Compliance*, edited by Thomas Risse, Stephen C. Ropp, and Kathryn Sikkink, 85–102. Cambridge: Cambridge University Press.

Dembour, Marie-Bénédicte, and Tobias Kelley, eds. 2011. *Are Human Rights for Migrants? Critical Reflections on the Status of Irregular Migrants in Europe and the United States.* New York: Routledge.

Donnelly, Jack. 1986. "International Human Rights: A Regime Analysis." *International Organization* 40 (3): 599–642.

European Union. 2004. "Council Directive 2004/83/EC." *Official Journal of the European Union*, September 30. Available at http://eur-lex.europa.eu/legal-content/en/TXT/?uri=CELEX:32004L0083.

Groenendijk, Kees. 2008. "Local Voting Rights for Non-nationals in Europe: What We Know and What We Need to Learn." Migration Policy Institute, April. Available at https://www.migrationpolicy.org/research/local-voting-rights-non-nationals -europe-what-we-know-and-what-we-need-learn.

Hafner-Burton, Emilie M., and Kiyoteru Tsutsui. 2007. "Justice Lost! The Failure of International Human Rights Law to Matter Where Needed Most." *Journal of Peace Research* 44 (4): 407–425.

Hathaway, James C. 1991. "Reconceiving Refugee Law as Human Rights Protection." *Journal of Refugee Studies* 4 (2): 113–131.

Hyndman, Jennifer, and Bo Viktor Nylund. 1998. "UNHCR and the Status of Prima Facie Refugees in Kenya." *International Journal of Refugee Law* 19 (1–2): 21–48.

Inder, Claire. 2017. "The Origins of 'Burden Sharing' in the Contemporary Refugee Protection Regime." *International Journal of Refugee Law* 29 (4): 523–554.

Ireland, Patrick. 2004. *Becoming Europe: Immigration Integration and the Welfare State.* Pittsburgh, PA: University of Pittsburgh Press.

Lebovic, James H., and Erik Voeten. 2009. "The Cost of Shame: International Organizations and Foreign Aid in the Punishing of Human Rights Violators." *Journal of Peace Research* 46 (1): 79–97.

Mattila, Heikki S. 2000. "Protection of Migrants' Human Rights: Principles and Practice." In *The Human Rights of Migrants*, edited by Reginald Appleyard, 53–71. Geneva: International Organization for Migration.

Money, Jeannette. 1999a. "New Citizens: Immigrant Electoral Participants and the Host Polity." In *In Defense of the Alien*, vol. 22, edited by Lydio F. Tomasi, 101–115. New York: Center for Migration Studies.

———. 1999b. "Pauline Hanson and the Counterbalancing of Electoral Incentives in Australia." *People and Place* 7 (3): 7–19.

Money, Jeannette, Shaina Western, and Edith Yuh. Forthcoming. *Compendium of Nationality Legislation.* Geneva: International Organization for Migration.

Morris, Lydia. 2001. "Stratified Rights and the Management of Migration. National Distinctiveness in Europe." *European Societies* 3 (4): 387–411.

North, Douglass. 1990. *Institutional Change and Economic Performance.* Cambridge: Cambridge University Press.

Rutinwa, Bonaventure. 2002. "New Issues in Refugee Research: Prima Facie Status and Refugee Protection." UNHCR Working Paper no. 69. Available at https://www .unhcr.org/3db9636c4.pdf.

Sanderson, Matthew. 2010. "International Migration and Human Development in Destination Countries: A Cross-national Analysis of Less-Developed Countries, 1970–2005." *Social Indicators Research* 96 (1): 59–83.

Stasiulis, Daiva K. 1997. "International Migration, Rights, and the Decline of 'Actually Existing Liberal Democracy.'" *Journal of Ethnic and Migration Studies* 23 (2): 197–214.

Stern, Steve J., and Scott Straus, eds. 2014. *The Human Rights Paradox: Universality and Its Discontents.* Madison: University of Wisconsin Press.

UNDP (United Nations Development Programme). 1990. *Human Development Report, 1990.* New York: Oxford University Press.

———. 2012. *Human Development Report, 2012.* New York: UNDP.

UNHCR (United Nations High Commissioner for Refugees). 1951. "Convention and Protocol relating to the Status of Refugees." Available at https://www.unhcr.org/en -us/3b66c2aa10.

———. 2001. "The International Protection of Refugees: Complementary Forms of Protection." Available at https://www.refworld.org/pdfid/3b20a7014.pdf.

———. 2008. "UNHCR Statement on Subsidiary Protection under the EC Qualification Directive for People Threatened by Indiscriminate Violence." Available at https://www.unhcr.org/protect/PROTECTION/479df9532.pdf.

———. n.d. "Solutions." Available at http://www.unhcr.org/uk/solutions.html (accessed March 1, 2019).

United Nations. 1948. "Universal Declaration of Human Rights." Available at http://www.un.org/en/universal-declaration-human-rights.

World Bank. 2017a. "Net Migration." Available at http://data.worldbank.org/indicator/SM.POP.NETM.

———. 2017b. "Refugee Population by Country or Territory of Asylum." Available at http://data.worldbank.org/indicator/SM.POP.REFG.

———. 2017c. "Refugee Population by Country or Territory of Origin." Available at http://data.worldbank.org/indicator/SM.POP.REFG.OR.

———. n.d. "Worldwide Governance Indicators." Available at http://info.worldbank.org/governance/wgi/index.aspx#home (accessed March 1, 2019).

Conclusion

HEATHER SMITH-CANNOY

This project began as an exercise to survey scholars working on topics in international relations and human rights to understand the connections between emerging threats to rights and to evaluate whether these threats are generating mass migration. The results show a clear and interconnected vision of threats to human rights. Resource deprivation in the form of pollution and climate change undermines rights in many indirect ways: cutting off access to water, eroding coastal zones, displacing populations, and inhibiting farming (McAdam 2012). Yet we see in Part I that mass migration in large numbers due to environmental devastation is not yet occurring.[1] Instead, populations subject to the effects of climate change and water pollution have found innovative ways to adjust without fleeing or to fight back, either through the United Nations (UN; as Chapter 2 illustrates) or through coordination with other states across the Global South (as Chapter 1 shows in regard to the environmental-justice movement).

In contrast, victims of state-sponsored violence, perhaps unsurprisingly, are fleeing from their homes, generating the largest ever-recorded number of migrants. Flight appears to be their greatest hope for survival, yet Part II shows that if they successfully escape, their prospects for improved human rights conditions remain dim. Xenophobic violence against migrants in host countries (as Chapter 4 illustrates) becomes a significant threat to those who successfully escape. Deprivation of citizenship also causes people to flee in search of a better life, but those who flee without the benefits of identity documentation become susceptible to traffickers and hostile host countries unwilling to grant them asylum. In these cases, intergovernmental organizations (IGOs) appear to be the best agents of change in prodding reluctant governments to change course (as Chapter 7 shows regarding the UN in Burma and Chapter 8 shows on the European Union [EU] in Europe).

When the emerging threats to rights are slow or invisible, such as environmental degradation, communities find ways to stay and fight, but when governments use violence or rescind citizenship, people flee, often into even more dangerous situations. For those who flee, their prospects for a better life may depend critically on three characteristics of the host state: level of human development, quality of governance, and access to citizenship (as Chapter 9 discusses). In other words, not all host states are equal in the provision of rights and benefits for migrants. The rest of the Conclusion develops the two central arguments of book, drawing on insights from contributing chapters: using a human rights frame to look at intersections between issue areas (environment-violence and violence-citizenship) and examining whether and to what extent environmental degradation, violence, and deprivation of citizenship serve as drivers of displacement. The final section proposes directions for future research.

Human Rights: Looking across and between the Issues

In the Introduction I argue that by grouping environmental degradation, violence, and deprivation of citizenship, we can deemphasize the traditional frameworks applied to these issue areas and instead focus on human rights. Traditional approaches to these areas tend to examine political factors while neglecting human rights. For example, an international law approach to the study of environmental degradation emphasizes the factors that impede successful agreements or hasten the collapse of such agreements (Battaglini and Harstad 2016; Susskind and Ali 2014; Gupta 2012). Lost in this discussion is the impact of a warming climate on the populations of island-nations, as Chapter 1 details. Greenhouse gas emissions, the chapter argues, are responsible for both extreme climatic events (such as hurricanes) and slow-onset events (floods, water shortages, drought, heat waves). Victims of climate change–related events can be displaced from their homes, unable to work or attend school, making even the most basic human rights out of reach. Our work in this book reframes the conversation around these topics to make human rights the central focus.

Similarly, with respect to state violence, research in international relations tends to examine causes of state violence against civilian populations (Eck and Hultman 2007; Azam and Hoeffler 2002; Balcells 2010). Such work also looks at the motivations of rebels willing to take up violence against their state. This work falls squarely in the field of international security but often fails to consider the ways in which widespread violence subverts virtually all aspirations for human rights. As rates of generalized violence increase and more people are exposed to dangerous conditions at home, it becomes more important for us to think about not only why the violence is occurring (the traditional security framework) but also what effect widespread generalized violence has on the prospects for human rights more generally.

Finally, a more traditional framework for examining questions of citizenship, refugee status, and statelessness tends to be found within international law. The legal framework is used by scholars and practitioners of refugee law to understand when and under what conditions an asylum seeker can expect to be granted asylum in a sanctuary country. Yet even within the most well-developed legal regime in this area (the Convention relating to the Status of Refugees [Refugee Convention]) there are important gaps that imperil the human rights of asylum seekers. When asylum seekers are denied formal refugee status but fear returning to their country of origin or habitual residence, they live in a legal limbo—unable to work and in many cases confined to squalid refugee camps. Even for those who are merely awaiting an asylum decision, the process often takes years, and in the interim prospects for rights remain very dim. Here, focusing on the legality of asylum decisions neglects the human costs associated even with long delays in processing refugee applications. Where will children go to school? How can parents earn a living to support the family? The most basic questions surrounding the human condition are not the focus of work in this field. *Emerging Threats* seeks to fill this gap by redirecting the way that we think about these threats to human rights today.

Environment-Violence Connections

When we look across these issue areas, we can begin to make human rights the focus of our analysis. Chapter 5 shows that the Communist and Karen insurrections in Myanmar were facilitated by the availability of timber and gems. Cash from the sale of such lootable resources can be used to purchase weapons and continue the fight. The availability of these resources prolonged the insurrections and ultimately the suffering of the Burmese population. In Myanmar, groups that successfully negotiate a cease-fire with the government, referred to as "cease-fire groups," often receive economic incentives from the government: business opportunities, import-export licenses, or cash transfers. An example is the government's chief negotiator distributing envelopes to leaders of cease-fire groups in 2014 that contained very valuable automobile import licenses. Government support undercuts the fundraising needs of cease-fire groups, thereby diminishing their fund-raising abuses directed at civilians, such as theft, extortion, and kidnappings. But cease-fire groups do not then become less likely to commit abuses against civilians. Instead, they start engaging in different types of abuses aimed at terrorizing civilians, because once they coordinate with the government, they are expected to join in and terrorize enemies of the government. Terrorizing civilians consists of very serious human rights violations, including rape and torture.

Chapter 5 shows that this shift from abusing civilians for revenue generation to terrorizing civilians to suppress government opposition is not unique to Myanmar. The statistical analysis tests the human rights consequences of cease-fires from twenty-three Asian countries between 1985 and 2014. The findings overwhelmingly suggest that citizens are frequently subject to worse conditions following cease-fires. A more traditional security framework neglects the contribution of abundant natural resources on the duration of conflict and the duration of conflict on the specter of human rights for civilians.

Chapter 2 challenges standard assumptions in the literature about the predicted relationship between resource scarcity and violence. When groups have to compete over scarce or dwindling resources, there are good reasons to expect that violence will break out (Homer-Dixon 1994). Even if scarce resources are not a direct cause of violence, they may activate latent ethnic tensions and ultimately contribute to violence among enduring rivals (Goldstone 2002; Baechler 1999). Paradoxically, when the UN contaminated the Haitian water supply with cholera, Haitians did not respond with violence. Instead, the Bureau des Avocats Internationaux (BAI), a major Haitian human rights organization, worked with victims through a grassroots outreach effort to fight the actor responsible for the pollution of their water supply. The UN denied that spillover from the peacekeeping base in Meille, a small village in central Haiti, was the cause of the cholera outbreak. An international investigation by a renowned cholera expert suggested that the UN's improper sewage management on the Meille base and Nepalese peacekeepers infected with a particular South Asian strain of the disease were the causes of the outbreak.

Though the UN should have acted quickly to investigate and contain the outbreak, it instead issued a series of denials and engaged in coverups for a year as the outbreak spread across Haiti. The UN is immune from prosecution in national courts by virtue of the Convention on the Privileges and Immunities of the UN, which grants blanket immunity to the UN, similar to a Status of Forces Agreement, which is a standard agreement granting immunity to peacekeeping forces in exchange for their work. In theory, civilians wronged by the UN have the ability to file claims before a commission of inquiry, which may be convened, but in practice, the UN has never convened such a commission; in spite of the well-documented abuses carried out by UN peacekeepers, no systematic compensation has ever been provided.

But unlike in the past, the UN was not successful in shielding itself from responsibility in the case of the cholera outbreak in Haiti. The BAI flooded the UN Stabilization Mission in Haiti (MINUSTAH) with more than five thousand claims associated with the outbreak. In coordination with human rights attorneys and journalists, they filed a class-action lawsuit in New York challenging the UN's professed immunity and waged a social media campaign designed to show the tragic effects of the UN's negligence. They also engaged the UN's own human rights oversight system, filing complaints with the Universal Periodic Review and the UN Special Procedures bodies that triggered investigations of wrongdoing by the UN Secretariat with the special rapporteur on the human right to safe drinking water and sanitation. These efforts led the UN to change course; in August 2016 it finally admitted its role in the outbreak and agreed to provide support and assistance to all those affected. In this case the moral consciousness raising, social media pressure, and careful coordination among lawyers and Haitian activists successfully contributed to justice for the Haitian victims of the cholera outbreak. The chapter shows that even in the most challenging case, where lack of access to clean water could have contributed to violence, Haitian activists instead mounted an aggressive political action campaign at the global level using foreign courts, UN human rights tribunals, and moral consciousness-raising tactics in the media.

Chapter 3 examines a series of issue areas connected to the depletion of the physical environment—resource consumption, resource distribution, population control, food distribution, and energy consumption. The chapter deftly illustrates that when two passionate sets of activist movements (human rights and environmental rights) confront unacceptably low levels of protection in their respective fields, competition rather than coordination may emerge. The competition creates pressure on national politicians to give bold speeches and create hollow policy that seems to do little to address these challenges and may themselves contribute to severe human rights consequences.

Poorly managed water conflicts in the Tigris-Euphrates River basin have the potential to create cascading human rights violations in the region. When governments competing over access to water cannot negotiate agreements over water rights, the human rights of these populations can suffer. As water supplies become more variable and altered sediment flows to agricultural land and marshland reduce resiliency to floods and droughts, the absence of interstate cooperation or coordination can mean that once-fertile farmland can dry up. In reframing these conflicts to better account for human rights concerns, the chapter makes it clear that reduced food

security, crop failure, and water pollution are but some of the many consequences people endure when environmental conflicts are mismanaged.

Chapter 1 addresses the human rights consequences of climate change,
illustrating its disproportionate human impact on peoples in the Global
South. The chapter makes clear that for those in the Global South, the issue
not about scarce resources leading to violence but rather that the aged,
women, and children lack the resources to flee the effects of climate change
and therefore become victims of environmental violence. With higher average incomes and greater resources, people in the Global North have a greater
capacity to adapt to the consequences of climate change. The chapter argues
that the Sustainable Development Goals are the international community's
response by trying to rectify the disproportionate impact that climate change
has on people in the Global South.

Violence-Citizenship Connections

Examining the relationships uncovered between violence and citizenship
across these chapters can yield similarly interesting lessons. Violence can
motivate people to flee their country of origin, but on arrival in asylum
countries, asylum seekers can be met with new forms of violence and discrimination as a consequence of their citizenship or its lack. Chapter 4 shows
that xenophobic violence against refugees in sanctuary countries imperils
basic human rights of asylum seekers in Africa. Once asylum seekers arrive
in a sanctuary country, they may experience extreme discrimination because they are foreigners. The analysis flips the more traditional approach of
thinking about refugees as causes of security threats to the states in which
they seek asylum to considering the security challenges that the refugees
themselves experience in asylum countries.

The case presented on anti-refugee violence in South Africa illustrates
the backlash that asylum seekers can experience once they flee to a host state.
South Africa's population of refugees quadrupled between 2004 and 2014,
leading to anti-immigrant sentiment among the native population (UNHCR
2006, 2015). While the refugees come from more than forty countries across
Africa, the majority are from Somalia, the Democratic Republic of the
Congo (DRC), and Ethiopia. The chapter documents twenty-one major attacks on migrant and refugee populations undertaken by nationals with the
goal of systematic "national cleansing." The analysis suggests that the lack of
citizenship or the perception of the asylum seeker as a foreigner plays a key
role in motivating the attacks against this population.

Chapter 6 provides another important insight on the relationship between citizenship and violence. The findings demonstrate that human rights
indeed improve when states experiencing a democratic transition employ

truth-and-justice mechanisms. The discussion follows the literature in differentiating between the effects of two distinct types—those that prioritize
peace (such as truth commissions) and those that prioritize justice (such as
tribunals and prosecutions). Truth-and-justice mechanisms that use trials
and prosecutions to punish the guilty are associated with better human
rights outcomes than those that rely exclusively on truth commissions and
amnesty. With the exception of the Liberia Tribunal and the International
Criminal Tribunal for the former Yugoslavia, transitional justice processes
have typically neglected the rights of refugees. Yet citizens forced to flee violence at home should, the chapter argues, be incorporated into the reconciliation process at home. Such populations are uniquely poised to build
narratives around truth and reverse past human rights atrocities simply by
returning home.

In examining the relationship between violence and citizenship, this
book also shows that the deprivation of citizenship can pave the way for violence and human rights atrocities. Chapter 7 shows that deprivation of citizenship can be a precursor to violence: as the Burmese government slowly
dissolved the Rohingya's citizenship rights, virtually all of their basic human
rights were also stripped away. The tragic case of the Rohingya in Burma
serves as a cautionary tale. When a government begins targeting an unpopular minority group by depriving them of citizenship status, that group
becomes exceptionally vulnerable to additional human rights violations. The
Rohingya in western Burma are confined to camps and unable to work,
travel, or obtain medical care. By 2018, the UN, U.S. House of Representatives, and human rights organizations described the situation in western
Burma as genocide.[2] This chapter also shows that the process of escaping
one's home of habitual residence without documentation and citizenship
status carries with it extraordinary risk from a human rights perspective.
Subject to traffickers who exploit asylum seekers as they flee and to foreign
governments that detain and sell asylum seekers for profit, those without
citizenship are among the world's most vulnerable populations.

While Chapter 7 focuses on the ways in which deprivation of citizenship
can cause stateless populations to flee, Chapter 8 focuses on the challenges
that survival migrants experience after they have fled. The discussion shows
that those who successfully flee violence and arrive in Europe cannot count
on these liberal democracies to protect their rights—even in Europe, the lack
of citizenship can obstruct the realization of human rights. Among European states a mere seven have clear, well-established policies for determining
whether an individual should be considered legally stateless.[3]

Such procedures are critically important as a guarantor of rights for
people who lack citizenship, as the official legal status often carries with it
the right to legal residence, among others. Across Europe, there remain great

variations in other rights that may legally accompany stateless status. Some governments provide a path to naturalized citizenship, while others provide access to health care and education, but many fail to have established procedures for determining whether one is stateless. The lack of harmony between European states regarding stateless determination procedures calls into question the likelihood that escaping violence and successfully arriving in Europe will guarantee rights protections. In this way, the chapter shows that emigration without citizenship documentation makes for a very uncertain future for stateless asylum seekers.

Chapter 9 analyzes global migration trends, highlighting the mismatch between conditions in asylum countries and those necessary for migrants to thrive. Even when migrants and asylum seekers successfully escape violence, their prospects for thriving depend on three conditions in asylum countries: high levels of human development, good governance, and access to citizenship. A combination of these characteristics allows migrants to use their agency and thrive in their host countries. The chapter illustrates a series of paradoxes in the global refugee protection regime: countries in regions with the lowest levels of human development (sub-Saharan Africa, Afghanistan, and Pakistan) tend to both send and receive migrants at higher rates per capita than countries with higher development levels. Countries with the lowest levels of good governance indicators are taking in far more migrants and asylum seekers than countries with better governance indicators.

With respect to the third variable, there is a wide range in how difficult it is to obtain citizenship for asylum seekers. It is difficult to obtain citizenship in sub-Saharan Africa and the Middle East, where the overwhelming number of migrants and asylum seekers end up. In some countries in these regions naturalization can require up to fifteen years of residency, whereas in the Americas (a region with low receiving rates for migrants and asylum seekers) five years of residency for naturalization is the norm. Their findings support conclusions in Chapter 4 that states receiving large numbers of migrants and asylum seekers (such as South Africa) may indeed develop refugee fatigue, leading to xenophobic anti-immigrant policies. When asylum seekers flee their country of origin, their prospects for human rights and a life with dignity are inexorably tied to citizenship laws in their asylum country. Tragically, the overwhelming majority of migrant-receiving states lack high levels of human development and good governance and do not provide ready paths to citizenship, thus sowing the seeds of future discontent.

Human Rights Violations and Migration

This section examines whether and to what extent patterns of rights violations in a country of origin can be systematically linked to migration. Alexander Betts's (2013) concept of survival migration helps us think about whether rights falling below a certain threshold in a country of origin can serve as a driver of displacement. By differentiating between the issue areas covered in this book—resources, violence, and deprivation of citizenship— we aim to show that there are meaningful differences between these categories in assessing causes of migration. We differentiate between push factors, those conditions in a host country that fall beneath such a level that people are inclined to flee, and pull factors, those conditions in a foreign county that would improve one's way of life to such a degree that he or she is inclined to emigrate. Using illustrative cases from this book, I argue that we can situate the three potential drivers of displacement on a push-factor continuum: resource deprivation serves as the least likely to contribute to mass displacement, and violence is the greatest driver of displacement (see Figure C.1). In brief, the argument suggests that though resource degradation creates difficult situations endangering health, livelihoods, and in some cases survival, a lack of financial resources and willing host countries undercuts opportunities for flight. When we examine the most extreme driver of flight (violence), we see that the situation has become so desperate and dangerous that concerns about how refugees will escape and where they will land become secondary to ensuring survival. In the case of deprivation of citizenship, when governments intentionally deprive a particular group of nationality (as done to the Rohingya in Burma, discussed in Chapter 7), mass migration may indeed follow. But when governments simply fail to develop clear and consistent stateless determination procedures (the EU in dealing with migrants and refugees from Africa and Syria), we do not see mass migration, which in this case would imply migration from a European country to another host country.

The chapters on climate change, water pollution, and trade-offs between human rights and physical environments in Part I all suggest that resource deprivation or pollution of resources may serve as a push factor in migration

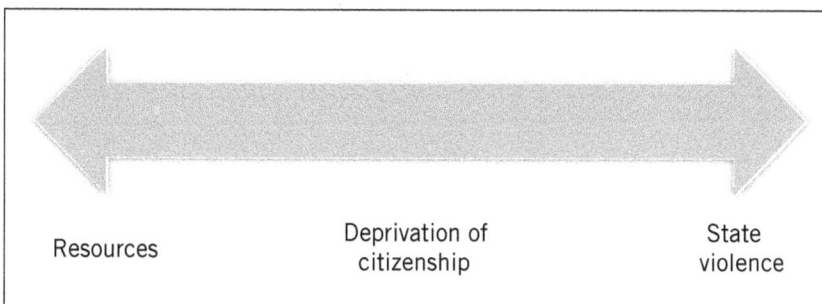

Resources   Deprivation of   State
                  citizenship   violence

Figure C.1 Push-factor continuum for displacement

decisions, but these decisions are constrained by economic resources. To be sure, people who live in especially dirty or polluted places (the Haitian population exposed to cholera in the water supply, for example) would most likely appreciate the opportunity to leave their country of origin to take refuge in a country with less polluted resources. In Chapter 1 we simply do not see Haitians fleeing their home in search of better environmental conditions abroad. But it would be erroneous to conclude that Haitians may not have wanted to leave—in other words, though the chapter documents the tooth-and-nail fight between Haitian advocates and the UN, we have no way of knowing how many Haitians may have opted to leave if given the opportunity. With more than nine thousand deaths resulting from the cholera epidemic, it seems likely that cholera may have been a push factor, but actual migration decisions are multifaceted and constrained by economic resources and opportunity (United Nations 2016). No countries threw open their border to Haitians seeking refuge, and because Haiti is the poorest country in the Western Hemisphere, with an average GDP per capita income of $846 per year, it seems likely that many Haitians simply could not flee their conditions at home (World Bank 2018).

Similarly, Chapter 2 illustrates that climate change has a disproportionate effect on the population of the Global South, leading to a type of climate injustice that renders its victims trapped in dirty, polluted, or degraded conditions. People in the Global South, who, like the Haitians facing cholera, lack the resources to adapt to coastal erosion, rising sea levels, and drought, may also lack the resources to flee. But the discussion shows that the injustice borne by victims of climate change results from more than a simple lack of adaptive capacity. Pressure to maintain low carbon footprints disproportionately affects underdeveloped countries because, if the world is to keep global warming below the two-degree-Celsius threshold, developing countries must employ negative-emission technologies. Such technologies, while good for the environment, can be prohibitively expensive. The result is that vulnerable populations may both lack the resources to adapt to or flee climate change and may also be trapped in places that are unable to develop because of the cost of green technology. Moreover, because the concept of climate refugee has yet to be accepted by governments, victims of climate change lack opportunities to immigrate to host countries.

Chapter 4 warns of a growing trend, best embodied in the Jordan River basin, where cases studied show that depleted groundwater resources, water pollution, and a lack of coordination between affected countries has contributed to out-migration. The chapter echoes warnings from military policy experts that climate change–related environmental changes may contribute to civil strife and conflict. A major drought in Syria between 2006 and 2011 contributed to out-migration into Jordan, which is now itself buckling under the weight of those Syrians who emigrated during the drought and refugees fleeing state violence. When human development needs are given precedence over environmental protection, the outcomes have been poor and frequently lead to refugee outflows.

Though the chapter warns that mass migration caused by climate change and environmental degradation has occurred in some areas in the Middle East, most findings across Part I imply that environmental degradation has yet to become a major driver of migration. As Chapters 1 and 2 demonstrate, structural factors such as poverty can inhibit adaptive capacities. Without financial resources one may find it especially challenging to leave home in search of more arable farmland. Without the technical expertise to clean polluted water, one may become ill with water-borne diseases. But even when poverty does not undermine one's capacity to adapt to these conditions, potential host states in the international community have yet to open their borders to environmental refugees. Countries in the Global North, which tend to experience fewer of the types of problems associated with environmental degradation that we see in the Global South, are not welcoming people fleeing from environmental degradation. If refugees do not have a country to escape to, environmentally induced flight may serve to undercut human rights rather than to secure them. For all of these reasons, we are not yet witnessing mass migration as a result of environmental degradation.

Similarly, with deprivation of citizenship, in some instances we see mass migration (the Rohingya in Burma), while in others we do not. I argue that deprivation of citizenship should be situated along the middle of the continuum as a push factor for migration. When a state rescinds the citizenship of a particular group, often the deterioration of basic human rights soon follows. But this process can be very slow and may contribute to mass migration only when human rights deteriorate precipitously. Betts's concept of survival migration is especially helpful in dealing with growing stateless populations because it suggests that rescinding or denying citizenship itself may not necessarily meet the threshold of rights violations for generating mass out-migration. But as Chapter 7 shows, the Rohingya's deprivation of citizenship can precede a more serious and targeted goal of cleansing a state or region of a particular group, which does embody the type of rights violations that, as the 2015 Rohingya refugee crisis demonstrates, certainly does contribute to mass migration.

Waves of Rohingya refugees sought to escape following the particularly nefarious human rights policies, but they did not do so immediately follow the implementation of the 1984 law revoking their citizenship. Such a finding is problematic because it undercuts one of the central conclusions of Chapter 9: access to citizenship in a host country is one of three key components to the full realization of rights for those escaping dangerous conditions at home. Moreover, Chapter 8 shows that survival migrants from Syria and Africa seeking to gain entry to Europe face legal challenges in their attempt to secure asylum and often also experience human rights violations associated with trafficking in the process of getting to Europe. Yet the pull to acquire asylum in Europe may be so great that even in absence of a clear stateless determination regime, migrants from across Africa and Syria remain in Europe in the hope that they will one day gain political asylum. While there may be variance in the ways in which deprivation of citizenship contributes to migration, there is no question that a lack of nationality is correlated with poor human rights protections once survival migrants cross international borders.

Across some of the chapters in Part II, we see that violence can serve as a more consistent push factor in migration decisions than either resource scarcity or deprivation of citizenship. While people may flee their country of origin for a variety of reasons, when threats to their basic rights to safety, security, and freedom emerge, the need to flee becomes more compelling. As of April 2018, the number of refugees fleeing the Syrian Civil War had swelled to 5.6 million (UNHCR 2018). Bashar Al Assad's use of chemical weapons and the weapons of the state against civilians creates a situation where people are pushed to flee to survive. When the state takes up arms against its own population, as Assad has, Betts's threshold for survival migration has clearly been crossed. Though technically such violence should be covered by the 1951 Refugee Convention, providing refugee status to those who successfully flee their country of origin, in practice we know that potential host countries are loathe to open their borders to refugees because of the often widespread public opposition to their presence. And unfortunately for the more than 465,000 people who have died or are missing as a result of the fighting in Syria, not everyone, even in the worst of conditions, flees (McDowall 2017).

Concerning the plight of refugees from Burundi and a variety of other African countries, Chapter 4 shows that in both instances violence in a country of origin contributes to mass migration. Following the 2015 election in Burundi, in which Pierre Nkurinziza was reelected to an unconstitutional third term in office, his government engaged in widespread violence against the opposition. Members of the opposition were killed and arrested, leading to an outflow of 265,000 Burundian refugees by June 2016 (Dobbs 2016). Between 2004 and 2014, the number of refugees in South Africa has quadrupled (UNHCR 2006, 2015). Protracted civil wars and violence in Somalia, the DRC, and Ethiopia have contributed to out-migration into South Africa, which has itself generated a national backlash against migrants and refugees. Together these cases suggest that violence in a country of origin can serve as a consistent push factor, compelling people to flee in search of safety and security.

Though not every chapter speaks directly to the causes of migration, those that do help us differentiate between the ways in which resource degradation, violence, and deprivation of citizenship may, to varying degrees, serve as drivers of displacement. Those rights violations that directly threaten survival seem to satisfy Betts's survival migration threshold. In these studies only violence seems to consistently endanger human rights to such a degree that large numbers of people make the difficult decision to flee their country of origin or habitual residence. A dearth of economic resources and welcoming asylum countries may undercut flight for those who would otherwise become environmental refugees. And when governments deny or rescind nationality for a particular group, flight may become necessary. The right to nationality has been described as "the right to have rights," meaning that many other human rights a government provides are reserved for citizens. When the body of rights reserved exclusively for citizens grows at the expense of rights for noncitizens and nonnationals, the critical drop in human rights for the noncitizen group may become so intolerable that it serves as push factor in migration decisions.

Future Research

A core theme that emerges from this investigation is that there is value in looking across issue areas to understand threats to human rights and causes of migration. Often the work in these fields tends to cluster—focusing on the rights violations experienced by particular groups (women, racial minorities, religious minorities) or thinking about very particular causes of migration (environmental degradation, state-sponsored violence, poverty). When we combine analysis of the causes of migration with the prospects for rights fulfillment in asylum countries, we see that merely escaping violence or persecution does not inexorably lead to improved human rights protections. If people escape state persecution in Burundi, they may well be subject to xenophobic violence once they have arrived in neighboring Tanzania. Alternatively, when stateless populations flee persecution, they risk having their rights violated by traffickers who promise safe passage to asylum countries. Even in democracies where there is political backlash against migrants, democratic governments may respond in ways that circumscribe migrant rights.

These findings suggest that one avenue for future research is to consider the intersections between migration and human rights as a process (Faist 2004). We know from the considerable volume of research on the causes of migration that people often flee in search of better economic opportunities

(Adhikari 2012; Moore and Shellman 2004; Karras and Chiswick 2002) or to escape violence (Davenport, Moore, and Poe 2003; Apodaca 1998). But migration can also be attributed to less commonly studied phenomena. It may be part of established cultural practices encouraging young adults to leave home (Geisen 2010) or occur when social capital develops between members of transnational communities separated by long distances, creating "safe" opportunities to journey away from home (Palloni et al. 2001). When thinking about the human rights of migratory populations, this book suggests that we should also be studying the types of experiences people have in transit. What sorts of experiences can they expect when they cross an international border? Does the cause of one's migration inform the likelihood that the migrant's rights will be respected in transit? This book shows that human traffickers can create significant and possibly lethal obstacles for rights fulfillment for those forced to flee their homes.

This work also suggests that across these very diverse issue areas, naming and shaming tactics can create opportunities for victims to seek justice. The utility of information politics to construct political will to improve human rights is a well-known tool for victims and advocates alike (Brysk 2013; Hafner-Burton 2008; Risse, Ropp, and Sikkink 1999). Indeed, Alison Brysk suggests, "Under the right circumstances, the naming and framing of rights can construct the political will to protect them. Speaking rights to power means gaining attention then empathy, and then evoking a powerful norm that persuades power-holders, allies, or fellow suffers to mobilize" (2013, 15). This book shows that without the innovative pressure campaign waged by Haitian human rights activists, it is unlikely that the UN would have accepted responsibility for the cholera outbreak. Without the work of Fortify Rights, which coordinated pressure on the member states of the Association of Southeast Asian Nations (ASEAN), it is unlikely that Burma would have granted the UN humanitarian access to the Rohingya. We build on important work on information politics, showing that it can help ease human suffering across a very wide range of issue areas.

As the world confronts problems of unparalleled scope and complexity that result in human rights crises never seen before, there is reason to question our traditional approaches. Naming and shaming in the face of a government hell bent on killing political opponents feels a bit like howling at the wind to stop a tornado. But this book demonstrates that with consistent efforts, even naming and shaming can lead to opportunities for aggrieved populations to seek justice. Thinking about not only the causes of forced migration but also the experiences of migrants in transit and their prospects for rights fulfillment in asylum countries can also shed light on methods for alleviating human suffering in the midst of emerging threats to human rights.

NOTES

1. This is not to suggest that climate change and environmental degradation are not often proximate causes of migration. Robert McLeman (2013) suggests that often environmental migrants themselves would not identify climate change as the true cause of their migration, preferring instead to point to the need to find work to support a growing family, for example. But if the cause of unemployment is drought in the agricultural industry, then climate change plays a direct role in such migration decisions.

2. In December 2018 the U.S. House of Representatives passed a resolution declaring the situation in western Burma as genocide. See Hansler 2018. The head of the UN fact-finding mission in Burma described the situation as genocide in the fall of 2018. See "UN Investigator" 2018. In December 2018 Human Rights Watch described the situation in Burma as genocide. See Sifon 2018.

3. These countries are France, Hungary, Italy, Latvia, Slovakia, Spain, and the United Kingdom.

REFERENCES

Adhikari, Prakash. 2012. "The Plight of the Forgotten Ones: Civil War and Forced Migration." *International Studies Quarterly* 56 (3): 590–606.

Apodaca, Clair. 1998. "Human Rights Abuses: Precursor to Refugee Flight?" *Journal of Refugee Studies* 11 (1): 80–93.

Azam, Jean-Paul, and Anke Hoeffler. 2002. "Violence against Civilians in Civil Wars: Looting or Terror?" *Journal of Peace Research* 39 (4): 461–485.

Baechler, Gunther. 1999. "Environmental Degradation in the South as a Cause of Armed Conflict." In *Environmental Change and Security*, edited by Alexander Carius and Kurt M. Lietzmann, 107–129. Berlin: Springer.

Balcells, Laia. 2010. "Rivalry and Revenge: Violence against Civilians in Conventional Civil Wars." *International Studies Quarterly* 54 (2): 291–313.

Battaglini, Marco, and Bard Harstad. 2016. "Participation and Duration of Environmental Agreements." *Journal of Political Economy* 124 (1): 160–204.

Betts, Alexander. 2013. *Survival Migration: Failed Governance and the Crisis of Displacement*. Ithaca, NY: Cornell University Press.

Brysk, Alison. 2013. *Speaking Rights to Power: Constructing Political Will*. Oxford: Oxford University Press.

Davenport, Christian, Will Moore, and Steven Poe. 2003. "Sometimes You Just Have to Leave: Forced Migration, 1964–1989." *International Interactions* 29 (1): 27–55.

Dobbs, Leo. 2016. "Number of Burundian Refugees Tops 250,000 since April." UNHCR, March 4. Available at http://www.unhcr.org/en-us/news/latest/2016/3/56d97f2d9/number-burundian-refugees-tops-250000-since-april.html.

Eck, Kristine, and Lisa Hultman. 2007. "One Sided Violence against Civilians in War: Insights from New Fatality Data." *Journal of Peace Research* 44 (2): 233–246.

Faist, Thomas. 2004. "Towards a Political Sociology of Transnationalization: The State of the Art in Migration Research." *European Journal of Sociology* 45 (3): 331–366.

Geisen, Thomas. 2010. "New Perspectives on Youth and Migration: Belonging, Cultural Repositioning and Social Mobility." In *Youth on the Move*, edited by David Cairns, 11–21. Wiesbaden, Germany: VS Verlag für Sozialwissenschaften.

Goldstone, Jack. 2002. "Population and Security: How Demographic Change Can Lead to Violent Conflict." *Journal of International Affairs* 56 (1): 3–21.

Gupta, Joyeeta. 2012. "Negotiating Challenges and Climate Change." *Climate Policy* 12 (5): 630–644.

Hafner-Burton, Emilie. 2008. "Sticks and Stones: Naming and Shaming the Human Rights Enforcement Problem." *International Organization* 62 (4): 689–716.

Hansler, Jennifer. 2018. "House Says Myanmar Crimes against Rohingya Are Genocide." *CNN*, December 13. Available at https://www.cnn.com/2018/12/13/politics/house-resolution-myanmar-genocide/index.html.

Homer-Dixon, Thomas. 1994. "Environmental Scarcities and Violent Conflict: Evidence from Cases." *International Security* 1 (19): 5–40.

Karras, Georgios, and Carmel Chiswick. 2002. "Macroeconomic Determinants of Migration: The Case of Germany, 1964–1988." *International Migration* 37 (4): 657–677.

McAdam, Jane. 2012. *Climate Change, Forced Migration, and International Law*. Oxford: Oxford University Press.

McDowall, Angus. 2017. "Syrian War Monitor Says 465,000 Killed in Six Years of Fighting." *Reuters*, March 13. Available at https://www.reuters.com/article/us-mideast-crisis-syria-casualties/syrian-war-monitor-says-465000-killed-in-six-years-of-fighting-idUSKBN16K1Q1.

McLeman, Robert. 2013. *Climate and Human Migration: Past Experiences, Future Challenges*. Cambridge: Cambridge University Press.

Moore, Will, and Stephen Shellman. 2004. "Fear of Persecution, Forced Migration: 1952–1995." *Journal of Conflict Resolution* 48 (5): 723–745.

Palloni, Alberto, Douglas Massey, Miguel Ceballos, Kristin Espinosa, and Michael Spittel. 2001. "Social Capital and International Migration: A Test Using Information on Family Networks." *American Journal of Sociology* 106 (5): 1262–1298.

Risse, Thomas, Stephen Ropp, and Kathryn Sikkink, eds. 1999. *The Power of Human Rights: International Norms and Domestic Change*. Cambridge: Cambridge University Press.

Sifon, John. 2018. "Myanmar's 'Genocidal Acts' Demand UN Action." Human Rights Watch, October 26. Available at https://www.hrw.org/news/2018/10/26/myanmars-genocidal-acts-demand-un-action.

Susskind, Lawrence, and Saleem Ali. 2014. *Environmental Diplomacy: Negotiating More Effective Global Agreements*. Oxford: Oxford University Press.

UNHCR (United Nations High Commissioner for Refugees). 2006. *Statistical Yearbook, 2004: Trends in Displacement, Protection and Solutions*. Geneva: UNHCR. Available at http://www.unhcr.org/statistics/country/44e96c842/unhcr-statistical-yearbook-2004.html.

———. 2015. *UNHCR Statistical Yearbook, 2014*. Geneva: UNHCR. Available at http://www.unhcr.org/en-us/statistics/country/566584fc9/unhcr-statistical-yearbook-2014-14th-edition.html.

———. 2018. "Syria Emergency." April 19. Available at http://www.unhcr.org/en-us/syria-emergency.html.

"UN Investigator Says Myanmar Genocide against Rohingya 'Ongoing.'" 2018. *Al Jazeera*, October 25. Available at https://www.aljazeera.com/news/2018/10/investigator-myanmar-genocide-rohingya-ongoing-181025035804009.html.

United Nations. 2016. "United Nations Response to Cholera in Haiti." Available at http://www.un.org/News/dh/infocus/haiti/CholeraFactsheetAug2016.pdf.

World Bank. 2018. "The World Bank in Haiti." Available at http://www.worldbank.org/en/country/haiti/overview.

Contributors

MAXIMILIAN AVILES is a graduate student at the University of San Diego and will be completing his M.A. in international relations in the spring of 2019. His academic research interests include transitional justice mechanisms, the political dynamics of the UN Security Council, and energy security in Europe and Latin America. As a Pickering Fellow, he will be joining the U.S. Foreign Service after completion of his graduate school career.

NEIL A. ENGLEHART holds a B.A. in history and East Asian studies from Oberlin College and a Ph.D. from the University of California, San Diego. He is professor and chair of the Political Science Department at Bowling Green State University. He works on human rights, state failure, state capacity, nonstate armed groups, and the politics of Asia. Currently he is working on projects on the impact of the UN Convention on the Elimination of All Forms of Discrimination against Women (CEDAW) and on the human rights behavior of nonstate armed groups. His most recent book is *Sovereignty, State Failure and Human Rights: Petty Despots and Exemplary Villains.*

KERSTIN FISK is assistant professor of political science at Loyola Marymount University. Her research broadly focuses on issues related to conflict and security, with emphases on civil war dynamics, violence against civilians, and state repression. She has forthcoming or published work in *Journal of Peace Research, Journal of Conflict Resolution, Civil Wars,* and *International Studies Perspectives.* Her most recent project investigates local-level patterns of communal violence related to refugee encampment.

BRIAN FREDERKING is professor of political science at McKendree University. His research interests include the UN Security Council, international law and organizations, nonproliferation, and transitional justice. He is the author of *The United States and the Security Council* and a coeditor of *The Politics of Global Governance*. He has published numerous articles in journals such as *International Studies Quarterly* and *American Political Science Review*.

BEATRICE LINDSTROM is staff attorney at the Institute for Justice and Democracy in Haiti. She manages advocacy and litigation to seek accountability and remedies from the UN for its peacekeepers' introduction of cholera to Haiti. She is lead counsel in *Georges v. United Nations*, a class-action lawsuit on behalf of Haitians and Haitian Americans injured by cholera. She regularly provides expertise on UN accountability and human rights in Haiti, as a former country expert for Freedom House, as a frequent guest lecturer at universities, and in the media.

ROBERT MANDEL is professor of international affairs at Lewis and Clark College. He is the author of fifteen books and more than fifty book chapters and articles pertaining to global security and conflict issues. His most recent book is *Global Data Shock: Strategic Ambiguity, Deception, and Surprise in an Age of Information Overload*. He has testified before the U.S. Congress and has worked for several intelligence agencies.

JEANNETTE MONEY is professor of political science at the University of California, Davis. Her research interests include various dimensions of immigration policy, such as immigration control, nationality legislation and immigrant incorporation, migrant rights, and international cooperation in migration. She has published numerous books and articles on migration, including *Fences and Neighbors: The Political Geography of Immigration* and *Migration Crises and the Structure of International Cooperation*.

PATRICIA C. RODDA is visiting instructor for international relations at Carroll University. Her research interests include international and public law, asylum protections, international intervention and nation building, statelessness, and LGBTQ rights and advocacy. Her newest project is a book examining the link between sex trafficking and women's rights.

MICHELLE SCOBIE is a lecturer and researcher at the Institute of International Relations at the University of the West Indies (UWI), St. Augustine, and coeditor of the *Caribbean Journal of International Relations and Diplomacy*. She has earned a Ph.D., LL.B., and L.E.C. Her research areas include international law, international environmental law, and developing states' perspectives on global and regional environmental governance, particularly in the areas of institutional architectures relating to biodiversity, climate change, tourism, sustainable development, marine governance, energy governance, private governance, environmental ethics, and trade and environment.

CHARLES ANTHONY SMITH is professor in political science at the University of California, Irvine, and associate dean of the Division of Continuing Education. His research is grounded in the American judiciary but encompasses work in both comparative and international frameworks using a variety of methodologies. He has published *The Rise and Fall of War Crimes Trials: From Charles I to Bush II* and *Gerrymandering in America: The House of Representatives, the Supreme Court, and the Future of Popular Sovereignty.*

HEATHER SMITH-CANNOY is associate professor and chair of the Department of International Affairs at Lewis and Clark College. Her research interests focus on human rights and international law with special focus on human trafficking. She is the author of *Insincere Commitments: Human Rights Treaties, Abusive States, and Citizen Activism.* Her current project examines sex trafficking and women's rights.

SHAINA WESTERN is lecturer on international relations and quantitative methods at the University of Edinburgh. Her research interests include international organizations, treaty ratification, migration, and human rights. She has published in top political science and international relations journals.

Index

Page numbers in italics indicate figures or tables.

www.ingramcontent.com/pod-product-compliance
Lightning Source LLC
Chambersburg PA
CBHW040147270326
41929CB00025B/3413